Nikolaos van Dam is a specialist on Syria and has served as Ambassador of the Netherlands to Indonesia, Germany, Turkey, Egypt and Iraq.

'[A] monumental work on Syrian power politics'
Robert Fisk, *The Independent*

'An excellent book'
Patrick Seale

'An admirable study ... invaluable for anyone with a serious interest in Middle Eastern politics'
Peter Mansfield

'The most informative explanation of the effects of sectarianism and regionalism on Syrian politics'
Philip S. Khoury, MERIP Reports

'[An] excellent study of the sectarian bases of Syrian politics'
Foreign Affairs

'Only a handful of important books have been written on modern Syria; and Nikolaos van Dam's The Struggle for Power in Syria is one of them'
Joshua Landis, *International Journal of Middle East Studies*

To the memory of my mother and father;
to Marinka;
to Nikolaos, Jan, Emma and Karel

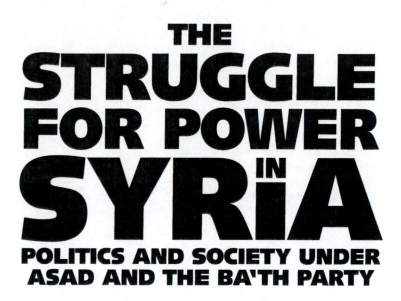

THE STRUGGLE FOR POWER IN SYRIA

POLITICS AND SOCIETY UNDER ASAD AND THE BA'TH PARTY

NIKOLAOS VAN DAM

I.B. TAURIS
LONDON · NEW YORK

Revised fourth edition published and reprinted twice in 2011 by
I.B.Tauris & Co Ltd
6 Salem Road, London W2 4BU
175 Fifth Avenue, New York NY 10010
www.ibtauris.com

Distributed in the United States and Canada
Exclusively by Palgrave Macmillan
175 Fifth Avenue, New York NY 10010

ISBN: 978 1 84885 760 5

A full CIP record for this book is available from the British Library
A full CIP record is available from the Library of Congress

Library of Congress Catalog Card Number: available

Printed and bound in Great Britain by CPI Antony Rowe, Chippenham

Contents

Tables

Map

Preface to the fourth edition

Sectarian, regional and tribal loyalties[1] have undeniably played a role in the political and socio-economic history of Syria in the twentieth century, but opinions vary strongly as to how significant that role has been. Many Western and non-Syrian authors are inclined to attach great consequence to it, being of the opinion that these factors continue to be important even since the country became independent.

Many socialist-oriented Arab nationalist writers and Syrian politicians, on the other hand, completely reject this view and publicly take a contrary stand, particularly if it concerns a regime which has their support. Nevertheless, these same writers and politicians sometimes attach great importance to sectarianism, regionalism and tribalism when the issue at stake is the activities of opposing or deposed regimes or of political opponents within their own regimes.

All these factors can naturally be over- or underestimated according to the stand that is taken. The truth lies somewhere in between and can only be revealed by critically testing the factual material on as broad a basis as possible.

Our aim is to investigate the extent to which and the manner in which particularist loyalties and commitments such as sectarianism, regionalism and tribalism have played a role in the struggle for political power in Syria. Attention will be focused mainly on developments within the military and civilian political power elite in the period since the break-up of the United Arab Republic in September 1961. In so doing, we shall attempt to answer the question of how important were sectarian, regional and tribal criteria in the formation of power factions within the Syrian Armed Forces and the party organisation of the Ba'th, which took over power in 1963. Above all, we shall investigate which factors and developments have encouraged the strong rise of religious minorities, in particular of Alawis, Druzes, Isma'ilis and Greek Orthodox Christians, in Syrian political life since 1963.

None of the works on Syria published so far has dealt so extensively with these matters. The studies by Be'eri, Biegel, Ma'oz, Van Dusen and others, all of which are listed in the bibliography, tend to stress one or other of the factors, neglecting the rest or leaving them out of consideration. Devlin, Petran, Rabinovich, Seale (1965), Torrey and others treat certain phases of Syria's politico-historical developments in detail, but give only brief or oblique attention to sectarianism, regionalism and tribalism, if only because the role of these factors was not chosen as the central thesis of their studies.

Sources used

For many reasons it is difficult to obtain reliable material dealing with the subject of this study. In the first place, most available sources appear to be extremely partial and biased and are often of a propagandist nature. More important, perhaps, is the fact that in Syria and other parts of the Arab world a kind of taboo obtains on overtly speaking and writing about sectarian, regional and tribal contradistinctions.[2] Such a taboo is practised particularly in Arab nationalist circles and is even stronger in the case of sectarianism than of either regionalism or tribalism. Political sensitivity prevents politicians from expressing themselves easily on a subject such as sectarianism, either orally or in writing, particularly if they have political aspirations for the future, in which case they have to allow for eventual repercussions should they express themselves openly about Syrian internal affairs that are usually considered to be 'confidential'.

Moreover, the Ba'thist organisation which has held power in Syria since 1963 is of a secretive character, while Syria has been in a situation of (semi-) war at varying intervals since 1948. It is only natural, therefore, that foreign researchers into contemporary political and social developments often meet with distrust as to their real purpose.

Documentation dealing with sectarianism, regionalism and tribalism in Syria has been drawn mainly from three categories of primary sources: internal Ba'th Party documents; biographies, memoirs and polemical writings; and the Arabic press and radio broadcasts. The information obtained from these sources has been supplemented by interviews.

Ba'th party documents

Many of the Ba'th Party documents used in this study have not yet been published. They have been issued by both the civilian and the military sectors of the party apparatus and consist mainly of internal party bulletins, circulars, brochures, minutes of party meetings, and other documents issued by the party's Syrian Regional Command, the National (i.e. pan-Arab) Command and their subordinate bureaus and sub-sections.

Many internal party documents which were previously classified as 'secret' have been published by Dar al-Tali'ah in Beirut in a series called *Nidal (Hizb) al-Ba'th (The Struggle of the Ba'th Party)*. This consists of eleven volumes in which the period up to 23 February 1966 is dealt with quite extensively. The Ba'th officially propagates an ideology that aims at realising the ideal of a united Arab society with a socialist system. Obviously, therefore, it is reluctant to admit that factors such as sectarianism, regionalism and tribalism – all considered as a negative residue of traditional society which hinders the awakening of a national and socio-economic awareness – have played any role in the struggle for power within the party's ranks. Most of the material about these factors has therefore been drawn from hitherto unpublished party documents which, in many cases, were classified as secret at the time or were intended for restricted use within the party apparatus.

Biographies, memoirs and polemical writings

Biographies and memoirs of Syrian and other Arab politicians offer details and indications that are indispensable if we are to obtain a reasonably complete impression of the role of sectarianism, regionalism and tribalism in the struggle for political power in Syria. Almost all biographies, autobiographies or memoirs used in this study, including those of Munif al-Razzaz, Sami al-Jundi, Muhammad 'Umran, Mustafa Talas, 'Abd al-Karim Zahr al-Din, Shibli al-'Aysami and others, all mentioned in the bibliography, offer a partial vision or interpretation of events and circumstances which were experienced and lived through by the respective authors. This aspect sometimes gives their writings a polemical character. Even more polemical are the works of Muta' Safadi, Khalil Mustafa, Fu'ad al-Atrash, of members of the Syrian Muslim Brotherhood and others which are listed in the bibliography and are indicated in the footnotes to the text. Such authors constitute, as it were, exponents of opinions and ideas prevailing among particular Syrian population groups and are for that reason incorporated in this study.

It should be noted here that the available number of published memoirs concerning the period of Ba'thist rule since 1963 has been extremely limited as a result of political circumstances. Many Syrian key-personalities, who were directly involved in the developments described, have not been able, or willing, to publish their personal interpretation of events, for instance because they were imprisoned, threatened, or even assassinated (as in the case of General Muhammad 'Umran, who therefore did not have the opportunity to publish the second volume of his memoirs as he had originally announced). Others simply did not have any inclination to write down their experiences for reasons of their own. The result of all this has been that the group of writers about Syria under the Ba'th has been restricted mainly to those few critical opponents who took the risk and had the courage to publish their accounts after being deposed themselves (like Munif al-Razzaz and Sami al-Jundi), or others who (like Khalil Mustafa) were subsequently imprisoned for long periods in reprisal for their publications; or those who were in power, and (like for instance Minister of Defence Mustafa Talas) occupied a position from which they could relatively easily publish accounts favourable to the regime.

The Arabic press and radio broadcasts

The Syrian government-controlled press and radio rarely offer any insight into the role which sectarian, regional and tribal loyalties and commitments play in Syrian political life, be it behind the scenes or in public. In the exceptional cases in which Syrian mass media have offered any information at all, it was usually in reaction to, or in denial of, reports which had appeared in the foreign press or foreign broadcasts.

Non-Syrian, and more particularly the Lebanese, mass media have much more to offer in this respect. The Lebanese press has served more than once as a kind of safety valve for various political factions or regimes in ventilating criticism and propaganda against political opponents and rivals. In the years following the takeover of power by the Ba'th in Syria in 1963, various Ba'thist party factions lost for different reasons the chance of unimpeded expression of their political views via the local mass media. They therefore sometimes resorted to establishing dailies and periodicals of their own in Beirut, such as *al-Ahrar* and *al-Rayah*, or, if they thought such action would be advantageous to their own position, deliberately leaked confidential or secret information concerning the party or the regime to existing Lebanese dailies such as *al-Hayat, al-Nahar, al-Jaridah, al-Muharrir* and *al-Anwar*.[3] In the period after Syria's intervention in Lebanon in 1976, Syrian influence was extended to such an extent that the Lebanese media gradually lost their former freedom to report about developments in Syria itself. Consequently the Lebanese press in this respect lost its role as an important source of information.

The tracing of material in the Arabic press and radio broadcasts which would be relevant to this study was facilitated through publications such as *The Arab World, al-Watha'iq al-'Arabiyah, Arab Report and Record, Middle East Record,* and *the Daily Report, Middle East and North Africa, of the Foreign Broadcast Information Service* (Springfield, Virginia).

Interviews

Through interviews with a number of Syrian, Jordanian, Palestinian, Iraqi and Lebanese Arab politicians, who were directly or indirectly involved in the political developments and events described in this study, it was possible to add new data and insights to the material distilled from the above-mentioned primary sources. It goes without saying that these people do not all wish to be mentioned here, but they included the following (ex-) politicians: 'Abd Allah al-Ahmad, Colonel Jasim 'Alwan, Dr Jamal al-Atasi, Shibli al-'Aysami, Salah al-Din al-Bitar, Dr Elias Farah, Lieutenant-General Amin al-Hafiz, George Saddiqni (Syria); Dr Munif al-Razzaz, Dr Fawwaz Suyyagh (Jordan); Tariq 'Aziz, Zuhayr Bayraqdar (Iraq); Malik al-Amin, Dr Bashir al-Da'uq, Eng. Nicola Firzili, Basharah Marhij, Munah al-Sulh (Lebanon) – none of whom bears any responsibility whatsoever for the interpretations laid down here.

Note on transliteration

The system used in this study for transliterating Arabic words is based upon that of the *International Journal of Middle East Studies*. Diacritical marks are omitted for the sake of convenience; at the beginning of Arabic words, the *'ayn* is maintained. The transliteration system used will be lucid to those who know Arabic and less relevant to those who have no mastery of that language.

Acknowledgements

The present study is a revised and updated version of a doctoral dissertation, originally presented to the University of Amsterdam in March 1977, entitled *De Rol van Sektarisme, Regionalisme en Tribalisme bij de Strijd om de Politieke Macht in Syrië (1961–1976)* (*The Role of Sectarianism, Regionalism and Tribalism in the Struggle for Political Power in Syria (1961–1976)*). I am indebted to Professor Dr S. Wild (University of Bonn), who supervised the preparation of the manuscript in its original form as a dissertation.

I am grateful to Professor Dr J. Brugman (University of Leyden) for his valuable comment and criticism of the initial English version and to Mr and Mrs P. C. Harnmeijer and Mrs J. Sanders for improving the English style.

My deepest gratitude goes to all those in the Middle East who helped me in collecting the data and material necessary for writing this book.

Chapter 6 and Tables 1–7 were earlier published in a different form as part of my article 'Sectarian and Regional Factionalism in the Syrian Political Elite' which appeared in *The Middle East Journal* (Vol. 32, No. 2,

Spring 1978, pp. 201–10). I am obliged to the Middle East Institute, Washington DC, which kindly allowed republication.

Finally, I am indebted to the Netherlands Organisation for the Advancement of Pure Research (ZWO) and the Oosters Instituut (Leyden), which financially supported this study.

Preface to the third edition

Since the demand for my book still persists after a period of more than sixteen years since its first publication in 1979, I found it appropriate to republish it in fully revised and updated form. The first edition has been substantially enlarged with four new chapters (7, 8, 9 and 10), as well as with several statistical tables, thereby covering the period of Syria under Ba'thist rule till 1996. Wherever necessary, the texts of the two earlier editions (1979 and 1980) have been changed and updated.

Since the publication of the first two editions, various studies have appeared which – mostly within the framework of a different context – give attention to the role of sectarianism, regionalism and tribalism, as well as to socio-economic and other factors. These have been taken into account, and include the works of Hanna Batatu, Alain Chouet, Alasdair Drysdale, Raymond Hinnebusch, Eberhard Kienle, Hans Günther Lobmeyer, Elizabeth Longuenesse, Volker Perthes, Elizabeth Picard, Patrick Seale and others, all mentioned in the bibliography.

Of those who contributed to the third edition, I wish to thank in particular my colleagues Ferdinand Smit, Gerben Meihuizen and Alan Goulty, for their valuable comments and criticism when writing the three final chapters; and Marcel Kurpershoek, for his valuable criticism of an earlier version of Chapter 7. I am grateful to Emma Sinclair-Webb, my editor at I.B. Tauris, for her valuable advice.

Although *Sectarianism, Regionalism and Tribalism in Politics* is still the central theme of this study, the original subtitle by that name has been altered to *Politics and Society under Asad and the Ba'th*, so as to reflect the somewhat wider framework of this newest edition. It is also to underline that the main period covered by this edition is that of the regime of President Hafiz al-Asad, who has now been in power for more than a quarter of a century, longer than any of his predecessors in modern Syria and indeed longer than any of his Damascus-based Arab predecessors as ruler of Syria since Mu'awiyah Ibn Abi Sufyan, the famous founder, in 661, of the Syrian-based Umayyad dynasty of caliphs.

Cairo, 1 January 1996

Preface to the fourth edition

As the demand for my book still persists after more than three decades since its first publication, I have decided to provide an update to the third edition of 1996 so as to include the takeover of Dr Bashar al-Asad as president. This new edition concludes that the Syrian regime as it exists since the death of President Hafiz al-Asad has retained the same characteristics which in the past were so essential for its survival and continuation. It also makes some observations about what amounts to approximately half a century of Alawi-dominated Ba'thist rule in Syria, including the period of President Bashar al-Asad. Chapters 9 and 10 have therefore been updated. The rest of the original text has been largely maintained with only some minimal changes. A new Chapter 11 has been added.

Detailed political developments of the era of President Bashar al-Asad itself fall outside the scope of this book and have already been covered in detail by other studies, such as those of Alan George, David Lesch, Flynt Leverett, Volker Perthes, Radwan Ziadeh and Eyal Zisser, all mentioned in the bibliography.

After the appearance of the previous edition, several important Syrian memoirs have been published which would have made my work much easier had they been available long before. These include the monumental works of General Mustafa Talas (4655 pages) and of former national guard commander Muhammad Ibrahim al-'Ali (1700 pages); of former deputy prime minister Muhammad Haydar; of General Walid Hamdun; of former National and Regional Command member Mansur al-Atrash; as well as the complete memoirs of Akram al-Hawrani (3770 pages). Some Syrian (ex-) politicians, such as former Syrian President General Amin al-Hafiz, have extensively given their views in television broadcasts. Others have published their detailed experiences in the electronic media, for example as did former Regional Command member Marwan Habash, Nabil Shuwayri and former prime minister Yusuf Zu'ayyin. An extensive review of these publications can be found in the new Chapter 11.

Various of the above-mentioned publications provide a much more detailed and precise picture than was available before, giving a clearer and more all-round view of developments, events and personalities. They have not, however, provided me with any reason to alter my historical and socio-political analysis of developments in Syria. My earlier analysis has only been confirmed by these memoirs.

The fact that my subject was considered to be taboo in Syria at the time did not make my research easier, but only whetted my academic appetite and added to my fascination. Looking back, I think the final results of my original study, which started some four decades ago, still stand firmly today.

Damascus, 20 September 2010

I

Introduction

Despite a great measure of cultural uniformity, Syria's present population is characterised by strong religious and ethnic diversity.[1] Subdivision of the population as to language *or* religion shows that 82.5 per cent are Arabic-speaking and 68.7 per cent are Sunni Muslims. In language *and* religion, the Arabic-speaking Sunni Muslims constitute a numerical majority of 57.4 per cent of the whole population. The remaining groups can be classified as ethnic and/or religious minorities.

The major *religious minorities* in Syria are the Alawis (11.5 per cent), Druzes (3.0 per cent), Isma'ilis (1.5 per cent) and the Greek Orthodox Christians (4.7 per cent), who constitute the most important community of all Christians in Syria (14.1 per cent).

The principal *ethnic minorities* are the Kurds (8.5 per cent), Armenians (4.0 per cent), Turcomans (3.0 per cent) and Circassians. Whereas the Kurds, Turcomans and Circassians are almost exclusively Sunni Muslims, and in that respect belong to a majority of the population, the Armenians are Christians and thus represent both an ethnic and religious minority. Of the religious minorities mentioned above, the Alawis, Druzes, Isma'ilis and Greek Orthodox Christians are almost exclusively Arabic-speaking.

Various factors have contributed to the existence of so many religious and ethnic groups in the area which today is called Syria, and to their survival:[2]

1. The three major monotheistic religions, Judaism, Christianity and Islam, all have their origins in the wider region of which Syria is part. The formation of sects and different schools within these religions led to a great diversity of faiths.

2. The Fertile Crescent, of which Syria is part, has in the past regularly been exposed to conquest by various population groups, such as the Arabs, Kurds, Mongols and Turks, and has always been a centre of tribal and individual movement.

3. At times the Middle East has been a place of refuge for people

who were persecuted in surrounding regions on political or religious grounds. Groups of these refugees were able to settle in Syria or its surroundings.

4. Tribal and national differences caused by all these developments often took on a religious aspect and contributed to the rise of different religious communities. It is only natural that political and religious diversities developed simultaneously as part of this process.

5. Religious, tribal and linguistic differences have frequently been preserved and strengthened as a result of localism, an intense local loyalty which in certain regions was fostered by the geographical structure. This was particularly true of the mountains and valleys of the Latakia region, and of the Jabal al-Duruz, with its difficult access.

6. Deficient communications in areas of difficult access and the lack of a strong central authority have helped to preserve the distinctive character and independence of religious and national groups. Communities which did not wish to be subjected to central state control were able to withdraw to less accessible regions where they could live more or less undisturbed. Central state authority rarely extended much further than the coast, river valleys and the more accessible plains, all of which were consequently usually inhabited by a majority of the traditionally dominant religious or national group, notably the Sunni Arabs. On the other hand, religious minorities, particularly those who have been severely persecuted in the past, such as the Alawis, Druzes and Isma'ilis, are found mainly in the less accessible regions.

7. Religious and ethnic diversities were also encouraged by the relative toleration shown by Islam towards Christians and Jews, and by the formal equality of national groups inside Islam. Arab and Islamic culture did not leave the Christian and Jewish communities undisturbed, however, and far-reaching assimilation took place.

Before nationalism became prevalent in the Islamic world, the major national groups such as the Arabs, Turks, Persians and Kurds were fairly tolerant in their attitudes towards one another. Thinking was not yet along 'national' lines, and the inhabitants of today's Syria considered themselves to be either Sunnis, Alawis, Druzes, Isma'ilis, Greek Orthodox Christians or Jews, etc. Most of them spoke Arabic, but this was of little or no political consequence. The majority of the population, i.e. the Sunnis, did not feel that they were 'enduring a foreign government' under Ottoman (Turkish) rule; the Alawis, Druzes and Isma'ilis and others did think so, but the Sunnis were certainly not 'at one' with them in this respect.[3]

Sunni Islamic intolerance was generally directed against the Shi'is and other heterodox Muslims, such as the Alawis, Druzes and Isma'ilis, rather than against Christians and Jews. Both the latter enjoyed a form of protection of minorities *avant la lettre* which has enabled them to maintain their respective identities until the present time, although at the cost of accepting second-class citizenship for their members.[4] Christians and Jews were recognised in Islam as *Ahl al-Kitab* (Peoples of the Book), i.e. people who had received divine revelations through prophets prior to Muhammad, and had been entrusted with earlier revealed books and scriptures. The status of *Ahl al-Kitab* allowed Christians and Jews to retain their religious organisation, their personal status, places of worship and religious trusts. This protected status was further institutionalised under the Ottoman Empire when their communities were officially recognised as *Millets* or (religious) 'nations'.

During the Ottoman Empire, Syrian society was considerably segmented into a number of closed communities, a situation described by Albert H. Hourani as follows:

> [The Ottoman Empire] was composed of a large number of groups, local tribal, linguistic and religious. On the whole, these groups formed closed communities. Each was a 'world', sufficient to its members and exacting their ultimate loyalty. The worlds touched but did not mingle with each other; each looked at the rest with suspicion and even hatred. Almost all were stagnant, unchanging and limited; but the Sunni world, although torn by every sort of internal dissension, had something universal, a self-confidence and sense of responsibility which the others lacked. They were all marginal, shut out from power and historic decision.[5]

The centuries-old rift between the various religious communities and between Sunnis and religious minorities in particular, widened during the nineteenth and twentieth centuries owing to various factors:[6]

During the nineteenth century the position of the religious minorities was strongly affected by political interference in the internal affairs of the Ottoman Empire by France, England and Russia, acting as self-appointed protectors of religious minorities. France claimed the right to protect the Maronite Christians of Lebanon, the Russian government claimed a similar right to protect the Greek Orthodox Christian subjects of the Ottoman Sultan, while England cultivated friendly relations particularly with the Druzes and Jews.[7] The situation of the religious minorities so protected was generally improved, but it was also negatively influenced by the fact that the protection drew upon them the hatred of the central Ottoman Government and of the Sunni population majority, who regarded them as 'potential traitors, sources of weakness and instruments of European policy: in general as dangers to the Empire and to the Islamic community'.[8] As a result, relations between Sunnis and the religious minorities actually worsened. Another effect of the political interference by the European powers was that it strengthened both the function of the religious minorities as political units and also their communal consciousness.

Under the French Mandate, sectarian loyalties were deliberately incited in order to prevent or suppress the rise of Arab nationalism.[9] On the other hand, the separatism and particularism of religious and national minorities were encouraged by the granting of autonomous status to areas where such minorities formed a local majority. As part of this policy, the Latakia region with an Alawi majority and the Jabal al-Duruz with a Druze majority had their own governments for some time under the Mandate; they were formally autonomous and independent of the Syrian Republic. The north-eastern Jazirah province, where a number of Christian communities were strongly represented and the Kurds constituted a local majority, was not given formal autonomy under the French Mandate but it was placed under direct French administration and local Kurdish aspirations for autonomy were encouraged.

As part of a divide-and-rule policy, the French favoured the military recruitment of special detachments among Alawis, Druzes, Kurds, Circassians and other minorities, who then formed part of the *Troupes Spéciales du Levant* used to maintain order and to suppress local rebellions. The fact that these troops were largely composed of minorities increased the resentment among the Arabic-speaking Sunnis. Discord between and within religious and ethnic minorities was also provoked by the fact that the French played off one tribal leader against another.[10]

The 'closed community' system was still very prevalent during the first half of the twentieth century; Jacques Weulersse observed it in the 1940s and defined it as a *minority complex*, as follows:

> a collective and pathological susceptibility which makes each gesture by the neighbouring community appear a menace or challenge to one's own [community], and which unifies each collectivity in its entirety at the least outrage committed against any one of its members.[11]

Three factors coincided to make regional loyalties and commitments a notable basis for political participation by many Syrians in the independence period. Michael H. Van Dusen has summarised them as follows:

> 1. The development of a political consciousness has stressed supranational [i.e. pan-Arab] and sub-national [i.e. regional] loyalties at the expense of a commitment to the nation state as a whole ... The many truncations of Syria since the turn of the century have stifled the development of any cohesive or definable loyalty to a Syrian nation state. The effects of these border changes on national integration may still be

seen: on the one hand, borders are only technically respected and Arab identity is much stronger than Syrian identity; on the other, the lack of any middle ground loyalty has meant that local political struggles have been projected to the national political arena, and, indeed, have dominated national politics.[12]

Thus, 'when Syria became independent in 1946 she was in many respects a state without being a nation-state, a political entity without being a political community'.[13]

2. The traditional self-sufficiency of Syria's various regional centres has not been greatly diminished by recent development schemes ... The traditional Arab agro-city is the focus of regional loyalties in countries such as Iraq and Syria ... [The agro-]cities have traditionally been the focus of political activity: in the independence period, this has meant that national politics is often defined in terms of sub-national, regional interests. Communication patterns within the country also reflect the agro-city mosaic: the link between Damascus as the political capital and a Syrian village is usually through the regional city in whose area it is located; communications between agro-cities are minimal.[14]

Syria's major agro-cities are: Damascus, Suwayda', Dar'a and al-Qunaytarah in the south; Aleppo and Dayr al-Zur in the north-east; and Hama, Homs and Latakia in the centre and north-west. Each of these functions as the hub of a network of several towns and hundreds of villages in the outlying rural areas. Idlib and Jisr al-Shughur are really part of the Aleppo agro-city, whereas al-Raqqah, Hasakah and al-Bu Kamal form part of the agro-city of Dayr al-Zur. During the last decades Tartus has developed into an agro-city alternative to Latakia, and many Alawis consider Tartus as their regional centre.[15]

3. The politicisation of Syrian youth in the late 1940s and early 1950s occurred at the high school level, and therefore occurred before these young men had moved into diverse careers or other sections of the country ... This fact has meant that their political and ideological loyalties reflect the local political situation in their particular agro-city. As a result, national parties have had to adapt to Syrian localism, becoming decentralised and cell-oriented; as a result, too, national parties continue to project [inter- and] intra-regional interests.[16]

Most Syrian political parties thus reflected regional interests and, irrespective of their political ideologies, were able to expand in specific areas or among some sections of the population while remaining negligible in others.

The rise of nationalism and continual social change have helped to weaken sectarian, regional and tribal ties, particularly since independence. Better means of communications and transport, for instance, have broken the isolation of particular communities. Modernisation and industrialisation bring members of different communities into contact more frequently and intensively than before. Sectarian, regional and other particularist mentalities have also been subdued by the vast expansion which education has experienced since independence and its national unification during the 1960s. In addition, urbanisation has caused family ties to weaken.

Notwithstanding increasing indifference towards religion as such, the significance of the religious community as a political and social unit continues. Organisations, clubs and non-political groups proliferate through the traditional social channels of the religious community, with all the consequences that this implies for the survival of sectarian loyalty and commitment.

People who were born into a specific religious community but have become areligious are nevertheless considered in this study as being members of that community. In practice, it still appears very usual to consider a person to belong to a religious community irrespective of his actual religious beliefs. Proselytism is rare.

Religious and ethnic groups are not distributed equally over the whole of Syria but usually concentrate to varying degrees in different administrative districts. In this respect a distinction should be made between 'compact' minorities and 'scattered' minorities. The former are those whose members are mainly concentrated in a particular district in which they form a local majority; the latter are those which are distributed over a number of regions without complying with the definition of compact minorities in any of them.[17]

Sunnis constitute a majority in all but two Syrian provinces, Latakia and Suwayda'.[18] Latakia has an Alawi majority (62.1 per cent), and the Greek Orthodox Christians, who mainly live in rural areas in the form of regional concentrations, are strongly over-represented with 12.8 per cent as compared to their national figure of 4.7 per cent. In al-Suwayda' (also called Jabal al-Duruz or Jabal al-'Arab) the Druzes form an overwhelming majority of 87.6 per cent, and relatively large Greek Orthodox and other Christian communities are also found. Sunnis are represented in al-Suwayda' by less than 2 per cent of the population, the least of all provinces.

In the province of Hama, where Sunnis constitute a majority of 64.6 per cent, Isma'ilis (13.2 per cent) and Greek Orthodox Christians (11.0 per cent) are relatively over-represented and are concentrated mostly in the rural areas surrounding the provincial capital, which is mainly Sunni. Most of Syria's Isma'ilis are concentrated in the districts (*mantiqah*'s) Salamiyah and Masyaf, where they constitute a local majority. Syrian Isma'ilis can therefore be classified as a compact minority, similar to the Alawis and Druzes. Most Syrian Kurds live in the northern areas bordering on Turkey, and may be defined as a compact ethnic minority.

Arab nationalists in Syria usually tend to avoid the use of geographical names which indicate the religious background of the inhabitants of an area. Thus, stressing that all Arabs are equal irrespective of their religion, they prefer the name *Jabal al-'Arab* (Mountain of the Arabs) to that of *Jabal al-Duruz* (Mountain of the Druzes). However, the mountains of the Latakia region until recently continued to be called *Jibal al-'Alawiyin* or *Jabal al-Nusayriyah* (The Mountains of the Alawis or Nusayris) in the Syrian Government's Statistical Abstract. Since 1976 the more neutral name of *al-Jibal al-Sahiliyah* (The Coastal Mountains) has been used.[19]

The *Wadi al-Nasara* (Valley of the Christians) is nowadays also called *Wadi al-Nadara* (Blooming Valley).

The compact religious minorities

Since the Ba'th took over power in 1963, members of the Arabic-speaking compact religious communities, such as the Alawis, Druzes and Isma'ilis, have played a prominent political role. Their social circumstances will therefore be discussed in some detail, albeit briefly.

The Alawis

About 75 per cent of all Syrian Alawis live in the Latakia region, where they constitute the local majority. Most of them work in the agrarian sector and thus represent the overwhelming majority of Latakia's rural population. In the coastal cities and towns they were until the 1970s in the minority as compared to the Sunnis and Christians. In the Latakia region, therefore, rural-urban and class contrasts more often than not coincided with sectarian differences.

In former times, the cities exercised economic and social domination over the rural population, who were forced to cede a major part of their revenues to urban landlords and traders. Urban-rural contrasts were sometimes so great that the cities seemed like settlements of aliens who sponged on the poverty-stricken rural population. In the 1940s, from the social and political point of view, coastal cities such as Latakia represented outposts of the mainly Sunni capital of Damascus.[20]

In the course of time, the Alawi community developed a strong distrust of the Sunnis, who had so often been their oppressors. Alawi suspicion of the Christians was slightly less strong, perhaps because the Christians had also been in a position of weakness and uncertainty.

With regard to social organisation, a rough distinction may be made between the Alawis living in the mountains and those inhabiting the Syrian plains and coastal areas. Tribal ties are more powerful among the former, having largely disappeared in the coastal plains, where the family constitutes the most important social unit and solidarity between the various branches of a family tends to be very strong indeed.

Whereas the Alawis in the lower plains and coastal areas were economically dominated and exploited by members of other religious communities, primarily by Sunnis and secondly by Christians, those in the inaccessible mountain regions were able to develop with greater independence. The socio-economic position of Alawi peasants was much the same in both regions, however, the main difference being that the mountain Alawi peasants were exploited by their co-religionists whereas the others usually were not.

Alawis can be subdivided tribally into four main confederations: the Khayyatun, Haddadun, Matawirah and Kalbiyah, who are scattered throughout the entire Latakia region and its surrounding areas. Of these four Alawi tribal confederations two important religious groups have split off, i.e. the Haydariyun, who constitute a religious unity but have maintained their original tribal ties, and the Ghasasinah, who emerged after the First World War under the leadership of Sulayman al-Murshid who set himself up as a religious leader and attracted a following of about forty thousand. After al-Murshid's death, most of his supporters rejoined their original tribes.[21]

Many villages and their lands are divided among families belonging to different tribes. The tribal confederations sometimes had more than one leader (singular: *ra'is* or *za'im*), and were in turn subdivided into tribes, each with its own 'foreman' (*muqaddam*). Although leadership of a tribe was usually acquired through inheritance, it was also possible to become a tribal leader due to personal qualities or through influence in Syrian power institutions at a national level. In this way, a few poor Alawi families, such as that of President Hafiz al-Asad, have been able to acquire great influence at the tribal level in their regions of origin because of the powerful position they have gained at the national level, for instance in the army or in other institutions of power.

Most Alawi tribes have their own religious leaders (shaykhs or *rijal al-din*) who, to a lesser extent than the tribal leaders, exercise great moral and social influence on the tribesmen. In some cases religious leaders have been so influential that they have been able to undermine the authority of tribal leaders by depriving them of their supporters, or have even replaced them. In some cases religious and tribal leaders have belonged to one and the same family.

Due to their land holdings, tribal leaders or shaykhs have been able to exercise enormous power over their peasant co-religionists. When tribal power was accompanied by feudal rights, and a tribal leader was simultaneously considered the religious leader of his tribe, the peasant tribesmen were little more than serfs. Under the French Mandate such a religious-tribal-feudal relationship existed between the powerful Alawi families 'Abbas, Kanj and Murshid and their subordinate co-religionists. The powers of these families extended far beyond the limits of their landed property.[22]

The 'Alawi Mountains' (*Jibal al-'Alawiyin*) were formerly one of Syria's most destitute and least developed areas and in several respects lagged behind the rest of the country. Although the cultivation of tobacco formed one of their most important sources of income, Alawi tobacco farmers were powerless and isolated, partly because their profits were greatly reduced by commission taken by the agents. In fact, the small tobacco farmers were forced to sell their crops to Sunni entrepreneurs on the coast, often for inadequate remuneration. A remarkable phenomenon, indicative of the extreme poverty of the Alawis, was that the poorest families indentured their daughters as house servants to the richer families, mostly urban Sunnis, who usually regarded the Alawi peasants with contempt.[23]

Since Syria became independent, and more particularly since the Ba'thist takeover of power in 1963, the socio-economic circumstances of the Alawi peasants have improved considerably. Since 1963, the Latakia region has even enjoyed disproportionate growth and development. Alasdair Drysdale has observed that 'the Ba'thi regime's commitment to reducing regional and urban-rural imbalances ... has been evident in efforts to improve life in the countryside ... It is noteworthy that al-Ladhiqiyah [Latakia] and Dar'a provinces have enjoyed disproportionate growth, possibly because of government favoritism.'[24]

Immediately after the 1963 revolution Alawis started moving eagerly into education. They were enabled to do so by their co-religionist Ba'thists who had assumed power. In increasing numbers Alawis were awarded scholarships and travelled abroad for higher degrees, becoming doctors, engineers, lawyers and university professors, so that in the 1990s they were strongly represented in the professions and senior cadres of the state, rivalling and sometimes displacing the Sunni and Christian intelligentsia.[25] The Syrian author Mahmud Sadiq has noted that under Alawi-dominated Ba'thist rule, the Syrian authorities occasionally practised strong favouritism towards Alawis in allocating foreign fellowships to students, or in selecting new members for the Syrian diplomatic service. Alawis were reportedly also preferred when appointing teachers for the more important schools in the bigger population centres; the same was apparently the case when appointing teachers of politically important subjects, such as 'history, nationalist and socialist education, social sciences and philosophy'.[26]

During the past decades, considerable migration has occurred among the mountain Alawis of the Latakia region. By settling elsewhere, many of them have forced other religious minorities, such as the Isma'ilis, to beat a geographic retreat. Others have migrated to the lower plains and the cities. In the provinces of Hama and Homs, in particular, Alawi villages have increased in number.[27]

Whereas in the early 1970s the most important coastal cities and towns such as Latakia, Tartus, Banyas and Jablah still had a Sunni majority, in the 1990s they had reportedly become Alawi by majority, as a result of a rapid process of 'Alawisation'. A similar trend of 'Alawisation' could be observed in some of the suburbs of Damascus.[28]

The Druzes

More than 90 per cent of Syria's Druzes live in the southern province of al-Suwayda', their regional concentration being even higher than that of the Alawis in Latakia (87.6 per cent and 62.1 per cent respectively). Most of the Druzes, like the Christians living in al-Suwayda' province, work in the agrarian sector.[29] They are fairly evenly distributed throughout the region, both the rural areas and the provincial capital being mainly Druze. Urban-rural contrasts, such as those in the Latakia region, do not occur in the Jabal al-Duruz. Another essential point of difference with the Latakia region is that the traditional elite of al-Suwayda' is entirely Druze, while that of the Latakia region is both Alawi and Sunni (and sometimes Christian). Consequently, the strong sense of regional identification that exists in both areas must be coupled with the relative lack of integration in the Latakia region on the one hand, and the stronger social cohesion in al-Suwayda' on the other. It is therefore not surprising that intra-regional tensions are greater in the Latakia region.[30] In the Jabal al-Duruz, therefore, the majority of the Druze population have not been dominated by members of another religious community and the feudal rule of prominent Druze families has usually not been accompanied by sectarian contrasts: socio-economic and class contrasts have been confined mainly to one and the same (Druze) community. Religious-tribal-feudal relations, such as those existing within the Alawi community, have not occurred among the Druzes.

Most of the Druzes who today live in the al-Suwayda' region are the descendants of seventeenth-century and particularly nineteenth-century migrants from Lebanon, Palestine or the Aleppo region. Entire families or parts of tribes settled in particular districts or villages which they subsequently came to dominate, either because they formed a numerical majority or because villages were composed almost entirely of members of one extended family.[31]

Leadership of the Druze community in the al-Suwayda' region was for long in the hands of the Hamdan family, who reportedly terrorised the Druze peasants, treated them as serfs and denied them any right to land ownership. In 1868, the Hamdan family lost that leadership to the prominent Druze family of al-Atrash, who continued to suppress the peasantry but were forced by an anti-feudal revolt (al-'Ammiyah), about 1890, to make a number of concessions including recognition of proprietorship of part of the land cultivated by the local peasants. Since that time many Druze peasants have been small or medium-sized landowners. Some of those who did not own land were forced to work as seasonal labourers, or migrated to the cities in the hope of improving their economic situation.[32]

A strict family hierarchy, based on such criteria as social importance and position, was long practised within the Druze community and was strictly adhered to in particular social events and activities.[33] Prominent Druze families such as the al-Atrash or Abu 'Asali used their traditional ranking within this hierarchy when competing for political power in local elections. The power of these great families has now largely been broken, however, particularly since the 1960s.

To outsiders, the Druze community of the al-Suwayda' region has usually shown great cohesion, particularly when the central Ottoman government, or the Syrian government situated in Damascus, has endeavoured to extend its authority over the Jabal al-Duruz.

The Isma'ilis

About eighty per cent of the Isma'ilis living in Syria inhabit the central province of Hama, mainly in the rural districts (mantiqah's) of Masyaf and Salamiyah, where most of them work in the agrarian sector. During the ninth and tenth centuries Salamiyah was a great centre of the Isma'ili sect, which was widely feared. In the eleventh century most Isma'ilis fled to the mountains of the Latakia region, where they found fairly safe refuge and settled mainly in and around the towns of Masyaf and Qadmus. In the course of time they were gradually forced from the countryside into these towns, which they were able to dominate socially and economically.[34] In the rural areas of the Latakia region, the Alawis were generally hostile towards the Isma'ilis, most of whom returned to their former religious centre of Salamiyah after the Ottoman Sultan 'Abd al-Hamid II granted them part of the Empire's domain there in 1845.

Since Syria became independent, the Isma'ilis in the Salamiyah district have advanced economically and socially much faster than their co-religionists in the Alawi mountains, who initially have remained relatively poor and backward. Many Isma'ilis have for some decades now worked as civil servants, in education, and in the professions, even in the period preceding the Ba'thist takeover of power in 1963.[35] Many Isma'ilis have migrated to the cities, particularly after 1963.

Sectarian, regional, tribal and socio-economic overlap

Categories such as sectarianism, regionalism, tribalism and class struggle are often used randomly and with little explanation in discussions of political trends, events and activities in the Arab world. The relevance of these categories is rarely demonstrated by those writers that employ them, and it is undoubtedly far easier to allege that sectarian, regional, tribal and/or socio-economic loyalties and commitments play an important role in a political power struggle when it is known that the rival factions belong to different groups within those categories than it is to demonstrate the validity of such an allegation. Quite different factors – ideology, inter-generational conflict, personal ambition and opportunism among them – can play an equally important role.[36]

Any stress on sectarian, regional and tribal categories in political or social analyses of the Arab world is usually interpreted by socialist-oriented Arab nationalist writers as an attempt to maintain discord in that world and to hinder its transformation from a feudal and/or capitalist society to a united Arab society with a socialist system focused on socio-economic interests and Arab identity. Sectarianism, regionalism and tribalism are then seen as dangerous social diseases which should be combated with all possible means, since they supposedly strengthen social divisiveness and hinder the class struggle.[37]

The present study is based on the assumption that Arab nationalist and class loyalties are developing in Arab society, thereby partially replacing traditional particularist loyalties and commitments. It does not assume, however, that Arab nationalist and class consciousness have always been present and were suppressed by those loyalties. Before the rise of Arab nationalism it was customary for people to think in terms of religious, regional or tribal communities rather than along socio-economic or national lines.[38]

Sectarian, regional and tribal categories can easily overlap, making it difficult to determine which play a role in a particular situation. In the event of such overlap, there is a danger of interpreting tribal loyalties as regional and/or sectarian loyalties, for instance, or vice versa. Overlap may be due to the regional concentration of particular religious communities and tribes in specific areas or provinces; to the fact that tribal groups as a whole usually belong to the same religious community; and to the fact that tribal and sectarian elements are sometimes inseparably linked to one another.[39] In this respect, the compact religious minorities, and the tribes belonging to these minorities, serve as clear examples.

Sectarian, regional and tribal groups may in turn partially overlap with socio-economic categories: one may be simultaneously a member of a specific social class, religious community or tribe, and an autochthonous inhabitant of a particular region. Even so, categories such as religious community and socio-economic class differ considerably. Thus, a socio-economic class may be thought of as a horizontal social stratum, the members of which comply with specific socio-economic characteristics. A religious community, on the other hand, usually comprises several socio-economic classes, and can be said to intersect vertically with parts of various classes. Thus, a socio-economic class may have a tangent plane with several religious communities.

On the one hand, the growth of class consciousness can specifically be impeded by solidarity with one's own religious community, since such a community usually comprises different socio-economic classes. On the other hand, sectarian loyalties can have a catalysing influence on the take-off of a class struggle if sectarian contrasts coincide with socio-economic differences. In such a case, the class struggle can be directed through sectarian channels. Thus, sectarian, regional, tribal and socio-economic loyalties, if they overlap, may complement and reinforce one another. In modern Syria such an overlap has been most evident in the case of the compact religious minorities.

The sectarian dimension of the urban–rural dichotomy in Syria is worthy of special attention. Whereas the compact religious minorities are concentrated mainly in the poverty-stricken countryside, the richer and larger cities are predominantly Sunni. In describing urban-rural contrasts in the 1940s, Jacques Weulersse wrote:

> The antagonism between urban and rural people reaches such an extent that one can almost speak of two different populations co-existing within the same political frame but without intermingling. The peasant pays all the costs of this antagonism, because the economic and social structure is based on the incontestable primacy of the cities.[40]

If these urban-rural contrasts are considered together with the *minority complex* mentioned earlier, it is easy to understand that the contrast between Sunnis in the larger cities and members of religious minorities in the rural areas must have been even greater than that between co-religionists in city and countryside. Sectarian and geographical factors are thus almost impossible to separate in any analysis of the relationship between the urban Sunnis and rural religious minorities. Similarly, it is difficult if not impossible to isolate sectarian, regional, tribal or socio-economic categories when they show strong overlap and apparently form an inseparable whole. This is particularly the case with members of compact religious minorities such as the Alawis, Druzes and Isma'ilis, who, as we shall show in the following chapters, have played a prominent and central role in the struggle for political power in Syria in the period since 1963.

2

The rise of minorities in the Syrian armed forces and in the Ba'th Party

We have seen in the introduction to this work that many Syrian political parties reflected regional interests, and that their supporters were usually concentrated in specific regions. Moreover, political groups, irrespective of their political colour, were frequently built up through traditional social channels. The latter factor, in particular, was largely responsible for the continued existence in Syrian political life of sectarian, regional and tribal loyalties. This is clearly illustrated by the Ba'th Party, which came to power in Syria in 1963.

The Constitution of the Arab Ba'th Socialist Party officially states:

> The Arab nation constitutes a cultural unity. Any differences existing among its sons are accidental and unimportant. They will disappear with the awakening of the Arab conciousness ...
>   The national bond will be the only bond existing in the Arab state. It ensures harmony among the citizens by melting them in the crucible of a single nation, and combats all other forms of factional solidarity such as religious, sectarian, tribal, racial and regional factionalism.[1]

Despite these ideological goals, which denied existing social realities and included the ousting of sectarian, regional and tribal loyalties in favour of Arab nationalist and socio-economic group sentiments, the Ba'th Party was built up to a significant extent through traditional social channels. The ways in which it developed into a political movement during its initial stages therefore had a decisive effect on the social composition of its membership in later periods.

The Ba'th Party was founded in Damascus in 1940 by Michel 'Aflaq, a Greek Orthodox Christian, and Salah al-Din Bitar, a Sunni Muslim, both of whom belonged to the Damascene middle class and were teachers at the al-Tajhiz secondary school, from which they recruited most of the initial party members. Although 'Aflaq and Bitar were

Damascenes, most of the original party members seem to have been rural migrants who had come to the Syrian capital for further education.

From Damascus the Ba'th party organisation spread spontaneously to other Syrian districts, apparently without any clear plan of action. The organisation's growth depended largely on personal initiatives taken by its original members in their native regions, and therefore in some regions, such as the Jabal al-Duruz, where its members could muster many supporters, it developed far more strongly than in others.[2] Muta' Safadi suggests that the strong Druze representation in the Ba'th Party was partially due to 'Aflaq's special relationship with some families of the Jabal al-Duruz:

> 'Aflaq had family friendships with some Druze families, because he himself belonged to a Christian family living in the al-Maydan Quarter of Damascus, which, like most of the families of al-Maydan, traded with the south, i.e. Hawran and the Jabal al-'Arab. In this way, the party spread swiftly among the well-educated Druze pupils who attended secondary schools in Damascus and al-Suwayda', the centre of the Jabal al-'Arab province.[3]

Few autochthonous inhabitants of the Syrian capital Damascus were initially attracted to the Ba'th Party. In fact its founding members made no serious effort to win the sympathy of the Damascene population for their ideals, being content for the time being with their success in recruiting rural students.[4]

Sami al-Jundi, one of the Ba'th's earlier members, wrote:

> The bulk of those who joined the party in Damascus were younger students [and pupils] from the countryside, who attended university and secondary school between 1940 and 1955. After graduating, they returned to their place of birth in order to pursue their activities.
>
> The social conditions in rural areas were favourable to the growth and spread of the Party. It expanded there and remained weak in the cities, especially in Damascus. In the course of time, therefore, it became a big body with a small head.[5]

Its socialist ideals made it easier for the party to obtain a firm footing in the rural towns and in the poverty-stricken rural areas than in the greater cities, where the political scene was dominated by the local bourgeoisie and traders. Since Arabic-speaking religious minorities are mainly concentrated in rural areas and the bigger cities are principally Sunni, it is only logical that minority members predominated among the Ba'thists. But whereas the socialist component of Ba'th ideology contributed only indirectly, i.e. because of an overlap between geographical and sectarian factors, to a proportionally strong representation of minority members in the Ba'th Party, there was also a direct cause: the secular character of Ba'thist Arab nationalism.

In the past, the Arab nationalist movement had always been interwoven with a kind of Sunni Islamism. And the Sunni Arabs, who usually played first fiddle in this movement, assigned in their Arabism such an important and central role to (Sunni) Islam that heterodox Muslims, let alone Christians, were allotted a secondary place: 'timid subordinates' tolerated by (Sunni Arab) 'superiors'.[6] In fact, many Sunni Arab nationalists tended to regard members of the Arabic-speaking religious minorities as 'imperfect Arabs' because they were heterodox Muslims or not Muslims at all. Equally, the religious minorities tended to suspect Arab nationalism as a disguise for unrestrained Sunni ascendancy, similar to the situation that pertained during the Ottoman Empire, the only difference being that Arab rather than Turkish Sunnis now held power.[7]

Ba'th ideology had a quite different basis. The Ba'th wanted a united secular Arab society with a socialist system, i.e. a society in which all Arabs would be equal, irrespective of their religion. This did not imply that Islam was of secondary importance to Ba'thist Arabism. In the Ba'thist view Islam constituted an essential and inseparable part of Arab national culture. Other than the Sunni variants of Arabism, however, the Ba'th considered Islam to be not so much an Arab national religion as an important Arab national cultural heritage, to which all Arabs, whether Muslim or Christian, were equal heirs apparent. In the opinion of Michel 'Aflaq, the Ba'th Party's ideologist, Christian Arabs therefore need feel in no way hindered from being Arab nationalists:

> When their nationalism awakens in them completely and they regain their original nature, the Christian Arabs will realise that Islam is their national culture with which they should satiate themselves, in order that they may understand and love it and covet it as the most precious thing in their Arabism.[8]

It was thus only natural that the Ba'th ideology appealed strongly to Arabic-speaking religious minority members, who may have hoped that the Ba'th would help them to free themselves of their minority status and the narrow social frame of their sectarian, regional and tribal ties.[9]

Finally, the minority members must have been attracted by the idea that the traditional Sunni-urban domination of Syrian political life might be broken by the establishment of a secular socialist political system as envisaged by the Ba'th, in which there would be no political and socio-economic discrimination against non-Sunnis or, more particularly, against members of heterodox Islamic communities.

After the takeover of Hafiz al-Asad in 1970, membership of the party apparatus was opened to all Syrians, including non-Arabs such as (Arabised) Kurds, Circassians and Armenians.[10] The number of non-Arabs in an Arab nationalist party like the Ba'th was bound to remain small, however. Although non-Arab ethnic minority members could officially join the Ba'th Party on an individual basis if they accepted Arabisation (i.e. they officially had to give up their original ethnic identity in favour of the Arab identity), they could not enjoy political emancipation similar to the Arab religious minorities. Deviant nationalist aspirations other than Arabism would be severely suppressed. And although non-Arab ethnic minorities living in the Arab world have been officially recognised in Ba'th ideology, non-Arabs in the Ba'thist political system are not considered as equals to Arabs in the nationalist sense, and consequently are politically – though not necessarily culturally – discriminated against.[11] Nevertheless it should be noted that in the 1990s many ethnic, tribal and social groups are represented in the Syrian Parliament, and thereby are provided with an official political outlet, however small the real political significance and power of the Parliament may be.[12]

Other Syrian political parties which have attracted relatively large numbers of Arabic-speaking minority members because of their secular ideologies are the Syrian Communist Party (SCP) and the Syrian Social Nationalist Party (SSNP). Similar to the Ba'th, the Syrian Communist Party is a clear example of an ideologically orientated party that was built up through traditional social channels. Due to the relatively strong representation of Kurds, the SCP failed to gain wide acceptance among other groups of the Syrian population. In the early 1970s, an SCP leader complained that his party organisation had not been able to win wide support among the Arab majority as a result of the 'narrow nationalist chauvinism' of Kurdish party members.[13]

Among the Christian Arabs, the Greek Orthodox have in the past generally taken a positive attitude towards Arab nationalism. Compared to other Arab Christian communities, their 'Arab identity' was least affected by the interferences of European powers in the internal affairs of the Ottoman Empire. In 1917, with the October Revolution, the traditional ties of the Greek Orthodox Christians with Russia were broken off. Afterwards, having lost their external 'protector', many of them chose to assimilate with the Arab nationalist movement.[14]

Traditional social barriers to a normal expansion of the Ba'th

The fact that relatively large numbers of the original Ba'thists came from rural and minoritarian backgrounds later formed a social impediment to the membership of urbanites and Sunnis, i.e. due to the traditional contrasts between urban and rural communities and between Sunnis and religious minorities. Such traditional social barriers impeded a normal country-wide expansion of the party organisation, and was still clearly manifest during the 1960s when the Ba'th Party had come into power. This can be illustrated by the Damascus and Hama party branches and by the party's Peasants' Organisation.

The Damascus Branch

Autochthonous Damascene party members had always been relatively few in number. An internal party document dating from 1965 went so far as to state that 'on a certain day Damascus had closed her gates in front of the party and the Revolution [of 8 March 1963]'.[15] According to Hanna Batatu, 'out of the 600 or so members of the Ba'th's Nationalist Guard in Syria's capital in 1964, only 12 were Damascenes.'[16]

Urban-rural and Damascene/non-Damascene contrasts were very evident among the members of the Damascus Branch, and in 1964 brought the party activities there to a virtual standstill. In other words, the fact that a majority of members of the Damascus Branch Command were non-Damascenes caused party activities in the Syrian capital to stagnate. Early in 1965, in an effort to stimulate party activities again, the Syrian Regional Command decided to replace three 'provincial' members of the Damascus Branch Command by autochthonous Damascenes.[17] Furthermore, it was decided to separate rural and urban people living in the Damascus district organisationally by uncoupling the sub-branch (shu'bah) of the Ghutatayn (i.e. two oases around Damascus) from the capital's party branch. In this way, the party activities of the urbanites and of the peasants could be more easily organised. At the same time the urban-rural contrasts which had earlier become visible within the party apparatus could be considerably lessened. Earlier, in 1963, a separate party branch, called Far' al-Atraf (Suburbs' Branch), had been set up for the other rural surrounding areas and suburbs of Damascus.[18]

The Hama branch

In the predominantly Sunni city of Hama, the Ba'th was given little support. Here, too, urban-rural contrasts formed an important factor, causing party activities to stagnate in 1964.

A significant difference with the situation in Damascus province, however, was that the urban-rural contrasts in Hama were accompanied and sometimes overshadowed by sectarian differences due to the fact that the surrounding rural districts were largely inhabited by members of religious minorities, among whom Isma'ilis, Alawis and Greek Orthodox Christians are numerically strong.

In April 1964, a sectarian-tinted anti-Ba'thist revolt occurred in Hama, with the local Muslim Brothers playing an important role. The bloody suppression of this revolt considerably increased the chasm between the predominantly Sunni city population and the predominantly minoritarian leaders of the Ba'thist regime. The harsh suppression of the insurrection in Hama was attributed by some to a sectarian blood revenge (*tha'r*) by the prominent Druze Ba'thist Colonel Hamad 'Ubayd. In February 1952 an insurrection in the Jabal al-Duruz had been bloodily suppressed by Sunni Hama officers who then supported the regime of Adib al-Shishakli, himself a Sunni from Hama.[19]

As a side-effect, Ba'th party activities in Hama city were seriously disturbed and came to a standstill. A number of local party leaders later proposed that a separate party branch be set up for Hama city, excluding the surrounding countryside with its religious minorities, apparently with the idea that this would end the deadlock in party activities. The proposal was rejected by the Syrian Regional Command, however, with the argument that 'this would only increase the regional and sectarian spirit existing within the party branch'.[20]

According to Mustafa Talas, the Hama revolt sparked over to Homs after the assassination of an innocent Sunni citizen by local Muslim Brotherhood militants, who had selected their victim on the false assumption that he was an Alawi member of the National Guard. Talas relates in his memoirs that when he was ordered to suppress the revolt, he 'decided on purpose to select the officers [for the operation] from one single religious group [i.e. only Sunnis like Talas himself], so as to prevent the people from fabricating lies' about the regime, i.e. accusing it of sectarianism, as had been done in the case of Hama.[21]

It is remarkable that the Regional Command, apparently in an effort to counter sectarian tendencies, would not allow a separate party branch to be set up for Hama city, whereas it had previously approved such a solution when dealing with difficulties in the Damascus Branch. The latter situation had been less complicated by sectarian problems, both the Damascene city dwellers and the people inhabiting the surrounding countryside being mostly Sunni.

The Peasants' Organisation

During the 1960s the Ba'thist Peasants' Organisation experienced organisational difficulties which, in various respects, were similar to those of the Damascus and Hama Branches. Its activities and further

growth were impeded by traditional social barriers which had penetrated the party apparatus as a result of faulty recruitment policies.
An organisational report published by the party's Peasants' Bureau in
1965 summarised the situation as follows:

> O comrades,
> During our work in the countryside, we have in many cases pursued
> an incorrect method, due to
> 1. Confining the party organisation to one family, or to one religious
> community, or accepting as members only those who were first to come
> forward. The effect [of adopting such recruitment methods] was that
> other groups in the village took a stand that was aimed not so much
> against the party as against those members of the village who had been
> taken into the [party] organisation; they alleged that it was they [rather
> than those recruited] who had supported the party. This is to say nothing
> of the weak elements that were organised ...
> 2. Concentrating all responsibility into the hands of one organised
> party member as though he had the standing of a *mukhtar* [village chief]
> and was empowered to propose others as members of the Peasants'
> Union or Confederation, the Chamber of Agriculture, etc., or as though
> no other sincere and respectable peasants were available but him.
> This caused (a) the creation of new notables among the peasants, and
> (b) a barrier to be thrown up between party members and the other
> peasants in the village.
> 3. An unsound selection procedure was used among the peasants who
> needed to be organised, due to the fact that party comrades who were
> active in the countryside did not have a careful and objective method in
> mind. For example, we took the village *mukhtar*, or those with medium
> land holdings, or heads of certain families into the party organisation.
> These former notables were consequently able to regain their previous
> prestige, albeit under cover of the party organisation. [They in turn]
> organised their peasant supporters, who accordingly felt very little serious
> or tangible change during the time that the [Ba'th] Party [was in power].[22]

Thus, for instance, when new members for the Peasants' Organisation
in a certain district were initially recruited only from among Isma'ili
peasants, this debarred Sunni peasants from joining the organisation
at a later stage.[23]

The following description of tribal and political interaction in the
Syrian countryside, given in the memoirs of former Ba'thist leader
Jalal al-Sayyid (from Dayr al-Zur), may serve as an explanation of the
political behaviour of some rural Ba'thists and others:

> The entire Arab countryside is dominated by tribal feelings, including
> the small and medium-sized towns. Intellectual, political and ideological
> currents which spread in such regions are, without exception, exposed
> to tribal traditions, and interact with them. These [intellectual and other]

currents are, however, much more affected by [tribal traditions] than that the latter are influenced the other way around.

I know of a small town in Syria which serves as a good example of what I say. Political currents there coincided with tribal currents and were in coherence and harmony with them. There was a tribe which consisted almost exclusively of Nasserists and another whose majority was Ba'thist. A [third] rival tribe wanted to emphasise its independence and presence, and considered that mere acceptance of Nasserism or Ba'thism would be considered as [an indication of its] subservience to the other [tribes]. Therefore it adopted a position in between, neither Ba'thist nor Nasserist, and tended towards currents opposed to both Ba'thism and Nasserism, such as that of the Syrian [Socialist] National [Party] [SSNP]. The tribe in question did not know anything about SSNP ideology, nor did it support it; it was merely Arab where its feelings were concerned. Its stance emanated merely from a spontaneous attempt and will to prove its independence.[24]

Particularist factionalism in the Ba'th civilian party apparatus

Before the unification of Syria and Egypt in 1958, the Ba'th had a large party organisation in Syria. In 1958, however, this was dissolved by the party's National Command at the request of the Egyptian President Nasser, who made the dissolution of Syria's political parties a precondition for union. Not until May 1962, i.e. more than half a year after the break-up of the United Arab Republic (UAR), did the Ba'th Party's National Command decide to rebuild the party apparatus in Syria. Many former Ba'thists did not join the reformulated Syrian party organisation but went over to other political movements, such as that of the Nasserists, or founded new political parties, like the Socialist Unionists (*al-Wahdawiyun al-Ishtirakiyun*).

When, on 8 March 1963, a group of Ba'thist and other officers seized power in Syria by means of a military coup, the civilian members of the Ba'th were too few (approximately 600) to cope with the great government responsibility which the Ba'thist military leaders had successfully claimed on their behalf.[25]

Some Syrian Ba'thists had remained secretly organised after the official dissolution of their party in February 1958, particularly in the districts of Latakia, Dayr al-Zur and Hawran. After the coup of 8 March 1963, these party members – who were known in party literature as the *Qutriyun* (Regionalists) – played a dominant role in the Syrian civilian party apparatus, thanks to their close ties with the leaders of the Ba'thist military party organisation which held actual power in Syria.[26]

Shortly after the coup of 8 March 1963, the newly formed Organisational Bureau of the Syrian civilian party sector decided that the number of civilian party members should be strongly increased, and passed a resolution to the effect that all 'supporters' (*ansar*) of the party were to be promoted at once to the rank of 'active member' (*'udw 'amil*), with the right to participate in party elections and to nominate persons for membership. This resolution was known to the party's rank and file as the 'advance regulation' (*Qanun al-Zahf*).[27] In the year following the coup of 8 March 1963, Ba'th Party members quintupled in number.[28] A party document dated 1965 shows that a new recruit would normally have had to wait much longer before becoming an active member: eighteen months as a 'supporter' and a similar period as an 'apprentice' (*'udw mutadarrib*).[29]

Some party leaders took advantage of these relaxed admittance procedures and had relatives, friends or acquaintances admitted to the party apparatus as active members without demanding that they should meet certain strict requirements such as a specific level of education or familiarity with, and adherence to, the ideological principles of the party. Moreover, in many cases there were no official party documents to testify to the number and identity of former party members, their party rank and manner of admission. It was thus not difficult for those party leaders and their supporters to transform drastically the composition of some party branches to their personal advantage.[30]

As a result, a number of party blocs came into being whose members were connected to each other by common sectarian, regional or tribal background rather than by ideological principles.

This had serious effects for the subsequent power struggle in both the civilian and military party organisation of the Ba'th, since it undermined party discipline, with all the negative consequences that this implied. An Organisational Report published in 1965 voiced the following complaints.

> The weakness of objective relationships within the Party, whether between members or between the [party] organisations, has most negative and dangerous consequences for its organisational cohesion, for its capacity for unity and action, and for its homogeneous development. These ineffectual relations are manifested in the lack of comradeship shown by the members, the presence of personal relationships rather than party relationships, and the division of loyalty between the organisation and the blocs that exist in the party. The result of all this is that the party is threatened by the infiltration into its midst of the disorders of bourgeois, feudal, tribal and sectarian realities. The result of these poor relationships within the party is inadequate party discipline.[31]

The Organisational Report also criticised the fact that rival blocs existed within the party which, in many cases, were not even based on ideological differences:

> O comrades, what has befallen the party, and is still affecting it, is not so much its being divided into rightist, leftist, revolutionary and opportunist wings, as the presence of groups which do not have a basic political line, or class content, through which their individual characteristics may be unambiguously specified.[32]

Regional party elections

Particularistic factionalism was also clearly evident during regional party elections. Various kinds of factionalism could be observed in almost all party branches during the elections held early in 1965 for the Second Syrian Regional Congress of the Ba'th Party. As a result, party members were not always free to choose their leaders, and sometimes the most capable members were prevented from attaining the commanding positions. The Organisational Report of 1965 mentions the following kinds of factionalism: *organisational bloc formation* (i.e. city against countryside; autochthonous people from the election district against people from other areas; residents of one district against those of another district); *sectarian bloc formation*; *tribal bloc formation*; the *formation of personal blocs* who sympathised with the *Munshaqqun*, and what was described as *opportunist bloc formation*.[33] The *Munshaqqun* were a former party faction who, under the leadership of Hammud al-Shufi, secretary-general of the first Syrian Regional Command of the Ba'th Party chosen after the coup of 8 March 1963, had been expelled from the party or had split off in the period after February 1964.[34]

In some areas, members of Ba'thist-dominated power institutions interfered in the elections in an effort to force specific electoral lists upon the party branches. In particular, members of the National Guard intervened in some instances, protected members of specific party blocs, and even made propaganda for them.[35] Non-party members also intervened during local elections. In one case, a tribal shaykh who supported a specific list reached an understanding with those who wanted to be elected, and transported voters to the election bureau in his car, following the electoral proceedings closely so as to be able to influence its results.

In two branches, observed irregularities caused the Syrian Regional Command to call for new elections; for instance, in the al-Raqqah Branch, party members were shown to have submitted a list with candidates to a peasant member and made him swear an oath on the Qur'an to vote for it.[36]

The final election results were afterwards described in the Organisational Report as follows:

> The election results, both negative and positive, to a great extent reflected the reality of each branch. This meant that junior party members exercised their suffrage democratically according to their actual circumstances, without the highest party command having exercised any influence.[37]

Localism in the Idlib Branch

In some branches, party activities were overshadowed by inter-village rivalries that penetrated into the party apparatus. An internal organisational report, written in 1967 and dealing with the situation in the Idlib Branch, showed that party activities were dormant there, partly due to an extreme form of *localism*: sub-branches were so numerous that almost every village of any significance had a party organisation at sub-branch level. As a result, many party members were incapable of visualising anything outside the confines of their own villages. Consequently, inter-village rivalries were not suppressed but continued to play their role within the party apparatus of the Ba'th, which officially aspired to a loyalty surpassing that of the village, tribe or religious community.

To break the deadlock in the party activities of the Idlib Branch, the Syrian Regional Command decided in 1967 to unite various subbranches into new and larger units in order to broaden the previously narrow basis of individual village organisation.[38] Another problem that negatively affected the activities of the Idlib Branch was that many of its members were illiterate because, for purely electoral reasons, many literate members had been purged before the party elections of 1965, to be subsequently replaced by illiterates.

The Latakia Branch

Before the Second Syrian Regional Congress of the Ba'th Party, held in March and April 1965, it was decided that each Syrian party branch should be represented by a minimum of five and a maximum of nine delegates; this was to prevent the larger party branches numerically dominating the smaller ones at the Congress. Nevertheless, the Organisational Report presented to the Congress noted that members of the party branch of the Province of Latakia, in particular, were far too numerous as compared to those of other branches.[39] This raised doubts as to whether the Latakia leaders had applied party regulations dealing with the admission or purge of members as strictly as had been the case in other regions.[40] Since the highest leadership of the Ba'thist military party organisation was mostly in the hands of Alawi officers originating from the Latakia region, it is hardly surprising that the civilian party branch had grown strongly in that particular region.[41] In the period after 8 March 1963, a great many Qutriyun were admitted into the civilian party apparatus with the help of the Alawi General Salah Jadid, one of the leaders of the Ba'thist military party organisation. The Qutriyun were strongly represented in the Latakia region, as well as in Dayr al-Zur and Hawran.

Several leaders of the military party organisation had tried to organise their own civilian party factions by filling the civilian party apparatus with their supporters, so as to obtain a stronger position than their military rivals within the party framework. On the other hand, several civilian party members tried to obtain the support of a military party faction of their own, for instance by exploiting rivalries among the military Ba'thists, and by playing them off one against the other.[42] After the takeover of power by the Ba'th in 1963, the groups involved in the power struggle consisted of ever-changing coalitions of military and civilian Ba'thists who continuously tried to exploit one another in order to increase their own power, while simultaneously trying to remove their opponents from the political scene.[43]

Pre-1963 minority members of the Syrian armed forces
Under French rule (1920–46)

Several politico-historical and socio-economic factors contributed to the strong representation of minorities in the Syrian armed forces before Ba'thist officers took over power in 1963. One such factor dates back to the time when Syria was under French Mandate. As was mentioned in the introduction, the French favoured recruitment from the various religious and ethnic minorities, such as the Alawis, Druzes, Isma'ilis, Christians, Kurds and Circassians, in the *Troupes Spéciales du Levant*, which later developed into the Syrian and Lebanese armed forces. At the same time, however, members of the Sunni Arab majority of the Syrian population were not encouraged to enlist. This implied a 'divide-and-rule' policy that was intended to prevent any of the communities from obtaining a position so powerful as to be able to endanger the position of the central administration. This French recruiting policy followed a tradition established by colonial powers in their various dependencies, i.e. first to recruit enlisted personnel, and later officers too, from tribal groups remote from the central capital, from minority groups and especially from groups with limited independence aspirations. Frequently these groups came from economically less-developed areas and were therefore attracted by the opportunities in the army.[44]

On the other hand, the French also tended to enlist members of large and influential families into the *Troupes Spéciales* in order to secure the allegiance of the minority communities from which they were primarily drawn.[45] Bou-Nacklie has noted that 'despite the fact that the French overrecruited from the 'Alawis and the Druze, they did so with great finesse ...' The French for example rarely recruited from tribes or clans which had rebelled against them. 'Rather, over-representation of the 'Alawis and the Druze came from those groups and faction[s], tribes and clans that had either remained neutral or were loyal to the French ... In 1944 ... the 'Alawis were over-represented among the soldiers but poorly represented in politics, the officer corps, the gendarmerie, and the police.'[46]

The wealthy Sunni Arab landowning and commercial families, who led the Arab nationalist movement during French occupation, indirectly reinforced the trend towards strong representation of minorities in the Syrian army by refusing to send their sons for military training, even as officers, in a force which they viewed as serving French imperial interests.[47] Moreover, they often despised the army as a profession, and considered the Military Academy of Homs – as Patrick Seale puts it – 'a place for the lazy, the rebellious, the academically backward, or the socially undistinguished. Few young men of good family would consider entering the [military] college unless they had failed at school or been expelled'.[48]

A socio-economic factor that even further accentuated the strong representation of minorities in the Syrian Army was that many people from the poor rural areas (where most minoritarians live) saw a military career as a welcome opportunity to climb the social ladder and to lead a life that would be slightly more comfortable than that within the agrarian sector. This incentive was of less significance for people from the larger cities, which were mainly Sunni.

Finally, people in urban areas frequently found it easier than their rural counterparts to avoid military service by paying a redemption fee.[49]

The Independent Syrian Republic (1946–58)

After Syria became independent in 1946, admissions to the Military Academy at Homs increased strongly each year, mainly due to a vast expansion in the number of schools which opened up educational opportunities to the sons of the lower classes in hundreds of villages and small towns.

The new secondary schools were especially significant because a secondary school diploma was required for entrance to the Military Academy. Whereas Academy applicants had previously been few in number and almost exclusively from the middle and upper classes, in the 1950s and 1960s they could be numbered in the hundreds and were mainly from the lower middle class and the rural areas.[50] Indirectly, this trend again helped to increase the numbers of (ex-peasant) minority officers.

Once having moved into command positions, these officers brought in relatives and others from their sectarian, regional and tribal communities, helping them to advance and tending to favour their applications to the army, navy and air academies.[51]

It is thus understandable that many members of minority communities were among the military who, especially after 1949, when the first of a long series of military coups took place, started to dominate Syrian political life.

A military report describing the situation of the Syrian Army in 1949 reportedly stated, perhaps with some exaggeration, that 'all units of any importance as well as the important parts (*'Anasir*) stood under the command of persons originating from [religious] minorities'.[52] Batatu has noted, however, that

> [on] the level of the officer corps the 'Alawis, contrary to a widespread impression, were not as important numerically as the Sunnis prior to 1963. They derived much of their real strength from the lower ranks of the army. In the arithmetical sense, they had a plurality among the common soldiers and a clear preponderance among non-commissioned officers. As early as 1955 ... Colonel 'Abd al-Hamid Sarraj, chief of the Intelligence Bureau, discovered to his surprise that no fewer than 65 per cent or so of the non-commissioned officers belonged to the 'Alawi sect.[53]

Notwithstanding the fact that members of religious minorities showed a disproportionately strong representation in the Syrian army and occupied politically and strategically important military functions, the most prominent factions in power before the takeover by the Ba'th in 1963 were mostly led by Sunni officers.

Thus, the leaders of the three first military coups d'état in Syria – Generals Husni al-Za'im (1949), Sami al-Hinnawi (1949) and Adib al-Shishakli (1949–54) – were all Sunnis. In maintaining power, al-Za'im and al-Shishakli in particular relied on the support of officers who had similar ethnic or regional backgrounds. Under al-Za'im's rule Kurds and Circassians played an important role. For example, al-Za'im's bodyguard, stationed around the Presidential Palace in Damascus, was completely Circassian.[54] Under al-Shishakli numerous officers from his region of birth, Hama, were able to climb swiftly in the military hierarchy.[55]

Al-Shishakli imposed numerous regulations during his reign, aiming at the creation of a homogeneous Arab-Muslim state. 'Kurds, Assyrians, Armenians, Alawis, and Christian minorities of all sorts were harried by a swarm of decrees'.[56] Nasserist Colonel Jasim 'Alwan (Sunni from Dayr al-Zur) later recalled that al-Shishakli had urged him to give clear preference to Sunni-Arab Muslims in his classes at the Military Academy of Homs, and to limit the number of religious and ethnic minority members to the 'absolute minimum'. 'Alwan, who at the time was instructor of the class which included Alawi officers like Hafiz al-Asad, 'Ali Aslan and Muhammad Nabhan, rejected the idea.[57]

In the period February 1954 to February 1958, when the Syrian–Egyptian union was established, the Syrian officers' corps was strongly divided into rival factions. These also were led mainly by Sunnis. The sixteen Syrian officers who, on 11 January 1958, made the so-called 'union pledge' were all Sunnis.[58]

The Separatist Period (1961–63)

In the years preceding the Syrian-Egyptian union, Damascene officers had played an important political role. During the so-called Separatist Period (*Fatrat al-Infisal*), Sunni Damascene officers, led by Lieutenant-Colonel 'Abd al-Karim al-Nahlawi, reached the climax of their power.[59] It was no coincidence that Damascene Sunni officers were able to stage a successful coup on 28 September 1961, and caused Syria's separation from the United Arab Republic. During the union, whether purposely or not, military command over Syria's military districts had mainly been entrusted to these Damascene Sunnis, who therefore occupied an exceptionally strong position.

The prominent position of the Damascene officers was reflected in the composition of the Syrian Army Command, formed shortly after the coup of 28 September 1961. Of its ten members five were Sunni Damascenes. Of the other five members four were Sunni (of whom one was Circassian) and one a Druze.[60] Because of the strong opposition within the Syrian officers' corps against the Damascene officers' group of al-Nahlawi, the leaders of the 28 September 1961 coup were forced to appoint a non-Damascene as commander-in-chief of the armed forces. They found the Druze Major-General 'Abd al-Karim Zahr al-Din, then fourth in seniority, willing to accept this important military position. Of the three most senior officers two were excluded because they were Christians; the third, an Alawi, was considered unsuitable because he reportedly lacked the necessary personal qualities.[61]

Also important was the fact that, in the period preceding the coup of 28 September 1961, the Sunni Damascene al-Nahlawi occupied the key military position of deputy director of officers' affairs – his direct superior being an Egyptian. From that position he could transfer officers who supported him to army units that were of political and strategic importance to the plans for the coup, which he had drawn up together with a number of his fellow Damascene officers. The coup was consequently almost exclusively a 'Damascene' affair.[62]

During the Separatist Period, however, the power position of al-Nahlawi's faction of Damascene officers crumbled quickly, partly because al-Nahlawi never received the full support of the non-Damascenes. On 28 March 1962, he tried in vain to tighten his slackening grip on the army and government apparatus by way of a military coup. Following this abortive attempt, he was expelled from Syria together with five of his most prominent Damascene military colleagues. The events around 28 March 1962 clearly showed how the Syrian officers' corps had become polarised on a Damascene/non-Damascene basis. The weakened position of the Damascene officers was clearly expressed in the composition of the Syrian Army Command chosen after 2 April 1962. Only one of its eight members was from Damascus.[63]

When al-Nahlawi's military coup, which started on 28 March 1962, resulted in a stalemate that threatened to deteriorate into violent confrontation, it was decided to convene a Military Congress in Homs on 1 April in order to avert the danger of bloodshed. Attended by representatives from all military regions and major units (41 officers in all), the congress represented, as it were, the corporate identity and interests of the Syrian officer corps, as it then existed. It is interesting to note that of the 41 officers, Sunnis were most strongly represented, with 36 members, whereas from a regional point of view the Damascene officers (13 in all, and all Sunnis) were the biggest group. Also present were four Christians (three from the Latakia region and one from Hama Province), and one Alawi officer from the Alexandretta region. The representation of Alawi officers in leading military positions was to change greatly after the 8 March 1963 coup. At the Homs Military Congress, the Damascene Lieutenant-Colonel Muti' al-Samman, secretary-general of the Ministry of Defence and representative of the Damascus Region Military Command, demanded the expulsion of six non-Damascene officers from Syria – irrespective of whether they had been 'wrong' or not during the events around 28 March 1962 – as compensation for the expulsion of al-Nahlawi and five of his Damascene officer colleagues.[64]

During the subsequent period the majority of Damascene officers were gradually purged from politically strategic army units around

Damascus and elsewhere. They were replaced – as the then commander-in-chief of the Syrian Armed Forces, the Druze General Zahr al-Din, put it – 'by officers who harboured nothing but hatred and aversion towards Damascus and its inhabitants'.[65] These were probably mostly officers from the Syrian countryside, who had so often been held in contempt by the people from Damascus.

The numerous army purges resulting from the struggle for political power between the senior (and mainly Sunni) officers greatly weakened Sunni representation in the upper echelons of the officer corps.[66] Whereas officers of Arabic-speaking religious minority groups had been less active in the political sphere in the 1950s and consequently had suffered less from its wear and tear, in the early 1960s they were able to occupy important positions of command which had become vacant through the successive dismissals of Sunnis by one side or the other.[67]

Ba'thist monopolisation of power (1963)

On 8 March 1963 a military coup by a coalition of Ba'thist, Nasserist and independent unionist officers brought down the 'separatist regime'. Shortly after, minority members in the Syrian officer corps again increased strongly in numbers at the expense of the Sunnis. A principal reason for this was that the Ba'thist military leaders involved in the coup had called up numerous officers and non-commissioned officers with whom they were related through family, tribal or regional ties to consolidate their newly achieved power positions quickly.[68]

Most of the military called up in this way were of minoritarian background, especially Alawis, Druzes and Isma'ilis, which is not surprising since most members of the Ba'thist Military Committee which supervised the activities of the military organisation were themselves minority members.[69] This method of recruitment was later explained in a Ba'th internal party document as follows:

> The initial circumstances following the Revolution and its attendant difficulties urged the calling-up of a large number of reserve military (officers and non-commissioned officers), party members and supporters, to fill the gaps resulting from purges of the opponents and to consolidate and defend the Party's position. This urgency made it impossible at the time to apply objective standards in the calling-up operation. Rather, friendship, family relationship and sometimes mere personal acquaintance were the basis [of admission], which led to the infiltration of a certain number of elements who were alien to the Party's logic and points of departure; once the difficult phase had been overcome, this issue was exploited as a weapon for slandering the intentions of some comrades and for casting doubts on them.[70]

The latter part of this quotation obviously refers to charges that some members of the Military Committee had, on sectarian grounds, packed the army with members of their own communities.[71] According to one report, many Alawis were among those officers who, directly after the coup of 8 March 1963, were to fill the gaps in the army resulting from purges of political opponents. About half the approximately seven hundred officers who were dismissed were reportedly replaced by Alawis.[72] According to Mahmud Sadiq, the representation of Alawis among the newly appointed officers was as high as 90 per cent. How extremely important the purges of 1963 turned out to be in the longer term can be concluded from the fact that the origins of a significant number of the officers holding senior positions in the Syrian armed forces in the mid-1990s could still be traced to this batch.[73]

It should be noted that at the time of the coup five of the fourteen members of the Ba'thist Military Committee were Alawis, so that it is hardly surprising that Alawi officers subsequently played an important role in the army. Moreover, the highest leadership of the Military Committee lay in the hands of three Alawis, notably Muhammad 'Umran, Salah Jadid and Hafiz al-Asad.[74] Jadid was chief of staff of the Syrian army between August 1963 and September 1965; al-Asad became commander of the Syrian air force; and 'Umran, the eldest of the three, commanded the crack 70th Armoured Brigade, stationed south of Damascus, which was to be the backbone of the Ba'thist military organisation for some time to come. From these military positions the three Alawi leaders of the Military Committee played a paramount role in the post-8 March 1963 'Ba'thist' transformation of the Syrian armed forces.

If the strong representation of members of religious minorities in the Syrian armed forces is left out of consideration, the fact that nine of its fifteen members had minoritarian backgrounds can appear more or less accidental. Several writers, particularly opponents of the Ba'th regime, have argued, however, that minoritarian members of the Military Committee were drawn together on sectarian grounds.[75] General Amin al-Hafiz later even considered that the communal backgrounds of the members of the Military Committee at first played no role at all, not even in bringing them together into one secret organisation.[76]

The leaders of the Military Committee were swiftly able to consolidate their newly achieved positions of power, thanks to their efficient organisation and planning and to all the military supporters who had been called upon. Within a few months they succeeded in purging their most prominent Nasserist and Independent Unionist military opponents. These, once again, whether coincidentally or not, happened to be mainly Sunnis.[77]

The climax of the Ba'thists' power monopolisation came on 18 July 1963, when a group of predominantly Sunni Nasserist officers, led by Colonel Jasim 'Alwan, staged an abortive coup. Most of the officers who suppressed this coup, not without bloodshed, were of minoritarian backgrounds, and among them Alawis played a prominent role.[78] This had little or nothing to do with sectarianism but was exploited as such by Sunni political opponents of the Ba'th, who resented the many minority members among the new rulers and tried to give the impression that the repeated purges of Sunni officers were based primarily on sectarian motives. In this way they tried to discredit and to undermine the position of the Ba'th Party in the eyes of the Sunni majority of the population.

The fact that a senior Alawi officer had been among the leaders of the abortive Nasserist coup did not, according to these opponents, with their typical fervour for detecting plots and intrigues, discredit their view. The involvement of the Alawi officer Muhammad Nabhan was interpreted by them as indicative of his desire 'in reality' to serve the interests of his Ba'thist co-religionists by provoking the Nasserist officers to a coup from within. The Alawi Ba'thist officers might subsequently have seized the opportunity to purge the remaining (mainly Sunni) Nasserist officers from the army.[79] The distrust which such interpretations engendered among many of the Sunni population against those Ba'thists who originated from religious minorities, was difficult to neutralise from this point on.

After the abortive Nasserist coup of 18 July 1963, in particular, anti-Ba'thist publications started to appear stressing the so-called sectarian character of the Syrian Ba'thist regime. Muta' Safadi's book *Hizb al-Ba'th: Ma'sat al-Mawlid Ma'sat al-Nihayah* ('The Ba'th Party: The Tragedy of its Beginning and the Tragedy of its End') is a typical example in this respect.[80]

3

Sectarian polarisation in the Syrian armed forces between Sunnis and religious minorities

Sectarian, regional and tribal factionalism in the Ba'thist military elite

After the abortive Nasserist coup of 18 July 1963, a struggle for power started among the leaders of the Ba'thist Military Committee. To strengthen their positions, these leaders had gathered around them military men with whom they were connected through sectarian, tribal or regional ties. As a result, the command structure and discipline in the armed forces and the military party organisation were seriously undermined. In a report dated 19 October 1965, the secretary of the Ba'thist Military Organisational Bureau described this process as follows:

> After the Revolution of 8 March the party leaders found it essential to set up an extended military party organisation within the Army that would bring together all military friends of the Party as well as those who sided with it and had participated in the Revolution. It should be pointed out, however, that mistakes were made in the manner and method of organising, and that the qualification of membership was presented as a gift to tens, nay to hundreds, because the foundations on which the organisation was based were aimed not so much at belief in the Party but, unfortunately, at the protection of the organisation's leaders, at different levels, from section (*firqah*) commanders to the highest leaders, and at the gathering of followers and protégés in general, especially after 18 July [1963]. But the matter did not end there, nay, it went much further than that when the followers became leaders in the organisation and organised as they pleased; nay, even further than that, when they started to correct the party members who had lived through the whole struggle of the Party and had given their lives for it. And if we were to examine the organisation of any section, we would find that it was set up by the section secretary, who [at the same time] is commander of that

unit, *according to his personal, political, regional or sectarian inclinations.* And this section secretary is [at the same time] party instructor of his section *(firqah).* But the question is from where he got the party education and knowledge that qualified him for that [task]. The answer is that at the time even the highest party leaders were isolated from supervising and directing the organisation because at first they were preoccupied with confronting the hard circumstances of the Revolution. Afterwards they became submerged in authority affairs, as well as in a fierce struggle for power, which created a weakness of discipline and education in the Party, and subsequently [resulted in] a lack and loss of unity in thought, spirit and orientation. This caused the organisation to end up in a state of mutilation which the comrades could not tolerate. *Thus party loyalty was replaced by loyalty to a person or bloc.*[1]

Anti-Sunni sectarian discrimination in the Syrian armed forces

According to Dr Munif al-Razzaz, secretary-general of the National Command of the Ba'th Party in 1965 and 1966,

the smells of deliberate sectarian bloc formation started to emanate. At first it was whispered about, but later the voices became louder, as it appeared that there were real indications that the accusations [stating that in their struggle for power, the military had exploited sectarian ties in such a way as to have specifically negative results for the Sunnis] were well-founded.[2]

Thus it appeared that sectarian criteria had been applied in the dismissal of officers and non-commissioned officers who had been called up to the army early in the 8 March 1963 coup: Sunni military in particular were affected by the dismissals.[3] Muta' Safadi gave the following, somewhat exaggerated, description of these dismissals:

Dismissals by the hundreds were all aimed at officers originating from the bigger cities, and especially the Sunnis. Thus the most important officers of complete sections of the armed forces, such as the Air Force, the Navy and motorised troops, were dismissed. The same plan was followed with regard to non-commissioned officers and soldiers, so that it became commonplace for complete brigades, with their general staffs, their non-commissioned officers and their soldiers, to become dependent on [members of] specific religious communities, as for instance the 70th and 5th Brigades.[4]

Furthermore, it seemed that Sunnis were being discriminated against when applying for the Military Academy and other military training centres.[5] The same applied when new military people were allowed to become members of the military party organisation of the Ba'th, or new members were recruited for the Ba'thist National Guard, the 'Political Branch' (al-Shu'bah al-Siyasiyah), the intelligence services, or other Ba'thist-dominated power institutions, while Alawis, Druzes, Isma'ilis and (Greek Orthodox) Christians in many cases were given preferential treatment.[6] According to Muta' Safadi's polemical work, 'the doors of the Military Academies and the various military schools were closed to Sunni youths from the cities. Even [those who had attended] complete courses were collectively dismissed from the service before having graduated'.[7]

Similar discrimination to the disadvantage of Sunni military was apparent in the transfer of officers within the armed forces. Officers who were 'trusted' because of their sectarian ties with military leaders originating from minority communities were usually stationed in politically-strategically important army units close to Damascus, whereas those who were 'not trusted' on the same grounds or were considered to be potentially unreliable because they were Sunnis were in many cases transferred to the Syrian–Israeli front or to other army units far away from the capital, such as those in Aleppo and Latakia.[8] This sectarian-tinged military transfer policy resulted in the army units stationed around Damascus being dominated by minority members, whereas Sunnis were more strongly represented in specific army units far away from the capital. The result of this transfer policy was to become clear during the military coup of 23 February 1966.

Sectarian ties played an important role not only in the appointment of officers in high military positions but also at lower levels. Some armed units came to be composed mainly of members of a specific religious community, whereas their commanding officers might have different origins. Some tank battalions, for instance those of the 70th Armoured Brigade, stationed near al-Kiswah south of Damascus, had mainly Alawi crews, while their commanders were Sunnis.[9] Muta' Safadi described this situation as follows: 'Teachers became officers and peasants became soldiers and non-commissioned officers, with the result that the 70th [Armoured] Brigade in particular became almost [completely] Alawi, as to both its command and its rank and file'.[10]

The authority of these Sunni commanders over their Alawi crews could easily be brought to naught if Alawi officers serving in other armed units instructed their co-religionists not to carry out their orders. Some officers exercised active control in this way over a far larger part of the Syrian armed forces than they were formally entitled to do under the official military command structure.

The existence of such prohibited 'collateral contacts' (ittisalat janibiyah) was clearly demonstrated by the words of the Alawi General

Muhammad 'Umran, who, early in 1966, declared during a party meeting:

> Mahmud Hamra [a Sunni officer from Hama] cannot command his battalion [of the 70th Armoured Brigade], because 70 per cent of the non-commissioned officers in his battalion are led by 'Ali Mustafa [Alawi battalion commander in the same brigade and supporter of 'Umran]. The same applies to Muhammad al-Hajj Rahmun [Sunni] and Kasir Mahmud [Alawi] respectively.[11]

Another example of the fact that the army command structure and discipline were undermined by the manipulation of sectarian loyalties was the suspension of one non-Sunni officer's membership of the Ba'th military party organisation in October 1965. The principal reason for his suspension was that he had set different groups within his military unit against each other on a sectarian basis, and also that he had instructed an aide-de-camp belonging to his own religious community to be ready to arrest all Sunni NCOs in his army unit as soon as he had given the order by telephone to do so.[12] In a speech broadcast during this period by Radio Damascus, President Amin al-Hafiz referred to the fact that 'friendship and other ties had undermined military discipline in the Armed Forces' and stressed the necessity for absolute and strict obedience among the military.[13]

To undermine the authority of military commanders by manipulating the sectarian loyalties of their men was not a new phenomenon in the history of the Syrian Army: similar tactics had been used, for instance, during the 'Separatist Period'. Early in 1963 the Damascene Lieutenant-Colonel al-Nahlawi had tried unsuccessfully to regain control over the Syrian Army through a military coup with the aid of some of his Damascene followers who had not been dismissed. One reason for his failure was that some of the officers had lost control over their own men, who had refused to take further orders from their Damascene commanders, or had simply left their armed units, at the instigation of Alawi and Sunni Shaykhs.[14]

Apparently the appointment of Sunni officers to high military posts was sometimes principally intended to satisfy their Sunni army comrades, as well as to diminish their distrust of military men from religious minorities. Such appointments helped to counter the impression that key positions in the armed forces were occupied mainly by members of specific religious communities. But to hold a high military function did not imply having independent power.[15]

Overt sectarianism fails as a tactic:
the expulsion of 'Umran

The sectarian practices described above caused power relations within the Syrian armed forces to be largely determined by personal alliances between leaders of officers' factions who, in turn, mostly attracted their followers from sectarian, regional and tribal connections and adherents. The officer corps as a whole, however, was not yet divided along sectarian lines. Thus in 1965 the Alawi chief of staff of the Syrian Army, Major-General Salah Jadid, was backed by Alawi officers with whom he had strong personal ties. This did not imply that all Alawi officers supported Jadid, nor that he had only Alawi followers. The military intelligence chief, Lieutenant-Colonel Ahmad Suwaydani, a Sunni from Hawran, for instance, was one of Jadid's many non-Alawi supporters at the time. Suwaydani, in his turn, could rely on the support of his own (mainly Sunni) Hawrani officers. The latter, of course, did not form one compact bloc either but were divided into different factions, led by officers such as Ahmad Suwaydani, Mustafa al-Hajj 'Ali and Musa al-Zu'bi, all members of the Ba'thist Military Committee. Numerous other Ba'thist officers did not belong to any sectarian and/or regional officers' bloc; their sectarian or regional backgrounds played no role and they did not exploit organisationally prohibited 'collateral contacts' (*ittisalat janibiyah*) to strengthen their positions on sectarian, regional and/or tribal bases. Alliances between leaders of officers' factions often cut across factors such as common religion, tribe, region of origin or ideology. Personal interests often played an important role in forming or breaking up bonds with other officers. Alliances could easily be broken and ideological principles set aside by officers whose power positions or personal interests were threatened.

Examples of abruptly changing loyalties and alliances between military officers have been described in detail in various studies.[16] An extreme case was Mustafa Talas's switch of loyalty in 1965 from President Amin al-Hafiz to Salah Jadid following his entanglement in a nightclub brawl. Amin al-Hafiz initiated disciplinary action against him but Jadid managed to help him and thus won him over to his own side.[17] Later, Sunni supporters of Amin al-Hafiz ascribed Talas's switch to sectarian motives, circulating rumours that his mother was of Alawi origin.[18] These rumours were obviously spread with the intention of strengthening the 'sectarian' solidarity of Amin al-Hafiz's Sunni supporters. Another explanation for Mustafa Talas's joining the side of Salah Jadid (and Hafiz al-Asad) could have been his reportedly strong personal relationship with Hafiz al-Asad dating back to the beginning of their military life in 1953, when they both joined the Military Academy.[19] Officers who changed alliances easily could nevertheless have clearcut ideological ideas.[20]

Describing the situation in the latter half of 1965, Munif al-Razzaz wrote:

> Coalitions in this struggle for power started to assume strange shapes which had nothing to do with principles ... The principles with which the struggle was concealed were nothing but a weapon with which to attack rivals, and a place of refuge serving as a protection against the rival. [The principles] were at each stage open to change.[21]

Officers' factions, even though made up mainly of people from the same religious community, could thus easily belong to opposing political camps. This was clearly demonstrated in December 1964, when the Alawi Major-General Muhammad 'Umran was expelled from Syria by the other members of the Military Committee, under the accusation of having built up a sectarian (Alawi) bloc in the army, and of being the principal person responsible for the atmosphere of sectarian distrust which then existed.[22] Not only senior Sunni officers such as President Amin al-Hafiz and Musa al-Zu'bi accused 'Umran of spreading sectarianism but also prominent Alawi officers such as Salah Jadid and Hafiz al-Asad.[23]

Although, like 'Umran, Jadid and al-Asad depended largely on personal Alawi military supporters to maintain their positions of power and very probably profited from sectarian, regional and tribal loyalties to strengthen those positions, they were wise enough not to speak about this openly, as 'Umran had done.

'Umran had declared: 'The *Fatimiyah* must play its role' (*Inn al-Fatimiyah yajib an ta'khudh Dawraha*),[24] obviously with the intention of playing off the heterodox Muslim officers (i.e. the Alawis, Druzes and Isma'ilis being the *Fatimiyah*) on sectarian grounds against his most prominent rival, the Sunni president and commander-in-chief of the armed forces, Amin al-Hafiz.

Most Ba'thist officers could not tolerate the use of such overt sectarian-tinged declarations since, according to the secular Arab nationalist Ba'th ideology, Ba'thists should strive to banish sectarian, regional and tribal group feelings. In later periods of the power struggle among Ba'thist officers it was repeatedly proven that, in the final analysis, those who spoke openly in favour of strengthening the position of their own religious group weakened their own positions rather than those of their opponents, who also reinforced their positions on a sectarian basis but did not openly speak about it.

Personal ambitions were among the most important reasons for the power struggle between 'Umran and other members of the Military Committee, headed by Sunni President Amin al-Hafiz. 'Umran's overt exploitation of sectarian ties was not the main cause of his banishment by the other members, but was gratefully seized upon as an argument that could be used against him.[25]

The sectarian aspect of the power struggle between 'Umran and the others could not be hidden for long from the Lebanese press. The anti-Ba'thist conservative Lebanese daily *al-Hayat* went so far as to ascribe the rivalries between the most prominent Alawi Ba'thist military leaders to tribal contrasts, pointing out that Muhammad 'Umran was from the Alawi tribal confederation of the *Khayyatun*, whereas Salah Jadid was from the *Haddadun*. *Al-Hayat* furthermore drew the conclusion that the position of Alawi officers had been weakened as a result of the expulsion of 'Umran, stating that these had remained divided and had not all gone over to the side of Salah Jadid.[26] Such allegations, whether true or false, did not pass unnoticed by the Syrian Ba'thists, as was shown by the fierce manner in which the *al-Hayat* article was criticised in the Ba'thist-dominated Syrian daily *al-Thawrah*:

> British-sponsored papers such as *al-Hayat* always stirred up sectarian differences ... They distinguished each Syrian ruler, officer or official by saying to what particular religion or tribe he belonged, giving the impression that tribal and other differences between government officials would eventually lead to the breakdown of the regime in Syria.[27]

Internally, the Syrian Ba'thist rulers later admitted that the rumours spread, *inter alia*, by the Lebanese mass media had created the impression among some party members that the Sunnis (under the leadership of President Amin al-Hafiz) had scored a victory against the Alawis when the Alawi General 'Umran had been expelled from the country.[28] In reality, however, prominent Alawi officers such as Salah Jadid and Hafiz al-Asad remained in the Syrian armed forces and had the support of powerful military factions which, even without 'Umran and his military supporters, constituted a dangerous threat to President Amin al-Hafiz, as was to become clear in 1965.

It may be noted that 'Umran on the one hand and Salah Jadid and Hafiz al-Asad on the other were from different regions. Michael Van Dusen has stressed the importance of regional loyalties in explaining the 'Umran–Jadid rivalry:

> Muhammad 'Umran was an articulate 'Alawi from the Hama area; he had been close to the Hawrani movement but he never was an al-Hawrani man nor motivated by religious considerations, the latter reflecting the greater assimilation of 'Alawis in the Hama area. (Both the 'Alawis and

Isma'ilis of the Hama area were better assimilated than those on the coast.) For many officers, he represented Hama at a time when the major Hama factions in the fourth generation [of Syrian officers since independence] had already been eliminated in intra-generational quarrels. Salah Jadid, on the other hand, led the increasingly important al-Ladhaqiya [i.e. Latakia] faction in the army.[29]

Sectarian polarisation in the armed forces

After Amin al-Hafiz and Salah Jadid had successfully eliminated Muhammad 'Umran, their most prominent rival in the Military Committee, they had to face each other.

An incident that woke their slumbering rivalry into an open power struggle took place in 1965 between Jadid and Major Salim Hatum, who commanded elite paratroops stationed near Damascus.

Since the Ba'thist takeover of power in 1963, tensions had developed between the senior leaders of the Military Committee and the junior members of the military organisation. Some of the latter, foremost among them the Druze Major Salim Hatum, had taken an active part in the 8 March 1963 coup and subsequently held sensitive military command posts. Unlike the leaders of the Military Committee, however, they were not appointed to the highest military ranks or to high party and state positions. 'Apparently these officers envied not only the leaders of the Military Committee but also civilian party militants who enjoyed an elevation of rank and status while they themselves had only a share of anonymous power which not everyone is able to enjoy and appreciate.'[30]

In an internal party document these tensions among the military were later explained as follows:

Considering the leading role played by the first *Military Committee* following the Revolution and the many competences and roles it filled in the party, Army and government, and the particular positions thus acquired by its members, all this created a certain sensitivity between these comrades and other comrades holding lower ranks who had carried arms on the morning of the Eighth of March, and between them and other comrades of various ranks who for a number of reasons predating the Revolution could not carry arms ... This sensitivity among the comrades grew daily and the Military Committee's neglect of the Organisation's affairs, its preoccupation with the affairs of government, its entry into the endless struggle among the leaders of the Party and the Revolution, and its aloofness from the military rank and file, caused that sensitivity to deepen.[31]

This tense situation exploded in April 1965 when a fierce quarrel broke out between Salim Hatum and Salah Jadid. Hatum had forced his way into the other's house and, threatening him with a pistol, demanded Jadid's immediate resignation as Chief of Staff of the Syrian Army.

Apparently, Hatum considered Jadid to be responsible for the fact that he himself, in spite of his lion's share in the execution of the 8 March 1963 coup, unlike the senior leaders of the Military Committee, had not been appointed to one of the higher military ranks or party positions and had not obtained the status accompanying these positions. In reaction to Hatum's threats, Jadid offered his resignation to the supreme commander of the armed forces, President Lieutenant-General Amin al-Hafiz. His offer was rejected, however, since it was considered unacceptable that a chief of staff should be forced to resign in such a way. Amin al-Hafiz, who should have taken disciplinary measures against Hatum after this incident, did not do so. Munif al-Razzaz later gave the following explanation for this omission:

> Amin al-Hafiz supported Salim Hatum. Earlier, he had started to have doubts about Salah Jadid's loyalty towards himself and now he laughed up his sleeve about the new situation that had developed. Amin al-Hafiz did not want to take punitive measures against Hatum so as to create a kind of alliance with him against Salah Jadid. Salah Jadid had from the start had the feeling that his basic support had to come as much as possible from the Alawis. These [Alawis] felt that people like Salim Hatum wanted to get rid of Salah Jadid by working on the basis of [the Army being divided into factions composed of] Alawis, Druzes, Sunnis, etc.[32]

In the second half of 1965 the confrontation between the regime's most important military rivals was clearly expressed during party and military meetings; al-Hafiz continually brought up the subject of sectarianism, and fiercely and critically accused Jadid of building his own sectarian (Alawi) bloc within the Army. Such accusations did not gain support for al-Hafiz but had rather the reverse effect, resulting in his further estrangement from Alawi officers in general; the latter, out of self-preservation, went over in even larger numbers to the rival camp of Jadid. On the other hand, and for similar reasons, many Sunni officers rallied around al-Hafiz, feeling more secure in a military camp dominated by co-religionists, however much they may have opposed sectarian bloc formation.[33]

Within the army, Sunni followers of Amin al-Hafiz deliberately tried to create a cohesive Sunni bloc, opposing Alawi and Druze officers in particular. As became evident from later interrogations, a number of these Sunni officers tried to encourage sectarian strife within their own and other army units, telling NCOs and lower ranks that the Alawi and Druze military were preparing a coup with the aim of deposing Sunni President Amin al-Hafiz and, subsequently, of dominating and humiliating the Sunni population. These *agents provocateurs* continuously tried to give the impression that the power struggle was about a religious question rather than the opposite, namely, that religious feelings were stirred up with the aim of achieving political power.[34]

With the help of some of his Sunni supporters in the Syrian Intelligence Service, Amin al-Hafiz tried to strengthen his position, supplying weapons and support to various (predominantly Sunni) groups which in earlier periods had turned against the Ba'th regime. In an internal party document dated 1966, they were labelled as 're-actionaries, Nasserists, Hawranists and neutrals', and al-Hafiz was even accused of encouraging these groups to stage a 'civilian revolt'. Al-Hafiz's Sunni supporter, Major 'Abd al-Ghani Barru, was accused of having 'distributed arms to a number of civilian supporters of Akram al-Hawrani in Hama and others who had taken part in the [sectarian-tinged] Hama revolt' of April 1964 against the Ba'th regime, and 'urged them to undertake sabotage activities.' According to the same source, Badr Jum'ah, head of the Aleppo Security Branch and a staunch (Sunni) supporter of al-Hafiz, made efforts to supply weapons to 'unionist Sunni groups' for an eventual 'sectarian war in the interest of the Lieutenant-General' (Amin al-Hafiz), who was also from Aleppo.[35]

The fact that many Alawi officers went over to Jadid's camp as a result of these developments did not necessarily imply that they now supported him and his views. It did mean, however, that together with Jadid they turned against al-Hafiz.[36]

While Amin al-Hafiz, without clearly wanting to, had driven most Alawi officers into the opposing camp, in the second half of 1965 he also lost the support of his most important military Druze supporters, notably Salim Hatum and Hamad 'Ubayd, who were manipulated to Jadid's side for reasons that had little or nothing to do with the sectarian aspect of the power struggle. Hamad 'Ubayd was appointed Minister of Defence in September 1965. Jamil Shayya, the only civilian Druze member of the Syrian Regional Command in this period, also switched loyalties from al-Hafiz to Jadid.[37]

The most prominent (but not all) Isma'ili Ba'thist officers, such as Ahmad al-Mir and 'Abd al-Karim al-Jundi, already supported Jadid.[38] Despite al-Hafiz's accusations of sectarianism directed towards Jadid, the latter's most prominent Sunni military supporters such as Mustafa Talas and Ahmad Suwaydani remained firmly at his side.

During the power struggle between al-Hafiz and Jadid, the manipulations with sectarian, regional and tribal loyalties caused the tension within the Syrian armed forces to increase to such an extent that far-reaching polarisation resulted between Sunnis and members of religious minorities. Sectarian contradistinctions among the military consequently began to overshadow almost all other differences.[39] The officer corps became divided into two rival camps, with a heavy representation of Sunnis on the one side and Alawis, Druzes and Isma'ilis on the other. This sectarian polarisation was based not so much on sectarian unanimity among military men from the same religious community as on common opposition and sectarian distrust.[40] This was directed against military men from other religious communities, who, it was felt, were threatening the other's position, and whose behaviour was interpreted as a form of sectarianism, regionalism and/or tribalism aimed at strengthening their own position as a religious, regional and/or tribal group to the disadvantage of other groups.

The al-Hafiz/Jadid rivalry was reflected not only in the armed forces and the military party organisation, but also in relations between the major civilian party institutions of the Ba'th. In particular, it was expressed in rivalry between the Syrian Regional Command, controlled by Jadid and his supporters, and the (pan-Arab) National Command, dominated by Amin al-Hafiz, and the Ba'thists of the 'older' party generation led by Michel 'Aflaq. In the years subsequent to 1963 the National Command almost completely lost its control over the Syrian party apparatus, which was formally subordinate to it.

In the second half of 1965 the National Command tried to mediate between Jadid and al-Hafiz. In an effort to strengthen its own position, it had tried to exploit the al-Hafiz/Jadid rivalry so as to play one off against the other. When, in 1965, al-Hafiz was isolated in the Syrian Regional Command by Jadid's supporters he in turn – just like 'Umran in December 1964 – sought rapprochement with the National Command, hoping thus to reinforce his position in the Syrian regional party apparatus.[41] In an effort to break Jadid's dominance over the Syrian party apparatus, the National Command decided on 19 December 1965 to take over all authority by dissolving the Syrian Regional Command.[42] After doing so, the National Commmand stated that military discipline in the Army was to be restored and, in an internal statement issued to the military, declared:

> The National Command sharply criticises the purge of comrades, and will protect them all against any attempt to that end. At the same time, it will not allow the 'appropriation' (*istimlak*) of army units and their transformation into personal blocs. The National Command will oppose

any loyalty other than that to the Party. It is against sectarianism, against raising [the question of] sectarianism, against personal loyalty, as well as against the tribal blocs. It only recognises loyalty to the Party. At the present stage, the National Command, together with the Premier and the Minister of Defence, is the competent authority for solving the problems of the Army, for eliminating its interference in politics and government affairs, and for returning it to its militarism. The National Command, together with the Premier and Minister of Defence, are to effect the military transfers necessary to do away with the situation of tension, fear and interference.[43]

The sectarian polarisation of the Syrian armed forces into rival camps made it extremely difficult for the National Command to find a new minister of defence who would be acceptable to both groups and would also be capable of restoring military discipline.[44]

According to al-Razzaz, only two of the higher Ba'thist officers, i.e. Muhammad 'Umran and Fahd al-Sha'ir (Druze), were qualified to become minister of defence because they did not belong to either of the rival parties. 'Umran was the only senior Alawi officer who had not sided with the Jadid-dominated camp, since Jadid (like al-Asad and al-Hafiz) had been among those responsible for 'Umran's expulsion from Syria in December 1964.[45] The appointment of a Sunni officer as minister of defence would probably have been interpreted as a personal affront by the Alawi officers and would consequently have accentuated the sectarian character of the power struggle. A proposal to appoint Muhammad Rabah al-Tawil (a Sunni from Latakia city) as minister of defence was therefore rejected.[46] A majority within the National Command, including Amin al-Hafiz, finally gave their preference to 'Umran as minister of defence, and on 2 January 1966 he was included in Salah al-Din Bitar's newly formed cabinet in this capacity.

The main argument used in favour of 'Umran's appointment was that it might diminish the sectarian character of the power struggle by putting the Alawi officers at their ease. An additional argument for Premier Bitar to have 'Umran appointed was that he was personally supported by some of 'Umran's Alawi followers.[47] His appointment also had tactical advantages for Amin al-Hafiz and the majority of the National Command, however: it might cause a rift in the relative unanimity among Alawi officers, of whom one part might rally around 'Umran while the other might remain loyal to Jadid. Such a split would strengthen the position of Amin al-Hafiz and the majority of the National Command, who would then be able to effectuate their plans.[48] Hafiz al-Asad later declared in an interview that the National Command at the time had suggested the appointment of 'Umran as minister of defence 'to profit from the ties which 'Umran and Amin al-Hafiz had with factions within the armed forces, in order to purge the Regional Command with their help, and subsequently to distance itself from 'Umran and Amin al-Hafiz by playing them off against each other.'[49]

Amin al-Hafiz's hostile attitude towards the Alawi officers, the majority of whom he now strongly distrusted, made any fruitful co-operation between him and Muhammad 'Umran extremely unlikely. Within a few days of 'Umran's appointment as Minister of Defence, tense relations had developed between them, making it very difficult to transfer to less sensitive military units those officers who most threatened the regime of the National Command, i.e. Salim Hatum, 'Izzat Jadid (Alawi) and Ahmad Suwaydani.

Munif al-Razzaz was of the opinion that the transfers of these three officers could have been effected around 20 February 1966 with the help of 'Umran's most prominent Alawi supporter, 'Ali Mustafa, a battalion commander of the 70th Armoured Brigade, who supported the majority of the National Command. But Amin al-Hafiz, who in the meantime had acquired almost an anti-Alawi complex and had started to consider virtually all Alawis as personal enemies, refused to accept that an Alawi supporter of the National Command – who as such opposed military men like Hatum, Jadid and Suwaydani – should mobilise his military units. When 'Ali Mustafa nevertheless did so on the suggestion of al-Razzaz, Amin al-Hafiz demanded that the move should be cancelled immediately.

It was thus impossible to take the precautionary measures that were necessary for the transfer of the National Command's most dangerous military opponents, and the way was open for Jadid's supporters to carry out a successful military coup.[50]

The bloc of Alawi officers who rallied behind 'Umran after his return from exile proved relatively weak. In other words, his appointment had not caused a serious split among the Alawi officers, as had been hoped and expected by Amin al-Hafiz and the majority of the National Command.

Within the armed forces 'Umran's appointment met with strong criticism, and he did not appear to be *persona grata* either among the non-Alawi officers or among the vast majority of Alawi officers. They strongly criticised his sectarian practices and intrigues behind the scenes, and preferred to see him go rather than serve in such an important military post.[51]

A principal task allotted to 'Umran as minister of defence was to restore military discipline in the armed forces. It seems doubtful, however, whether members of the National Command such as 'Aflaq really thought 'Umran capable of restoring military discipline in the armed forces, since he had a reputation for exploiting sectarian group feelings in order to strengthen his own position. Sectarian tensions increased rather than diminished after 'Umran's appointment. Some military party members demanded his expulsion from both the party and the government on account of his overt sectarian practices. They disapproved of any kind of sectarianism and regionalism and even proposed that people should be executed if they let themselves be influenced by such factors.[52] All in all, a clear indication of the crisis situation that then existed in the Syrian armed forces.

On 23 February 1966, President Amin al-Hafiz and Jadid's other opponents on the National Command were deposed by a military coup, in the execution of which Salim Hatum and 'Izzat Jadid played central roles.

The armed units stationed around Damascus, which were mostly dominated by Alawi and Druze officers, immediately rallied behind the coup. Major opposition came from army units stationed far away from the capital, e.g. in Latakia, Hama, Homs and Aleppo, where several Sunni officers who supported Amin al-Hafiz tried to turn the military and political situation to their own advantage.[53]

The fact that army units stationed directly around Damascus offered little resistance to the coup was clearly a result of the earlier-mentioned tactics of minoritarian members of the Syrian military command: officers who were 'trusted' on sectarian grounds, because they came from the same religious minority communities, were placed close to Damascus, whereas those who, for similar reasons were 'not trusted' – because they were Sunnis – were stationed near the Israeli front, or far away from the Syrian capital more to the north of the country.[54]

The new coup resulted in the purge of some of the more prominent Sunni officers' factions. The most important members of 'Umran's faction were also dismissed. In the course of 1966 they were officially purged from the military party organisation, under such accusations as having been guilty of sectarian, regional and/or tribal bloc formation within the armed forces. Mustafa 'Umran, a nephew of Muhammad 'Umran, was accused of 'participation in the leadership of a sectarian and tribal bloc' or, in other words, participation in the leadership of an Alawi officers' faction in which the 'Umran family played an important role.[55]

Those who were purged in this way showed a strikingly high percentage of Sunnis.[56] This resulted once more in increased representation of members of religious communities, especially the heterodox Islamic, to the disadvantage of the Sunnis.

4

The purge of Druze officers in the Syrian armed forces

The deposed National Command's secret organisation

After the coup of 23 February 1966, Munif al-Razzaz, secretary-general of the deposed National Command, managed to evade arrest and went into hiding in Damascus. From his ever-changing hiding places he started to form a new party organisation made up of separate military and civilian sections, the obvious aim being the reinstatement in power of the National Command. The civilian section was led by al-Razzaz himself, and the Druze Major-General Fahd al-Sha'ir was found willing to take on the task of setting up a military bureau and leading the military party organisation. Although in principle al-Razzaz's newly formed party apparatus accepted individuals from all religious communities as members, this was not the case in the military party section, which specifically excluded Alawis.

In the power struggle which took place in the Syrian army before 23 February 1966, sectarian loyalties were so important, and the confidence between officers from different religious communities so shaken, that members of Fahd al-Sha'ir's Military Bureau at first refused to allow Alawis into their organisation, fearing that to do so would probably result in their plans being discovered by Alawi supporters of Salah Jadid and Hafiz al-Asad.[1]

Early in 1967, a number of officers were tried in Damascus, accused of having been involved in the plot of the deposed National Command which had ended in failure in September 1966. Munif al-Razzaz was then accused by supporters of the Syrian Regional Command's regime of having instructed some officers, notably Major Mustafa al-Hajj 'Ali and Lieutenant-Colonel Salah Namur (both Sunnis), 'to accept into their organisations members from specific communities only', and 'to stimulate and exploit sectarian feelings' in an effort to cause the fall of the Syrian Regional Command.[2] In an interview held later, Munif al-Razzaz commented as follows on these accusations of sectarianism:

48

I did not exclude Alawis. On the contrary: the civilian party organisation which we started to set up after 23 February 1966, and which was opposed to the existing situation and was against the blocs of Salah Jadid, Hafiz al-Asad and Salim Hatum, included a great many Alawis. When we started to set up the military organisation and had entrusted Fahd al-Sha'ir with the task of building it up and he had begun to form the command of the Military Bureau, I suggested – as did professeur Michel ['Aflaq], who had written a letter from Beirut – that [the Alawi officer] 'Ali Mustafa would be included in the Military Bureau. As a matter of fact, the attitude which had originated shortly before 23 February 1966 gave the power struggle a predominantly sectarian character, and caused the military officers leading the Military Bureau to bear a grudge against having an Alawi take part in their activities as long as these were secret. They feared that the admittance of Alawis into their organisation would probably lead to its discovery.

Thus, in spite of several letters exchanged between them and me regarding the acceptance of 'Ali Mustafa as a member of the Military Bureau, they decided unanimously that they would dissolve the existing military command if he were to be admitted. In this way I was forced to accept. I agreed to postpone ['Ali Mustafa's admission to the Military Bureau] for as long as there was any lack of confidence.

We particularly had 'Ali Mustafa in mind. Although he had been removed from the Army [and appointed abroad in the Syrian Foreign Service], he used to come to Syria and see Hafiz Asad. I believe that at that time it would have been possible to utilise his presence in order to separate Hafiz Asad from Salah Jadid. Notwithstanding his having been expelled from the Army, 'Ali Mustafa was a protégé of Hafiz Asad. At first he was a protégé of Muhammad 'Umran, and his attitude was sympathetic towards the National Command.

It was possible to profit from his presence, but the Military Bureau refused to take Alawis into the leadership for fear of being discovered, because at that time Alawi ties were stronger than ever. The civilian organisation, on the other hand, did have Alawi members. So we were not against their admission. But the officers said: 'We definitely do not want Alawis at this stage' – because the military organisation was very vulnerable. This did not imply that the military excluded them because they were Alawis. At that stage a special kind of confidence was needed, however, and therefore they refused to admit Alawis.[3]

In fact, the efforts of the deposed National Command to have 'Ali Mustafa join the Military Bureau led by Fahd al-Sha'ir resembled the earlier appointment of Alawi General Muhammad 'Umran as Minister of Defence in January 1966. In both cases the appointment of a prominent Alawi officer – who was supposed to sympathise with some members of the National Command – was apparently proposed with the intention of causing a split among other Alawi officers.

Salim Hatum's secret organisation

Shortly after the 23 February 1966 coup, the new Syrian rulers held an Extraordinary Regional Congress of the Ba'th Party in Damascus to discuss the reasons which had led to the coup. It was decided that all those who had taken standpoints based on sectarian, regional or tribal loyalties should be severely punished, particularly if party members. Further, it was declared that the 'Movement of 23 February' had not only been an answer to the so-called 'rightist and dictatorial mentality' of the deposed members of the National Command and General Amin al-Hafiz, but was also intended to put a stop to sectarian manipulations. Accusations against those who had taken over power on 23 February, to the effect that their power was based on sectarian and regional ties, were strongly rejected on the grounds that the coup had been undertaken by people 'from all Syrian provinces'. The same was said to apply to those who had been arrested or expelled from the country, and who were stated to be neither 'a separate group' nor members of a 'specific religious community'.[4] In the previous chapter, however, we have demonstrated that sectarian, regional and tribal bloc formations played an important role in the two major opposing camps in the power struggle during the months that preceded the coup.

It was striking that at the end of the Extraordinary Regional Congress two of the most important Druze officers of the regime's military organisation, Hamad 'Ubayd and Salim Hatum, who had both been members of the Provisional Syrian Regional Command which officially assumed power on 23 February 1966, were not re-elected to the new Regional Command.[5]

Hamad 'Ubayd lost his prominent position in the party (and the Army) as a consequence of the attitude he took shortly after the 23 February 1966 coup. 'Ubayd had been minister of defence in Dr Yusuf Zu'ayyin's Cabinet, which resigned on 22 December 1965 following the dissolution of the Syrian Regional Command, and he had thought that he had the right to regain this former government position in reward for his support of Jadid against al-Hafiz since September 1965, when he was first appointed minister of defence.[6] Moreover, al-Hafiz and the National Command had now been deposed. 'Ubayd's lack of leadership qualities and rumours about his corrupt nature, however, made it obvious that the important Ministry of Defence could not be entrusted to him again, the more so as his support was no longer essential to Jadid. Even before 'Ubayd's appointment as minister of defence, rumours had circulated about his corrupt activities. His lack of leadership qualities – necessary for such an important position – was also well known within the officer corps. Officers of the Qatana garrison, where 'Ubayd had commanded two brigades before becoming minister of defence, complained about his weak personality and the fact that he was incapable of leading his men. This gave rise to a situation in which the other commanding officers of the two brigades at Qatana were, according to their own description of the situation, 'running their army units on a basis of self-rule (*Tasyir Dhati*)'.[7]

The appointment of Hafiz al-Asad as minister of defence on 23 February 1966 (even before the new cabinet had been announced) was therefore strongly criticised and disapproved of by Hamad 'Ubayd, who as a result got into difficulties with the leaders of the new regime.[8]

Shortly after the coup, supporters of Amin al-Hafiz prevailed upon the disappointed Hamad 'Ubayd to create conditions in Aleppo which would be favourable to a counter-coup from their side.[9] The plans for this counter-coup failed, however, and 'Ubayd and most of the others involved were arrested by supporters of the new regime.[10]

Salim Hatum's position in the party was weakened due to severe criticism of the savagery with which Amin al-Hafiz had been taken prisoner.[11] Salim Hatum, who in fact had had a lion's share in the execution of the 23 February 1966 coup, not only was not remunerated for his active and decisive role but lost ground in the party. He felt that he had been deceived by Salah Jadid, whom he had supported in the coup, and felt wronged at not being rewarded with the military functions and power he coveted. Major Hatum, who commanded the army's elite commando battalion (*Maghawir*), aspired to the position of commander of an armoured brigade, combined with responsibility for the army's security affairs.[12] All this made him a willing conspirator against the new regime, which he had so recently helped to put in power. In the hope of realising his ambitions after all, Hatum started to build up his own military organisation, of which the junior officers and men were almost exclusively from the Jabal al-Duruz, and in the majority of cases were members of the Druze community. In addition to some important Druze officers such as Lieutenant-Colonel Talal Abu 'Asali, commander of the Syrian army units at the front with Israel and secretary of the corresponding military party branch, the leadership included some non-Druzes such as Mustafa al-Hajj 'Ali, the Sunni commander of the Military Intelligence Service, who was from Hawran, Syria's southern province bordering on the Jabal al-Duruz.

In the civilian sector Hatum got in touch with members of the so-called Shufi group, which also consisted largely of Druzes. The Shufi group (in Ba'thist party literature also known under the name of *Munshaqqun*, i.e. those who 'broke away' from the party) was a former Syrian Ba'th Party faction led by Hammud al-Shufi (Druze from al-

Suwayda'), who had been secretary-general of the Syrian Regional Command from September 1963 until February 1964, in which period he played an important role in rebuilding the civilian party apparatus of the Ba'th in Syria. The Shufi group had a strong, specifically Marxist, ideological orientation and had many supporters in several Syrian party branches. Its followers were by far the most numerous, however, in the party branch of Hatum's home district: the Jabal al-Duruz. Their critical attitude towards most leaders of the Military Committee had caused some prominent members of the Shufi group (including Hammud al-Shufi) to be purged from the Ba'th Party in 1964 and 1965.[13] In 1966 a number of the group's supporters were still within the party apparatus of the new regime, and Salim Hatum acted more or less as their representative in the Army.[14] Hatum's relationship with the Shufi group dated as far back as 1963, when they started to lose power within the party and chose Hatum to act as their military *patron*.[15] Hamad 'Ubayd also sympathised with the Shufi group for some time.[16]

The fact that many prominent members of the Shufi group originated from the Jabal al-Duruz, like Salim Hatum himself, probably induced them to cooperate with him notwithstanding the fact that he did not hold a clearly defined ideological point of view.

Hatum's military organisation and that of the deposed National Command were in themselves not strong enough to cause the fall of the regime of Jadid and al-Asad. For purely tactical reasons, Hatum and members of the Military Bureau led by Fahd al-Sha'ir therefore decided to cooperate. The two military organisations continued to exist separately, however, and only their leaders worked together to a certain extent.[17] Several meetings between representatives of both groups were held at which a plan was worked out with the aim of deposing the established regime.[18] According to Munif al-Razzaz, Hatum was informed of the details of the plans for a coup, worked out mainly by Fahd al-Sha'ir, only a few days before the planned date. He had not been informed earlier of these details to prevent him knowing exactly which army units contained members of the National Command's military organisation. Hatum, in fact, had never been really trusted by the leaders of the National Command's Military Bureau.[19] In view of the earlier relationship between Hatum and the National Command, which had been deposed with his help, it is clear that the two groups only cooperated with the idea of each disposing of the other afterwards.[20]

Alawi–Druze sectarian polarisation and Salim Hatum's abortive coup (8 September 1966)

On 10 August 1966 the Syrian Regional Command, more or less by accident, discovered the plans for the coup by the deposed National Command and Salim Hatum. During the rest of that month it gradually came to know the names of the other people involved.

Fahd al-Sha'ir had selected 3 September 1966 as a suitable date for a military coup. Between 25 August and 3 September 1966, however, the major part of the deposed National Command's secret military organisation was discovered, including the composition of its Military Bureau. Since many of its officers were arrested, there was little likelihood of its undertaking action against the regime of the Regional Command with any reasonable chance of success. Fahd al-Sha'ir therefore went into hiding on instructions from al-Razzaz, and abandoned any further plans for military cooperation with Hatum. Hatum himself, however, continued with his plot against the Regional Command, and this culminated in an abortive coup on 8 September.[21]

Early in September 1966, Salim Hatum, Talal Abu 'Asali and Mustafa al-Hajj 'Ali started to criticise openly the arrests that had been carried out in August of officers who had been involved in the recently discovered plot. In their criticism they stressed that there was, reportedly, not a single Alawi among the officers arrested or wanted for arrest, but only members of other religious groups. This, according to Hatum, Abu 'Asali and al-Hajj 'Ali (as it was later described), was a 'sensitive affair' for which the onus lay with the leadership of the army and the party.[22]

Salim Hatum was able to exploit the sectarianism issue by pointing to the fact that since the coup of 23 February 1966, prominent Druze officers such as Hamad 'Ubayd had been purged from both the party and the Army, and that now other Druze military bosses, such as Talal Abu 'Asali and Fahd al-Sha'ir – the highest-ranking Druze officer in the Syrian Army – were wanted for arrest by the Army Command on accusations of involvement in the recently discovered plot.[23]

It is hardly surprising that a relatively large number of Druzes were among the officers arrested in connection with this plot, since they formed the principal membership of Hatum's secret military organisation. Moreover, Fahd al-Sha'ir, when building up the secret military organisation of the deposed National Command, had as a matter of course drawn recruits from his own Druze religious community, since this offered additional advantages in preserving secrecy. Anyone who recruits from his own religious community, especially in situations where sectarian distrust and tension play an important role, runs less risk of his plans leaking out to members of other religious communities.

Reasons of secrecy, security and lack of trust in Alawi officers had caused the Military Bureau of the deposed National Command from the beginning to refuse to admit members of this religious community to their military organisation, so that it was only natural that Alawis were not among those arrested in relation to the plot. Why this was so was practically unknown outside the Military Bureau concerned and the leadership of Hatum's military organisation. Since the power struggle between Amin al-Hafiz and Salah Jadid, sectarian distrust towards a number of Alawi officers had increased within part of the Syrian officer corps. It was not difficult for Hatum and his supporters to exploit and strengthen this distrust among their own co-religionists, of whom the Druzes were by far the most numerous.

Hatum and his close Druze associates thus created the impression – which to some extent had the effect of a self-fulfilling prophecy – of an Alawi–Druze sectarian polarisation in the Syrian armed forces.

Together with Talal Abu 'Asali, Hatum succeeded in gaining the support of the majority of the (almost exclusively Druze) civilian party branch of the Jabal al-Duruz, and of the members of the deposed National Command's secret military organisation who were stationed in the Jabal al-Duruz.[24]

The arrest of Druze officers who had originally supported and participated in the coup of 23 February 1966, as well as the efforts of the Army Command to appoint supporters of Salah Jadid and Hafiz al-Asad to politically-strategically important positions within specific army units which were dominated by (Druze) members of the Hatum group, caused great alarm and unrest in the Jabal al-Duruz party branch.[25] On 7 September 1966, its command consequently presented a special memorandum to Salah Jadid in which they elucidated the viewpoint of the majority of members of the al-Suwayda' Branch.[26]

These members, it was declared, still supported the purge of so-called 'rightist elements'[27] from the party, as long as those involved did not include officers who had participated in the 23 February 1966 coup on the side of the Regional Command. The al-Suwayda' Branch Command apparently referred in particular to transferred or dismissed Druze officers from the al-Suwayda' region. With regard to these officers, the al-Suwayda' Branch demanded that all those who had in the meantime been transferred to less important posts or had been arrested should be reappointed to their former posts until their supposed involvement in the plot against the Regional Command could definitely be demonstrated to the lower-ranking party members. It was further proposed that a Regional Congress or meeting be convened at a lower level to discuss the party crisis. The Jabal al-Duruz members finally threatened in their memorandum to ignore any further instructions from the Regional Command and to boycott future party elections if the purges of officers originating from the Jabal al-Duruz who had taken part in the coup of 23 February 1966 should continue prior to the proposed meeting.

During trials held in Damascus early in 1967 of those charged with involvement in the plot against the regime of the Syrian Regional Command, members of the Hatum group were accused of having deliberately stimulated sectarian group feelings. The Public Prosecutor at the trial argued:

> On the discovery of the plan, the conspirators in al-Suwayda' started to spread rumours via conspirator 'Abd al-Rahim Bathish, chief of the [local] intelligence branch, with the aim of stirring up sectarian feelings; this caused a number of party members in al-Suwayda' to submit a memorandum to the Regional Command of the Ba'th Party.[28]

In reaction to that memorandum, the Regional Command decided to send to al-Suwayda' a high-level party commission consisting of the Syrian president and secretary-general of the Syrian Regional Command, Dr Nur al-Din al-Atasi, its assistant secretary-general, Salah Jadid, and Jamil Shayya, the Regional Command's only Druze member. The commission's purpose was to expound the background of the so-called 'party crisis' to al-Suwayda' party members.

In the event, when the commission arrived, Hatum and his supporters seized the opportunity to arrest Jadid and al-Atasi, and to use them as hostages in their subsequent negotiations with the party and army authorities, including Hafiz al-Asad, who had stayed behind in Damascus. Other prominent officers, for example the Alawi Commander of the National Guard, Captain Muhammad Ibrahim al-'Ali, were arrested in al-Suwayda' by the Druze Lieutenant 'Abd al-Rahim Bathish, head of the local military intelligence branch, who set a trap by falsely inviting them to a meal. At the same time, other military supporters of Hatum succeeded in taking the al-Suwayda' Brigade by surprise. Jamil Shayya, the only Druze member of the Regional Command's commission, was not arrested by his co-religionists and thus was in a position to mediate between Jadid and Hatum.[29]

It is a striking fact that, in crises with a sectarian character, mediators are by preference chosen from the same religious community (and if possible from the same region) as the person(s) with whom negotiations are to be held. The reason for this is obvious, namely, that in such crises people from the same religious community (and region) frequently have greater confidence in each other. It may be noted that following the 23 February 1966 coup Jamil Shayya had been sent to Aleppo to mediate between the new regime and his co-religionist Hamad 'Ubayd, who opposed it.

In his negotiations (by telephone) with Minister of Defence Hafiz al-Asad and with Premier Yusuf Zu'ayyin, Salim Hatum made a number of demands, including: the return of his most important supporters to the military positions from which they had been dismissed or transferred after 23 February 1966; the release of his followers or associates who had recently been arrested in connection with the discovery of the plot against the Regional Command; the purge of some of Salah Jadid's most prominent military supporters from the Army; the readmittance of what Hatum called the 'leftists' (i.e. the Shufi group) to the party; the resignation of the Syrian Regional Command, chosen in March 1966, and the appointment of a new Provisional Regional Command which was to include, as well as some members of the existing Regional Command, at least five members of the Shufi group.[30]

The Army Command flatly refused to give in to any of Salim Hatum's demands, and instead sent military units, including a rocket battalion, to al-Suwayda', with the threat that the provincial capital would be bombarded.[31]

As a result of these effective counter-measures, Salim Hatum's coup failed on 8 September 1966 and Hatum and Abu 'Asali finally decided to flee to Jordan in order, as Abu 'Asali declared later, 'to avoid an armed clash at such a close range to the front with Israel'.[32] In Jordan, Hatum and Abu 'Asali together with their followers were given political asylum.

Anti-Alawi sectarian propaganda

On 13 September 1966 Hatum held a press conference in Amman and gave his version of what had happened in al-Suwayda'.[33] He declared that 'the situation in Syria was being threatened by a civil war as a result of the growth of the sectarian and tribal spirit, on the basis of which Salah Jadid and Hafiz al-Asad, as well as the groups surrounding them, ruled'.[34] Hatum stated further:

> The sectarian spirit is spread in a shameful way in Syria, particularly in the Army, in the appointment of officers and even recruits. The ruling group is embarking upon a purge of officers and of groups which oppose it and these are being replaced by its own followers at different levels ... The [filling of] powerful places in the state and its institutions is limited to a specific class of the Syrian people [i.e. the Alawis]. Thus, the Alawis in the Army have attained a ratio of five to one of all other religious communities.[35]

Hatum's remarks in Amman about the sectarian atmosphere in Syria's armed forces were not concealed from the members of the Ba'th Party of the Syrian Regional Command. In fact, they were reproduced in the party's internal monthly organ *al-Munadil* in mid-September 1966, albeit in a strongly weakened form.[36]

In an interview which Hatum and Abu 'Asali gave to *al-Nahar* on 14 September 1966, Hatum stated that they had fled to Jordan in order to struggle from there in one way or another 'to save the [Syrian] Army, and to eliminate the sectarian spirit which dominates it'.[37] He declared further:

> Whenever a Syrian military man is questioned about his free officers, his answer will be that they have been dismissed and driven away, and that only Alawi officers have remained. The Alawi officers adhere to their tribes and not to their militarism. Their concern is the protection of Salah Jadid and Hafiz al-Asad. The latest arrests comprised hundreds of officers of all groups, with the exception of the Alawis.[38]

In view of the fact that Alawi officers had been excluded from the military organisation of the deposed National Command, it was not surprising that there was, reportedly, not a single Alawi among those arrested. Hatum's accusations, addressed to Hafiz al-Asad and Salah Jadid and implying that these Alawi Ba'thist leaders were guilty of carrying out a sectarian policy in the army by having only non-Alawi officers arrested, were therefore not quite justified; Jadid and al-Asad could not directly be blamed, though they were probably the indirect cause, for the fact that Alawis were, on principle, not admitted to the military organisation of the deposed National Command.

Talal Abu 'Asali added to Hatum's remarks that the situation in the Syrian Army was extremely delicate and serious,

> because all sons of the fatherland are anti anything Alawi. This division is so prevalent in the Army that men may start to fight one another at any moment. This would be a natural answer to the Alawi bloc formation which has become a distinguishing mark of the party.
>
> Alawi supremacy has pervaded all levels to such a degree that you see Alawi women act without restrictions as if they were the [official] authorities. And the neighbours of all houses inhabited by Alawis can see clearly how they dominate in the name of the [official] authorities and the Party. Every Alawi, big or small, knows what will happen as regards developments, transfers and arrests, even earlier than some of the high officials.[39]

Finally, Abu 'Asali related that 'when the arrests took place of officers at the front' (who were involved in the plot against the regime of the Regional Command) the Alawi women uttered shrill, long-drawn and trilling sounds [as a manifestation of joy], and shouted with joy *la illah illa Allah* ['there is no god but God'], so that the women of the arrested officers could hear them. And this is a simple picture of the atmosphere in the country.[40]

Two weeks later, on 28 September 1966, Salim Hatum issued a declaration which – according to *al-Hayat* – included the accusation that the group ruling in Damascus

intended to execute a sectarian plan to establish an opportunist regime, carrying the slogan of 'an Alawi state with an eternal mission', in which *al-'Amid* [chief] Salah Jadid and *Nur al-Anwar* [the light of lights] Ibrahim Makhus would glitter.[41]

'An Alawi state with an eternal mission' was clearly a play upon the Ba'thist slogan 'One Arab nation with an eternal mission', while *Nur al-Anwar* and *'Amid* are Alawi religious terms and ranks. Ibrahim Makhus (Alawi) was at the time Syria's minister of foreign affairs.

With the aid of such declarations Hatum and his followers tried to increase the sectarian tension among the Syrian population and within the Syrian Army, making Hafiz al-Asad and Salah Jadid and other Alawi leaders suspect in non-Alawi eyes, with the aim of undermining their power positions.

Hatum's insinuations strongly resembled the accusations and insinuations that were expressed in the (false) declaration circulated in Syria early in 1969 by opponents of the Ba'th regime then in power. In that declaration the prominent Alawi Shaykh 'Abd al-Rahman al-Khayyir was said to have summoned the Syrian Alawis to resist Salah Jadid's so-called misuse of the Alawi religion for purely political purposes. The same declaration accused Jadid of wanting to establish an Alawi state. This declaration was first published in the anti-Ba'thist conservative Lebanese daily *al-Hayat* on 19 May 1969, and was reproduced later by Jordan's former Prime Minister, Sa'd Jum'ah, in his book *Mujtama' al-Karahiyah* ('Society of Disgust').[42] The declaration may have been distributed by opponents of the Syrian Ba'th regime for motives similar to those of Hatum: stirring up sectarian unrest and tensions.[43]

The purges following Hatum's abortive coup

After Salim Hatum's abortive coup, purges on an extensive scale were held in the Syrian army and the Ba'th Party. Those purged included many Druze officers, which was quite natural since Hatum and Abu 'Asali had relied mainly on Druze supporters.[44] Command of the purged military units was subsequently entrusted to Alawi officers in many cases.[45]

The abortive plot set its imprint on political events in Syria deep into 1967, during which year the purges continued. For more than six months after Hatum's failure, the Jabal al-Duruz party branch was almost completely paralysed in its activities.[46]

The unsuccessful action, and the subsequent purges and arrests, stirred the Syrian Druze community to such an extent that the veteran leader Sultan al-Atrash – leader of the Syrian revolution against the French in 1925, who was still held in great respect – sent an open telegram to the Syrian general staff in December 1966 with the following text:

> Our sons strike in the prisons, and we hold you responsible for the consequences. The Jabal [al-'Arab] has been – and still is – accustomed to carry out revolutions and to drive away the traitor and foreign invader. But his creed prohibits him from revolting against his brother or from acting treacherously towards a son of his [Arab] nation. This is the only deterrent [that forces us] to confine ourselves in principle to negotiations [with the official authorities].[47]

It would not be a simple matter for the (predominantly Alawi) rulers in Damascus to pacify the Druze community after its trust in the central authorities had been severely shaken.[48]

In March 1967 a great many people who had been involved in the abortive plot were tried – many *in absentia* – by a special military court formed in Damascus.[49] Two of the main charges brought against the accused were: participation in a plot to overthrow the regime, and instigation of civil war and sectarian division.[50] For five of the accused, all Druze officers,[51] the prosecutor demanded the death sentence.

A significant consequence of the abortive plot was that – apart from the leading Sunni officers' factions which had already been purged or neutralised following the 23 February 1966 coup – the most important Druze officers' factions were now also purged, and those that were left were no longer in a position to form separate power blocs which could seriously threaten the regime.

When the June 1967 War broke out, Salim Hatum returned to Syria, where he was arrested by the authorities and accused of having plotted with 'Anglo-American and West German imperialist circles' to overthrow the Syrian regime as part of a 'comprehensive imperialist plot'. Hatum was tried by a special military court, sentenced to death, and executed on 24 June 1967.[52]

Elimination of prominent Hawrani factions

The purge of many prominent Druze officers and of a lesser number
of officers from the province of Hawran strengthened the positions of
a number of Alawi officers. The inter-communal sectarian and regional
feelings of tension and distrust which had flared up during the power
struggle within the Ba'thist political elite caused a number of party
members to become alarmed about the predominance of Alawis in the
party and the armed forces.[53] During the early months of 1967, leaders
of some party branches, sub-branches and sections resigned from their
party functions, refusing to participate any further in party meetings
and other activities in expression of their concern about the inter-
communal sectarian and regional tensions in the party apparatus and
the armed forces, and also to demonstrate their concern about the
predominance of specific – especially Alawi – sectarian, regional or
tribal factions.[54]

Externally these tensions found expression when all three ministers
from the Hawran region threatened to resign from the Syrian government.[55] Shortly after the Arab–Israeli War of June 1967 some of the
most prominent civilian Ba'thists from Hawran lost their positions in
the party commands and the government.[56] On 15 February 1968 the
chief of staff of the Syrian army, Ahmad Suwaydani – who was from
Hawran and who had once been a prominent supporter of Salah Jadid
– was relieved of his army functions.

Mustafa Talas has related how Salah Jadid was put under pressure
in November 1967 by his major Sunni civilian allies from Dayr al-Zur,
who threatened to accuse him openly of sectarianism if he would not
fully support Suwaydani in his conflict with al-Asad. Thus, Fawzi
Rida (Sunni from Dayr al-Zur) during a meeting openly stated:

> If you [i.e. Salah Jadid] do not side with Major-General Ahmad Suway-
> dani with all your force and weight in his conflict with Major-General
> Hafiz al-Asad, we shall all accuse you of sectarianism, and [allege] that
> there is a higher council of the [Alawi] sect which takes the decisions,
> and that the [Ba'th] Party is nothing but throwing dust in the eyes ...
> and that the sons of the Alawi sect cannot forsake one another.[57]

Salah Jadid, who rejected these allegations, did not, however, now
have enough influence in the army to prevent the dismissal of Suwaydani, which meant the removal of the principal remaining military
figure from Hawran.

Musa al-Zu'bi and Mustafa al-Hajj 'Ali, the two other Sunni
Hawrani members of the former Ba'thist Military Committee, were
dismissed from the Army in 1967 and 1968 respectively. In fact, it

implied that civilian and military Ba'thists from Hawran had mostly been neutralised or eliminated from the party apparatus and the army as separate power blocs. This did not mean that hardly any Hawrani officers were left in the army, or that Ba'thists from Hawran ceased to occupy high functions in the party apparatus; it meant the end of their role as significant power groups. Later, they were not to be given another chance to regroup as powerful factions in the armed forces so as to constitute a serious threat to other (e.g. Alawi) factions within the armed forces or the party. Previously, the Hawrani factions had derived their influence and power mainly from existing alliances with other groups, such as those of Salah Jadid or Salim Hatum.[58]

In August 1968, Ahmad Suwaydani was reportedly involved in an abortive coup. In July 1969, he was arrested by Syrian authorities when his plane stopped at Damascus airport en route to Cairo from Baghdad – where he had found political refuge in 1968.[59] Following Suwaydani's arrest, many of his military supporters from Hawran, who were still in the army, were reportedly also arrested. In May 1970, new arrests were made of civilians and military who were accused of planning the overthrow of the Syrian regime in favour of the rival Ba'th regime of Iraq. The arrested officers included many from the Hawran, Aleppo and Idlib provinces, almost all Sunnis. The arrested officers from Aleppo and Idlib were mainly supporters of Lieutenant-General Amin al-Hafiz, who was from Aleppo and since 1968 had lived in exile in Baghdad.[60]

After almost twenty-five years in captivity, Ahmad Suwaydani was released in February 1994, having been one of the longest-held political prisoners in the world.[61]

5

The struggle for power within the Alawi community

The al-Asad/Jadid rivalry

Following the fall of the National Command in February 1966, and more particularly after Hatum's abortive coup, most Ba'thist officers and civilian party members clustered around either Salah Jadid or Hafiz al-Asad, who were at the time Syria's most important political bosses.

Although Jadid ceased to have an official function in the Syrian Army in August 1965 – when he exchanged his position as chief of staff for the key civilian function of assistant secretary-general of the Syrian Regional Command – he managed for some time to maintain his grip on a large part of the officer corps, partly through his supporters in the Military Bureau, which supervised the military party organisation. Since April 1966 this Bureau had also included civilian members. Jadid also controlled part of the armed forces through direct personal, though organisationally prohibited, collateral contacts (*ittisalat janibiyah*) with a number of military officers.[1] As minister of defence, Jadid's rival al-Asad was in a more advantageous position from which to influence the officer corps, part of which was already personally linked to him. Al-Asad had been commander of the air force since 1964, and had been largely responsible for its build-up; he was therefore able to appoint many of his personal supporters to strategically important positions. Moreover, al-Asad had been a senior leader of the Ba'thist Military Committee, which for several years had been responsible for the activities of the military party organisation.

After the 23 February 1966 coup the tension between Jadid and al-Asad was repeatedly shown, but open confrontation did not occur. The conflict situation took more serious proportions after the Arab military defeat in June 1967, partly due to differences of opinion over the military, foreign and socio-economic policies which were then to be pursued.[2]

Ideological controversy between the major Ba'thist factions and groups usually focused on the question of whether priority was to be given to an inner-directed socialist policy or to a more outwardly-directed Arab nationalist policy aimed at inter-Arab cooperation and unity, in the interest of confrontation with Israel. A major problem was which would be the most suitable combination of these socialist and Arab nationalist policies in order to produce results which, in the long run, could be considered as optimal from a Ba'thist point of view.

Differences of political opinion between Jadid and al-Asad became obvious at the Regional and National Ba'th Party Congresses held in Damascus in September and October 1968, where two main political trends were manifest. One advocated top priority for the so-called 'socialist transformation' (*tahwil ishtiraki*) of Syrian society, and was dominated by civilians, including Salah Jadid, 'Abd al-Karim al-Jundi, Ibrahim Makhus, the (Alawi) minister of foreign affairs, and Premier Yusuf Zu'ayyin as prominent members. This socialist-oriented group openly rejected the idea of political or military cooperation with regimes which it branded as 'reactionary, rightist or pro-Western', such as Jordan, Lebanon or Iraq, even if this should be at the expense of the struggle against Israel. This group had no objection to increased dependence on the Soviet Union and other Communist countries of the Eastern Bloc, as long as this would be of benefit to the socialist transformation.[3]

The second trend showed strong Arab nationalist leaning and demanded top priority for the armed struggle against Israel, i.e. a strengthening of the Arab military potential, even if this should have temporarily negative effects on Syria's socialist transformation. A policy of military and political cooperation and coordination was advocated with other Arab states such as Jordan, Iraq, Egypt and Saudi Arabia, without much concern for their respective political colours, as long as this would be in the interest of the Arab struggle against Israel. This nationalist trend was represented at the congresses by most of the military delegates, the most important being Hafiz al-Asad, Minister of Defence, and Mustafa Talas, chief of staff of the Syrian Army.

Proposals made by al-Asad, suggesting that negotiations be opened with the rival Ba'th regime of Iraq – which had come to power in July 1968 and was dominated by Ba'thists connected with the National Command that had been deposed in Syria in February 1966 – in the interest of military cooperation against Israel and with the intention of reducing Syria's political isolation in the Arab world, were strongly rejected by the majority of 'socialist-oriented' civilians at the congress. These vehemently objected to any rapprochement with the Ba'thists who ruled Iraq, maintaining that they were 'rightist' dissidents who had been ousted from the party as a result of the 23 February 1966 Movement.[4]

Jadid and his supporters obtained a clear overall majority during the congress, and managed to get their political ideas accepted as official party policy resolutions.

Hafiz al-Asad did not accept the results of the party congresses, and refused to attend any further meetings of the Regional Command or Joint Meetings of the Syrian Regional Command and the National Command. Notwithstanding his election to the Regional Command he resigned *de facto* from that institution.[5] He decided to perfect his control of the armed forces by cutting off the military party apparatus from the civilian party leadership and issued orders forbidding Regional Command members and other civilian party officials to visit any sections of the military party organisation, or to entertain direct contacts with the military party sector.[6] Army officers were in turn forbidden to have direct contact with civilian party politicians other than through the official chain of command of the military party organisation.[7] In addition, military intelligence institutions prevented normal relations between the civilian and military party sections by opening party mail and by hindering the normal distribution of party circulars issued by the Syrian Regional Command to the party apparatus.[8]

Following the party congresses of September and October 1968, some of Jadid's military supporters (predominantly Alawis) were transferred to less sensitive positions in the armed forces without prior consultation of the Military Bureau; this was dominated by Jadid's supporters and under normal circumstances took the decisions regarding most military transfers.[9]

The prerogative of the Army Command to effectuate transfers of army officials above a certain rank was officially laid down by the Joint Meetings of the Syrian Regional and National Commands. It had been decided, for instance, that the transfer of army brigade commanders fell under the jurisdiction of the Joint Meeting.[10] Notwithstanding this, al-Asad continued with his plans and reportedly relieved the Alawi Lieutenant-Colonel 'Izzat Jadid – one of Salah Jadid's most prominent military supporters – of command of the 70th Armoured Brigade, which was of great political and strategic importance.[11]

While al-Asad thus succeeded in obtaining control over the major part of the Syrian armed forces, Jadid tightened his grip on the civilian party apparatus by filling most civilian party key positions with his supporters. A 'duality of power' (*izdiwajiyat al-sultah*) was thus created: the two major Syrian power institutions, i.e. the armed forces and the civilian party apparatus of the Ba'th, were controlled by different party or army factions which actively opposed each other and pursued different policies.

The power struggle within the Alawi community

In the preceding chapters we have shown that since the break-up of the United Arab Republic in 1961, sectarian, regional and tribal loyalties have played an important role in the power struggle in Syria. It is a reasonable conclusion that the power of military officers and civilian politicians at the national level depended largely on the influence they had been able to build up on the regional, sectarian, and/or tribal levels: to be successful in national politics, one needed first to be politically successful among people of one's region, religious community or tribe. A struggle for power between people from different regions and/or religious communities was often expressed in the form of inter-regional and/or inter-sectarian conflict. Power struggles between persons from one and the same region and/or religious community were often expressed in the form of intra-regional and/or intra-sectarian conflict.[12]

Thus, the power struggle which raged in 1964 between the most prominent Alawi officers of the Ba'thist Military Committee, i.e. Muhammad 'Umran, Salah Jadid and Hafiz al-Asad, was clearly reflected in internal dissension in the (Alawi-dominated) party branch of Latakia region.[13]

Similar dissension in the same branch was demonstrated in 1969 and 1970, when the power struggle between al-Asad and Jadid – both being from Latakia – reached a climax: in order to enlarge their power within the Ba'th Party on the national level, both wanted to increase their grasp on the party branch and other Ba'thist-dominated power institutions in their home region.

In February 1969, when Jadid's supporters, who dominated the Latakia party branch, tried to eliminate al-Asad's influence by purging some of his prominent supporters, fierce counter-measures followed: Hafiz al-Asad ordered the arrest of the Latakia Branch Command, and had its members replaced by some of his own supporters who had previously been purged. The newly appointed members of the Latakia Branch Command also included supporters of al-Asad who had previously been purged from the party for having stood as candidates in trade union elections as rivals to the electoral list produced by the Branch Command. When they were subsequently purged by way of punitive measures, al-Asad reacted by closing the entire local trade union.[14] The Governor of Latakia Province – also a member of the local party branch command – was placed under house arrest on 27 February 1969 and forbidden to visit his office or local party headquarters. Furthermore, the offices of the (predominantly Alawi) Tartus party branch and local sub-branches were raided by a commando battalion which was charged with guarding vital installations in that Province, with the intention of arresting members of the party branch command.

'Adil Na'isah, secretary-general of the Latakia Branch and a Jadid supporter who was the Syrian Regional Command's only Alawi member in addition to al-Asad and Jadid, was arrested in Tartus and forced to leave the province immediately under military escort. Afterwards, 'Adil Na'isah was released for some time, to be imprisoned again in 1972. Twenty-two years later, in 1994, he was released.

Al-Asad instructed the military intelligence services in various provinces to prevent members of the party's command from getting in touch with the civilian apparatus of the party branches by warning them and threatening them with arrest. The measures taken were by far the most drastic in Latakia and Tartus Provinces. In effect, these measures which al-Asad took in late February 1969 resembled a military coup; as a result, the Syrian Regional Command lost most of its powers, notwithstanding the fact that it was formally continued and tolerated in office. Al-Asad's troops occupied the buildings of the Damascus and Aleppo radio stations, as well as the offices of the two major Syrian (Ba'thist-controlled) newspapers, *al-Ba'th* and *al-Thawrah*; military control was imposed on news broadcasts, political commentaries and all political, cultural and information programmes.[15] On 20 March 1969, Salah Jadid's Ba'thist faction started to publish an alternative paper in Beirut, *al-Rayah*, since it had almost completely lost the *al-Ba'th* and *al-Thawrah* dailies as its mouthpieces in Syria.

At the request of the Syrian Regional Command an Extraordinary Regional Congress was convened in March 1969 in Damascus at which efforts were made to reach a compromise between the factions which had clustered around al-Asad and Jadid respectively. No real conciliation was achieved, however. To ensure al-Asad's position during the congress, his troops occupied strategically important points in Damascus and its surroundings. The congress ended in stalemate, and the previously mentioned 'duality of power' (*izdiwajiyat al-sultah*) continued: al-Asad kept his supremacy in the Syrian armed forces, while Jadid largely succeeded in maintaining his grip on the Syrian civilian party apparatus.

Shortly before the Extraordinary Regional Congress, al-Asad's military supporters had surrounded and besieged the headquarters of

Colonel 'Abd al-Karim al-Jundi (a staunch Isma'ili supporter of Jadid), who was then chief of the national security and general intelligence services. They abducted a number of his aides and supporters and confiscated cars belonging to his office. 'Abd al-Karim al-Jundi committed suicide.[16]

Al-Jundi's death brought to an end a period in which Jadid's most prominent non-Alawi military supporters – including Ahmad Suwaydani and Ahmad al-Mir – had been either neutralised or purged. Ahmad al-Mir, a founding member of the Ba'thist Military Committee, had been commander of the military units on the Syrian-Israeli front during the June 1967 War. Shortly after the war he had been relieved of his function, and in September 1967 he had been chosen as a member of the National Command of the Ba'th Party. In October 1968, al-Mir had been replaced in that position and appointed to the Syrian Embassy in Madrid. As an indirect result, the subsequent power struggle between Jadid and al-Asad supporters was more or less confined to members of the Alawi community.[17]

In 1969 and 1970 Jadid and his supporters tried to regain some of their lost influence by placing the Ba'thist commando organisation *al-Sa'iqah*, set up in Syria after the June 1967 War, under the direct supervision of the Syrian Regional Command. The objective was to transform the organisation into an alternative power instrument which could eventually be used as a counterweight to al-Asad's military force.[18]

In September 1970, Syria's political leaders decided in favour of armed intervention in the Jordanian civil war on behalf of the Palestinian commando organisations which at the time were fighting a losing battle against the regular army commanded by King Husayn. This intervention failed and sparked off a new confrontation between al-Asad and Jadid and their respective supporters and allies.

The Tenth Extraordinary National Congress of the Ba'th Party was convened in Damascus towards the end of October 1970 to try to find a solution to the renewed party crisis. Shortly beforehand, however, al-Asad had some of Jadid's military supporters transferred so as to be ready for any eventuality and to be able to impose his will on his political adversaries if the congress should be to his disadvantage.[19] During the congress it became clear that al-Asad and his most important military supporter, Mustafa Talas, were almost completely isolated, whereas Jadid and his allies enjoyed the support of the majority of congress members. In the armed forces, relations between the major political camps were just the reverse. When the congress majority finally passed an unrealistic resolution that Defence Minister al-Asad and Chief of Staff Talas should be relieved of their military posts, charging them with such tasks in the party as would be decided upon by its command, the two were able to take effective counter-measures easily and swiftly.[20]

On 13 November 1970, al-Asad ordered his military to occupy the offices of the civilian party section as well as those of the Ba'thist-dominated 'people's organisations', and furthermore to arrest prominent civilian party leaders, including Salah Jadid and President Nur al-Din al-Atasi. Several congress members fled to Lebanon in order to avoid arrest and from there continued to oppose the new Syrian regime. Salah Jadid was held in captivity in al-Mazzah prison (Damascus) from November 1970 until his death on 19 August 1993, to be buried the following day with full honours in his home village near Latakia. Dr Nur al-Din al-Atasi was released in 1992 after more than twenty years in prison, to die shortly afterwards. Several other civilian and military Ba'thist opponents of al-Asad suffered a similar fate.

Under al-Asad's rule the civilian party section of the Ba'th was not able to regain the powerful position it had held for some time during the preceding period. On 13 November 1970, political power was almost completely monopolised by the officers' faction of Hafiz al-Asad, who, in February 1971, became Syria's first Alawi president. This ended the Syrian tradition of having a Sunni president. It also symbolically represented the political evolution of the Alawis from being a discriminated-against socially and economically backward religious community to a nationally emancipated group in a position of dominance.

After 13 November 1970, Hafiz al-Asad relied largely on his own officers' faction to maintain his power. This included a number of senior officers who, together with their supporters, held strategically important positions in the Syrian armed forces. Officers belonging to non-Alawi religious communities also occupied high military functions as a matter of form, but they were in no position to offer a serious threat to the Alawi president, whose personal followers were well able to deal with any sign of insurrection. Major-General Naji Jamil, for instance, a Sunni from Dayr al-Zur who commanded the Syrian air force from November 1970 until March 1978, was in no position to use that air force effectively in any military revolt against the president, partly because Hafiz al-Asad's Alawi supporters were then in charge of the major air bases. This also applied to other Sunni senior officers such as Major-General Mustafa Talas, who was appointed minister of defence in March 1972 and was succeeded as chief of staff by Major-General Yusuf Shakkur, a Greek Orthodox Christian from the Homs area.

Officers such as Talas, Jamil and Shakkur were able to exercise considerable power so long as they followed the president's policies. If they should deviate from his line in any way, however, they could fairly easily be pushed aside by his military supporters, who were mainly Alawis, particularly in view of the fact that they themselves did not have a strong personal following in the armed forces.

In fact, the appointment of Sunni officers such as Talas and Jamil to such high military posts could very well have been done with the idea of placating the Sunnis and dispelling the impression that the most important posts were exclusively held by Alawis.[21]

As we have seen, the most prominent Sunni, Druze and Isma'ili officers' factions had been neutralised or purged from the armed forces prior to 1970. The supremacy which Hafiz al-Asad's faction held after November of that year considerably reduced the chances for non-Alawis to form independent power blocs which would have any potential to endanger the position of the established regime. Although Lebanese newspapers and periodicals repeatedly reported that al-Asad's position was threatened by Sunni officers, the reliability of such accounts is doubtful and their veracity was not sufficiently proved at the time.[22]

Any risks of a challenge to al-Asad's position in fact originated mainly within the Alawi community. From the arrests and dismissals that have taken place, we can deduce that Alawi officers and civilian Ba'thists from the Latakia region were mainly involved in the conspiracies that have been uncovered since November 1970. In June 1971, for instance, a number of Jadid's supporters were arrested and accused of involvement in subversive activities against the regime, and these included several prominent civilian party members of the Latakia Branch Command.[23]

The Alawi Major-General Muhammad 'Umran was murdered on 4 March 1972 in Tripoli in Lebanon, where he had lived in exile since 1967. Traces left by the killers reportedly indicated the possible involvement of one of Syria's Intelligence Services. 'Umran may well have maintained contact with possible military supporters in Syria, in the hope of a future political comeback. His murder, and the rumours that the Syrian regime had been involved, may well have undermined the confidence which Alawi officers, in particular, felt for al-Asad.[24]

In December 1972, more civilian and military supporters of Jadid and his allies were arrested on the charge of plotting against the regime, and once again those arrested showed a strikingly high percentage of Alawis: al-Rayah reported the arrest of fifteen officers, at least twelve of whom were Alawi. Moreover, according to the same source, most of the civilians who were arrested came from the Latakia, Tartus and Damascus party branches.[25]

Since challenges to al-Asad's regime came mainly from within the Alawi community, it is hardly surprising that he placed increasing reliance on persons with whom he had a close relationship, such as members of his own family, tribe or village and its surroundings, in order to secure his position even against people from his own religious community. His five brothers were all active party members and occupied eminent positions in the army, the party organisation or the government. Rif'at al-Asad was foremost. After the November 1970 coup he was in command of the Defence Companies (*Saraya al-Difa'*), elite army units of political and strategic importance which were stationed around Damascus and with which he was able to protect his elder brother's regime. Military troops under his command were reported as playing an important part in the October 1973 War against Israel, and on 4 March 1974 he and a number of other officers were awarded military decorations for having shown extraordinary distinction during the war.[26]

After the November 1970 coup in particular, rumours circulating in the country and outside its borders suggested rivalry between the two brothers and even that, from time to time, Rif'at had threatened his brother's position. Thus, when the Army Command reportedly attempted to transfer Rif'at and his units away from Damascus, it was rumoured that he had repeatedly revolted.[27] In April 1975, however, at the Sixth Syrian Regional Congress of the Ba'th Party in Damascus, Rif'at al-Asad was elected a member of the Syrian Regional Command, next to his brother Hafiz.[28]

At the same Congress another brother, Jamil, was made a member of the Twelfth National Congress of the regime's party organisation[29] after having already been elected to membership of the Syrian People's Assembly in May 1973.[30] Jamil apparently also held an important military position, although less prominent than that of Rif'at. The other three brothers of the president were Isma'il, Muhammad and Ahmad 'Ali Sulayman. The latter for some time held a function in Latakia's provincial governing council.[31]

In Beirut, Jadid's supporters continued to attack al-Asad's regime through the pages of their newspaper *al-Rayah*, giving special attention to the regime's sectarian and tribal aspects. In an article entitled 'Who Are the Rulers of Baghdad and Damascus?' one editor wrote:

> We can state here that the two groups which are at the top of power in Damascus and Baghdad belong to blocs which have come into existence within the Army and the Party, and which in reality are sectarian or tribal blocs [such as] that of Tikritis in Iraq ... The rulers of Damascus and Baghdad have both seized power by means of military coups which depended on alliances between tribal or sectarian blocs.[32]

In another article, entitled 'Meeting between al-Qardahah, Tikrit and al-Manufiyah', *al-Rayah* mockingly described the political rapprochement between Syria, Iraq and Egypt in 1972 as a rapprochement between three regimes in which the rulers with real power were predominantly from the native regions of the respective presidents: Hafiz al-Asad was from al-Qardahah, President Ahmad Hasan al-Bakr of Iraq was from Tikrit, and the Egyptian President Anwar al-Sadat from the al-Manufiyah district.[33]

In their articles directed against al-Asad, Jadid's Ba'thist supporters did not mention that their own previous power positions in Syria had also depended on sectarian, tribal and regional blocs in the armed forces and the party.

After his November 1970 coup, Hafiz al-Asad tried to end Syria's political isolation in the Arab world, which had been particularly severe in the period since 23 February 1966. He sought rapprochement with the 'confrontation states' Egypt and Jordan, as well as with more conservative states such as Saudi Arabia, for the purpose of building up a unified military and political front against Israel. Jadid and his allies had previously rejected almost all serious cooperation with Nasser's Egypt, as well as with the more conservative states, arguing that only the progressives could win the final struggle against Israel. Al-Asad's new inter-Arab policy showed decided results in the October 1973 War, during which Syrian and Egyptian armed forces effectively coordinated their military efforts against Israel.

The developments described in this book suggest a clear relationship between political stability and the degree of sectarian, regional and tribal factionalism among the political power elite: if these factions showed great diversity, the result was political instability.

The relatively long period of stability that Syria has enjoyed since November 1970 can be largely attributed to the fact that military and party discipline during this period have not been undermined by as much sectarian, regional and tribal factionalism as previously; moreover, only one relatively homogeneous Alawi officers' faction, that of Hafiz al-Asad, remained and it was able to hold supreme power and impose its will on the others. The undermining influence which factionalism can exert on military discipline has been illustrated by the achievements of the Syrian armed forces: during the October 1973 War these were considerably better than in that of June 1967, when the officer corps and the Ba'th party organisation were deeply affected by sectarian, regional and tribal faction formations.

In 1976, Hafiz al-Asad's position was seriously undermined for the first time since his 'Corrective Movement' in November 1970, mainly due to his order that the Syrian Army should intervene in the Lebanese civil war. This war, which had raged on and off since April 1975, was between Lebanese rightist political parties, composed mainly of Maronite Christians, and leftist political parties, whose adherents were mostly from the various Muslim communities and which at a later stage were given military support by most of the Palestinian commando organisations.

Al-Asad intervened in the Lebanese fighting in the hope of attaining a situation where constitutional and legal means could be used to achieve a peaceful settlement between the opposing parties. This attempt failed, however: the fighting escalated in a fashion that may not have been entirely foreseen, and the Syrians were initially entangled in fierce military confrontation with Palestinian commandos and leftist Lebanese militia, traditional allies of the Syrian Ba'th regime.[34] This aspect in particular had a corrosive effect on al-Asad's position at home. Strong opposition was voiced against his intervention in Lebanon; after plots to bring down the established regime were discovered and frustrated, many arrests were reported to have been carried out in the armed forces and in the Ba'th civilian party apparatus.[35]

Following Syria's military intervention in Lebanon, a whole series of political assassinations and attacks on Ba'thist political leaders took place in Syria. At the time it was not clear whether these were due to internal political opposition against Syria's military intervention in Lebanon, for example, or to the rivalry between the Ba'thist regimes which ruled respectively in Baghdad and Syria, or even whether they were intended to provoke 'sectarian divisions'. In any case, it could be noted that almost all the assassinated were Alawis.[36] Radio Damascus accused what it called the *'tribal Tikriti fascist clique'* ruling in Baghdad of responsibility for some of the killings.

The Iraqi Ba'thist regime, on the other hand, accused what it called 'the al-Asad family regime', and in particular Rif'at al-Asad, of being behind the assassinations.[37] In their propaganda campaigns against the Syrian regime the Iraqi Ba'thists did not at the time exploit the sectarianism issue, and did not go much further than elaborating on the family ties between some of the regime's leaders. It may be interesting to note that in 1977 it became official Iraqi policy to omit tribal or regional references in personal names. This measure, which was not obligatory for non-officials, was obviously taken with the aim of blurring tribal or regional loyalties. Another aim must have been to prevent the general public from easily recognising the regional or tribal origin of the Ba'thists who ruled Iraq.

Anti-Syrian sources ascribed the efforts to bring down al-Asad's regime not only to political motives but also to supposed resentment against Alawi dominance in Syria. For example, on 26 April 1976,

Radio Cairo alleged that the so-called abortive coup attempted by Syrian officers earlier that year could be traced largely to what it called a 'mutiny by the Ba'th Party rank-and-file against the party leadership for imposing the authority of the Alawi religious community on the country'.[38] In another transmission, on 5 June 1976, Radio Cairo described Hafiz al-Asad's regime in propagandist terminology as 'the Syrian Ba'th Alawi regime'. And in March 1978, President al-Sadat of Egypt, severely criticised by Syria for visiting Israel in November 1977 and for starting negotiations with Israeli Premier Menahem Begin, went so far as to state that the Syrian Ba'th regime was 'firstly Alawi, secondly Ba'thist, and thirdly Syrian', and to insinuate that President al-Asad had 'the intention of setting up an Alawi state'.[39]

Contrary to what might be concluded from all this sectarian propaganda, the potentially most dangerous opposition to Hafiz al-Asad's regime could be exercised primarily by officers who belonged to the Alawi community and only secondarily by others.

In 1977 another development in Syria contributed to al-Asad's deteriorating position. On 18 August 1977, probably in the hope of re-establishing some of the prestige his regime had lost through its military intervention in Lebanon, al-Asad announced the formation of a Committee for Investigation of Illegal Profits, 'to investigate crimes of bribery, imposition of influence, embezzlement, exploitation of office and illegal profits'.[40] The anti-corruption campaign which then started was apparently intended to dispel popular discontent with the government's handling of economic policy and with the widespread corruption that reportedly plagued both the government bureaucracy and the public sector. The campaign was doomed to failure from the very beginning, since some high-placed military officers in the direct entourage of President Hafiz al-Asad, who constituted an indispensable part of the hard core of his (mainly Alawi) officers' faction, were also found to have been guilty of involvement in corrupt practices. According to some reports, local public opinion regarded the President's brother, Lieutenant-Colonel Dr Rif'at al-Asad, as one of the standard bearers and main beneficiaries of corrupt activities in Syria.[41] To purge such officers from the Army or to take severe disciplinary action against them could have directly undermined the power position of al-Asad's faction and consequently of the whole regime. It was thus thought preferable not to harm the positions of the most prominent officers, with the result that the regime's credibility in handling the anti-corruption campaign was at stake and its prestige once again damaged.

It may be concluded that the failure of the anti-corruption campaign was yet another example of the paradigmatic situation in which the Syrian Ba'thist regime had repeatedly found itself since its seizure of power in 1963. This was due to the composition of the hard core of the political power elite: i.e. a political party or a faction of that party which, although pursuing an ideology that wanted to do away with sectarian, regional and tribal loyalties, found itself more or less forced to revert to those traditional loyalties when it took power in order not to lose the strength that was needed to realise its ideology.

The problem became a vicious circle: on the one hand, power was essential if the necessary drastic social changes entailing the suppression of sectarian, regional and tribal loyalties, were to be effected; on the other hand, maintenance of that power entailed dependence on those same loyalties thus hindering their suppression.

6

Sectarian and regional factionalism in the Syrian political elite: a statistical analysis

In this chapter we present some results of research into the composition of the Syrian political power elite by means of a statistical analysis of the sectarian, regional, socio-economic and political backgrounds of members of important political power institutions.

Syrian cabinets between 1942 and 1980 have been investigated, as well as the Syrian Regional Commands of the Ba'th Party in power in Syria since 1963 (see Tables 1–7).[1]

Special attention is given to the military members of the Ba'th because they have been Syria's most important rulers since 8 March 1963, and their backgrounds most closely approximate to those of the 'core' of the political power elite of the time.

The results of this statistical research reflect and confirm the trends and developments which have been described in detail in the preceding chapters.

In the introduction it was noted that sectarian, regional and tribal categories can overlap to a great extent with socio-economic categories, and that urban-rural contrasts can equally coincide with sectarian contrasts. Furthermore, an overlap of sectarian, regional, and tribal and socio-economic loyalties can result in their elements becoming inseparably inter-connected, as well as in their complementing and reinforcing each other. This applies specifically to the case of the compact minorities, where the categories involved show the greatest coincidence. It may therefore be incorrect to attribute the representation of specific religious communities in power institutions, at any level, to the existence of sectarian loyalties, or to explain it on that basis, without taking into account the regional, tribal, socio-economic and politico-historical backgrounds of the people involved. Similarly, it may be incorrect to attribute the representation of specific regional groups in power institutions principally to the existence of regional loyalties.

A historical revolution in the Syrian political elite (1963)

The year 1963 was clearly an important turning point in modern Syrian history, with regard to the representation of specific sectarian, regional, socio-economic and political groups.

The relationship between Sunnis and non-Sunnis, urban and rural people, richer and poorer classes, and conservative and progressive political groups underwent abrupt change when the Ba'thists took over power on 8 March 1963, a change that was expressed in the new composition of the Syrian political elite.

From 1942 until 1963, Sunnis, urbanites (primarily Damascenes, with people from the rival city of Aleppo in second place) and people from the more well-to-do classes and conservative political parties had occupied the senior and most powerful positions. Members of religious minorities (especially the heterodox Islamic ones) and people from rural areas were heavily under-represented in important institutions, and were politically and socio-economically discriminated against as compared to other population groups (see Tables 1 and 4).

After 8 March 1963, the relation between these groups underwent a radical reversal, as is shown by the fact that members of heterodox Islamic communities (especially Alawis, followed by Druzes and Isma'ilis) and people from the poor rural areas (especially from the Latakia region) rose strongly and gained relative over-representation in the principal power institutions (see Tables 2–7). Furthermore, after 1963 Syrian political life came to be heavily dominated by persons from the lower middle class and from progressive political parties.

Sami al-Jundi, a founding member of the Ba'th, who became minister of information in the cabinet formed directly after the coup of 8 March 1963, has provided a vivid description of the abrupt change of personnel in the ministries which then took place:

> Three days after my entering the Ministry, the [party] comrades came to ask me for an extensive purge operation ... The measure of a minister's success [was determined by] the lists of dismissals, since party members as well as their relatives and the members of their tribes [came to] demand their campaign and kinship rights. From the time the party appeared on the stage, caravans of villagers started to leave the villages of the plains and mountains for Damascus. And while the alarming *qaf* started to predominate in the streets, coffee houses and the waiting rooms of the ministries, dismissals became a duty so that [those who had newly come] could be appointed.[2]

By the 'mountains' Sami al-Jundi must have meant the mountains of the Latakia and al-Suwayda' regions: the *Jibal al-'Alawiyin* (Mountains of the Alawis) and the *Jabal al-Duruz* (Mountain of the Druzes). The *qaf*, described by al-Jundi as 'alarming', apparently because it appears to be so predominant, is an Arabic letter which is pronounced in certain rural dialects of Syria, but not in urban Syrian Arabic, where a glottal stop (or *hamza*) is used instead. People pronouncing the *qaf* are therefore easily recognisable as coming from specific rural regions. The Alawis and Druzes are *qaf*-speakers.[3]

The rise of the religious minorities and rural people after 8 March 1963 can be considered as a kind of national emancipation.

A great deal of Syria's political instability in the twentieth century has been caused by a so-called 'traditional' intra-elite conflict, i.e. a struggle for power between socio-economic elites originating from roughly the same classes, who tried to cause the fall of their political rivals in order to realise their own limited self-interests. Prior to 1963, this struggle for power was carried on almost entirely without the involvement of the rural masses and lower urban classes.

After the Ba'th had taken over power in 1963, the struggle between rival political elites who had very similar socio-economic backgrounds continued in the 'traditional' way. The major difference with the period preceding 1963 was that the socio-economic, sectarian and regional backgrounds of the new political elites differed considerably from those of their political predecessors, since political power was now mainly held by people from the countryside and the lower middle class, and by members of religious minorities.[4] Van Dusen has defined the core of the new political elite that came to power after 1963 as 'simply those Syrians of the lowest socio-economic background to whom a high school education was available'.[5]

This opened the way for drastic political and socio-economic changes which now gave primary attention to the interests of the rural population and of members of religious minorities who had previously been discriminated against.

The Syrian cabinets and the Regional Commands

A comparison of the sectarian backgrounds of members of Syrian cabinets since 1942 shows the striking fact that during the Syrian–Egyptian union (1958–61) no Christians held posts in the regional cabinets, whereas Sunni representation (94.7 per cent) was stronger than in the periods preceding or following that of the union. In the central governments of the United Arab Republic (UAR) the relative percentage of Syrian Sunnis was even higher.[6] This might be explained by the strong Sunni acculturation which took place during the Syrian–Egyptian union, mainly due to the dominating position of the (predominantly Sunni) Egyptians. During the periods before and after the

UAR, Christians (and especially the Greek Orthodox) had been duly represented in the cabinets.

While Syrian cabinets to some extent reflected the backgrounds of the political power elite, the Regional Commands of the Ba'th Party, in whose hands political power was concentrated after March 1963, give a far more accurate picture of the increased representation of the lower classes, the rural areas, the Latakia region, and the religious minorities.

Between February 1966 and November 1970 this representation reached its zenith, both in the cabinets and in the Regional Commands. In fact, the latter showed no representation at all of people from the major cities of Damascus and Aleppo during that period. On a regional basis, the Command's members were mostly from the rural Latakia region (29.7 per cent), the southern province of Hawran (20.3 per cent) and Dayr al-Zur (15.6 per cent) in the north-east. This was no mere coincidence: Alawi General Salah Jadid, then at the summit of his power, owed his prominence in the Syrian Ba'th party apparatus mainly to the support of party factions from those regions.[7] The Alawis showed the strongest representation among religious minorities at 23.4 per cent.

In the period after November 1970, Sunnis and urbanites again increased their percentage in the Syrian cabinets and the Regional Commands at the expense of rural people and members of religious minorities.

Among Sunni urban members of the Regional Commands, the number of Damascenes increased remarkably in the period 1970–95, notwithstanding the fact that the Ba'th Party had always had relatively few followers among the autochthonous inhabitants of the Syrian capital. This might be explained by the fact that in the period in question the Alawi president, General Hafiz al-Asad, cooperated with some high Damascene Ba'thist officers and tried to win the urban population to his side, much more than had the Ba'thists who were in power before him. Moreover, al-Asad engaged in a somewhat more liberal domestic economic policy towards part of the Syrian bourgeoisie. In the era of General Salah Jadid (1966–70), a tough line had been followed against the Syrian bourgeoisie and the remaining large land-owners, and this was slackened somewhat after 1970.

The military in the Syrian Regional Commands

Examination of the regional and sectarian backgrounds of military members of the Syrian Regional Commands after 8 March 1963 provides even stronger evidence of the increased representation of rural people and religious minorities than in either the Syrian cabinets or the entire Syrian Regional Commands (including both civilians and military) of that period.

Officers from the Latakia region showed the greatest representation, at 48.4 per cent of all military members. In the 'Jadid Era' (1966–70) this even reached the peak of 63.2 per cent. With regard to religious minorities, Alawi officers in the post-8 March 1963 period were most strongly represented in the Syrian Commands, with an average of 38.7 per cent, followed by Druze officers (8.1 per cent) and Isma'ili officers (8.1 per cent) (see Tables 6 and 7).

Sunni officers were represented at 45.1 per cent, but, as we have seen, this says little about their actual degree of power in the armed forces. Moreover, most of the officers in question, other than their colleagues who originated from compact minorities, were born in different regions. Eventual sectarian loyalties thus could not be supported or strengthened by common regional ties, and as a result they were unable to form a power bloc on a regional basis as could the officers belonging to compact minorities.

Christian officers are not found among the military members of the Syrian Regional Commands, although they sometimes occupied very high positions in the Syrian armed forces. Their importance was mostly in the military–technical field; in the political field they could play an important role on an individual basis, but never as a group. Like the Sunnis, Christian officers originated from various regions.

The preceding chapters have given a detailed description of how power struggles among the Ba'thist military since 1963 resulted in purges of successive prominent Sunni (1966), Druze (1966), Hawrani (1966–68), and Isma'ili (1968–69) officers' factions, and ended in the supremacy of some Alawi officers' factions. The course of these purges can be traced in the composition of the Syrian Regional Commands.

After 23 February 1966 the last Sunni officer from Aleppo, Amin al-Hafiz, and the last Druze officers, Salim Hatum and Hamad 'Ubayd, were removed. Since October 1968 officers from Hawran have not been represented, and there have been no Isma'ili officers since March 1969, after which date only Alawi and Sunni officers remained as military members, the Alawis enjoying almost complete supremacy. They represented strong army factions, whereas the Sunni officers – though they slightly outnumbered the Alawi officers in the Regional Commands – did not. Rif'at al-Asad's election as a member of the Syrian Regional Command in April 1975 could be interpreted as a reflection of the fact that, after 1970, President Hafiz al-Asad relied to an important extent on officers from his own family, tribe or village neighbourhood.[8]

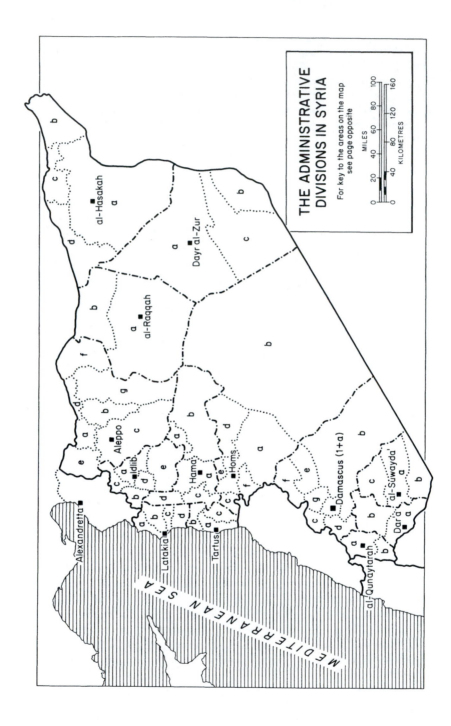

THE ADMINISTRATIVE
DIVISIONS IN SYRIA

For key to the areas on the map
see page opposite

MILES
0   20   40   60   80   100
KILOMETRES
0   40   80   120   160

MEDITERRANEAN SEA

b

c

al-Hasakah a

d

b

Dayr al-Zur a

c

b

al-Raqqah a

f

g

b

b

d

Aleppo c

a

a

b

d

e

Idlib a

c

Hama e

d

b

Homs a

d

c

b

f

e

c

f

b

Damascus (1+a) a

al-Suwayda a

b

g

c

c

d

a

Dar'a a

b

e

c

a

d

c

d

b

a

c

a

Latakia a

Tartus b

al-Qunaytarah

Alexandretta

Administrative divisions in Syria, as used in *Statistical Abstract 1992*

Provinces (*muhafazah*'s) are indicated by numbers 1–13, and districts (*mantiqah*'s) by letters a–g.

1. Damascus: a al-Ghutah; b Duma; c Zabadani; d Qatana; e al-Qutayfah; f al-Nabk; g al-Tall.
2. Homs: a Homs; b Tadmur (Palmyra); c Talkalakh; d Mukharram; e al-Rastan; f al-Qusayr.
3. Hama: a Hama; b al-Salamiyah; c Masyaf; d al-Ghab.
4. Latakia: a Latakia; b al-Haffah; c al-Qardahah; d Jablah.
5. Idlib: a Idlib; b Jisr al-Shughur; c Harim; d Ariha; e Ma'arrat al-Nu'man.
6. Aleppo: a I'zaz; b al-Bab; c Jabal Sam'an; d Jarabulus; e 'Ifrin; f 'Ayn al-'Arab; g Manbij.
7. Al-Raqqah: a al-Raqqah; b Tall Abyad.
8. Dayr al-Zur: a Dayr al-Zur; b al-Bu Kamal; c al-Mayadin.
9. Al-Hasakah: a al-Hasakah; b al-Malkiyah (Dijlah); c al-Qamishli; d Ra's al-'Ayn.
10. Al-Suwayda' (Jabal al-Duruz): a al-Suwayda'; b Salkhad; c al-Shahba'.
11. Dar'a (Hawran): a Dar'a; b Izra'.
12. Tartus: a Tartus; b Banyas; c al-Shaykh Badr; d Draykish; e Safita.
13. Al-Qunaytarah (Golan): a al-Qunaytarah; b Fiq.

Table 1 Regional and sectarian representation in Syrian Cabinets (1942–63)

Cabinet No.: Period:		31–65 1'42/2'58	66–69 2'58/9'61	70–75 9'61/3'63	31–75 1'42/3'63
District	Religion				
Damascus	Sunni	36.9% (117)	36.8% (21)	37.1% (33)	37.3% (171)
(21%)*	Christian	6.1% (19)	–	7.9% (7)	5.7% (26)
	Shi'i	–	–	–	–
	Total	43.6% (136)	36.8% (21)	44.9% (40)	43.0% (197)
Aleppo	Sunni	17.0% (53)	14.0% (8)	13.5% (12)	15.9% (73)
(20%)	Christian	5.8% (18)	–	2.2% (2)	4.4% (20)
	Total	22.8% (71)	14.0% (8)	15.7% (14)	20.3% (93)
Idlib	Sunni	1.0% (3)	–	–	0.7% (3)
(7%)	Total	1.0% (3)	–	–	0.7% (3)
Hama	Sunni	5.8% (18)	8.8% (5)	5.6% (5)	6.1% (28)
(8%)	Isma'ili	0.3% (1)	–	–	0.2% (1)
	Alawi	–	–	–	–
	Christian	–	–	–	–
	Total	6.1% (19)	8.8% (5)	5.6% (5)	6.3% (29)
Homs	Sunni	8.0% (25)	7.0% (4)	3.4% (3)	7.0% (32)
(10%)	Alawi	–	–	–	–
	Christian	–	–	–	–
	Total	8.0% (25)	7.0% (4)	3.4% (3)	7.0% (32)
Latakia	Sunni	1.9% (6)	–	10.1% (9)	3.3% (15)
(13%)	Alawi	2.6% (8)	1.8% (1)	2.2% (2)	2.4% (11)
	Isma'ili	–	–	–	–
	Christian	–	–	4.5% (4)	0.9% (4)
	Total	4.5% (14)	1.8% (1)	16.9% (15)	6.6% (30)
Dayr al-Zur	Sunni	6.7% (21)	7.0% (4)	6.7% (6)	6.8% (31)
(12%)	Total	6.7% (21)	7.0% (4)	6.7% (6)	6.8% (31)
Dar'a	Sunni	–	1.8% (1)	2.2% (2)	0.7% (3)
(4%)	Christian	–	–	–	–
	Total	–	1.8% (1)	2.2% (2)	0.7% (3)
Qunaytarah	Sunni	–	–	–	–
(2%)	Druze	1.0% (3)	–	–	0.7% (3)
	Total	1.0% (3)	–	–	0.7% (3)
Suwayda'	Sunni	–	–	–	–
(3%)	Druze	1.9% (6)	3.5% (2)	3.4% (2)	2.4% (11)
	Total	1.9% (6)	3.5% (2)	3.4% (2)	2.4% (11)
Non Syrian	Sunni	4.2% (13)	–	–	2.8% (13)
	Christian	0.3% (1)	–	–	0.2% (1)
	Total	4.5% (14)	–	–	3.1% (14)
Unknown	Sunni	–	19.3% (11)	1.3% (1)	2.6% (12)
TOTAL		100.0% (312)	100.0% (57)	100.0% (89)	100.0% (458)

* The percentages placed directly after the regional names indicate the respective parts of the total population by region.

Table 2 Regional and sectarian representation in Syrian Cabinets (1963–76)[1]

Cabinet No.:		76–83	84–88	89–95	76–95
Period:		3'63/2'66	2'66/11'70	11'70/8'76	3'63/8'76
District	Religion				
Damascus	Sunni	20.2% (34)	20.0% (24)	20.0% (36)	20.1% (94)
(21%)[2]	Christian	4.2% (7)	–	–	1.5% (7)
	Shi'i	–	0.8% (1)	–	0.2% (1)
	Total	24.4% (41)	20.8% (25)	20.0% (36)	21.8% (102)
Aleppo	Sunni	13.1% (22)	4.2% (5)	5.0% (9)	7.7% (36)
(20%)	Christian	0.6% (1)	–	–	0.2% (1)
	Total	13.7% (23)	4.2% (5)	5.0% (9)	7.9% (37)
Idlib	Sunni	3.0% (5)	2.5% (3)	3.3% (6)	3.0% (14)
(7%)	Total	3.0% (5)	2.5% (3)	3.3% (6)	3.0% (14)
Hama	Sunni	7.1% (12)	10.0% (12)	7.8% (14)	8.1% (38)
(8%)	Isma'ili	3.6% (6)	0.8% (1)	1.1% (2)	1.9% (9)
	Alawi	1.2% (2)	–	2.8% (5)	1.5% (7)
	Christian	–	–	–	–
	Total	11.9% (20)	10.8% (13)	11.7% (21)	11.5% (54)
Homs	Sunni	7.1% (12)	5.0% (6)	10.6% (19)	7.9% (37)
(10%)	Alawi	1.2% (2)	–	–	0.4% (2)
	Christian	0.6% (1)	2.5% (3)	–	0.9% (4)
	Total	8.9% (15)	7.5% (9)	10.6% (19)	9.2% (43)
Latakia	Sunni	7.1% (12)	9.2% (11)	16.7% (30)	11.3% (53)
(13%)	Alawi	4.8% (8)	12.5% (15)	6.7% (12)	7.5% (35)
	Isma'ili	1.2% (2)	2.5% (3)	11.1% (2)	1.5% (7)
	Christian	–	1.7% (2)	1.1% (2)	0.9% (4)
	Total	13.1% (22)	25.9% (31)	25.6% (46)	21.2% (99)
Dayr al-Zur	Sunni	4.2% (7)	9.2% (11)	4.4% (8)	5.6% (26)
(12%)	Total	4.2% (7)	9.2% (11)	4.4% (8)	5.6% (26)
Dar'a	Sunni	8.9% (15)	8.3% (10)	6.7% (12)	7.9% (37)
(4%)	Christian	1.2% (2)	4.2% (5)	2.8% (5)	2.6% (12)
	Total	10.1% (17)	12.5% (15)	9.4% (17)	10.5% (49)
Qunaytarah	Sunni	–	3.3% (4)	2.2% (4)	1.7% (8)
(2%)	Druze	–	–	–	–
	Total	–	3.3% (4)	2.2% (4)	1.7% (8)
Suwayda'	Sunni	–	–	–	–
(3%)	Druze	6.0% (10)	3.3% (4)	2.2% (4)	3.8% (18)
	Total	6.0% (10)	3.3% (4)	2.2% (4)	3.8% (18)
Non Syrian	Sunni	–	–	–	–
	Christian	–	–	–	–
	Total	–	–	–	–
Unknown	Sunni	4.8% (8)	–	5.6% (10)	3.8% (18)
TOTAL		100.0% (168)	100.0% (120)	100.0% (180)	100.0% (468)

Notes [1] See chapter 7, note 40. [2] The percentages placed directly after the regional names indicate the respective parts of the total population by region.

Table 3 Regional and sectarian representation in Syrian Regional Commands of the Ba'th Party (1963–2000)

Regional Command No.: Period:		1–4 9'63/2'66	5–8 3'66/11'70	9–13 11'70/6'2000	1–13 9'63/2000
District	Religion				
Damascus	Sunni	2.0% (1)	–	21.4% (21)	10.4% (22)
(21%)'	Christian	–	–	–	–
	Shi'i	–	–	–	–
	Total	2.0% (1)	–	21.4% (21)	10.4% (22)
Aleppo	Sunni	8.0% (4)	–	6.1% (6)	4.7% (10)
(20%)	Christian	–	–	–	–
	Total	8.0% (4)	–	6.1% (6)	4.7% (10)
Idlib	Sunni	4.0% (2)	–	5.1% (5)	3.3% (7)
(7%)	Total	4.0% (2)	–	5.1% (5)	3.3% (7)
Hama	Sunni	–	–	4.1% (4)	1.9% (4)
(8%)	Isma'ili	10.0% (5)	9.4% (6)	–	5.2% (11)
	Alawi	–	–	3.1% (3)	1.4% (3)
	Christian	–	–	1.0% (1)	0.5% (1)
	Total	10.0% (5)	9.4% (6)	8.2% (8)	9.0% (19)
Homs	Sunni	10.0% (5)	9.4% (6)	6.1% (6)	8.0% (17)
(10%)	Alawi	2.0% (1)	–	1.0% (1)	1.0% (2)
	Christian	–	–	–	–
	Total	12.0% (6)	9.4% (6)	6.1% (7)	9.0% (19)
Latakia	Sunni	10.0% (5)	6.3% (4)	5.1% (5)	6.6% (14)
(13%)	Alawi	12.0% (6)	23.4% (15)	16.3% (16)	17.4% (37)
	Isma'ili	–	–	–	–
	Christian	–	–	5.1% (5)	2.4% (5)
	Total	22.0% (11)	29.7% (19)	26.5% (26)	26.4% (56)
Dayr al-Zur	Sunni	12.0% (6)	15.6% (10)	7.1% (7)	10.8% (23)
(12%)	Total	12.0% (6)	15.6% (10)	7.1% (7)	10.8% (23)
Dar'a	Sunni	6.0% (6)	14.0% (9)	9.2% (9)	9.9% (21)
(4%)	Christian	2.0% (1)	6.3% (4)	1.0% (1)	2.8% (6)
	Total	8.0% (4)	20.3% (13)	10.2% (10)	12.7% (27)
Qunaytarah	Sunni	2.0% (1)	6.3% (4)	1.0% (1)	2.8% (6)
(2%)	Druze	–	–	–	–
	Total	2.0% (1)	6.3% (4)	1.0% (1)	2.8% (6)
Suwayda'	Sunni	–	–	2.0% (2)	1.0% (2)
(3%)	Druze	20.0% (10)	9.4% (6)	4.1% (4)	9.4% (20)
	Total	20.0% (10)	9.4% (6)	6.1% (6)	10.4% (22)
Non Syrian	Sunni	–	–	–	–
Unknown	Sunni	–	–	1.0% (1)	0.5% (1)
	Total	–	–	1.0% (1)	0.5% (1)
TOTAL		100.0% (50)	100.0% (64)	100.0% (98)	100.0% (212)

Note ' The percentages placed directly after the regional names indicate the respective parts of the total population by region.

Table 4 Sectarian representation in Syrian cabinets (1942–1976)[1]

Cabinet No.: Period: Religion	31–65 1'42/2'58	66–69 2'58/9'61	70–75 9'61/3'63	31–75 1'42/3'63	76–83 3'63/2'66	84–88 2'66/11'70	89–95 11'70/8'76	76–95 3'63/8'76
Sunni	82.1% (256)	94.7% (54)	79.8% (71)	83.2% (381)	75.6% (127)	71.7% (86)	82.2% (148)	77.1% (361)
Alawi	2.6% (8)	1.8% (1)	2.2% (2)	2.4% (11)	7.1% (12)	12.5% (15)	9.4% (17)	9.4% (44)
Druze	2.9% (9)	3.5% (2)	3.4% (3)	3.1% (14)	6.0% (10)	3.3% (4)	2.2% (4)	3.8% (18)
Isma'ili	0.3% (1)	–	–	–	4.8% (8)	3.3% (4)	2.2% (4)	3.4% (16)
Christian	12.2% (38)	–	14.6% (13)	11.1% (51)	6.5% (11)	8.3% (10)	3.9% (7)	6.0% (28)
Shi'i	–	–	–	–	–	0.8% (1)	–	0.2% (1)
TOTAL	100.0% (312)	100.0% (57)	100.0% (89)	100.0% (458)	100.0% (168)	100.0% (120)	100.0% (180)	100.0% (468)

Note [1] See Chapter 7, note 40.

Table 5 Sectarian representation in the Syrian Regional Commands of the Ba'th Party (1963–2000)

Regional Cmnd No.:	1–4	5–8	9–13	1–13
Period:	9'63/2'66	3'66/11'70	11'70/6'2000	3'63/2000
Religion				
Sunni	54.0% (27)	51.6% (33)	68.4% (67)	59.9% (127)
Alawi	14.0% (7)	23.4% (15)	20.4% (20)	19.8% (42)
Druze	20.0% (10)	9.4% (6)	4.1% (4)	9.4% (20)
Isma'ili	10.0% (5)	9.4% (6)	–	5.2% (11)
Christian	2.0% (1)	6.3% (4)	7.1% (7)	5.7% (12)
TOTAL	100.0% (50)	100.0% (64)	100.0% (98)	100.0% (212)

Table 6 Sectarian backgrounds of the military members of the Syrian Regional Commands of the Ba'th Party (1963–2000)

Regional Cmnd No.:	1–4	5–8	9–13	1–13
Period:	9'63/2'66	3'66/11'70	11'70/2000	9'63/2000
Religion				
Sunni	35.0% (7)	42.1% (8)	56.5% (13)	45.1% (28)
Alawi	30.0% (6)	42.1% (8)	43.5% (10)	38.7% (24)
Druze	25.0% (5)	–	–	8.1% (5)
Isma'ili	10.0% (2)	15.8% (3)	–	8.1% (5)
Christian	–	–	–	–
TOTAL	100.0% (20)	100.0% (19)	100.0% (23)	100.0% (62)

Table 7 Regional and sectarian backgrounds of the military members of the Syrian Regional Commands of the Ba'th Party (1963–2000)

Regional Command No.: Period:		1–4 9'63/2'66	5–8 3'66/11'70	9–13 11'70/2000	1–13 9'63/2000
District	Religion				
Damascus	Sunni	–	–	13.0% (3)	4.8% (3)
Aleppo	Sunni	15.0% (3)	–	13.0% (3)	9.7% (6)
Hama	Isma'ili	10.0% (2)	15.8% (3)	–	8.1% (5)
Homs	Sunni	5.0% (1)	10.5% (2)	21.7% (5)	12.9% (8)
	Alawi	5.0% (1)	–	–	1.6% (1)
	Total	10.0% (2)	10.5% (2)	21.7% (5)	14.5% (9)
Latakia	Sunni	15.0% (3)	21.1% (4)	–	11.3% (7)
	Alawi	25.0% (5)	42.1% (8)	43.5% (10)	37.1% (23)
	Total	40.0% (8)	63.2% (12)	43.5% (10)	48.4% (30)
Dayr al-Zur	Sunni	–	–	8.7% (2)	3.2% (2)
Dar'a	Sunni	–	10.5% (2)	–	3.2% (2)
Suwayda'	Druze	25.0% (5)	–	–	8.1% (5)
TOTAL		100.0% (30)	100.0% (33)	100.0% (38)	100.0% (101)

Table 8 Party apparatus distribution on 31 October 1984*

District	Full Members	Supporters	Total party apparatus
Damascus	6,963	31,832	38,795
Rural Damascus	6,693	29,148	35,841
Dar'a	4,837	15,766	20,603
Suwayda'	5,586	16,975	22,561
Qunaytarah	4,842	14,491	19,333
Homs	9,994	47,541	57,535
Hama	7,378	45,387	52,765
Tartus	9,259	35,013	44,272
Latakia	8,489	43,255	51,744
Idlib	6,572	27,240	33,812
Aleppo	7,564	45,529	53,093
Raqqah	3,915	18,088	22,003
Dayr al-Zur	3,468	14,599	18,067
Hasakah	6,533	28,119	34,652
Security Forces	4,205	3,900	8,105
Damascus University	3,301	8,640	11,941
Aleppo University	1,466	5,438	6,904
Tishrin University	1,327	4,511	5,838
TOTAL	102,392	435,472	537,864

* *Al-Taqrir al-Tanzimi* 1985, p. 57. See Chapter 9, note 21.

Table 9 Distribution of party apparatus and population according to branches and percentage of party apparatus in population eligible by age at the end of October 1984*:

Party distribution & population	Party distribution	General population		Population eligible by age		Party % in population eligible by age	Total party
Branches		no.	%	no.	%	%	%
Damascus	51,314	1,057,073	9.49	837,000	13.02	6.13	9.54
Rural Damascus	36,420	845,285	7.59	621,000	9.66	5.86	6.77
Dar'a	21,182	428,838	3.85	232,000	3.61	9.23	3.94
Suwayda'	23,140	294,076	2.64	140,000	3.18	16.53	4.30
Qunaytarah	19,912	229,928	2.06	141,000	2.19	14.12	3.70
Homs	58,114	1,033,965	9.28	546,000	8.49	10.64	10.81
Hama	53,344	974,343	8.75	551,000	8.57	9.68	9.91
Tartus	44,851	556,336	5.00	302,000	4.70	14.85	8.34
Latakia	58,161	702,861	6.31	390,000	6.07	14.91	10.81
Idlib	34,391	837,613	7.52	384,000	5.98	8.96	6.39
Aleppo	60,576	2,485,637	22.32	1,117,000	17.37	4.60	11.26
Raqqah	22,582	371,812	3.34	244,000	3.79	9.25	4.20
Dayr al-Zur	18,646	637,774	5.73	293,000	4.54	6.36	3.47
Hasakah	35,231	681,533	6.12	468,000	7.28	7.53	6.56
TOTAL	537,864	11,137,114	100.00	6,430,000	100.00	8.36	100.00

We note that the percentage of party members in the population eligible by age amounts to 8.36%. When the Seventh Regional Congress was held, it was 8.20%, with an increase of 0.16%. It is also noted that Damascus University was added to the Damascus branch, Aleppo University to the Aleppo branch and Tishrin University to the Latakia branch, while the Security branch was distributed on all branches.

* *Al-Taqrir al-Tanzimi 1985*, p. 56. See Chapter 9, note 11.

7

Sectarian provocation and confrontation

> Having consolidated his bases within the army, [Alawi] Major-General Salah [Jadid] was wise enough not to bring up the weapon of sectarianism. He preferred to profit when his [Sunni] opponents brought it up, thus proving that from the point of view of the Party and of the nationalists, he was more sincere than those who raised the sectarian banner. Notwithstanding all this, I do not know which of the two is the more serious crime: causing sectarianism or exposing it. [Munif al-Razzaz, *al-Tajribah al-Murrah* ('The Bitter Experience'), p. 160.]

Sectarian provocation: The Aleppo massacre

Chapter 5 showed that a long series of political assassinations and attacks on Ba'thist political leaders started in Syria after that country's military intervention in Lebanon in 1976. Almost all those put to death were Alawis, and at first it was not clear who was behind the killings. After the temporary Syrian–Iraqi reconciliation in October 1978, however, it was realised that these were the responsibility of Sunni Muslim extremist opposition groups who, among other things, resented what they perceived as the 'anti-Islamic' and 'infidel' Alawi sectarian and repressive character of the Syrian regime. A group calling itself the *Mujahidin* (Strugglers), apparently composed of Muslim Brothers but not identical with the organisation of the Syrian Muslim Brotherhood, claimed responsibility for the assassinations. In an editorial in their clandestine newsletter *al-Nadhir*, entitled 'The *Mujahidin*: who are they and what do they want?', they identified themselves and their motives:

> Three years ago, to be exact on 8 February 1976,[1] the first bullet was fired for the sake of Allah, thereby opening the gate for the organised *Jihad* [Holy War], which has now started to produce positive results. This first bullet, however, was the result of long and persistent suffering

89

from oppression and terror. The prisons of Syria were packed with
[Sunni] Muslim prisoners ... The *Zabaniyah* [i.e. angels who thrust the
damned into hell] of suppression and tyranny attacked and wandered in
the people's quarters, schools and universities; general liberties and civil
rights were trampled underfoot ...

The ordeal reached its climax, however, when oppression became
concentrated against the [Sunni] Muslims and against the Islamic religion
in particular: mosques were destroyed; religious scholars were arrested;
educational programmes were banned; Islamic law schools were closed;
atheist and disintegrative information and instruction were published;
sectarian party domination increased steadily; the psychological and
military destruction of the armed forces was planned; the country was
handed piece by piece to the Jews [i.e. Israel]; the [Alawi] sectarian party
militia were allowed to take the place of the regular armed forces; the
riches of the nation were plundered by way of corruption, embezzlement,
illegal trade, doubtful transactions, and the unlawful enrichment of a
handful of people at the cost of the overwhelming majority.

Syria's modern history has never before witnessed such despotism
and intellectual and administrative immorality as that which it witnesses
today in the shadow of the regime of Hafiz Asad and his reckless gang.
It is necessary, therefore, that the dead be resurrected from the sleep of
non-being, that ambition and honour be activated, and that it be loudly
acclaimed: 'Allah is great; on to the *Jihad*': *Permission to take up arms is
hereby given to those who are attacked, because they have been wronged.
God has power to grant them victory* [Qur'an, Surah 22, verse 39].

The *Mujahidin* are young people who believe in Allah as their Lord,
in Islam as their religion, and in our master Muhammad, Allah bless
him and grant him salvation, as prophet and messenger. They sacrifice
themselves to liberate their religion and their nation from tyranny,
infidelity, injustice and aggression; and to actively raise the words 'There
is no God but Allah' and to make the magnanimous *Shari'ah* the com-
passionate [Islamic] law for all peoples, and for the Syrian people in
particular. They have tried to do this in various ways, and only the *Jihad*
remains.[2]

In other articles published in *al-Nadhir*, which the *Mujahidin* introduced as 'The Voice of the Islamic Revolution', they left little doubt
as to what they thought of the Alawis, speaking of them as 'the Nusayri
[i.e. Alawi] enemy', and as the 'infidel Nusayris who are outside Islam'.
They stated that 'the *Mujahidin* are entering the noblest of battles
against [Alawi] atheism ruling in Syria'; and they defined their struggle
against the regime as 'between the suppressed [Sunni] Muslim majority
and the infidel Nusayri minority'.[3] Elsewhere the *Mujahidin* accused
the Alawis of 'having made Islam their traditional enemy'.[4]

The intention of the Sunni Muslim extremists was obviously to
polarise the antagonisms in Syrian society around the confessional axis.

They showed little discrimination in their choice of target: it was apparently sufficient that the victims be Alawis, Ba'thists or not.[5]

One of the worst incidents occurred on 16 June 1979 at the Aleppo artillery school, when at least 32 cadets were murdered and 54 wounded. The majority of the victims were said to be Alawis.[6] This was denied, however, by the (Alawi) Syrian minister of information, Ahmad Iskandar Ahmad, who stated that they also included Christians and Sunni Muslims.[7] But although it may well have been true that those killed or wounded were not all Alawis, it was more important that the general public thought that it was so. And this must have been the intention of the murderers, because such thinking would encourage sectarian polarisation and consequently destabilise the Alawi-dominated Ba'th regime.[8] In the words of a captured deputy leader of the so-called 'Muslim Brotherhood' in Syria, who was made to 'confess' on Damascus television: 'these acts were bound to splinter the domestic front and to sow sectarianism similar to that in Lebanon.'[9]

An alarming aspect of the Aleppo mass slaughter was that it seemed to demonstrate that the army was now penetrated by Sunni activists whose hatred of Alawi domination made them ready to murder. Not less disquieting for the regime was the fact that the (Sunni) officer who had led the Aleppo massacre was himself a member of the Ba'th Party.[10]

In an official statement issued on 22 June 1979, the Syrian minister of the interior accused the Muslim Brotherhood of being behind the killings. He also suggested that there was a direct link between the assassinations and outside opposition to Syria's rejection of the idea of a partial agreement with Israel similar to that entered into by President al-Sadat of Egypt:

These people moved immediately after the [Egyptian-Israeli] Sinai agreement [signed in September 1975]. Their criminal actions escalated following al-Sadat's visit to Jerusalem [in November 1977], and again following the signing of the shameful and humiliating agreements with the Zionist enemy. They began a series of assassinations in Syrian cities, in Aleppo, Hama and Damascus. The victims included innocent citizens in various walks of life and of diverse employment.

The latest of these assassinations was that in the artillery school in Aleppo, where they were able to bribe a member of the armed forces, Captain Ibrahim Yusuf, who was born in Tadif, a village in the Governorate of Aleppo. They utilised his presence and his powers on the day when he was duty officer at the school. On the evening of Saturday 16 June, Yusuf was able to bring a number of criminals of the Muslim Brotherhood organisation into the school. He then called the cadets to attend an urgent meeting in the mess hall. When they rushed from their beds in response to his order and came to the hall, he ordered his criminal accomplices to open fire. Automatic weapons were fired and hand grenades were thrown. In a few moments, 32 unarmed young cadets were killed and 54 wounded.

Are we asked to believe that these criminals who killed young men in their prime are training to go soon to the battlefield, to resist Israeli aggression and perhaps to be killed by the enemy in defence of our noble homeland and of our national dignity? Is it possible to imagine that they are bound to this homeland by even the weakest of ties? Is it possible to imagine that such action can be anything but a service to Israel and to all other enemies of our nation?[11]

Immediately after the Aleppo massacre, a country-wide campaign was started to uproot the Muslim Brotherhood organisation. As a beginning, fifteen of its members already in prison were executed. The decree issued by the Supreme State Security Court on 27 June 1979 stated that 'imperialism and Zionism incited their agents in our country to perpetrate criminal deeds including murder and destruction, and to sow the seeds of sedition among the sons of our people, all under the guise of religion, which dissociates itself from them'. The decree further accused 'al-Sadat and Zionism' of having 'relied on the Muslim Brotherhood gang' to 'fulfil al-Sadat's aim of dealing a blow to internal unity'.[12]

It should be noted, however, that the Syrian Muslim Brotherhood had strongly condemned President al-Sadat's dealing with Israel.[13] In a reaction, Radio Cairo commented on the anti-Muslim Brotherhood campaign in Syria as follows:

> The Syrian authorities have tried to put the blame for the massacre on the Muslim Brotherhood so as to divert attention from the covert conflict between Alawis and Sunnis within the Syrian party ... The members of the Muslim Brotherhood who were executed recently had been detained in Syrian prisons since 1977 and had no connection with the artillery school incident.[14]

Many other assassinations occurred. For example, those in August 1979 of two prominent Alawi leaders in Latakia city, i.e. Shaykh Yusuf Sarim and Nadir Husari, sparked off Alawi–Sunni sectarian clashes which reportedly were brought rigorously under control by armed forces under the command of Rif'at al-Asad. Alawi-dominated local security forces also reportedly discriminated in favour of the Alawi community, thus further accentuating the sectarian dimension of the clashes.[15]

Anti-Alawi sectarian propaganda

Syrian accusations that President al-Sadat was attempting to undermine Syria's internal unity were not unfounded. Ever since the Syrian–Egyptian controversy over Egypt's signing of the second Sinai disengagement agreement with Israel in September 1975, President al-Sadat, supported by the Egyptian mass media, had devoted a good deal of attention and propaganda to the fact that the Syrian Ba'th regime was dominated by Alawis.[16] In this respect, Egypt surpassed the other regional radio stations which were then most hostile to Syria: Radio Israel and the clandestine Voice of Lebanon run by the right-wing Maronite-dominated Lebanese Phalangist Party.

In many of his speeches President al-Sadat referred to the Syrian regime as that of the *'Alawi Ba'th'*.[17] On 1 May 1979, he went further than ever before in his attacks on the Alawi Ba'thists in power in Syria, indiscriminately assailing the whole Alawi community as such and no longer distinguishing between Ba'thists and non-Ba'thists:

I was prepared to speak on behalf of the Golan. But no. Let these dirty Alawis speak for it. These are people who have lost all life's meaning. By God, let them face their people in Syria and let them solve it. We shall see what they will achieve. I could have brought them the Golan, but I am not responsible for it while the Alawis are in power ... We all know what the Alawis are in the eyes of the Syrian people. The Syrian people will deal with them. Afterwards things will be different ... The attitude of Syria – it is not right to say Syria, because the Syrian people are powerless in this – the attitude of the Alawis is known ... [King] Faysal [of Saudi Arabia] told me that Hafiz al-Asad is Alawi and Ba'thist, and the one is more evil than the other ... Faysal also told me: How can you hold hands with the Syrian Ba'thists? Al-Asad is an Alawi and Ba'thist; one is more evil than the other.[18]

In addition to the sectarianism that was practised by members of the Ba'thist regime, all this propaganda may well have helped to foment further sectarian unrest and tensions and to stimulate sectarian clashes. Radio Cairo was widely listened to in the Arab world, if only out of interest in Egypt's dealings with Israel. In line with Egyptian propaganda, which identified the ruling Ba'th Party with the Alawi community as such, the Cairo daily *al-Akhbar*, in an editorial entitled 'The Sea of Blood in which Syria Lives', commented on the Aleppo massacre:

If the news of this massacre came as a surprise to some people and aroused fear and consternation, it was no surprise to those who are conversant with the facts of the situation in Syria and the atrocities which Alawi Ba'thist rule is committing against the Syrian people. This massacre was only one link in a long chain of crimes and assassinations and of other acts of suppression and coercion to which the Alawi Ba'th Party resorts in order to humiliate the Syrian people and to guarantee its own rule. The Syrian people were bound to rise against such humiliation and to defend themselves.

The Ba'thist minister of the interior, in a statement issued in his own defence, said that the massacre was the latest crime in what he called a chain of conspiracies against Syria, all of which are hatched abroad. It is natural that a Ba'thist minister should make such a claim.

But the truth, the truth of the tragedy through which the Syrian people are living and of the circumstances and conditions surrounding the Aleppo massacre, is now common knowledge to all people. The majority of the massacre's victims, more than 50 killed and scores injured, were Alawis, that is, of the same faction [sic] to which the Ba'th Party belongs. The Ba'th Party represents only a small minority of the people of not more than 11 per cent.

According to the news agencies, revenge against the Alawis was the motive behind the massacre, whose perpetrators deliberately sought a large gathering of Alawi military personnel as their target. The massacre took place ten days ago but was kept secret, so that henchmen of the Alawi regime could go on a murder rampage among non-Alawis or Sunnis. News agencies have said that most of those recently killed were Sunnis and that killing in revenge for the massacre of Alawis in Aleppo is continuing. As a result, Syria is in danger of becoming the victim of inter-communal strife and civil war, similar to the Lebanese civil war.[19]

On 30 June 1979, in an effort to counter the sectarian propaganda and the unrest surrounding the Aleppo massacre, and to widen support for the Ba'th regime's campaign against the Muslim Brotherhood, President Hafiz al-Asad for the first time commented in public on the Aleppo incident and elaborated on the Ba'th Party's stand on religion and politics:

The concept of 'homeland' loses its meaning if its citizens are not equal. This equality is an integral part of Islam. We are leading the country in the name of the Arab Ba'th Socialist Party. I lead it in my capacity as Secretary-General of the Party and as President of the Republic, not in the name of a religion or of a religious community, despite the fact that Islam is the religion of the majority. Ba'thists and those who believe in their homeland all believe in the principles of freedom, unity and social-ism ... Those who consider religion to be a matter of ritual and neglect its essence cause it to become an obstacle to progress. Since the start of the Corrective Movement [of November 1970], we have always affirmed that religion means love, work, and achievement. What matters is the presence of moral values and ethics. We have always worked to strengthen religious values in the hearts of the citizens. We have affirmed that Islam is a religion of life and progress. But now we are facing a conspiracy against our country, and a criminal act which was committed not by an individual whom we can forgive, but by a political organisation called the Muslim Brotherhood, which has a pre-planned policy of committing crime. This gang would have adopted the same position if we were angels. It considers a third of the people to be non-Muslims [i.e. the heterodox Muslims, such as the Alawis, Druzes and Isma'ilis, and the Christians]. Its members want to monopolise Islam for themselves, despite the fact that no party has the right to monopolise Islam or any other religion ...

They have exploited the atmosphere of freedom in order to tempt some young people into committing crimes and to cause them to become enemies of Islam. We cannot be lenient with this group, which has committed various acts of murder and one of the most odious massacres ever known in the history of Islam ...

Assassination attempts cannot overthrow this regime and we will not permit sectarian acts. The Brotherhood made their decision in 1975, when the dividing line between us and the al-Sadat regime became clear. Their decision at that time was to implement a strategy to create sectarian fighting, and this was admitted by Muslim Brotherhood members during interrogation ... Those who advocate sectarianism must be punished and their organisation in Syria must be liquidated because they oppose prosperity and tradition.

President al-Asad concluded by urging the population to abandon all sectarian prejudices:

Islam is one thing and this gang is something else again. The Arab Ba'th Socialist Party is a nationalist socialist party that does not differentiate between religions. As a faithful Muslim, I encourage everyone to have faith and to fight rigidity and fanaticism, because they contradict Islam. I believe that a true Muslim is the brother of his Muslim and Christian brothers, and that a true Christian is the brother of the Christian and Muslim. If Syria had not always been above sectarianism, it would not now exist.[20]

In general, however, the regime's subsequent propaganda and its campaign to root out the Muslim Brotherhood was seen as so crude and strident that it antagonised rather than won over the larger part of the devout population. President al-Asad's description of the Muslim Brothers as 'traitors, renegades and heretics', for instance, must have had a counter-productive effect and encouraged the further alienation of the Sunni Muslim majority of the population in particular; his words: 'May God curse them and their Islam. We shall not have one Islam with them. They are murderers of Islam and Muslims. They are traitors of Islam and Muslims',[21] must have had a similar effect. This applied also to utterances by his brother Rif'at and other Ba'thist leaders who, in public speeches, labelled the Muslim Brotherhood (*al-Ikhwan al-Muslimun*) 'Traitors of the Muslims' (*Khuwwan al-Muslimin*), which was clearly a word-play.[22]

The Muslim Brotherhood not unjustifiably claimed that the regime's propaganda against them only helped to strengthen their position: 'The regime's decision to blame the Muslim Brothers [for the assassinations] and its disgraceful method of accusing them, as well as its naive propaganda against them, means nothing other than their nomination to the leadership of the Syrian people to bring them through their great ordeal'.[23]

Later, in early 1980, country-wide bloody civil disturbances occurred which were apparently inspired by the Sunni Muslim extremists, and which for varying reasons were supported by a great many of the conservative and devout population. The regime's leaders then hastened to state that in fact they considered only a limited faction of the Muslim Brotherhood organisation to be responsible for the assassinations and the ensuing unrest. President al-Asad declared on 23 March 1980:

> I would like to clarify a point on the Muslim Brotherhood in Syria. The Muslim Brotherhood in Syria do not all sympathise with the assassins. The great majority of them condemn murder and are opposed to the killers, believing that they should work for the sake of religion and not for any other objective. We have absolutely no dissension with these people. On the contrary, we encourage them. We encourage everyone who works for religion and who upholds religious values. These are entitled, in fact it is their duty, to make suggestions and to demand anything from us that might support and uphold religion. We will not shirk from our duty, nor allow anyone to surpass us in this respect. We encourage those who work for religion and fight those who exploit it for non-religious objectives. We also fight the reactionaries who try to exploit the faithful in our country for their foul political designs.[24]

In a clear departure from the Ba'th Party's earlier secularism, under which religion and official politics were kept strictly divided, President al-Asad opened some of his speeches in this period with religious phrases such as '*Allah Akbar*' ('God is great'), and even quoted verses from the Qur'an to underline some of his arguments.[25] On some occasions the president even deemed it necessary to state explicitly that he was a Muslim, apparently because most of the Sunni majority of the population believed Alawis to be non-Muslims, and, for that reason alone, had considerable doubts about the legitimacy of al-Asad's rule.[26]

It may well have been true that President al-Asad and his more prominent Alawi (and other) Ba'thist colleagues considered themselves in principle to be above sectarianism. But even if the regime's Ba'thist leaders of Alawi extraction, for instance, had theoretically not held any sectarian inclinations, and if, during the struggle for power, they had indulged in favouritism only on a regional or tribal basis, as in the early stages of the 8 March 1963 revolution, this would not have prevented their Alawi subordinates, supporters or clients from holding sectarian motivations for their support for their leaders. They would thus have seen their leaders not only as tribally or regionally related party bosses but also, and particularly during crises in which sectarian tensions played an important role, as fellow-Alawis, leading and representing that section of the Alawi community with which they could identify, and defending Alawi interests when necessary.

Moreover, many Alawis who had non-ideological motivations seem to have 'adopted Ba'thism as their instrument of supremacy',[27] so as to benefit from a regime in which co-religionists, tribal relatives and acquaintances from their home region were already heavily represented, though in many cases for quite different reasons.

Threats of sectarian civil war

Although it is incorrect to say that Syria during this period (or in any previous period) was ruled by 'the Alawi community' as such, this did not hinder many non-Alawis (and even some Alawis) from identifying the regime in just such terms. And this was exactly what the Sunni Muslim extremist opponents of the Syrian Ba'th regime, who were responsible for the Alawi assassinations, tried to encourage. By deliberately provoking sectarian polarisation, they tried to portray the regime as being purely sectarian, with the aim of winning wide support among the non-Alawi majority of the population against the Alawi-dominated Ba'th regime. In this way they tried to force direct sectarian confrontation between the Alawi minority and the Sunni majority, which they probably thought could be won on the basis of superior numbers. In view of the fact, however, that Syrian Alawis numbered about one million, many of them holding sensitive positions of power in the army, police and security forces, such sectarian confrontation could only be expected to be extremely bloody and violent, and its outcome far from certain. Given the impression, whether true or false, of being threatened by the Sunni majority, many Alawis, including many of the regime's initial opponents, might well have felt forced to cluster together for self-preservation, fearing the unattractive and all too likely prospect of political and socio-economic discrimination on a sectarian basis, as had been the case before the rapid national emancipation of Alawis and other minoritarians following the Ba'thist takeover in 1963.

The Syrian Communist Party faction opposing the Ba'th regime, gave the following analysis of the situation:

> Being patriots, it hurts us that the banners of sectarianism are being raised in our country, which [even] France failed to do ... The sectarian method of the regime seems to constitute one of the greatest dangers to the country. In dealing with it, we must distinguish between it and the situation of the Alawi community, because that community does not rule the country, just as the Sunni community did not rule the country in the past. The country is ruled by classes, social groups and families. As to religious communities, these contain both poor people, workers, and others who are honest, and these are in the majority; they contain also rich people and those who profit from their positions in the regime or from their positions in the field of production, and these are a minority. The rich people and the profiteers of the regime in our country, notwithstanding their differences, have interests in common; just as the poor, the workers and the suppressed should be united by their interests, irrespective of their religious communities. The [sectarian] methods of the regime, however, whether intentionally or not, have generally led to a kindling of the spirit of sectarianism and to sectarian tension. If no steps are taken to prevent this danger, it may lead to confrontation between religious communities.[28]

Notwithstanding these dangerous and bloody prospects, the Sunni Muslim extremists seemed ready to lead the country into Lebanese-style civil war if this were the only way to bring down the al-Asad regime. With this aim in mind, their reportedly openly professed strategy early in 1980 was one of increased violence against the regime in an effort to force its leaders to commit the regular army to fighting the population, arguing that since the army was 'mostly Sunni, its loyalty to the regime could, under sufficient pressure, be cracked'.[29]

The officers and men of the most sensitive and strategically important armed units, however, were Alawis; and the regime realistically preferred to trust only these units with the task of dealing with popular disturbances.

As long as the Sunni Muslim extremists and their temporary Sunni and other non-Alawi allies were unable to control large quantities of arms and strategically important army units, these schemes to end Alawi domination seemed unlikely to be successful. Under these circumstances, and contrary to what might be concluded from sectarian propaganda, the potentially most dangerous opposition to Hafiz al-Asad's regime came primarily from Alawi officers who were part of the Ba'th regime's inner circle; only secondarily did it come from other sources. It seemed that only Alawis who were 'privy to the inner workings of the system, [could] command the resources of organisation and information to launch a clean-cut coup',[30] with or without the help of officers from other communities.

Ironically enough, the Alawi-dominated factions in the Army and in the Ba'th Party owed their powerful positions partly to purges of sectarian and/or regionally based military Ba'thist factions as well as to other opposition groups, such as the Sunni Muslim extremists, who resented the disproportionately strong representation of Alawis in power institutions but whose open opposition helped to strengthen the trend which they opposed.[31]

Following the Aleppo massacre, many people feared that sectarian civil war might not be far off unless drastic reforms were soon enacted to end the regime's sectarian and despotic character. With this in mind, declarations were issued by various leftist political groups which opposed the regime. Dr Jamal al-Atasi's faction of the Party of the Arab Socialist Union in Syria, for example, issued the following internal memorandum:

> This is a crisis of national fragmentation and divisiveness which threatens to kindle the fire of sectarian struggle and civil war ... The terrible chain of events which keeps spreading not [only] shows us a struggle between terrorist groups motivated by fanaticism and a despotic regime which emphasised a particular [i.e. Alawi] *esprit de corps* and thus feeds fanaticism; nay, it is also the loud expression of a national crisis that threatens the existence of our country, pushing it along the road to bloody sectarian clashes; i.e. the road towards the Cyprusisation and Lebanonisation of Syria; i.e. the road towards national divisiveness to which the sectarian struggle led in Lebanon; just as it is the realisation of the dream of Zionist imperialism that the Arab East should explode through its own internal struggles, beginning in Lebanon, passing through Syria, and finishing in Iraq.
>
> But whatever the official explanations and propaganda to minimalise the seriousness of these phenomena, or to link them to external factors such as imperialism, Zionism, reactionism, Sadatism, Chamounism and Haddadism, this does not obscure the role which the present regime is playing through its method and composition, kindling these phenomena as a reaction, through nourishing these divisions. For the regime bears full responsibility for what the situation has become; even for the national divisiveness and for terrorist phenomena in particular.

The party circular continued by warning that those who opposed the Alawi-dominated regime should not blame the whole Alawi community for the present situation. If they did so, they would help to strengthen the position of the conservative Sunni Muslim extremist opposition and encourage sectarian conflict:

We deem ourselves as well as all other patriots to be above calling this regime (in spite of everything its composition and its formation include as to discrimination and open favouritism) one of a religious community [i.e. of the Alawis] as such; and above 'assigning' responsibility for the policies and measures of the ruling group to the account of that [Alawi] religious community; even if that dominating group tries to exploit the religious community and to bind it through fanaticism and clannishness, or through inspiring fear of clannishness among others [i.e. the non-Alawis] and of their reactions towards them, so as to present itself as if it were the protector [of the Alawi community] and the source of its advantages and interests, by presenting gains and privileges to this or that [Alawi] individual or this or that [Alawi] family; so as to fill its power institutions as well as its repressive and intelligence institutions with many of its members. Nevertheless, the majority of the [Alawi] community, with all its farmers, workers, teachers and various social groups, remain just as other groups, and more so, crushed by the despotism, suppression and exploitation of the regime; whereas in its patriotic and national outlook, it aspires to national integration and not to discrimination and divisiveness, since its general interests are tied to the general interest of all patriots and the masses of our whole nation.[32]

Thus, although it was not 'the Alawi community' as such which ruled Syria, it was nevertheless correct to speak about Alawi-dominated Ba'thist rule. In practice, however, effective participation in this regime was limited to a fairly restricted tribally and regionally related section of the Alawi community; many other Alawis were able to profit from this as a result of a greater or lesser degree of sectarian favouritism practised by Alawis belonging to the ruling establishment, thus strengthening its Alawi sectarian character. David Hirst goes as far as to state that

it is not, in any real sense, the Ba'thists who run this country. It is the Alawites ... In theory they run it through the party, but in practice it is through their clandestine solidarity within the party and other important institutions ... Behind the facade, the best qualification for holding power is proximity – through family, sectarian, or tribal origins – to the country's leading Alawite, President Assad.[33]

Sectarianism, corruption and lack of party discipline

The strong Alawi representation in Syrian power institutions could not in itself account for the instability which the Syrian regime had encountered since the mid-1970s. Alawi Ba'thists had been dominant since the takeover by the Ba'th in 1963, and this was strengthened in the post-November 1970 period, when al-Asad's Alawi-dominated officers' faction monopolised power and at first achieved a relatively long period of stability.

The deeper causes of the instability with which the Syrian regime had to contend, therefore, should not be sought only in the sectarian backgrounds of its ruling elite but rather in a *combination* of corruption, economic difficulties, undemocratic and repressive methods, lack of party discipline and forms of sectarianism which came to the fore particularly in the period after Syria's military intervention in the Lebanese civil war. As a result, popular discontent and socio-economic tensions could be directed and even stimulated through sectarian channels, as was clearly demonstrated, for instance, by the violent and bloody country-wide civil disturbances in spring 1980.

In September 1979, a second anti-corruption drive was started with the intention of improving the country's deteriorating political and socio-economic climate. But the structural obstacles which had hindered the radical execution of the first anti-corruption campaign in 1977 were still present, and prospects for the successful implementation of thorough reform measures seemed dim as long as the regime's party organisation remained weak. In December 1979, Hammud al-Shufi commented as follows:

> In the absence of genuine democratic processes, rampant practices of corruption, extortion and bribery have remained unchecked. Assad's recently announced and much-publicised campaign to wipe out corruption from his government had to be halted as soon as it became clear that it would implicate personal friends and relatives for whom he had secured choice governmental and military positions.[34]

In 1980, the Ba'th party organisation still suffered from many of the weaknesses it had had to contend with since it came to power in 1963. Despite seventeen years of rule by various Ba'thist factions, it had not been able to solve these weaknesses, as was made clear in the Organisational Report presented to the Seventh Syrian Regional Congress of the Ba'th Party, held in Damascus from 22 December 1979 to 6 January 1980. This report summarised what it called the greatest difficulties which had hindered the Party's organisational activities:

1. Insufficient experience and educational level of comrades in the party commands, and occasional lack of harmony among them.
2. Inadequate ideological education among the party apparatus; lack of willingness to undertake self-education; and the growing tendency towards dissipation among the [younger] generation.
3. Lack of careful selection in appointments to the chain of commands, and of direct knowledge among the leadership about those proposed as candidates by branch commands.

4. Inadequate degree of *al-Jihaz al-Mutafarrigh* among commanding party institutions [i.e. the apparatus by which members are freed from any other duty and are expected to devote themselves exclusively to party work].

5. Other important phenomena include: indifference; no feeling of responsibility; lack of enthusiasm and Party spirit; opportunism; misunderstanding of democracy; and the growth of inherited *illnesses of society* [i.e. sectarianism, regionalism and tribalism].[35]

The weakness of the Ba'th Party in Syria from the ideological point of view was evidenced by the Organisational Report's description of the major difficulties which it confronted in instructing the party's thought to the party apparatus: 'Scarcity of educational material which accurately expresses the party's thought; the difficulty of training educational instructors; and scarcity of sources dealing with socialist nationalist thought.'[36] In fact, Arabic sources dealing with socialist Arab nationalist thought were superabundant, but since many of its writers belonged to the rival Ba'th Party in power in Iraq and had previously been expelled or had fled from Syria, their books were generally not available. The works of Michel 'Aflaq were generally banned in Syria during this period.

During the Seventh Regional Congress the decision was taken to set up a 75–member Central Committee which was to 'maintain the Regional Congress's constant control of the Regional Command in the period between congresses'.[37] Not surprisingly, and in line with the statistical analysis of Syrian power institutions given in Chapter 6, Alawi officers were strongly represented among the military members elected to the Central Committee. They included President Hafiz al-Asad and his most prominent Alawi supporters, including his brother Rif'at, 'Ali Aslan (deputy chief of staff), 'Ali Duba (chief of military intelligence) and 'Ali Haydar (commander of the Special Forces).[38]

The Central Committee chose from among its ranks a new 21–member Regional Command. Among those re-elected were, of course, President Hafiz al-Asad and his brother Rif'at.[39] From a statistical point of view the composition of this Regional Command was in line with those of its three predecessors since November 1970, as described in Chapter 6: they all showed a relatively strong representation from the Latakia region, and of Alawis.[40]

At the end of the Seventh Regional Congress, President al-Asad announced a number of guidelines for drastic reforms, intended to help the regime and the country to ameliorate the critical situation in which they found themselves.[41] During the first stages of its efforts to carry out its reform programme, however, the regime met with country-wide opposition and riots on a larger scale than had been encountered since 1963.

The regime's failure to carry out the necessary reforms to re-establish political and socio-economic stability, as well as its inability to undo its sectarian character, once again emphasised the paradoxical situation in which it had repeatedly found itself since seizing power in 1963.[42] The Alawi-dominated Ba'th regime was caught up in a vicious circle from which there was apparently no way out.

The structural failure to curb sectarianism

In countries such as Syria, reliance on regional and tribal ties is apparently a prerequisite for the maintenance of power. Theoretically, regionalism and tribalism need not necessarily give rise to sectarianism, even when there is a strong overlap between the three categories, as is the case with the compact religious minorities of Alawis, Isma'ilis and Druzes.[43]

Under favourable circumstances sectarianism might be curbed and gradually fade away, notwithstanding efforts by groups excluded from power to encourage it for their own political purposes. In the case of the Syrian Ba'th regime, sectarianism might have been curbed successfully if party discipline had been continuous, if there had been no corruption, and if the party's elite composition had been gradually widened, in combination with socio-economic and democratic reforms, and educational development.[44]

Even if the strong Alawi representation in the power elite at first had little or nothing to do with sectarianism but rather with regionalism and tribalism, as was apparently the case in the early stages of the 8 March 1963 revolution, this could not prevent the Sunni and other non-Alawi opponents from seeing it as an Alawi or minority-dominated sectarian regime. Similarly, Sunni and other non-Alawi opponents of the secularly inspired Ba'th regime could not be prevented from exploiting the theme of sectarianism for their own political purposes, so as to undermine its position. In the latter case, political ideas created their own realities, and sectarianism started a life of its own, irrespective of whether or not the dominant political group really derived its power from sectarian solidarity.

Had the Ba'thist elite been composed mainly of tribally and regionally related Sunnis, thereby also giving the regime a 'minority rule' dimension, the sectarianism theme would have been more difficult to exploit. Since the more powerful members, however, belonged largely to a religious minority that was traditionally discriminated against, whose religion was not even recognised by most Sunni Muslims as being Islamic, sectarianism was fairly easy to exploit. As far as criticism from the side of the Sunni opposition was concerned, the Alawi-dominated regime found itself in a kind of 'no win' situation, described by Stephen Humphreys as follows:

> In Syria, we have a government whose legitimacy is always in question, whatever the success or failure of its policies. The Sunni majority of the population remains profoundly resentful of a Ba'thist government which is both Secularist in orientation and dominated by men of Nusayri background, and this resentment (as we have seen) is easily mobilized.[45]

On the other hand, once the Alawis, so often disdained by the Sunnis, had gained power or had powerful protectors in the regime, they could hardly be expected to remain completely objective and to refrain from the sectarian practices of which they had so often been the victims. Given this situation it was only natural that Alawi revanchism should also play a role, a role which was strengthened in the post-1976 period as a result of the sectarian provocation and Alawi assassinations by Sunni Muslim extremists. The latter, in turn, considered that they had been provoked into undertaking the assassinations because of the regime's repressive, undemocratic, corrupt, and what they perceived as 'infidel' Alawi sectarian character. In the words of one who was brought to trial in Damascus in September 1979: 'Assassination is the only language with which it is possible to communicate with the state'.[46] All this caused sectarian action and reaction to become almost indistinguishable.

Members of the Special Forces, under the command of 'Ali Haydar, on various occasions undertook revanchist actions against the inhabitants of Aleppo and Hama. Following bloody disturbances in March and April 1980, both cities were cordoned off and rudely and thoroughly combed out by units of the Special Forces and the Defence Companies of Rif'at al-Asad in search of Sunni Muslim extremists responsible for earlier assassinations, and their sympathisers. Many were killed and wounded in these actions.[47]

The favourable circumstances under which sectarianism might possibly be curbed and would eventually disappear have not materialised under Ba'thist rule in Syria. In spite of almost two decades of secularly inspired but sectarian minority-dominated Ba'thist rule, by the early 1980s Syria paradoxically and tragically appeared to be more distant than at any time since independence from the Ba'thist ideal of a secular society in which all Arabs, irrespective of their religion, could participate equally.[48]

8

Sectarian showdown: eradication of the Muslim Brotherhood

The only occasion since the early seventies on which the Syrian regime was really shaken by its internal enemies was when the confrontation with the Syrian Muslim Brotherhood *Mujahidin* (Strugglers) reached a climax with the insurrection in Hama in February 1982, which was bloodily suppressed by the Syrian military.

In order to confront more effectively the sectarian provocations and attacks by the Syrian Muslim Brotherhood *Mujahidin* described in Chapter 7, the Regional Command began after the Seventh Regional Congress (January 1980) to arm and train thousands of Ba'th party members and supporters (*ansar*) in the various party branches all over the country. The military Ba'th organisation played a crucial role in the process of training.[1] From now on not only the armed forces but also the civilian party apparatus, equipped with arms, participated in crushing any armed opposition. As a result, violence and counter-violence became even more widespread. The Seventh Regional Congress marked the rise of Rif'at al-Asad to a position in the state second only to President al-Asad's. Patrick Seale has noted that Rif'at's iron-fist methods probably saved the regime, but also changed its character. Matching and even exceeding the brutality of their enemies, the authorities now made more use of military units equipped with heavy weapons to root out urban guerrillas. But the real innovation was the arming of the party members and its supporters.[2]

The Palmyra massacre (1980)

A decisive turning-point occurred in Damascus on 26 June 1980 when President Hafiz al-Asad narrowly escaped an assassination attempt by Muslim Brotherhood *Mujahidin*. A wave of fury swept through the Alawi community, and al-Asad's brother Rif'at vowed to take revenge. The next day two units of Rif'at al-Asad's Defence Companies were ordered by his (Alawi) deputy commander and son-in-law, Major Mu'in Nasif, to fly by helicopter to Palmyra and kill all Muslim Brotherhood members who were held in prison there. Major Mu'in Nasif briefed the men on their operation, and told them that they were to take revenge for what had happened:

> The Muslim Brothers have killed [Alawi] officers, they have killed [Alawi] religious shaykhs (*mashayikh*), they have killed [Alawi] doctors, and finally they have tried to kill President Hafiz al-Asad. Therefore we now entrust you with your first combat mission.[3]

About 550 Muslim Brotherhood prisoners were cold-bloodedly gunned down in their cells that day, some of them shouting *'Allahu Akbar'* during their last moments, and others crying in vain for help. Although the regime tried to veil the real character of the operation, details came into the open later, particularly after two of those involved were arrested in Jordan and made detailed confessions which were broadcast by Jordanian television. The captured Syrians had been sent to Jordan as members of a hit team with instructions to assassinate Jordanian Prime Minister Mudar Badran, who was accused of supporting the Syrian Muslim Brothers with arms and training.[4]

In reaction, the official Jordanian mass media lashed out against Syria, pointing at the Alawi character of the regime in their propaganda offensive:

> When the Arab people in Syria discovered the reality of the sub-sectarian regime dominating them, and the falsehood of the slogans and principles with which it distinguished itself; and when the Syrian regime which is built on the domination of a group of the Alawite sect began to confront the escalating popular opposition against it inside Syria, it resorted for the sake of survival to a policy of repression and terrorism inside and outside Syria. The Syrian regime worked to liquidate everyone who raised his voice against the regime. It assassinated [former Syrian Premier] Salah al-Din al-Bitar in Paris, it assassinated [the Lebanese Druze leader] Kamal Junblatt and [the editor-in-chief of the Lebanese magazine *al-Hawadith*] Salim al-Lawzi and many others in Lebanon and outside Lebanon. Inside Syria, the regime practised the ugliest methods to eradicate its opponents and to liquidate them through collective murder at some times and individual assassinations at others. It did not differentiate between man or woman, young or old, and even the Alawite sect did not escape its black malice, because it liquidated some of its leaders who opposed it, foremost of whom is Lieutenant-General Muhammad 'Umran, whom they assassinated in Lebanon.[5]

The Islamic Front in Syria

The repressive measures of the Syrian regime did not prevent the Muslim Brotherhood *Mujahidin* from continuing their opposition. On the contrary: by the end of 1980 various Sunni religious opposition groups formed an alliance called the 'Islamic Front in Syria', which was mainly dominated by the Muslim Brotherhood. In November 1980 the group published a political manifesto under the title *Declaration of the Islamic Revolution in Syria and its Programme*, signed by its Muslim Brotherhood leaders Sa'id Hawwa, 'Ali al-Bayanuni and 'Adnan Sa'd al-Din.[6]

In the *Manifesto* a special appeal was made to the Alawis 'to revise their accounts', and 'to come to reason before it would be too late.' At the same time, however, the situation was declared to have reached a point of no return as far as the Syrian Ba'th regime itself was concerned; there could, according to the *Manifesto*, be no truce until it had fallen and gone:

An Appeal to the Alawis

We hope that the followers of the 'Alawi sect, to which the imposed scourge Hafiz Asad and his butcher playboy brother belong, will positively participate in preventing the tragedy from reaching its sad end. We also appeal to the conscious elements in the sect to revise their accounts. We declare without deceit or intrigue that we shall be happy to see them shake off the guardianship of the corrupt elements which drove them to this critical predicament. There is still sufficient time left for them and the hearts of our people are big enough to welcome those who will come back.

We strongly believe that it is not absolutely necessary for problems to be resolved by violence. On the contrary, it is only natural for such problems to be solved through constructive dialogue and mutual confidence. However, what can be done if the other party insists on ignoring the others and refuses any dialogue, except that of force?

Because of this, and our belief that the present regime has reached the point of no return, and that it is now impossible for it to undergo a radical revision, we declare that there will be no truce, no laying down of arms, and no negotiation with those who are known for their deceit and for breaking their promises. We shall continue in our course, disregarding dangers and obstacles, until this oppressive regime has fallen and gone forever.[7]

According to the *Manifesto*, 'the rights of all religious and ethnic minorities will be guaranteed' (p. 18, paragraph 11). At the same time, however, the Muslim Brotherhood considered Alawis to be '*kuffar*' (disbelievers, rejecters of faith) and 'idolaters' (*mushrikun*), which implied that in the Islamic state they sought there could be no equal place for such minorities. The armed forces, according to the *Manifesto*, had to be freed from what was called their 'sectarian composition' (*Tarkib Ta'ifi*) (pp. 43–4), apparently implying that the Alawis, and for that matter other minority members too, would have to give up their key positions, which were subsequently to be taken over by Sunnis. All these propositions could not but be generally rejected by Alawis and members of other religious minorities, whether Ba'thists or not, including those Alawis who opposed the regime themselves. From the fact that the indiscriminate killing of Alawis by Muslim Brotherhood *Mujahidin* continued it could be concluded that the proposed 'constructive dialogue' was not really meant seriously.[8]

On the other hand, the proposals made in the *Manifesto* appeared to be all the more attractive to Sunni opponents who felt suppressed by the Alawi-dominated Ba'th regime, and hoped to improve their positions through the Islamic Front in Syria, either being convinced of its principles, or, no less important, merely using it as a vehicle with the aim of overthrowing the regime.

In the period following the formation of the Islamic fundamentalist alliance, violence escalated even further. The Islamic Front succeeded in carrying their terrorist war to Damascus itself in the form of bombing governmental institutions such as the prime minister's office (August 1981), the air force headquarters (September 1981), a Soviet experts' centre (October 1981), and a military recruitment centre in al-Azbakiyah district (29 November 1981) which caused the injury of hundreds of passers by. After President Anwar al-Sadat of Egypt was assassinated by Islamic terrorists in Cairo on 6 October 1981, leaflets were distributed in Damascus, threatening President Hafiz al-Asad with the same fate.[9]

Sunni religious propaganda against Alawis

As described in earlier chapters, Sunni propagandists generally claimed that the policies of the Alawi-dominated Syrian Ba'th regime were in fact determined by the sectarian background of its rulers. But whereas from the mid-1960s until the end of the 1970s the alleged interaction between political behaviour and Alawi sectarian background was often dwelt upon in Sunni polemical writings, this theme had gradually become so self-evident to its authors that by the 1980s some of them started to concentrate more on formulating purely religious arguments, thereby reducing the discussion mainly to whether Alawis should be considered as Muslims or not. When in religious debates the terms 'Alawi' and 'Nusayri' were used, the term 'Nusayri' (derived from the name of Muhammad Ibn Nusayr, who has been described as the ninth-century founder of an extremist Shi'i sect in Iraq which later spread into Syria) would be preferred by those who wanted to imply that Alawis were non-Muslims, whereas 'Alawi' (derived from the name of 'Ali Ibn Abi Talib, son-in-law of the Prophet Muhammad) would be favoured by those holding the opinion that Alawis could be considered as Muslims (in this case Twelver Shi'is). Such anti-Alawi writings were intended not so much to stimulate a purely religiously motivated theological discussion as to prepare the ground for a religiously motivated large-scale Sunni Muslim movement aiming at toppling the Alawi-dominated Ba'th regime by force. The latter would in their view be 'legitimised' on the basis of the anti-Alawi radical Sunni thesis – derived from the fourteenth-century Hanbali jurist Ibn Taymiyah – that it would be permissible to liquidate Alawis.[10]

The Syrian Ba'th regime hardly ever employed religious arguments in its response to anti-Alawi propaganda and polemical writings. There were two main reasons for this: firstly, as the Ba'th considered itself a secular Arab nationalist organisation, it generally refused to enter into a religious debate. Secondly, official reactions to anti-Alawi sectarian polemics and propaganda in similar 'religiously inspired' language, would not only appear to confirm the allegations that the regime was dominated and inspired by the Alawis, but, even worse, would most probably stimulate sectarian controversy and antagonism. Nevertheless, reprints of a number of earlier publications which were regarded as shedding a favourable light on Alawi history were occasionally allowed to be sold in Syrian bookshops.[11]

These books generally did not elaborate on the anti-Alawi propaganda of the kind reflected in polemical writings published in the late 1970s and early 1980s. The first exception to this rule was, however, the study published in Beirut in 1980 by a Syrian Alawi lawyer from Latakia, Hashim 'Uthman, under the title al-'Alawiyun bayna al-Usturah wa al-Haqiqah ('The Alawis between Legend and Truth'). This book has been described as an 'unofficial reaction' to the confessional attacks of the radical Sunni opposition.[12] Although Hashim 'Uthman does not refer directly to the various anti-Alawi publications which appeared in this period, he does go into the arguments put forward by the Syrian Islamic fundamentalist opposition, and seeks to refute them.

It was only much later that for the first time an official study of the religion and status of the Alawis was published by an Alawi religious authority himself and widely circulated: In his book 'Aqidatuna wa Waqi'una; Nahnu al-Muslimin al-Ja'fariyin 'al-'Alawiyin' ('We, the "Alawi" Ja'fari Muslims: our faith and our reality'), Shaykh 'Abd al-

Rahman al-Khayyir explicitly took issue with those who proclaimed Alawis to be non-Muslims:

> Throughout a period of about half a century ... during my many en-counters with both Muslims and non-Muslims, I was most unfortunately struck by and am still struck by their wrong-thinking, which evolved as a result of their reading iniquitous books of bile which quote antagonists and opponents and were written in periods of sectarian fighting and blind fanaticism. Contents of books with such unjust accusations have been passed on and handed down without any argument, as if they were the revelation (of God), the Lord of the Worlds. Such falsities were being ridiculed, magnified and embellished with fantasies of novelists and exploiters, and were also the result of dealings with illiterate and semi-educated 'Alawi' Muslims whose words and deeds were taken as so-called proof of the correctness of the accusations contained in such iniquitous books of bile; or they resulted from conversations with some inexperienced school pupils of the new generation and some parvenus amongst them ... in whom religious beliefs have been replaced by im-ported partisan principles, inherited through a tradition of ignorance, and not through the teachings of venerable religious scholars.
>
> Throughout this long period, I was always and am still encountering the incorrect notion ... according to which it is decisively maintained that 'Alawis' are non-Muslims, who neither recognise Islam, nor subject themselves to the [Islamic] Shari'ah law, and ... and ... etcetera, until the end of this iniquitous recital, which has been composed by the internal enemies who are dividing, exploiting or executing the nation, in collaboration with the external enemy (colonialism), which seeks to usurp the abundant resources of our country by relying on these internal enemies and conspiring with them in order to rip apart our everyday unity, decreed by our nation, language, history and religion ...
>
> On all the above-mentioned occasions, I was always and am still forced to enter into debates, disputes and communications, in order to refute such unjust accusations, and to demonstrate with arguments and proof that the 'Alawis' are Muslims of the Ja'fari school, and that they have eminent personalities who teach them their Islamic knowledge, religious observance and procedures, basing themselves thereby on the original texts of the Ja'fari jurisprudential books, which are equally relied upon by the 'Twelver' Imami Muslims ...
>
> Thus, I consider it my religious, patriotic and social duty towards my brothers in faith, my brothers in Islam, in all-embracing Arabism, and in still more all-embracing humanity to publish this concise epistle, hoping that those who are sincere will resort to it as a categorical reply to the tendentious rumours which during the past years have been propagated against us by Zionists, colonialists, heretics and exploiters.[13]

How sensitive the issue of publicly discussing Alawi religion was considered can be concluded from the fact that the text of the above-

quoted book of Shaykh 'Abd al-Rahman al-Khayyir was only posthumously published in Damascus in 1991, after it had been kept in
manuscript form for almost twenty years.[14] Some thirty years earlier
the publication of an official book on Alawi religion such as that of
Shaykh al-Khayyir had still been considered rather unusual. During a
discussion in 1963 between the then Minister of Information Sami al-
Jundi and the powerful Alawi Chief of Staff General Salah Jadid, the
former proposed to have the Alawis publish their secret religious books
in order to help rebut all kinds of wrong ideas which circulated about
Alawis in Syria, and thereby to solve the issue of sectarianism. Jadid
reportedly reacted by saying that 'if we do that, the [Alawi] religious
Shaykhs will crush us'.[15]

The battle for Hama (1982)

The sectarian confrontations between Muslim Brotherhood *Mujahidin*
and the Alawi-dominated Ba'th regime continued, and reached their
climax in Hama in February 1982 with the bloodiest showdown in
modern Syrian history. The city of Hama was considered a traditional
stronghold of Islamic fundamentalist forces, where the Muslim Brotherhood *Mujahidin* had entrenched themselves in an extensive network of
fortified hide-outs. According to a detailed report of 400 pages, entitled
Hamah, Ma'sat al-'Asr ('Hama, the Tragedy of the Era'), published
afterwards by the Muslim Brotherhood, the Syrian regime had been
planning to comb out the city of Hama quarter by quarter, following
a method it had practised earlier in Aleppo, Homs and Hama itself,
where the authorities had cordoned off whole areas, carrying out mass
arrests, and allegedly massacring numerous people in the process. The
difference with Hama in February 1982 was that the confrontation
between the regime and the Islamic fundamentalist opposition forces
turned into an armed uprising involving a whole city and its population. The battles in Hama raged for almost a month (2–28 February
1982), and could be distinguished from earlier confrontations by their
unprecedented level of violence, bloodshed and destruction. Estimates
of the number killed vary between 5,000 and 25,000, mainly victims
from the population of Hama itself. Taking one of the higher estimates
would mean that about 10 per cent of the total population of approximately 200,000 people was killed. Whole densely populated
districts, including their mosques, suqs and networks of traditional
streets, were heavily shelled and later levelled to the ground.[16]

Muslim Brotherhood sources also mention several bloody confrontations with the Syrian regime prior to the battle for Hama in February
1982, including what they describe as 'the massacre of Jisr al-Shughur'

(10 March 1980), 'the first massacre of Hama' (5–12 April 1980), and 'the second massacre of Hama' (21 May 1980).[17] According to the Muslim Brotherhood publication *Majzarat Hamah* ('The Massacre of Hama'), the people of Hama had undergone severe forms of repression in the years leading up to 1982. In what the study calls 'April, the bloody Spring (1981)', death squads of the Defence Companies reportedly executed more than 200 people, including whole families, in various quarters of Hama. Apparently the lists of those killed included various full members of the Ba'th Party who had shown their membership cards to the death squads but were nevertheless shot. During a heated debate which later, at the request of the Hama party branch, took place with a higher party delegation sent from Damascus, the Hama (*Hamwi*) party members reportedly asked for an explanation of the fact that the Alawi-dominated Defence Companies had been killing not only Hamwi opponents of the regime but even party members from the city: had it been their explicit intention to kill Hamwis as such? The delegation from Damascus apparently refused to respond satisfactorily, however, and later all those Hamwi members who had complained during the meeting and had questioned the intentions of the regime were reportedly arrested.[18]

According to the Muslim Brotherhood's report *Hamah, Ma'sat al-'Asr*, the Syrian regime prepared for the 'final' battle of Hama by concentrating Alawi elite troops around the city with the aim of a subsequent wide-scale armed attack against the (Sunni) opposition forces. The regime's forces included units of Rif'at al-Asad's Defence Companies (*Saraya al-Difa'*), commanded in Hama by the Alawi Lieutenant-Colonel 'Ali Dib, as well as units of the Special Forces (*al-Quwwat al-Khassah*) of Alawi Major-General 'Ali Haydar, the 47th Tank Brigade, commanded by the Alawi Colonel Nadim 'Abbas (which constituted part of the Third Armoured Division, commanded by Alawi Major-General Shafiq Fayyad), the 21st Mechanised Brigade, commanded by the Alawi Colonel Fu'ad Isma'il, Military Intelligence units commanded by the Alawi Colonel Yahya Zaydan, as well as armed Ba'th party units. The number of troops involved on the side of the Syrian regime was estimated to be between 12,000 and 25,000.[19] The battle of Hama had begun when, on 2 February, a group of Muslim Brotherhood *Mujahidin* was completely surrounded by the regime's forces during their combing-out operations in the city, and decided to launch a full-scale counter-attack.[20]

While the Muslim Brothers afterwards claimed that they had been provoked into the large-scale confrontation, and that they finally came out in self-defence, they had earlier announced, for example in their *Declaration of the Islamic Revolution*, published more than a year before, that they would continue their armed struggle until the regime was deposed. When starting their counter-offensive, the Muslim Brotherhood *Mujahidin* proclaimed a wide-scale Islamic revolt against the Ba'th regime, calling through the loudspeakers of the mosques of Hama for a *Jihad*. They stormed into homes, killing some seventy officials and party leaders, they overran police posts, and ransacked armouries in a bid to seize power in the city, which they next day declared 'liberated'. During the first day the Muslim Brotherhood *Mujahidin* laid siege to the residences of the (Sunni) Governor of Hama, Muhammad Harba, and of other security, army, and party chiefs, including the local Party Secretary Ahmad al-As'ad. They succeeded in holding out until security forces had fought their way into the city to relieve them. Although the Ba'th regime had been confronted with previous revolts in Damascus, Aleppo, Homs and Hama itself, a full-scale urban insurrection of such dimensions had never been witnessed before under Ba'thist rule in Syria.[21] Patrick Seale has described this critical situation as follows:

> In Damascus there was a moment of something like panic when Hama rose. The regime itself shook. After battling for five long years it had failed to stamp out an underground which had killed the flower of the 'Alawi professional class and had tarred Asad's presidency with the charge of illegitimacy. Fear, loathing and a river of spilt blood ruled out any thought of truce. Hama was a last-ditch battle which one side or the other had to win and which, one way or the other, would decide the fate of the country. Every party worker, every paratrooper sent to Hama knew that this time Islamic militancy had to be torn out of the city, whatever the cost. Some such understanding that this was the final act of a long-drawn-out struggle may serve to explain the terrible savagery of the punishment inflicted on the city. Behind the immediate contest lay the old multi-layered hostility between Islam and the Ba'th, between Sunni and 'Alawi, between town and country.[22]

Loyalties in the Ba'th Party and the armed forces and other security institutions involved in the armed confrontation were tested to the limit. As on earlier occasions, the Muslim Brotherhood *Mujahidin* had tried to provoke a sectarian polarisation between Alawis and Sunnis in the armed forces, hoping to win to their side the Sunnis who constituted a majority in the regular army. The regime's elite troops involved in the confrontation were, however, essentially Alawi in composition, and with some exceptions they held firm. They were also generally able to maintain control and discipline in the regular armed forces. According to the Muslim Brotherhood, all military men originating from Hama were expelled from key units, such as the 21st Mechanised Brigade and the 47th Tank Brigade, just prior to their assault on the

city.[23] The Ba'th Party *Organisational Report* of 1985, however, described the maintaining of solidarity and coherence within the armed
forces as if no serious disciplinary incidents had occurred at all:

> All this appeared clearly in the heroic role which those [Ba'th Party]
> comrades played in the confrontation with the hired criminal Muslim
> Brotherhood gang, when they eradicated its roots and rid the homeland
> of its crimes and sins, without committing any violations or displaying
> any signs of irresolution in carrying out orders. Neither did there appear
> any abnormal phenomena in their ranks despite the presence of quite a
> high percentage of non-party members amongst the ranks of these forces.
> This constituted a glorious episode in the history of our armed forces,
> in which their internal cohesion and unity were clear.[24]

The above statement did not mean, however, that the regime's forces
did not commit wide-scale atrocities during their recapture of the city,
in which tanks, heavy artillery, rocket launchers, and helicopters were
used. And on various occasions soldiers refused to carry out their
orders.

Although the Muslim Brotherhood's report of the events in Hama
does not mention any serious sectarian split in Ba'thist military ranks
at the time, it nevertheless gives several accounts of incidents where
Sunni Ba'thists from the city of Hama itself were allegedly slaughtered
by the regime's forces just because of their *Hamwi* origin, irrespective
of the fact that the victims happened to have a reputation as loyalist
Ba'thists, or otherwise were supporters or informers of the regime.[25]

According to the Muslim Brotherhood's analysis of the military
operations against Hama, the Syrian military command had carefully
taken precautionary measures to prevent the possibility of any collective
revolt within the Army by maintaining a certain sectarian balance in
key units surrounding the city. In all cases the mainly Alawi Defence
Companies of Rif'at al-Asad were kept close by, so that they could
intervene swiftly whenever necessary. According to the Muslim
Brotherhood's analysis, the Alawi-Sunni ratio in the mobilised armed
units surrounding Hama was determined by political-strategic factors.
Thus, the soldiers of the 47th Tank Brigade were estimated to be
composed of 70 per cent non-Alawis and 30 per cent Alawis loyal to
the regime, whereas the ratio among its officers was the other way
around: 70 per cent Alawis and 30 per cent non-Alawis. In the 21st
Mechanised Brigade the ratio of Alawi officers was supposed to be
even higher than 80 per cent, whereas the ratio among its soldiers was
estimated to be roughly similar to that of the 47th Brigade: i.e. 70 per
cent non-Alawis and 30 per cent Alawis. The Alawi element in the
Special Forces of Major-General 'Ali Haydar was estimated by the

Muslim Brotherhood to be 45 per cent among the soldiers and 95 per cent among the officers. The Alawi percentage among Rif'at al-Asad's Defence Companies was supposedly the highest: both officers and soldiers were estimated to constitute 90 per cent of the whole force. The strong Alawi representation was, according to the Muslim Brotherhood's analysis, intended to prevent any possibilities of large-scale military revolt:

> The [sectarian] distribution according to these ratios indicates that the regime feared the possibility that insubordinate actions might be carried out by certain units and formations: the mentioned [sectarian] percentages made collective revolts impossible. Collective insubordination under the leadership of a group of officers who shared an understanding and harmony in their mode of thinking, and who shared the same social background, was thereby made completely impossible. In case the regime were afraid of [Alawi] sectarian elements who were not followers of the Asad family, the tribal distribution in the Special Forces and the Defence Companies would be altered, and elements of the Defence Companies would then be chosen exclusively from the Asad family, their relatives and followers, to such an extent that they would constitute more than 80 per cent of all detachments. This series of percentages, including security officers, non-commissioned security officers and privates of the secret service, made the occurrence of a collective revolt an impossibility. If, nevertheless, it happened, the Defence Companies would be ready to thwart any such revolt in the appropriate time, because they were participating in the siege operation, and would be close to the theatre of operations in the city ... [26]

Batatu also suggests that in all probability a considerable number of the non-commissioned officers and rank-and-file of *Saraya al-Difa'* and *Saraya al-Sira'* belonged to the same tribe as President Hafiz al-Asad:

> The members of these units were chosen with great care and it seems unlikely that preference in selection would not have been given to men with close tribal links to Hafiz al-Asad. Many of them are even said to be from his birthplace, the village of Qardahah ... But of course, Asad does not rely exclusively on his own tribe.[27]

In the civilian ranks of the Ba'th Party the situation was apparently completely different: cohesion and solidarity were far less developed than among the military, as can be concluded from the fact that more than half (52 per cent) of all 'supporter members' expelled in 1982 from the Syrian party apparatus were from the Hama branch.[28]

Following the showdown in Hama and the eradication of the Muslim Brotherhood strongholds there, it became clear that opposition to the regime had been dealt a major blow. Shortly after the Hama uprising had been quelled, the National Alliance for the Liberation of Syria was founded, composed of a number of opposition groups, including the Muslim Brotherhood, and Syrian Ba'thists linked to the Ba'th regime in Baghdad.[29] However, the Alliance, renamed in 1990 the National Front for the Salvation of Syria, remained weak and ineffective.[30]

On 7 March 1982, in a speech during the first celebration after the Hama showdown of the anniversary of the Ba'thist 8 March Revolution, President Hafiz al-Asad lashed out against the crushed Muslim Brotherhood:

> Brother compatriots, sons: nothing is more dangerous to Islam than distorting its meanings and concepts while you are posing as a Muslim. This is what the criminal Brothers are doing. They are killing in the name of Islam. They are assassinating in the name of Islam. They are butchering children, women and old people in the name of Islam. They are wiping out entire families in the name of Islam ...
>
> Sons, brother compatriots, the masses in every town and village in this country will defend this homeland and Islam as revealed, the Islam of Muhammad, may the peace and blessings of God be upon Him. Sons, we are the ones who will defend Islam as revealed; the Islam of the Prophet's followers; the Islam of 'Umar and 'Ali, the Islam of justice; the Islam of equality; the Islam of love; the Islam of patriotism, the Islam of progress; the Islam of revolution; the Islam of struggle against reaction and feudalism ...
>
> Sons: Death a thousand times to the hired Muslim Brothers, who linked themselves with the enemies of the homeland and who were employed by the imperialist, Zionist and reactionary enemies. Death a thousand times to the Muslim Brothers, the criminal Brothers, the corrupt Brothers.[31]

The eradication of the Muslim Brotherhood strongholds did not mean that inter-communal relations in Syria now became peaceful. Whereas the Islamic fundamentalist opposition had been severely hit, Alawi–Sunni sectarian tensions were as severe as ever, if not stronger. The massive repression in Hama and elsewhere may very well have sown the seeds of future strife and revenge.[32]

Thomas Friedman has argued, with hindsight, that the Hama massacre could among other things be seen as:

> the natural reaction of a modernising politician [i.e. President Hafiz al-Asad] in a relatively new nation-state trying to stave off retrogressive – in this case, Islamic fundamentalist – elements aiming to undermine everything he has achieved in the way of building Syria into a twentieth-

century secular republic. That is also why, if someone had been able to take an objective opinion poll in Syria after the Hama massacre, Assad's treatment of the rebellion probably would have won substantial approval, even among many Sunni Muslims. They might have said, 'Better one month of Hama than fourteen years of civil war like Lebanon.'[33]

9

The power elite under Hafiz al-Asad

In the thirty years after Hafiz al-Asad assumed power – de facto in 1968/9, and officially in 1970 – very little changed in the power structure of the Syrian regime. Most of the prominent Alawi officers mentioned earlier as being in command of key positions in the armed forces and security and intelligence services in the early and mid-seventies were still, some twenty to twenty-five years later, in the same or similar key positions. This meant that the regime during this period could be characterised by a great degree of continuity. It also implied that the main supporters of al-Asad generally remained loyal, as during a period of more than twenty years the president apparently felt no need to make any radical changes in the power apparatus. Al-Asad's reported obsession with loyalty paid off in both the short and long term, as apparently no substantial purges were considered to be necessary in the Syrian armed forces since 1970, the only exception being the purge of his brother Rif'at, which will be dealt with hereafter. President Hafiz al-Asad's strong preference for continuity and his extraordinary reluctance to change the faces around him also meant that most of the senior army top commanders, like the president himself, by the mid-nineties had reached an age – mostly around sixty-five – at which they would normally have been retired.[1] A few of the highest commanding officers of the 'old guard' have been retired, only to be recalled by President al-Asad to duty at a later stage, apparently because he considered their reliability to be unquestionable, and on that basis preferred them for the time being to younger successors.

The al-Asad brothers

The only time since the early 1970s when the regime has really been shaken from within its own organisation was in November 1983, when President Hafiz al-Asad fell seriously ill and the question of his succession

appeared to become acute.[2] The power structure which President al-Asad
had built, wholly depended on himself, and now appeared to break down
without him. From his sick-bed al-Asad gave instructions to form a
six-man committee to which he entrusted the day-to-day running of
affairs: foreign minister 'Abd al-Halim Khaddam, assistant
secretary-general of the Ba'th Party National Command 'Abd Allah
al-Ahmar, minister of defence Mustafa Talas, chief of staff Hikmat
al-Shihabi, prime minister 'Abd al-Ra'uf al-Kasm, and Zuhayr
Mashariqah, assistant secretary-general of the Ba'th party Regional
Command (all of them Sunnis). From a strictly formalistic point of view,
the choice of the above men seemed to be quite natural, as they were
after the president officially among the highest ranking members of the
Ba'th party Regional Command, who at the same time occupied key
positions in the Ba'th party apparatus, government or the armed forces.
President al-Asad's formal decision at the time corresponded with the
picture he later portrayed of himself during one of his interviews with
Patrick Seale, when he remarked: 'I have always been a man of
institutions'.[3] When taking into account the real power centres within
the armed forces, however, it was less natural that Rif'at al-Asad, who
was officially part of the same party upper ten, was not also appointed
by the president to the steering committee. After all, Rif'at al-Asad was,
next to the president, by far the most powerful member of the Regional
Command, having a formidable base in the armed forces with his 55,000-
strong heavily armed Defence Companies, which may in theory have
been subservient to the army chief of staff or the minister of defence,
but in practice were not and behaved as independent formations. But it
was perhaps just because of this factor, combined with Rif'at's sometimes
reckless, less sophisticated and notoriously corrupt behaviour, that he
was not trusted by his brother to become a member of the six-man
committee.

It seems likely that President Hafiz al-Asad, in view of Rif'at's
characteristics, in fact did not want his brother to succeed him, and
therefore thought it better not to include Rif'at in the six-man committee.
Moreover, the other powerful Alawi generals were not included either,
although without Hafiz al-Asad the regime's continued existence seemed
to depend on them as well as on Rif'at.

According to another version, described by Mahmud Sadiq, rumours
circulated at the time saying that a division of military and civilian
powers had been established, giving supervision over military and security
affairs to General 'Ali Aslan, the deputy chief of staff and most senior
Alawi officer after the president, and supervision over civilian government
and Ba'th party affairs to the Sunni minister of foreign affairs, 'Abd
al-Halim Khaddam. If the president should pass away, Khaddam was to

take over as Head of State, albeit on the condition that he would refrain from military affairs, which were to remain the domain of the Alawi military. Even if these rumours were false, they are still worth mentioning, as they reflect the kind of sectarian thinking which prevailed at the time.[4]

Fearing that the president was dying, and alarmed at the changes his death might bring, the most powerful Alawi generals – according to Seale's study – turned to Rif'at for leadership, considering him under the emergency circumstances of the moment, to be the better alternative. According to another version, the Alawi generals, including 'Ali Duba, 'Ali Haydar, Ibrahim Safi, and Shafiq Fayyad, only pretended to support Rif'at, whereas in fact they were preparing themselves to prevent Rif'at from taking over and succeeding his brother as president.[5] The Alawi generals were apparently unhappy with the six-man committee put up by President al-Asad, as they considered its members no more than frontmen. At their instigation, and in the absence of President Hafiz al-Asad himself, a full meeting of the Syrian Regional Command was convened, during which it was decided that it was to substitute itself for al-Asad's six-man committee. In this way Rif'at al-Asad was officially brought back into the centre of affairs.

In the meantime, however, the president had been making unexpected recovery, and he turned out to be extremely displeased with the behaviour of the Alawi generals who had deviated from unquestioning obedience. Rif'at had misinterpreted the rallying of the Alawi generals around him as signifying a total commitment to his leadership. On that basis he had started to prepare for a takeover should his brother pass away. Once the president showed signs of recovery, however, the Alawi generals not only withdrew their support for Rif'at but also started to see him as a threat to themselves. The Alawi generals who had first rallied around Rif'at had included the division commanders Shafiq Fayyad and Ibrahim Safi, as well as 'Ali Aslan, deputy chief of staff and chief of operations, and 'Ali al-Salih, head of the missile corps. They now started to turn against Rif'at, and early 1984 began manoeuvring to hold him in check. After having sufficiently recovered, President Hafiz al-Asad gave orders to General 'Ali Duba, the head of military intelligence, to put Rif'at and his principal supporters under surveillance, and to 'Ali Haydar, commander of the Special Forces, together with Shafiq Fayyad, to bring their military units to Damascus, to serve as a counterweight to the Defence Companies of Rif'at. The president intended to bring Rif'at under control. Rif'at in turn, seriously alarmed, sought to protect whatever power he had left.

At the end of February 1984, heavily armed units of Rif'at's Defence Companies on the one side, and 'Ali Haydar's Special Forces and the Presidential Guard commanded by 'Adnan Makhluf on the other, confronted one another at strategic points in the centre of the capital, and Syria seemed on the verge of a bloodbath. The Regional Command met in emergency session to find a way out of the internal crisis and finally agreed to the solution that by presidential decree on 11 March 1984 three vice-presidents were to be nominated: firstly 'Abd al-Halim Khaddam, secondly Rif'at al-Asad, and thirdly Zuhayr Mashariqah.

Rif'at al-Asad's promotion to vice-president was in fact a demotion, as his duties were left unspecified, and by another presidential decree the command of the Defence Companies was taken away from him. Refusing to comply with the new situation, Rif'at decided on 30 March 1984 to order the Defence Companies, which in practice were still under his effective control, to move in strength on Damascus and seize power. The tanks of Shafiq Fayyad's armoured brigade, together with the Special Forces shock troops of 'Ali Haydar were swiftly deployed to prevent a coup by Rif'at. Only upon the personal intervention of President al-Asad himself could a bloody confrontation be avoided, and Rif'at be persuaded to step down.[6] Finally, on 28 May 1984, some seventy senior officers were banished by plane from Syria for a cooling-off period, including Rif'at, 'Ali Haydar and Shafiq Fayyad. None of them had any assurance of when they would be back, save that it would fully depend on the will of the president. In fact all were soon recalled to resume their duties, except for Rif'at. His Defence Companies had in the meantime been cut down in size, and their remaining men were subsequently redistributed over several other units, including the Presidential Guard and the Special Forces. Some of their members were arrested.

During the period of his strong influence within the armed forces, Rif'at had also built up an alternative network of organisations, which were deeply embedded in the Ba'th party but at the same time were independent from it, such as the League of Higher Studies Graduates (*Rabitat Khirriji al-Dirasat al-'Ulya*). The League included thousands of people with an academic degree throughout Syria, and constituted a kind of anti-establishment debating forum outside the Ba'th Party.[7] Following the crisis, measures were taken to dismantle Rif'at's alternative power networks. Ba'th Party members were ordered to leave the League, which later was dissolved.

The long struggle between Hafiz and Rif'at was brought to its conclusion during the Eighth Regional Congress of the Ba'th Party, held in Damascus from 5 to 20 January 1985. Rif'at was formally re-elected to the new Syrian Regional Command, but remained in fact isolated and soon left for Europe again, not to return from exile to Syria until 1992,

on the occasion of the funeral of his 82-year-old mother Na'isah. Back
in Syria, Rif'at still officially retained the function of vice-president, but
in this function did little more than occasionally receive newly accredited
foreign ambassadors for protocol visits. At the same time he was kept
well away from important official public occasions and ceremonies, where
only the two other members of the vice-presidential trio, Vice-Presidents
Khaddam and Mashariqah were to appear. Nor was he seen in Syrian
media coverage of meetings of the Syrian Regional Command, of which
he was formally still a member.

In 1995, the Syrian minister of defence General Mustafa Talas
revealed in his memoirs details of such a nature that they would not have
been published had Rif'at al-Asad not fallen from grace with President
Hafiz al-Asad. Talas relates that when he was appointed as head of the
examination commission of the Tank Academy in April 1965, he found
out that Rif'at al-Asad, brother of the then air force commander Hafiz
al-Asad, had, according to the ('Alawi) academy director 'Izzat Jadid,
obtained the best marks of his class, to be followed as second best by a
younger cousin of Talas. Suspecting that this was the result of a put-up
job, Talas demanded things to be put straight. Rif'at al-Asad subsequently
ended up as the 31st of his class of 37 students, while Talas's cousin
ended as 15th. Hafiz al-Asad at the time did not criticise the demotion
of his younger brother, but on the contrary approved of it as apparently
being justified.[8]

According to the analysis of Mahmud Sadiq, the internal power
structure of the Syrian regime was changed essentially by the dismantling
of the Defence Companies and the banishment of Rif'at al-Asad, because
subsequently the Defence Companies and the other elite units could no
longer be played off one against the other by President al-Asad.[9] In
practice no other serious differences surfaced within the Syrian officer
corps in the years after the expulsion of Rif'at in 1984. This did not
imply, however, that the remaining elite units could not be played off one
against the other as well.

In the wake of the struggle between Rif'at and Hafiz, another brother
of the president, Jamil al-Asad, also had his wings clipped. In 1981 Jamil,
who was also a member of the Syrian People's Assembly, had founded
the Alawi *'Ali al-Murtada Association*, a political grouping behind a
religious facade. It had been active in mobilising part of the Alawi
community through purely sectarian channels different from and
sometimes even contrary to the Ba'th Party. In December 1983 it was
disbanded on the president's orders.

According to Mahmud Sadiq, the Murtada Association even tried to
convert or, what he calls, 'Alawise' (*'Alwanah*) Bedouin and farmers from
the Jazirah, Homs and Hama semi-arid and desert regions with the

argument that the people from these regions had originally been Alawis who had been forced by the Ottoman authorities to become Sunni muslims. Members of the Murtada Association were occasionally also armed through the Defence Companies of Rif'at al-Asad, which gave rise to the creation of some armed gangs in several Syrian cities, with consequences for internal security and stability. For some time the regime had tolerated all kinds of violent illegitimate activities of Jamil al-Asad and other younger members of the al-Asad extended family, including of Jamil's son Fawwaz, particularly in the Latakia and Tartus regions. These activities, which undermined the Ba'th party's authority and did no good to the regime's reputation, were later curbed, albeit only partially.[10]

The Ba'thist military power elite

The sectarian and regional backgrounds of the members of the Syrian Regional Command and the Central Committee of the Ba'th Party installed during the Eighth Regional Congress held in Damascus in January 1985 – and still in power more than fifteen years later, although elections were supposed to have been held every 5 years – remained more or less the same as before, implying a continued extremely strong representation of Alawi officers, and of personalities from the Latakia region in particular.[11] The new Central Committee was personally appointed by President Hafiz al-Asad, and expanded from 75 to 90 members, half of whom (mostly civilians) had not been members of the previous Central Committee. As was to be expected, most of the military members retained their seats.

The military members of the Central Committee represented the Ba'thist military party elite and were the most prominent supporters of President al-Asad, commanding some of the most essential military positions, units and power institutions. Of the seventeen clearly identifiable military members of the Central Committee, at least ten (i.e. almost 60 per cent) were Alawis.[12] Many of the officers belonging to the inner circle of the regime were reportedly from the same tribe, or were otherwise related.[13]

The president stipulated that the minister of defence and the chief of staff were both to be members of the Regional Command, whereas the senior military commanders were to be members of the Central Committee and of the Military Party Committee and to hold other key party functions in the armed forces, such as secretaries of military party branches and sections.[14] As a result of this measure, the real power structure in the armed forces and the military party organisation was now much more clearly reflected and visible in the composition of the official

Ba'th Party institutions than had earlier been the case, for instance during the days of the secret Ba'thist Military Committee.

Various scholars have suggested that a considerable part, if not a majority, of Hafiz al-Asad's most important military supporters belong to the same tribal confederation as the president himself. Volker Perthes even notes that 'all military units as well as most security services that might be in a position to stage a coup are under command of Alawi loyalists from the president's own tribal and regional background.'[15] According to Alain Chouet's detailed analysis, President al-Asad had since 1970 surrounded himself with Alawi military loyalists originating in particular from three specific Alawi family or tribal circles, one closer to the president than the others. Each circle was, in turn, composed of three different elements in such a manner that specific subtle tribal-confederational balances and rivalries were carefully maintained and respected. On those rare occasions when a member of one of the circles of Alawi intimi was substituted by someone else, replacements were, according to Chouet, effected in such a way that the succeeding person had a family or tribal-confederational profile as close and similar as possible to that of his predecessor.[16]

Since the number of mutations among the highest-ranking Alawi supporters of al-Asad have been so remarkably few since 1970, it seems difficult, however, to justify talk about a *system* of maintaining a precise tribal-confederational balance within the armed forces and various security institutions. Studying the tribal composition of the al-Asad regime and its Ba'thist predecessors leads me to conclude that extended family relations, and for that matter membership of tribal *sub-sections*, have been of essential importance. Membership of a tribal *confederation*, however, generally seems to be too loose, wide, and vague a concept to be of serious consequence in contemporary power politics.[17] The Alawi top military leaders (like their opponents and the political prisoners of the regime) turn out to belong to all different tribal confederations, i.e. the Khayyatun, Kalbiyah, Haddadun and Matawirah. No clearly distinguishable pattern seems to occur among the Alawi military power elite in favour of membership of one specific tribal confederation, whether it be that to which the president belongs or not. Differences of opinion among serious scholars concerning even the tribal background of President Hafiz al-Asad himself, illustrate to some extent the vagueness of the concept of tribal confederation as a political-social unit. According to Hanna Batatu and Mahmud Faksh, al-Asad belongs to the Numaylatiyah section of the al-Matawirah, whereas according to Patrick Seale and Haytham Manna, who questioned the villagers of al-Asad's hometown al-Qardahah, the president belongs to the Kalbiyah.[18] The latter is correct. Seale notes in this respect that:

'Alawis today are not always comfortable with the subject of tribal affiliation as the Ba'thist state has striven to replace such categories with the modern notion of citizenship, but if pressed every village boy could tell you to which tribe his family belongs. Asked to name the leading tribes and families of [al-Qardahah], the head of the municipality replied, 'We have no tribes or families here. We are all members of the Ba'th family under the leadership of Hafiz al-Asad.' Only then, after some coaxing, did he mention the Kalbiya[h] clans which trace their lineage back hundreds of years.[19]

The many social cross-links existing today between members of the different sections of the Alawi community seem to be too many and too complex for the tribal confederations themselves to be decisive in determining patterns of tribal-confederational loyalties. Whereas originally the four big tribal confederations were concentrated in more specific parts of the Alawi mountains, over time they have intermingled to such an extent that even small hamlets may be composed of different tribes living side by side, if perhaps not in harmony.[20]

The civilian Ba'th party apparatus: a statistical analysis

An analysis of the statistics provided in the Organisational Report (1985) confirms the findings concerning earlier periods, indicating that Ba'th party membership was lowest in the bigger cities such as Damascus and Aleppo, and greater in rural areas. A comparison of the geographical distribution of full party members with that of the whole local population clearly confirms that in the eighties the Ba'th party continued to be strongly represented in the (mainly Alawi) Latakia region, as well as in the southern rural provinces.

As mentioned earlier, today's provinces of Latakia and Tartus have for practical reasons been dealt with as one in this study. When taking them as two separate provinces, however, as they are today, an analysis of the Organisational Report (see table 8) provides the following conclusions: a comparison of the population of specific regions with the number of local full members, leads to the conclusion that the Ba'th party in Tartus was statistically 'overrepresented' to a degree of 201 per cent (i.e. proportionally more than twice as many party members as could be expected on the basis of the local population if the Ba'th party had been evenly spread over the whole Syrian population), and in Latakia by 146 per cent. The lower figure for Latakia province can be explained by its relatively bigger (to a great extent Sunni) *urban* population (41.8 per cent urban in Latakia as against only 20.2 per cent in Tartus). Combined, Latakia and Tartus were overrepresented by 170.5 per cent.

In the cities of Damascus and Aleppo, full Ba'th party members were relatively 'underrepresented' by a factor of respectively 71 and 41 per cent. This percentage may even be overstated, as rural Ba'thists who migrated to these bigger cities generally had their membership transferred to their respective new (mainly urban) party branches. Of the other rural provinces, only the southern districts were clearly overrepresented as well: the (mainly Druze) party branch of al-Suwayda' was overrepresented by an exceptionally high 202 per cent, whereas (mainly Sunni) Dar'a (Hawran) was overrepresented by 131 per cent. The rural al-Qunaytarah (Golan) branch was strongly overrepresented by as much as 186 per cent. The latter high representation was apparently related to the Israeli occupation of the Golan, which induced its (mainly Sunni) inhabitants, many of whom had been made refugees as a result of the 1967 War, to be relatively more politically active. Moreover, the al-Qunaytarah branch was being dealt with as a separate unit irrespective of the fact that most of its members perforce lived outside their home province, and did not have their membership transferred to the branches of the provinces to which they had moved.[21]

It should be noted that the strong representation of Druzes and the southern rural provinces in general was not in any way reflected in the higher echelons of the all-powerful Alawi-dominated military party organisation.

When comparing the figures on membership as a percentage of the population in each province *eligible by age* (i.e. 14 years and older) to become members (see table 9), a similar picture appears. Whereas the country-wide average membership is 8.36 per cent of the whole population, the branches of Latakia (14.91 per cent), Tartus (14.85 per cent), al-Suwayda' (16.53 per cent) and al-Qunaytarah (14.12 per cent), turn out to be the most strikingly overrepresented. Taken together, the mainly Alawi Latakia and Tartus branches also in terms of absolute numbers (19.15 per cent) constituted the biggest part of the overall party organisation (see table 9).

The Organisational Report of 1985 notes that in the period before the Seventh Regional Congress (held in January 1980) the party apparatus had been flooded by thousands of newly recruited members having the status of 'supporters' (*ansar*), because it did not apply objective admission rules and standards. As a result the party was enlarged to such an extent that it could no longer responsibly absorb the new members, who thereby became a burden to the party leadership.

Subsequently, in the period between 1980 and 1984, it was decided to expel (*fasl*) as many as 133,580 'supporter' members from the party. This meant that almost a third of the total number of 'supporters' were purged. Over the same period a total of 3,242 full members were purged, implying a much lower proportion of expulsions of just over 4 per cent.[22]

In the Organisational Report (1985) the situation was described as follows:

> The phenomenon of indiscipline amongst the ranks of the supporters appeared before the Seventh Regional Congress, through the application of a policy of expansion, in which quantity became more important than quality. As a result, thousands of citizens became affiliated [i.e. 'supporter' members], without due consideration being given to the established affiliation criteria laid down in the Internal Regulations.
>
> Consequently, the expansion of the supporters' organisation exceeded the capacity of party institutions to absorb, manage and adequately supervise. This was due to lack of place and space at party locations, lack of leading cadres qualified in advance for this objective and lack of party action prerequisites demanded by such an expansion. All this led to negligence, withdrawal and the gradual appearance of the phenomenon of indiscipline. This matter heavily burdened and confused the successive party leaderships, forcing them into taking collective dismissal decisions and dismissing thousands of people. Thus ... comrades dismissed during this period amounted to one hundred and thirty three thousand, five hundred and eighty (133,580) supporters.
>
> It was said in this matter that the affiliation [process] which occurred in some branches was erroneous. In fact, upon scrutinising and investigating, it became evident that the affiliation was not erroneous, but qualitatively speaking arbitrary, with the aim of reaching the figures set in plans and striving towards achieving higher numbers of affiliates, so that the affiliates would actually be there, well and alive, whereas their presence inside the party was merely ink on paper.
>
> In spite of the fact that this phenomenon [of indiscipline] was studied, it was only treated through the dismissal of great numbers. A great deal of attention needed to be given to the phenomenon so that it could be put right in various ways: dismissal should have been the last resort.[23]

According to the statistics published in the Organisational Report (1985), about 39.5 per cent of the 133,580 new 'supporter' members were expelled during the first two years (1980–81) after the Seventh Regional Congress. Whereas the expulsion measures during this period were carried out relatively evenly in most Syrian districts, expulsions in the Latakia region were clearly above the average. This implies that the application procedures had previously been applied there even less strictly than elsewhere. Of the total number of expelled 'supporter' members in 1982 (14,584), more than half (52 per cent) were from the Hama party branch. This should not be surprising, as in February 1982 social relations in Hama were put to the utmost test by the bloody confrontations in the provincial capital between the Muslim Brotherhood and the Syrian armed forces. When the Muslim Brotherhood tried to provoke a sectarian polarisation in the Syrian armed forces and the Ba'th regime, many civilian 'supporter' members who had been recruited earlier on an irregular basis apparently turned out be disloyal and unreliable, and therefore had to be expelled.[24]

Another reason why many 'supporter' members and others had to be expelled was the phenomenon of opportunism which in the mid-1980s still plagued the party due to the fact that so many had succeeded in becoming part of the regime, with the aim of profiting from material and other advantages which it supposedly offered. Earlier anti-corruption campaigns had apparently been unsuccessful. The Organisational Report (1985) described the situation as follows:

The phenomenon of opportunism

When quantity became more important than quality, as we previously mentioned, opportunists infiltrated into the party ranks and constituted a dangerous phenomenon. These people never miss meetings and are never late in settling their subscription fees. They proclaim obedience, loyalty and commitment. They are mercurial types, with no personal opinions, whether right or wrong. Their main concern is to attain leading and responsible positions, in order to realise moral and material gains and to reap the fruit at the cost of the party's reputation and its combatants. They believe that the existence of the party is temporary and that it will eventually vanish. Hence, they seize opportunities to make illegitimate profits by purchasing houses, precious objects and agricultural lands, speculating in real estate, acting as stockbrokers, smuggling and exploiting the party and state mechanisms for their own personal purposes, without any consideration for the party revolutionary and combative principles. The treatment of this destructive phenomenon is the responsibility of your Congress and of the different leaderships in the future. These people should be deprived of any sort of privileges and they should be questioned. Leadership tasks and responsibility should be assumed by the combative comrades, according to established criteria of struggle.[25]

Party membership by October 1985 had grown to a total of 537,864, of whom 102,392 had the status of full member ('*udw 'amil*) and 435,472 that of 'supporter' (*nasir*). This implied that in the period between 1978 and 1985 the number of civilian party members had more than doubled, notwithstanding the numerous purges mentioned above.[26] The privilege of attending the Regional Ba'th Party Congresses was in 1985 restricted to those who had been both 'full members' for a period of at least ten years and members of the Regional Command, the Central Committee, representatives of party sections (*shu'ab*), and a few other sectors.[27] The tightening of such rules, however, did not exclude the many other alternative ways for Syrians to play an effective part in the Ba'th party apparatus and regime.

It may be concluded that the civilian party apparatus was more a reflection of the power structure of the Ba'thist military, than the other way around. As among the military, rural people, particularly from the Latakia region, were strongly represented among the civilian Ba'thists. However, the strong representation among the civilians of the southern rural regions, including the predominantly Druze province of al-Suwayda', was not noticeably reflected in the Ba'thist military apparatus. The civilian Ba'thists' function was to support and complement the all-powerful military rulers. Without the support of the latter, the civilians would be more or less powerless. The fact that 30 per cent of the civilian members could be purged from the party within a relatively short period without any serious repercussions for the internal stability of the regime constituted a clear indication of the full subservience of Ba'thist civilians to military members: civilian Ba'thists did not have any alternative power-base. Raymond Hinnebusch has argued that 'however much the centre may be weakening, it is linked to society by a dense network of structures which have incorporated a deep rooted village base.' Nevertheless, the military clearly play the pivotal role in the leadership of the Syrian state, and without them the Ba'thist populist/rural networks would lose their power base.[28]

The succession question

The al-Asad Sons

In the early 1990s, many Syrians believed that Basil al-Asad, President al-Asad's eldest son, was being groomed to succeed his father. Officially, however, nothing of the kind was ever mentioned or confirmed. It was only in 1990 that President al-Asad was for the first time publicly referred to as the father of Basil (Abu Basil), who was then twenty-eight years old. Previously Hafiz al-Asad had always been more anonymously referred to as Abu Sulayman, although he never had a son by that name. Basil had apparently become the president's right-hand man, someone he could trust and was reputed to be one of the few prominent figures in the regime who was not tainted with corruption. Basil was entrusted with special missions, for instance combating corruption and smuggling and intervening in feuds, including some involving members of the al-Asad family itself. As staff member of the Presidential Guard and chief of presidential security, Basil al-Asad was entrusted with the command of an elite armoured brigade, though only at the rank of major. Due to his outstanding characteristics as an apparently honest, sincere, hard-working, and highly active many-sided personality, who was always prepared to help others, Basil to some extent fulfilled the symbolic function of a national ideal for a new Syrian generation. At the time many Syrian youths even started to imitate his style and outward appearances, such as wearing a short shaven beard. On 21 January 1994 the then nearly thirty-two-year-old Basil was killed in a car accident, and speculations about the possibility of his succeeding his father came abruptly to an end.[29]

Although none of President al-Asad's other sons had earlier been portrayed as having qualities similar to those of Basil, his second son, Dr Bashar al-Asad, was mentioned by various high Syrian officials during commemorating speeches as the natural person to inherit Basil's role.[30] The Syrian media widely reported Bashar's taking over of functions earlier performed by his elder brother. On 17 November 1994, during the celebration of the twenty-fourth anniversary of President Hafiz al-Asad's 'Corrective Movement' of 1970, Bashar al-Asad (at the age of twenty-eight) officially graduated as 'commanding officer' (i.e. captain) from the Military Academy in Homs, after having successfully completed a course as tank battalion commander as the best of his class. Bashar's cousin, the son of Presidential Guard Commander 'Adnan Makhluf ended as second best. It appeared as if a younger (Alawi) generation, consisting partly of sons and other younger relatives of the senior Alawi generals, was being prepared to eventually succeed the older one. Various nominations, transfers and dismissals, effectuated in the armed forces and intelligence and security branches in 1994 and 1995 pointed to such a trend, and contained at the same time potential elements for inter-generational conflicts within the Alawi community.

It should be noted that relatives of other prominent Alawi figures, including sons of for instance Rif'at al-Asad and 'Ali Duba, preferred to go into business, commerce or construction, instead of pursuing military careers similar to those of their fathers. Many sons of the Alawi elite established cross-links with other communities through intermarriage or other social relationships, and thus contributed to substantial change in the originally closed character of the Alawi community.[31]

During the ceremony of 17 November 1994, Bashar's admission to the ranks of the armoured forces was officially welcomed by the minister of defence, General Mustafa Talas, who did so 'on behalf of the armed forces'. It should be noted, however, that Bashar's performance as leading personality had been criticised and thrown into question; for this, Alawi General 'Ali Haydar was placed under temporary arrest in summer 1994. Another reason for his arrest was reportedly his apparent violation of the taboo on sectarianism: during a meeting of senior officers with chief of staff General Hikmat al-Shihabi, who intended to discuss possible regional security scenarios after a peace agreement with Israel, Haydar protested that '*we* [i.e. the Alawis, as interpreted by al-Shihabi] who have built the regime do not only wish to discuss contingency planning but want to have a say in the peace process itself'. Although all the officers present (many themselves Alawi) must have been fully aware of the crucial role of Alawis in the regime, it was nevertheless considered unacceptable to speak openly about it, even indirectly. Moreover, Haydar's remarks could be interpreted as indirect criticism of the line followed by President Hafiz al-Asad in the peace negotiations with Israel.[32]

Like Basil before him, Bashar was apparently entrusted with heavier military responsibilities than would be justified by his junior rank. In January 1995 he was promoted to major in the Presidential Guard.[33] Gradually Bashar's military and political activities were given more publicity by the official Syrian media. In a press report from Damascus, clearly inspired by the regime, it was announced, for instance, that

> Bashar al-Asad had launched a ferocious campaign against corruption, smuggling and the possibility of drugs trafficking across Syrian territory ... He set up integrated work teams to receive citizens' complaints throughout the country and to provide the necessary follow-up so as to help find solutions ...
> Many have vested 'great hopes that [Bashar's] military future shall be no less important than his political future' ... It is no surprise to find Major Bashar leading or supervising a [military] field action somewhere, following its results, and being eager for it to be successful and distinguished. For many officers this has made him a source to consult and seek advice from ... [34]

Bashar was also reported to be receiving Lebanese politicians in Damascus, both ministers and members of the opposition, and in May 1995 he visited Lebanese President Elias al-Harawi in his palace at Ba'abda as well as the president of Lebanese Parliament, Nabih Birri, in Beirut, to discuss the political situation in Lebanon. Bashar's visits to Lebanon were portrayed by Syrian officials as 'personal' and 'unofficial'. The fact that Bashar was accompanied by the commander of the Syrian forces in Lebanon (Alawi) Major-General Ibrahim Safi, and the Head of the Syrian security apparatus in Lebanon (Alawi) Brigadier Ghazi Kan'an, gave an official dimension to the visits, however, just as the presence of these most prominent Syrian generals in Lebanon symbolised Syrian hegemony over the country. A former member of Lebanese Parliament, Albert Mukhaybar, even openly criticised Bashar's visit to the Lebanese president because it happened to take place during a Lebanese cabinet crisis. Mukhaybar commented that 'the Lebanese know very well that they are still under [Syrian] tutelage; the Lebanese people reject it and resist it with peaceful means, and they are not in need of a message which reminds them of it.'[35]

Although Bashar himself denied that he was a candidate for the Syrian presidency, his activities could hardly be seen otherwise than as a preparation for assuming higher political responsibilities.[36] A senior Syrian official reportedly commented in this respect:

> Bashar enjoys great vitality and dynamism. He belongs to the deep-rooted al-Asad tree ... Major Bashar is a guarantee for both stability and the [continuation] of the 'school' of President al-Asad. He is very much the like of his father, the Syrian president.[37]

After Basil's death in 1994, innumerable posters and wall paintings appeared all over Syria, portraying President Hafiz al-Asad together with his late son.[38] In 1995 paintings started to appear on which President al-Asad was portrayed with both his late son Basil and Bashar.

Bashar Hafiz al-Asad as president

In an interview with *Time* on 13 November 1992 President al-Asad gave a very formal answer to the question who would be his successor:

> I have no successor. The successor is decided by all those institutions, state and constitutional organisations and party institutions. These, I believe, have deep roots because they have a twenty or twenty-two years long experience, and they are able to cope with this prospect.[39]

When President Hafiz al-Asad died on 10 June 2000 as a result of heart failure, this scenario was, more or less, literary followed up in the sense that 'all those institutions, state and constitutional organisations and party institutions' bent everything in such a way that the succession of his son Bashar could be easily accommodated and the basis of the regime could be kept fully intact, be it without its former strong leader. It was as if a well-prepared protocol scenario had been lying in the waiting and was now meticulously carried out.

On 11 June 2000, Bashar was promoted by the Regional Command to Lieutenant-General and Supreme Commander of the Armed Forces. That same day, Bashar was unanimously chosen by the Ba'th Party Regional Command as a nominee for the presidency. On 24 June he was elected Secretary General of the Ba'th Party Regional Command. On 27 June the Syrian Parliament voted in favour of amending article 83 of the Syrian Constitution, decreasing the required age for president from forty to thirty-four so as to exactly suit Bashar's age. On 10 July 2000 Bashar's election as president was officially confirmed through a national referendum in which he reportedly obtained 97.20 per cent of the votes. On 17 July 2000 Bashar was officially inaugurated. In just over a month the transfer of power from father to son was fully formalised.[40]

Hafiz al-Asad's high-ranking Alawi military supporters and their respective dependents accepted President al-Asad's son Bashar as a unifying figure, symbolising their wish to continue the former president's legacy and to avoid premature dissension within Alawi ranks. In Syria the principle of collective military leadership has never been practised successfully for long, and accepting Bashar seemed to be the better alternative to prevent new intra-Alawi power struggles, including inter-generational ones.

The highest-ranking Alawi military supporters of Hafiz al-Asad had themselves, like the president, reached an advanced age and could not, therefore, be expected to outlast the late president for a very long period. They were gradually retired and their positions were taken over by a younger generation of Alawi officers with similar regional, tribal and family backgrounds. This transfer of power took place in a peaceful manner, as the Alawi military apparently decided to stick together for the sake of self-preservation and survival, and in order not to put at risk the enormous improvements which Alawis have generally experienced under Ba'thist rule, in social status, economic situation, privileges, military and civilian power.[41] Other rural minority groups for similar reasons abstained from interfering in the power struggle. Many Christians apparently preferred an Alawi-dominated al-Asad regime to any Sunni fundamentalist alternative.

An alternative scenario might have been that certain Alawi officers would have looked for military and political allies outside their own community in order to strengthen their positions against their Alawi rivals. The other way around, Sunni and other officers and politicians might well have tried to seek an alliance with certain Alawi officers with the aim of breaking open Alawi solidarity, and achieving alternative political aims. In such a case, the regime's structure might have been violently ripped open, and Alawi military supremacy might have been bloodily brought to an end. The possibility of people taking revenge for the suppression they had suffered under Alawi-dominated Ba'thist rule was also present. David Roberts has argued that

> the Alaouites [Alawis] have by now made so many enemies and created so many blood-feuds that it must be doubtful whether they dare risk letting the succession pass outside their own ranks for fear of a dreadful settlement of accounts.[42]

Personal ambitions within Alawi circles or other factors could, indeed, lead to a break-up of Alawi ranks and solidarity. Taking into account the enormous improvement of their positions under Ba'thist rule, the stakes for Alawis in general would be extremely high. A scenario in which the Alawi power elite were overthrown would therefore almost inevitably be extremely violent. As long as Alawi domination continues, Sunni opposition is bound to remain a potential danger to the regime.[43]

Initially it was believed that the existing pseudo-alliance between Alawi military and bourgeois Sunni civilians could further develop and broaden and give rise to greater pluralisation and democratisation.[44] This so-called alliance seemed to be based too much, however, on a temporary coincidence of mutual interests for such a scenario to be successful in the longer term. It should also be noted that economic liberalisation does not necessarily give rise to democratisation. During a conference on economic and political change in Syria held in London in 1993, participants tended to agree that:

> economic liberalization in Syria will most likely result in limited political change; in the absence of additional pressures, it will fall short of fully-fledged political liberalization or even democracy, even though there may be a 'return of politics'.[45]

Volker Perthes, one of the participants in the conference, noted in this respect that:

> the Syrian case contradicts the convenient argument, still often heard in western debates on development policy, that economic and political liberalization are inseparable, that economic liberalization both helps to further and eventually relies upon political liberalization and democratization ... Limited and selective pluralism, as granted by the regime, can be regarded as a manner of 'system maintenance' rather than democratization or substantial political liberalization ... Economic liberalization, the Syrian case tells us, is possible, and quite successfully so, without being paralleled by substantial political change.[46]

The first decennium of Bashar al-Asad in power has underlined the correctness of this thesis.

Taking into account the findings of this study, it appears to be very difficult to imagine a scenario in which the present narrowly based, totalitarian regime, dominated by members of the Alawi minority, who traditionally have been discriminated against by the Sunni majority, and who themselves have on various occasions severely repressed part of the Sunni population, can be peacefully transformed into a more widely based democracy, involving greater part of the Sunni majority. A transformation from Alawi-dominated dictatorship to democracy in Syria would imply that present repressive institutions should be dismantled, and that the regime would have to give up its privileged positions. As the Sunni majority in general has apparently not given up its prejudice and traditional negative attitude towards Alawi religion and Alawis in general – it might even be argued that Sunni grudges against Alawis have only increased as a result of Alawi-dominated dictatorship – it seems only logical to expect that the presently privileged Alawi rulers cannot count on much understanding from a more democratic (or less dictatorial, or perhaps even more repressive) regime which would for instance be dominated by members of the Sunni majority. Imaginable scenarios such as these make it all the more unlikely that the Alawi-dominated Ba'th regime will, without severe resistance, give up its present positions in favour of a more democratic regime which in the end – due partly to lack of any long-term democratic tradition in Syria – might turn into a Sunni or other kind of (possibly regional/minoritarian) dictatorship, members of which might wish to take revenge against their former Alawi rulers and oppressors.

Continuing forms of sectarian prejudice and discrimination have, during various critical stages of Syrian modern history, lead to sectarian polarisation, repression, and violent confrontation between Alawis and non-Alawis, irrespective of the fact that Syria has never been ruled by 'the Alawi community' as such. Many Alawis have themselves been suffering from Alawi-dominated Ba'thist dictatorship, often just as much as, or occasionally even more than, non-Alawis. As mentioned before, many Alawis, including many of the regime's initial opponents, might nevertheless feel forced to cluster together for self-preservation if they would be given the impression, whether justified or not, of being threatened by the Sunni majority.

10

Conclusions

In addition to the specific conclusions already drawn in the various chapters of this study, the following general points can be made about what amounts to about half a century of Alawi-dominated Ba'th rule in Syria.

The fact that sectarianism, regionalism and tribalism were major factors in the struggle for power does not imply that other elements, such as socio-economic and ideological factors, were not important too, or could be ignored.[1] On the contrary, it has been shown that socio-economic factors were important, and that in the case of the compact sectarian minorities such as the Alawis, Druzes and Isma'ilis, they coincided to a great extent with sectarian, regional and tribal factors. The overlap of sectarian, regional and socio-economic contrasts could have a mutually strengthening effect. Popular discontent and socio-economic tensions could sometimes be directed and even stimulated through sectarian channels.

Ideological differences were also important, even though during several crises sectarian, regional and tribal ties became the dominant means of self-preservation and retention of power. Once a political group had monopolised power and had provided itself with a solid base, it could give more priority to political and ideological ideas than to pure power politics. Those who were excluded from power, for instance because they had on idealistic grounds refused to apply sectarian power tactics, were consequently not in a position to put their ideals into practice. Others who had used sectarianism, regionalism or tribalism as a means to seize or maintain power, or were more or less forced by opponents to make use of them in order to maintain themselves, could later concentrate on their respective political programmes and ideals.

The developments described in this book suggest a clear relationship between political stability and the degree of sectarian, regional and tribal factionalism in the political elite: if these factions showed great diversity, the result was political instability. The period between 1963 and 1970 was dominated by intra-Ba'thist and related sectarian and regional rivalries. After Hafiz al-Asad's take-over in 1970 the Syrian political power elite attained a much higher degree of sectarian and regional homogeneity than on previous occasions, when contradictory forces jockeyed for power, even though this greater homogeneity also implied a narrower base. As a result of the fact that Syria was dominated by only one all-powerful political faction with a highly reliable and effective security apparatus (also effective in the sense of repression), the country experienced more internal political stability and continuity than ever before since independence.[2] The fact, however, that this continuity was linked to the absence of any substantial changes in the composition of the ruling political and military elite for a period of several decades also implied the serious future possibility of strong discontinuity and disruption of the regime, once its long-serving political and military leadership disappeared.

In the period after 1970, Syrian foreign policies have as a whole been more consistent and continuous. Syrian policies as such had nothing to do with the sectarian composition of the power elite.

In the al-Asad era Syria was able to develop into a major regional power in its own right, no longer subservient to the traditional power rivalries between other Arab countries in the region such as Iraq and Egypt, as had been the case in the past.[3] Consequently, Syria was bound to play a key role in any overall Arab-Israeli peace settlement.

However idealistic some Ba'thist leaders may originally have been, they could not evade the socio-political reality that without making use of primordial ties they could not monopolise power in Syria, let alone maintain themselves. Irrespective of the political line taken by the Syrian Ba'thist leadership after 1963, it should be noted that sectarian, regional and tribal ties have been so important that for about half a century they have constituted an inseparable and integral part of the power structure of the Syrian regime. Without their well-organised sectarian, regional and tribally-based networks within the Syrian armed forces, the security services and other power institutions, the Ba'thists who ruled Syria since 1963 would not have been able to survive for so long. Exploiting sectarian, regional and tribal ties was simply a matter of pure and elementary power politics. Nevertheless both Salah Jadid and Hafiz al-Asad could also be seen as *Ba'thist idealists*, who from their early youth, when they joined the Ba'th Party, had wanted to achieve their secular Arab nationalist and socio-economic ideals. In power, however, both developed opposing policies and ideas, al-Asad being more pragmatic than the radical Jadid. The outcome was that former party comrades and friends turned into serious rivals and lifelong enemies once it came to carrying the heavy burden of political responsibilities and of putting into practice under extremely difficult circumstances political ideas which earlier had just been theoretical ideals and ideology.

The pivotal role of sectarian, regional and tribal ties in the power structure of the Ba'th regime did not imply that the all-powerful Alawi rulers or others were eager to exploit these ties or would not have liked to do without them. In fact Ba'thist leaders as well as many less prominent Ba'thists strongly disliked the idea of exploiting sectarianism and other traditional social loyalties which they considered as being backward and contrary to the ideal of secular and egalitarian Arab nationalism. Many Alawi or other minoritarian Ba'thists had wanted to get rid of their minority status, and very much disliked being continuously reminded of and labelled by their sectarian backgrounds. In practice they were unsuccessful however, and in this respect their wishes were far from realised. Seale has noted that the interpretation resented most by Hafiz al-Asad is the political model portraying modern Syrian history as:

> the triumph of a sectarian minority, the long-repressed Alawis, over their rivals in a Levantine society profoundly divided on ethnic and religious lines ... Indeed he [i.e. al-Asad] has spent much of his adult life trying to escape from identification with his minority background, but the fact that his regime is still widely seen in these terms suggests he has been less than successful.[4]

This lack of success was partly due to the realities of Syrian power politics in which they got entangled from the very beginning of their take-over in 1963. During the process of consolidating their position in the early stages of the revolution, Ba'thist leaders for practical purposes relied heavily on people from their own communities, many of whom shared hardly any of their ideological ideals – such as getting rid of sectarianism, regionalism and tribalism – but rather saw these forces as a vehicle for their own advancement. It can even be said that it was only quite natural that the Ba'thists of rural origin, or those belonging to religious minorities tended to rely more heavily on their own people than on those outside their communities. Hanna Batatu has described this social behaviour as follows:

> When in Syria or Iraq disadvantaged or previously disadvantaged rural or partially urbanized people – representing a level in social evolution different than that of relatively long established urban groups – tend in their political actions to adhere to or cooperate more markedly with kinsmen or members of their own clan or people from their own sect or region, this is not so much a manifestation of narrow cliquishness, although their behavior bears this aspect, as it is they are really acting in a natural manner, merely obeying, so to say, the logic of their fundamental structural situation.[5]

Even if the strong Alawi representation in the Ba'thist power elite in the early stages of their take-over in 1963 had little or nothing to do with sectarianism, but rather with regionalism and tribalism, this could not prevent the Sunni and other non-Alawi opposition from seeing it as an Alawi or minority-dominated sectarian regime. It was only natural that Sunni and other non-Alawi opponents of the secularly inspired Alawi-dominated Ba'th regime exploited the theme of sectarianism as a weapon to undermine it. As has been shown, however, such anti-Alawi attacks generally only helped in achieving the opposite: i.e. furthering Alawi domination. In the process of exploiting sectarian loyalties, political ideas created their own realities and sectarianism its own dynamics, which could not be brought under full control by the dominant political elite.

The take-over by lower middle-class and poorer rural minoritarian Ba'thists in 1963 led to a social revolution: rural minorities which earlier had been discriminated against, and traditionally had belonged to the more if not most backward segments of Syrian society, went through an abrupt process of national emancipation. Traditional relationships were more or less completely turned upside down: people of rural origin and members of religious minorities started to dominate the predominantly Sunni people of the major cities, and relatively swiftly climbed the social and political ladders of society. Once in power, traditionally discriminated against Alawis, Druzes or other rural minoritarians, started to favour members of their own communities and began to discriminate against those whom they perceived as their former oppressors. This led to a certain levelling of society between poorer and richer classes, between rural and urban populations, and for that matter between religious minorities and Sunnis. Urban Sunnis particularly resented being dominated by people of peasant origin from the countryside, irrespective of whether these rural rulers were from religious minorities or Sunnis like themselves. The combination of rural and minoritarian domination only strengthened Sunni-urban resentment even further.

On the other hand rural domination did not really put the cities at a substantial disadvantage where social and economic development were concerned, as urban people in 1963 generally had a relatively better starting position. Moreover, in the period since 1963 the cities were further developed. Many rural people settled in the greater cities and gradually urbanised. New generations of families with rural and minoritarian origins were born in the cities, and thereby became urban themselves. This did not necessarily imply that these newly-born urban generations were socially fully accepted by the original urban inhabitants, or that they fully integrated. It could even be argued that some parts of the greater cities at first became temporarily ruralised to a certain degree, due to the great influx of rural people.[6] Hanna Batatu argues that the struggles that took place *within the cities* between the chief representatives of urban power on the one hand and former peasants or former country people on the other were generally of deeper structural consequence than the struggles in the countryside, where peasants sought to liberate themselves from the influence of the cities.

Connected with these struggles is a phenomenon that repeats itself: rural people, driven by economic distress or lack of security, move into the main cities, settle in outlying districts, enter before long into relations or forge common links with elements of the urban poor, who are themselves often earlier migrants from the countryside, and together they challenge the old established classes.[7]

Sectarian divisions which originally existed between urban and rural people continued to exist to some extent after the urbanisation of the latter, however, and it seems doubtful whether under the Alawi-dominated Ba'th regime similar common links and alliances as those described above, could be forged on a large scale between poor minoritarians of rural origin, Alawis in particular, and the *autochthonous* Sunni urban poor.[8]

During approximately half a century of Ba'th rule - a period spanning more than two generations - segments of the formerly less-developed minoritarian rural communities gradually became more educated, more developed, less poor, and sometimes even well-to-do and rich. The Alawis in general eagerly seized the new opportunities provided by the Alawi-dominated Ba'th regime in the fields of education, employment, economy, emancipation of women, etc. This led to a radical and far-reaching qualitative improvement of Alawi society. The strong social and political advancement of large segments of the Alawi community did not imply that other minoritarian rural communities were now strongly discriminated against as far as socio-economic opportunities were concerned. On the contrary, other minorities and rural people also harvested the fruits of Alawi-dominated Ba'thist rule, albeit sometimes somewhat less than the Alawis themselves.[9]

As a result of the above developments the rural-urban, and minoritarian-Sunni dichotomy which could be most clearly observed in the early years since 1963, gradually became blurred, and inter-communal and class relations became much more complex. Raymond Hinnebusch has analysed this complicated process and comes to the conclusion that:

> class provides the crucial key that drives change and links the major stages in the development of the contemporary Syrian state. The rise of the Ba'thists cannot be understood except as a function of broad class conflict rooted in major social dislocations ... The [Ba'thist] state itself seemed to be generating new poles of wealth and fostering a new stratification system in place of the old one it demolished. No new ruling class has yet crystallized or made the state its instrument, but this may be the next chapter in history.

None of these developments dispute the importance of sectarian politics in the short run ... When class conflict recedes, primordial solidarities tend to reassert themselves as crucial vehicles and the cement of political action. But class and raison d'état are each at least as important as sect in determining elite behaviour and public policy. Moreover in explaining political *change*, sectarianism per se gives little clue. Indeed, the importance of minority groups, notably the Alawis, has been their role as advance guard of an elite or as class coalitions rather than as sects per se. They played the role of class vanguard, then shield of state formation; they now appear as both spearheads of *embourgeoisement* and restratification, and as the target against which antiregime class coalitions have coalesced. It is this class/ state linked role of sect, rather than sectarian rivalries per se, which is by far of greater consequence for Syria's political development.[10]

In addition it can also be argued the other way around that when traditional primordial loyalties recede – for instance as a result of socio-economic changes such as economic development, modernisation, migration, urbanisation, etc. – class conflict is given a potential chance to assert itself as a crucial vehicle for political action. Under rural-minoritarian dominated Ba'thist rule, sectarianism at first constituted an important *catalyst* for class conflict, just because minoritarian-Sunni (i.e. sectarian) contrasts coincided to a great extent with socio-economic (rural-urban) and class (poor-rich) contrasts. In other words, sectarianism to a certain extent could become a vehicle for class struggle, instead of being a barrier against it.

During the al-Asad era, the Syrian regime continued to be confronted with a structural failure to eradicate corruption within the Alawi elite. Syrian socio-economic policies gradually became more pragmatic and liberal, and less rigid than during the earlier Ba'thist period which was dominated by the more leftist and dogmatic Salah Jadid. After 1970, and particularly in the period starting with the Syrian intervention in Lebanon (1976), the political and military elite used its power increasingly to enrich itself, and corruption started to infest the party apparatus and the regime. Various campaigns to eradicate corruption were successful only to a very limited extent, as the corrupt elements of the higher placed Alawi (and for that matter also non-Alawi) military elite belonging to the direct entourage of the president, as well as their clientele, were to a great extent left untouched. Disciplinary action against the most important supporters of the president could have directly undermined the regime, and therefore was not undertaken. Originally the Alawi elite had constituted one of the strongest forces in the regime favouring radical change. After having enriched themselves and having obtained all kinds of privileges to defend, the same elite turned into a major obstacle to the reform of abuses enveloping the state. As a privileged recruitment pool, 'parts of the Alawi community, in fact, have gone from the most-downtrodden to the most well-situated social segment.'[11] In the al-Asad era, the enriched Alawi officers and their families built up a kind of coalition with the rich urban bourgeoisie, the Sunni Damascene in particular, but others as well, including Christians. The latter gradually obtained a direct interest in helping maintain the Alawi-dominated Ba'th regime, at least as long as their businesses continued to prosper. Volker Perthes has noted in this respect that the change of regime in 1970 'also implied a change in developmental and socio-political strategy ... The new leadership did not any longer try to contend with the bourgeoisie, but much more tried to integrate it into its socio-political conception.'[12]

Corruption and discontent with its economic policies could cause sectarian grudges against the regime to become overshadowed by economic resentment.

Religion as such did not play as important a role as sectarianism. Efforts of Sunni religious opponents to mobilise opposition against the Alawi-dominated Ba'th regime through religious channels and theological arguments stimulated Alawi communal solidarity much more than that they caused purely religious debate and controversy. Nevertheless they also caused Alawis openly and officially to defend their position from a theological point of view, albeit in a relatively late stage in the 1980s and 1990s. Over the centuries, Alawi religious leaders had traditionally preferred to keep silent about their religion to outsiders. Under the newly created political circumstances they opened up, stressing, somewhat apologetically, orthodox dimensions of Alawi (Ja'fari) religion.

President Hafiz al-Asad also on numerous occasions made an effort to build up an orthodox religious image for the secular Ba'th regime, for instance by publicly performing prayers in, mostly Sunni, mosques (including the famous Umayyad Mosque in Damascus), or by appearing in public with high Sunni religious officials, or by quoting from the Qur'an in speeches. Al-Asad also had mosques built, including in his home town, al-Qardahah. It remains doubtful, however, whether all such actions were generally having a convincing effect on greater part of the Sunni population, however sincere the intentions of the Syrian president may have been.

The fact that sectarian favouritism and solidarity were in the first place social-communal and politically motivated, could not prevent many of the traditional Sunni population, as well as other non-Alawis, from experiencing Alawi-dominated Ba'thist rule as a kind of semi-religious repression, which it was not, as far as the dominant Ba'thists were concerned. It should be noted, however, that part of the traditional Sunni Muslim community perceived Ba'thist secularism in itself as anti-religious.

Prospects and possibilities for broadening the real power basis of the Alawi-dominated Ba'th regime in Syria are for the time being relatively limited. The vicious circle in which the Syrian regime has repeatedly found itself still persists: for the successive Ba'thist regimes in Syria it was essential to have a reliable power instrument with the support of which it would be possible to implement radical social changes, including the suppression of sectarian, regional and tribal loyalties; on the other hand, maintaining that power entailed dependence on those same loyalties, thus hindering their suppression. It can be concluded that radical social and economic changes have indeed been effected relatively successful under Ba'thist rule. Old traditions proved hard to eradicate, however, and efforts to suppress sectarian, regional and tribal loyalties have failed. The strategically and politically most sensitive positions in the armed forces, security services, and other power institutions remain the prerogative of members of the Alawi community, with only few exceptions.

Various scenarios of changing the regime's strong Alawi character are conceivable and have been described above. Although the possibility should not be excluded, it seems unlikely that the present Alawi domination will gradually and peacefully fade away and be replaced without violence by a much more widely based regime. Feelings of revanchism among people who have suffered from the repression of Alawi-dominated Ba'thist rule clearly remain, and Sunni opposition is bound to remain a potential danger to the regime in the longer run as long as Alawi domination continues.

In the Ba'thist era the ambivalent notion has developed that sectarianism, regionalism and tribalism are to be officially rejected as negative and backward, if their existence is not completely denied, whilst they are in practice accepted as facts of political and social life.

Since Syrian independence, the period of Ba'thist rule, starting in 1963, has already lasted much longer than the pre-Ba'thist period (1945-1963). As the overwhelming majority of Syrians are under 30 years old, most have experienced and known nothing else but Ba'thist rule, and have both at school and through the official mass media been extensively exposed to Ba'thist ideology and thinking. Ideas which in the past were specifically seen as particularly Ba'thist are now by many Syrians seen as a normal part of daily life. This does not mean, however, that Ba'thist ideology is generally accepted, nor that it is deeply rooted in society, except perhaps where some of the Arab nationalist ideas of the Ba'th are concerned.[13] It could even be concluded that the importance of the Ba'th Party, and for that matter of Ba'th ideology as such, has gradually decreased during the era of President Hafiz al-Asad. At the same time the personality cult around the president has gained strongly in importance, as has been the case with other Arab leaders in the region.

One of the biographers of Hafiz al-Asad has even coined the term *Asadiyah* ('Asadism'), which he described as meaning

> the *New Ba'th* led by Hafiz al-Asad, representing a new distinctive current in Syria which has been developed by him; it is a school of thought which has benefited from Nasserism, but has surpassed it, just as it has surpassed the traditional Ba'thist school, albeit that it does not contradict either of these schools of thought but has further developed them in line with contemporary needs.[14]

The al-Asad leadership cult was clearly reflected by the fact that in the 1990s tens of works have been published in Damascus on the Syrian president, all of them eulogies.[15]

Whereas sectarian and other communal identities and loyalties were in the heyday of secular socialist Arabism supposed to be gradually superseded by secular nationalist and socio-economic ones, it has over the years become much more common to argue that the former are natural and culturally specific bases of politics in the Middle East.[16] The political attention paid outside Syria to subjects such as sectarianism, regionalism and tribalism, as well as ethnic identity and diversity, has generally become much more prominent with the explicit resurgence of these and related factors in various conflicts all over the world.[17] In Syria itself, however, the taboo which originally obtained, particularly in Arab nationalist circles, on overtly speaking and writing about sectarian, regional and tribal loyalties, contradictions and rivalries, continues to generally exist for political reasons, notwithstanding the all too prominent awareness of their importance among the population.

Within Ba'thist circles it must have been common knowledge that sectarian, regional and tribal blocs played an important, if not essential, role during several stages of the party's history. Statements to the effect that certain groups, such as the Alawis, should have the right to claim a certain prominent role in the regime, or that Alawis misused their positions by exploiting sectarian ties, were mostly considered as strictly taboo, and were generally dealt with by severe measures, such as arrest or expulsion from the party or regime. Non-Ba'thist outsiders could be imprisoned for such allegations. Although the reality of primordial loyalties was inherently accepted as a well-established fact of political life and power politics, it was simultaneously considered as a kind of 'heresy' to openly admit that this could be the case.

Syrian Ba'thist memoirs

Introduction

Over the last four decennia various memoirs have been published by prominent Syrian and other Ba'thists who were leading the Ba'th Party organisation in Syria during crucial periods: during and after the Ba'thist takeover of 8 March 1963, the '23 February Movement' of 1966, the 'Corrective Movement' of 1970 and onwards. Some of the most important writings in this respect include (chronologically): *al-Tajribat al-Murrah* (*The Bitter Experience*) by former Ba'th National Command Secretary General Dr Munif al-Razzaz,[1] who in 1967 was the first Ba'thist leader to disclose a lot about the secretive inner workings of the Syrian regime. Sami al-Jundi's small book *al-Ba'th*[2] was also important in the period of its publication (1969) because so little had yet been published at the time. Although Jundi's book remains interesting as far as some details are concerned, it has in the meantime been overshadowed by several newer works and other memoirs.[3]

Muhammad 'Umran

General Muhammad 'Umran's book *Tajribati fi al-Thawrah* (*My Experience in the Revolution*), published during his exile in Lebanon in 1970,[4] is not really a memoir, but nevertheless contains relevant autobiographical details, as well as important analyses of Syrian internal events in the 1950s and 1960s. Only one volume was published, however, because 'Umran was assassinated in Tripoli in 1972 before he had been able to publish the, probably, more sensitive second volume which he had announced under the title of *Fi al-Istratijiyat al-Thawriyah wa al-Tatbiq* (*On Revolutionary Strategy and Practice*). 'Umran's work is also relevant because it is the only personal book published by one of the five founding leaders of the Ba'thist Military Committee which took power in Syria in 1963.

Additionally, Muhammad 'Umran's book is important in the sense that he himself corrects the picture usually provided of him by his former rivals as a man with mainly Nasserist inclinations, having no clear ideological vision, let alone solid Ba'thist ideas. 'Umran was generally considered by rival party members to be an opportunist with strong sectarian inclinations, being secretively active behind the scenes, showing a behavior which reflected an (Alawi) *batiniyah* attitude. But reading his *Tajribati fi al-Thawrah* justifies, in my opinion, the picture of a much more sophisticated politician with solid Ba'thist ideological ideals. Some people in Damascus turned out to be surprised at the time by its level of sophistication.

Former Ba'thist leader Mansur al-Atrash has noted in his memoirs that 'Umran wanted to obtain the reputation of a political intellectual in his struggle against the regime which assumed power on 23 February 1966 ('*Shubatiyin*'/'*Februarists*'), thereby wishing to give the impression that his original military capacity had become of lesser importance. This, according to al-Atrash, led to a situation in which 'Umran let pass by some opportunities to take power from the '*Shubatiyin*'. Al-Atrash reportedly told 'Umran, 'without wanting to belittle the importance of his intellectual efforts', that although these efforts were being appreciated, it would have been much more important for 'Umran to gather and unite those of the military who were hostile to the '*Shubatiyin*'.[5]

Mustafa Talas

More than twenty years later, in 1991, Syrian minister of defence General (al-'Imad) Mustafa Talas (born in 1932 in al-Rastan, near Homs) started publishing his memoirs in *Mir'at Hayati* (*The Mirror of my Life*).[6] Whereas previously it had been taboo to write about issues such as sectarianism or the secret intricacies of inner party history and its intrigues, this now became possible inside Syria.[7] This was not only because of Talas's position (although it certainly made it much easier), but also because speaking about such issues was not considered extremely sensitive anymore. Nevertheless, what was permitted for a select group of Ba'thists in power, or close to the regime, remained prohibited to others. Other memoirs (or other kinds of publications or statements) which only slightly hinted at sensitive phenomena could be strictly forbidden within Syria, and people could still be imprisoned for it for very long periods.

In an interview in 2007, Mustafa Talas called upon all officials, both military and civilian, to write down their memoirs 'because this is the only means to teach the generations the lessons gained from contemporary life'.[8] It was doubtful, however, whether others in Syria who were in a different position would have been permitted to write similar books.

In my view, Mustafa Talas's memoirs are indispensable to anyone wishing to seriously study the history of the Ba'thist era in Syria in great detail and depth. The memoirs give detailed pictures of the situations behind the scenes and of the secretive Ba'th organisation and their leading personalities. Some essential details, thus far unpublished, are provided.

Mustafa Talas was minister of defence for over thirty years (1972–2004) and personally took part in many important developments within the Syrian armed forces and the Ba'th Party since its early days.

Mir'at Hayati has become a monumental and impressive document consisting of five parts with a total of 4655 pages. Every part concentrates on a specific decennium. In an interview in 2007 Talas expressed his intention to publish the remaining decennium (1998–2008), which would then complete this work.

Part 1 (1948–1958) (824 pages, including a useful index not available in the subsequent volumes) deals in detail with Talas's early youth, the Military Academy, the Ba'thist Qatana revolt (1957), the unification with Egypt (1958), and many other topics. Next to giving a well studied analysis, Talas also provides many vivid descriptions, including those of his early days in the Military Academy, where he was together with Hafiz al-Asad, who was both respected and feared, also because he could, by way of disciplinary action, thrust his forehead (*yantah*) against those of his opponents in such a tough way that they would never want to experience this again (Vol. 1, pp. 307–09). Because of this story the book was reportedly not particularly welcome in Damascus on initial publication, although later on it turned out to be no problem.

Part 2 (1958–1968) (932 pages) describes the secretive life of the 'exiled' Syrian Ba'thist officers in Egypt during the Egyptian–Syrian union, and the formation of their secret Ba'thist Military Committee which later took power in Syria. Talas introduces some Military Committee members hitherto not generally known. He further covers the separation of Syria from Egypt in 1961, the 'Free Officers Movement' and their abortive coup in Aleppo in 1962, the Ba'thist 8 March Revolution 1963, the suppression of the Muslim Brotherhood insurrection in Hama (1964), many intricacies of the internal Ba'thist power struggles, including the expulsion of Military Committee leader Alawi General Muhammad 'Umran, the 23 February 1966 Movement, and the abortive 8 September 1966 coup of the ruthless Druze Major Salim Hatum, who tried to topple the regime by inviting the party leadership for a meal (*walimah*) in al-Suwayda' with the aim of taking them hostage, or even killing them. Talas reports that Hatum had tried to set up a similar trap before in October 1965, but then failed as well (Vol. 2, pp. 612–14).[9] Talas compares Hatum's effort with the slaughtering of the Mameluks by Muhammad 'Ali in 1811. The volume closes with a critical analysis (also as regards the Soviet Union) of the causes of the June War in 1967 and its consequences.

Talas describes how Salah Jadid after 1967 tried in vain to regain control over the Ba'th Party organisation in the army. He also notes 'with grief' that 'never in his life he shall forget the words of prime minister Dr Yusuf Zu'ayyin: *Praise be to God, al-Qunaytarah has fallen but the regime has not*' (Vol. 2, p. 874).

Part 3 (1968–1978) (1460 pages, two volumes) deals with the power struggle between Alawi Generals Hafiz al-Asad and Salah Jadid, and the suicide of National Security Chief 'Abd al-Karim al-Jundi (all three co-founders of the Ba'thist Military Committee). It also covers the Corrective Movement of Hafiz al-Asad (1970), foreign and inter-Arab relations, the October 1973 War, the 'Wars of Attrition', Syrian military intervention in Lebanon, the Israeli invasion of Lebanon (1978), various Ba'th Party congresses, Camp David, the Palestinian resistance movement, and a variety of other topics.

The book has had to undergo an amusingly minor type of censorship in *Part 3*, p. 1086, where President Hafiz al-Asad is quoted as having asked about an officer of Rif'at al-Asad's *Saraya al Difa'*: 'Where is that donkey [*himar*] from?' With a small piece of paper glued over it, the original word 'donkey' (*himar*) has been altered to 'officer' (*dabit*), making the text more respectful towards the speaker. All these details make Talas's book not only very informative, but now and then also very entertaining.

Part 4 (1978–1988) (528 pages) deals with Syria's relations with both Iran and Iraq (including Iraqi–Syrian unification efforts and internal Iraqi Ba'th affairs including some interesting encounters with then Vice-President Saddam Husayn and President Ahmad Hasan al-Bakr), the Muslim Brotherhood mass killing of Alawi recruits at the artillery academy near Aleppo (1979), 'lessons learnt' from the Iraq–Iran war, the assassinations of Presidents Anwar al-Sadat and Bashir al-Jumayyil, the Sabra and Shatila massacres, and many other subjects. The central part of this volume is the highly detailed and interesting account of Colonel Rif'at al-Asad's abortive coup against his brother Hafiz al-Asad (1984).

Part 5 (1988–1998) (911 pages, two volumes) gives a critical description of former Iraqi President Saddam Husayn and his policies. Talas provides interesting accounts of the Syrian position with regards to Iraq's occupation of Kuwait in 1990–91 and President al-Asad's efforts to convince Saddam Husayn to withdraw from Kuwait just before the expiration of the UN Security Council deadline of mid-January 1991. President al-Asad publicly promised to fully support Iraq and to fight on its side in case Iraq should be attacked after having withdrawn from Kuwait before the UN deadline. But Saddam Husayn refused, with disastrous consequences. Talas writes that he had predicted Iraq's aggression against Kuwait as early as 1988 (Vol. 5, p. 234). He reports about a plan by Iraqi nationalist officers to topple Saddam Husayn's regime directly after Operation Desert Storm in 1991 and to subsequently work closely together (and even planning to unite) with Syria, but it was rejected by the United States, who made it clear 'that they would fight such a new regime even more than was already the case with the regime of Saddam' (Vol. 5, p. 177).

President Hafiz al-Asad's efforts to prevent Western military attacks against Iraq in the 1990s are described by Talas as the 'biggest challenge with which [al-Asad] was confronted during his political life' (Vol. 5, p. 775).

Talas gives detailed insights into the Syrian position towards peace negotiations with Israel and the Middle East peace process, as well as into Syria's (generally bad) relations with Arafat, the PLO and Palestinian nationalist organisations. The book deals with a great many other issues, such as regional military battles and wars, water disputes in the Middle East, Turkish–Israeli cooperation, polemics with Salman Rushdi, and Princess Diana.

Most of Talas's work focuses on developments in which he himself personally participated. These are by far the most valuable parts of his work. Other sections are more like a kind of history writing concerning developments in which he was not himself a direct actor, but in which Syria nevertheless played a direct or indirect role.

Muhammad Ibrahim al-'Ali

The memoirs of the former commander of the National Guard and later the People's Army Muhammad Ibrahim al-'Ali, *Hayati wa al-I'dam* (*My Life and Execution*; 1700 pages),[10] are equally important and indispensable for those who want to obtain an in-depth understanding of Syrian Ba'thist history and its inner workings. They were privately published in Damascus between 2005 and 2007 (in several editions), and should make fascinating reading for those who are fond of detail and already have a solid background knowledge of the developments and issues concerned. The books are not always chronologically ordered, nor are they systematically organised. They also contain minor repetitions.

The first volume (638 pages) is almost exclusively devoted to the Arab nationalist 'Free Officers Movement' (Ba'thists, Nasserists and others) and their abortive coup in Aleppo in 1962. It has the character of a very detailed documentary study, which was originally planned as part of a wider Ba'thist history project about the Arab nationalist movement in Syria. It starts in the form of a lengthy interview taken by former Regional Command member George Saddiqni. Many of the participating officers, including Muhammad Ibrahim al-'Ali himself, were later to play a central role in the various Ba'thist regimes, and already had developed strong personal links amongst one another in this period, some of them going through the same dangers and fate of being imprisoned together. Muhammad Ibrahim al-'Ali was himself sentenced to death because of his role in the 1962 coup. As the date of his execution was scheduled for 9 March 1963, the Ba'thist Military Committee leaders, including Hafiz al-Asad, decided to carry out their coup a few days earlier than originally planned, in order to save Muhammad Ibrahim al-'Ali's life (Vol. I, p. 157).

The second volume (528 pages) gives a fascinating insight into Muhammad Ibrahim al-'Ali's difficult early youth in the countryside surrounding Hama, where his Alawi parents suffered the harsh conditions of poverty under Ottoman rule, and feudalism which suppressed the peasants. The book then proceeds through various stages of Muhammad Ibrahim al-'Ali's military career and his early, not unrisky, experiences as a member of the Ba'th Party. Of particular interest are his account of the bloody Nasserist coup (18 July 1963) of Colonels Jasim 'Alwan and Muhammad Nabhan (ex-Ba'thist Alawi), and the internal disputes within the Ba'th regime, involving President Amin al-Hafiz and Muhammad 'Umran (1963–66).

The third volume (534 pages) deals with the coups of 23 February and 8 September 1966. The latter coup is described in even more detail than by Talas, as Muhammad Ibrahim al-'Ali was personally taken hostage by Major Salim Hatum.

The abortive revolt in Qatana by Druze Major Muhsin al-'Aqabani (who was linked with Hatum) in the summer of 1966 is mentioned by both Muhammad Ibrahim al-'Ali (Vol. III, pp. 198–202) and Walid Hamdun (*Dhikrayat wa Ara'*, 1997, pp. 93–4), but no clear explanation is given as to the background of the al-'Aqabani revolt.

Neither Muhammad Ibrahim al-'Ali nor Talas makes a clear distinction between the secret military organisation led by Druze General Fahd al-Sha'ir, which was linked to the deposed National Command (led by Dr Munif al-Razzaz), and the group of Major Salim Hatum. Both originally operated separately from one another and were not aware of each other's existence until shortly before September 1966. Marwan Habash provides the most detailed account in this respect.[11]

Muhammad Ibrahim al-'Ali further deals with the June 1967 War, the Syrian military intervention in Jordan (1970) on behalf of the Palestinians (rarely described by direct insiders in such detail), the suicide of 'Abd al-Karim al-Jundi, the deposal and imprisonment of former Chief of Staff General Ahmad al-Suwaydani (which turned out to be for almost twenty-five years), various important Ba'th Party congresses and the final supremacy of Hafiz al-Asad in 1970 and afterwards. General Hafiz al-Asad is portrayed as a strong and solid statesman, with a principled personality, prepared to, short of being deposed himself (as he refused to accept in 1970), be unconditionally loyal to the party.

Both Muhammad Ibrahim al-'Ali and Mustafa Talas are familiar with all the key political and military players in Syria, which makes their memoirs all the more valuable and interesting. Muhammad Ibrahim al-'Ali's habit of visiting his comrades almost continuously gives his memoirs added value. Because of his position as commander of the National Guard, he considered it to be 'his duty to know what was going on in the party, the state and society' (Vol. III, p. 108). He has been described by others as the man 'who never sleeps' and always turns up everywhere. Muhammad Ibrahim al-'Ali's habit to continue having simultaneous contacts with various rivals within the regime sometimes led to suspicions of him siding with one party or the other: for instance with Salah Jadid and later with Rif'at al-Asad against Hafiz al-Asad.[12] Mustafa Talas writes that Muhammad Ibrahim al-'Ali frequented his office to such an extent that he finally closed his doors to him. Muhammad Ibrahim al-'Ali was, according to Talas, underappreciated by other leading officers, with the exception of Hafiz al-Asad (Vol. IV, p. 346).

Most interesting is Muhammad Ibrahim al-'Ali's relationship with the sect of the *Murshidiyin* and his apparently crucial role in helping abort the revolt of Rif'at al-Asad against his brother the president in 1984 (Vol. II, pp. 241–74). Muhammad Ibrahim al-'Ali, by coincidence, had started to cultivate a strong relationship with the *Murshidiyin* in 1963, who had been discriminated against since the hanging of their leader Salman al-Murshid in 1946 in the era of President Shukri al-Quwwatli. Muhammad Ibrahim al-'Ali helped bring about the lifting of discriminatory measures against the *Murshidiyin*, who could be considered as a sect separate from the Alawis in general. Rif'at al-Asad relied on members of the *Murshidiyin* to such an extent that they became the backbone of his *Saraya al-Difa'*. Rif'at's revolt in 1984 against President Hafiz al-Asad was therefore made toothless when the 3000 *Murshidiyin* military were requested by President al-Asad to withdraw from it, at the suggestion of Muhammad Ibrahim al-'Ali. Without these men, Rif'at's tanks and other armoured vehicles could not come into action, because the *Murshidiyin* occupied key positions in it. Muhammad Ibrahim al-'Ali's account of the event is confirmed by Talas (Vol. 4, pp. 345–9).[13]

As a result of showing his loyalty to President Hafiz al-Asad in such a crucial manner and period, Muhammad Ibrahim al-'Ali was later appointed as a member of the Central Committee of the Ba'th Party as a token of high appreciation.

Both Talas's and Muhammad Ibrahim al-'Ali's memoirs describe a situation in which the Ba'thist military and civilians, particularly in the period 1963–70, lived with strong mutual suspicions and deep mistrust. Faced by the real danger of a military coup which could occur at any moment, there were real threats of being personally killed or imprisoned until the end of life. Former Ba'th Party comrades and friends turned out, on various occasions, to become the most deadly enemies. The Ba'th regimes did not only severely suppress non-Ba'thist opposition but also internal Ba'thist rivals.

When having to choose which to read first – the memoirs of Mustafa Talas or those of Muhammad Ibrahim al-'Ali – I would prefer to start with the work of Talas. It is better organised and gives a more structured and analytical account. With regard to the three volumes of Muhammad Ibrahim al-'Ali's work, I would give priority to parts two and three. I am not normally eager to read such very long books, but for these works I am glad to have made an exception.

Walid Hamdun

The memoirs of another Ba'thist general, former deputy prime minister and Regional Command member Walid Hamdun (1937–2006), were posthumously published under the title *Dhikrayat wa Ara'* (*Memoirs and Opinions*).[14] His work is not of the same calibre as the memoirs of both Talas and Muhammad Ibrahim al-'Ali and they are less detailed. He also writes about developments in which he did not really participate himself. Hamdun's book is nevertheless useful if one wants to have the view of an inside observer concerning the positions of his party comrades like Muhammad Ibrahim al-'Ali in internal Ba'thist developments, for instance between Hafiz al-Asad and Salah Jadid in the late 1960s; or for vivid descriptions of personalities like Salah Jadid and Rif'at al-Asad. Hamdun also writes interestingly about his personal experiences during the Syrian military intervention in Jordan (1970), during the October War of 1973 as commander during tank battles on the Golan and with the Syrian military in Lebanon (dealing also with the illegal interventions of Rif'at al-Asad there). Also of particular interest are Hamdun's experiences with the Muslim Brotherhood opposition in Hama. Allegations made by an American magazine that he had forty-nine Israeli prisoners killed during the October War are strongly refuted by him as untrue and pure propaganda against the Syrian army (p. 145). According to Talas, Hamdun's book contains exaggerations and mistakes.[15]

Muhammad Haydar

Al-Ba'th wa al-Baynunat al-Kubra (*The Ba'th and the Great Disunity*), by former deputy prime minister and Regional Command member Muhammad Haydar,[16] provides a refreshing analytical synopsis of Ba'thist history in Syria from its early beginnings till 1970. He explains the dynamic interaction between its organisation inside Syria, Iraq and at the pan-Arab level. Muhammad Haydar was personally involved in various key developments and he provides many interesting autobiographical details. He gives an original and clear picture of the various internal ideological currents and the personalities involved. He noticeably labels the *Qutriyin* as being 'hostile towards Marxism, both in thought and composition' (p. 157), although 'they [according to Haydar] had been entrusted by the Military Committee after 23 February 1966 with the task of bringing the Marxist Ba'thist slogans of the Six National Congress into practice'. But taking the study of former minister of education Sulayman al-Khashsh (one of the *Qutriyin*) and Antun Maqdisi, *al-Marksiyah, 'Ard wa Tahlil* (*Marxism, and Exposé and Analysis*) (Damascus, 1968) as a reference, I do not really detect a hostility towards the subject of Marxism.

Haydar (himself Alawi) provides fascinating descriptions of various Ba'thist key personalities, for instance of the way Salah Jadid dealt with irregular inner party contacts when these did not suit him because they might undermine his authority (p. 154), and also gives examples of the oversensitivity of Jadid towards anything which could have given the slightest hint of sectarian behaviour (pp. 152–7). The Ba'thist period of 1963–66 is labelled by Haydar as the 'epoch of General Muhammad 'Umran'. In 2000 Haydar was indicted by a national state security court for acts which 'weaken the national feeling' (*Id'af al-Shu'ur al-Qawmi*).

Amin al-Hafiz

Other former Syrian politicians have been asked to air their views on television, such as former Syrian President General Amin al-Hafiz (1921–2009), who was interviewed in Baghdad by Ahmad Mansur for Al-Jazeera in *Shahid 'ala al-'Asr*, in a series of thirteen broadcasts in 2001 titled *Al-Inqilabat fi Suriya kama yaraha Amin al-Hafiz* (*The Coups in Syria as Seen by Amin al-Hafiz*).[17] Amin al-Hafiz does not add much new in these interviews, but nevertheless provides some interesting details. He refutes the claim (made in the memoirs of Akram al-Hawrani,[18] the Lebanese press and other publications) that the Druze Ba'thist Colonel Hamad 'Ubayd had been responsible for the severe bombardments of the city of Hama during the Muslim Brotherhood revolt in April 1964, which was at the time seen as a reprisal or blood revenge (*tha'r*) for the earlier bombardments of the Jabal al-Duruz in the era of Adib al-Shishakli. Apparently 'someone else' was responsible, also for the bombardment of the famous Sultan Mosque in Hama and the assassination of a son of the al-'Azm family. But al-Hafiz adamantly refused to mention his name. Four years later Talas disclosed in his memoirs that it was (Alawi) Major 'Izzat Jadid who had been responsible, at least for bombarding Hama, including the Sultan Mosque (2005, Vol. 5, p. 534). When 'Izzat Jadid afterwards reached out his hand in order to help Hama Muslim Brotherhood leader Marwan Hadid out of the rubble, he was reportedly bitten in it.

The Al-Jazeera interviews confirm the picture frequently ascribed to Amin al-Hafiz by his rivals and opponents, such as Mustafa Talas and Muhammad Ibrahim al-'Ali, notably that of a very straightforward military officer who is lacking the more sophisticated characteristics needed to be a good politician and statesman, let alone president. The higher ranking Amin al-Hafiz was at the time apparently used as a front man for the junior Ba'thist Military Committee officers. Amin al-Hafiz is occasionally described by Mustafa Talas as Abu 'Abduh '*al-Jahsh*' (the 'donkey'), showing his disdain for the former president. Muhammad Ibrahim al-'Ali notes that Salah Jadid once told him, 'Put books around him [i.e. Amin al-Hafiz], in front of him and behind him; cause a situation in which he will bump into books wherever he goes, in order to perhaps make him read ... His political horizon was zero' (Muhammad Ibrahim al-'Ali, Vol. 3, p. 119).

Also interesting are the remarks of Amin al-Hafiz about his discussions in 1963 with President Nasser. Apparently President Nasser gave the green light to Colonel Jasim 'Alwan to carry out his 18 July 1963 coup in Syria, even though he was told beforehand that the chances for success were very slim; and so it turned out to be, by their failure and bloodshed. Amin al-Hafiz also mentions that President Nasser, during the Non-Aligned Summit in 1964, provokingly addressed Muhammad 'Umran on the issue of Alawi sectarian military domination in Syria.

Finally, Amin al-Hafiz corrects various earlier publications about the Israeli spy Elie Cohen: Al-Hafiz never met him in Argentina, as is often alleged (also by Mustafa Talas, 'albeit only once': Vol. 2, p. 573). Cohen's intelligence information about Syria 'turned out to be worthless during the June 1967 War', as it was more than two years after he was executed in Damascus. The often 'romanticised' picture of Elie Cohen is cut down to size by both Amin al-Hafiz and Mustafa Talas, as well as by Marwan Habash.[19]

Marwan Habash

Other Ba'thists have written about their experiences in the electronic media or have given interviews, like Nabil Shuwayri and former prime minister Dr Yusuf Zu'ayyin.[20]

Most remarkable and very rich in detail are the writings of former minister and Regional Command member Marwan Habash, who published various series of articles in *Kulluna Shuraka' fi al-Watan* and other media, including *Harakat 23 Shubat ... al-Dawa'i wa al-Asbab* (*The 23 February Movement, its Motives and Reasons*); *Muhawalat 'Usyan al-Ra'id Salim*

Hatum fi al-Suwayda' Yawm 8 Aylul 1966 (The Revolt Attempt of Major Salim Hatum in al-Suwayda' on 8 September 1966); Harb Huzayran: al-Muqaddimat wa al-Waqa'i' (The June War: its Preludes and Facts); Qadaya wa Ara' (Issues and Views; 266 pages) and *al-Ba'th wa Thawrat Adhar (The Ba'th and the March Revolution)* (324 pages).[21]

Marwan Habash unveils many interesting details not published before. They deal with important developments in Syria in which the Ba'th Party played a central role. Habash deals extensively with the June 1967 War, including its prelude and aftermath and the proposal of Salah Jadid to change the Syrian armed forces command because of its defeat. This proposal was rejected by one vote in the majority against it. Habash also reports that then minister of defence, Hafiz al-Asad, proposed, in a joint military operation with Iraqi forces stationed in Jordan, to depose King Hussein during his confrontation with the Palestinian commando organisations in Jordan in September 1970. After Iraq rejected the idea, Syria intervened on its own.[22] Habash describes his ordeal in Syrian prisons for almost a quarter of a century (1970–93), being among the longest serving political prisoners in Syria. When interviewed by Human Rights Watch about his feelings when being imprisoned, Habash answered: 'Yesterday went by fast, today is very long, and tomorrow is very far away; and the characteristic they have in common is their killing monotony.' Habash writes about the personal torture which he himself and other imprisoned prominent Ba'thists had to undergo for long periods of time from former party comrades like, in particular, Naji Jamil, 'Adnan Dabbagh, 'Ali al-Madani and 'Ali Duba, and notes that the treatment of other prisoners was worse. Habash also describes the fate of others, like Nur al-Din al-Atasi and Salah Jadid. He provides the text of Jadid's highly personal letter to his daughter (who was born after he was imprisoned), shortly before he died in prison after twenty-three years in captivity.[23]

Habash gives his detailed insights on the internal history of the Ba'th Party from its early beginnings, the role of Michel 'Aflaq and Salah al-Din al-Bitar, Iraq, his early youth in the Golan (born in Jubata al-Zayt in 1938) and his role in the Qunaytarah party branch, as well as on many other topics. His writings (more than fifty articles and two books) deserve to be more accessible.

Mansur Sultan al-Atrash

The memoirs of former Ba'th National and Regional Command member Mansur al-Atrash (1925–2006), son of the famous Druze nationalist leader Sultan al-Atrash, were published posthumously by his daughter Rim in 2008 under the title *al-Jil al-Mudan. Sirah Dhatiyah (The Condemned*

Generation. Autobiography) (499 pages).[24] They describe his youth, his early experiences in the Ba'th Party, his opposition to Adib al-Shishakli, the times he was repeatedly forced to spend in prison, and his – for this study most relevant – role in the Ba'th Party leadership, including his participation in the first Revolutionary Command Council (1963) and his place in government from 1963 to 1966. Al-Atrash stresses that he always considered his role in the Ba'th Party before his status as belonging to a notable family, although this did not prevent others from seeing him primarily as the son of a notable. Al-Atrash's memoirs clearly reflect his intensive social network with people from southern Syria and members of the Druze community, both Ba'thist and non-Ba'thist.

He notes that 'whereas before the 8 March Revolution the idea of being proud of belonging to a certain religious community was considered to be shameful or even as a great sin, it had now [by the mid-1960s] come to be seen as a protection of one's present existence and as a guarantee for one's future life' (p. 367).

Al-Atrash reports how during the June 1967 War false rumourse were spread about Syrian Druze guiding Israeli war planes towards their targets inside Syria, with the intention of suggesting that Syrian Druze were co-responsible for Syria's military defeat. This led to some popular anger against the Druze within Syria, some of whom felt forced to temporarily flee their homes. Al-Atrash even gives the example of a Druze father ('Abd al-Karim Halabi) who was shot dead by a military guard after he had enquired about the fate of his son in the military camp of Qatana. The guard had become enraged upon hearing that the father belonged to the Druze community (pp. 378–9).

Al-Atrash notes that during the 23 February 1966 coup, Druze Major Salim Hatum, different from what had been originally planned, was at first left on his own to carry out the task of deposing President Amin al-Hafiz. The original plan had been for Hatum's commando troops to be substantially assisted by Colonel 'Izzat Jadid's tank battallion, but Jadid's tank support – apparently on purpose – was held up and came later than promised. As a result of the unassisted fighting, Hatum's units and military position were weakened and there was a lot of unnecessary bloodshed. The blame for this bloodshed was subsequently put on Hatum alone, and not on those who had apparently intentionally withheld their tank support. This, according to what al-Atrash describes as being 'purely hypothetical', may have been the main reason for Hatum's strong resentment against the (mainly Alawi) leaders of the 23 February coup, which in the end led him to take revenge and carry out his (abortive) 8 September 1966 revolt in al-Suwayda' (p. 372). But al-Atrash's hypothesis is undermined by the fact that Hatum had, reportedly, already made a similar attempt several months before the 23 February coup, in October 1965.

According to Marwan Habash the tank support came only later because their noise would have betrayed the coup in a premature stage. Hatum had been offered a ministerial or other important political post during a meeting of the Provisional Regional Command just before the coup of 23 February, provided he would give up his military position. Hatum refused such a political position as he prefered to remain in the military. Later, according to Marwan Habash, it turned out that Hatum had the hidden ambition to, in the end, dominate the country through an all-powerful combined command of the 70th armoured brigade and his own commandos (*maghawir*).

Had Hatum's coup succeeded, a Druze-dominated Ba'thist regime might have emerged, or at least it could have if the Druze community had had the capacity to fill the key positions of (among others) the much more numerous Alawi Ba'thists and their followers, who were so well embedded in the armed forces. It is doubtful, however, if such an operation would have been possible without much bloodshed, presuming that it would have been feasible at all.

Al-Atrash reports that General Muhammad 'Umran, after his release from prison after the June 1967 War, had settled in Tripoli, Lebanon, so as to be able to contact his military sympathisers more easily, as it was geographically closer to his (Alawi) home territory and less in the limelight than Beirut, where he expected to be under closer Syrian intelligence surveillance. 'Umran had hoped to regain his position within the regime with the help of his military supporters. Because of what was branded as 'the complot of Muhammad 'Umran', various Ba'thists, some of whom were prominent, were arrested. In the end 'Umran was ruthlessly hunted down and assassinated by supporters of the 23 February regime (pp. 383–4, 393).

It is remarkable that al-Atrash's memoirs contain various parts which are critical of Hafiz al-Asad, but that his book was nevertheless allowed to be distributed inside Syria (2010; pp. 366, 391–4).

The reliability of memoirs: the same events remembered differently

Sometimes articles by Syrian Ba'thist authors have been published in a different form: not really as memoirs, but nevertheless containing valuable detailed elements about Syrian history under Ba'th rule. Various publications describe the same events from different angles and the mentioned texts do not always tell the same story. Some authors explicitly dispute the different or 'deviant' versions of their former comrades, be it in their analyses or sometimes only in minor detail, particularly when their personal role is involved. It is not surprising that the role of the author is often portrayed by himself as more prominent than when his role is described by comrade colleagues or adversaries.

As a result, sometimes contradictory reports are provided, creating some uncertainty as to the real series of events. Muhammad Ibrahim al-'Ali, for instance, writes about the coup of 23 February 1966 that he himself played a pivotal role in gaining control over the 70th armored brigade south of Damascus (which provided the military backbone of the regime at the time). But Marwan Habash (who at the time was Head of the Ba'th Party Organisational Bureau) maintains that Muhammad Ibrahim al-'Ali did not play any role at all. Muhammad Ibrahim al-'Ali's claim that he was the person who conveyed the watchword for the 23 February coup is also disputed by Marwan Habash, as such a watchword, according to Habash, did not exist.[25] But Mustafa Talas (*Mir'at Hayati*, Vol. 2, p. 680) confirms that Muhammad Ibrahim al-'Ali had been given the task to overpower an infantry battalion of the 70th brigade. A substantial role for Muhammad Ibrahim al-'Ali therefore seems credible, although a centrally agreed watchword may not have existed.

What to do if writers contradict one another, or have rather different versions? A point in case is the suicide of National Security Chief 'Abd al-Karim al-Jundi. Mustafa Talas and Muhammad Ibrahim al-'Ali give slightly different accounts of the suicide of al-Jundi, and former Regional Command member Muhammad Haydar gives yet another (*Al-Ba'th wa al-Baynunat al-Kubra*, 1998, p. 180). They all heard the fatal shot themselves, but in the presence of a different combination of persons. Although the main lines are the same in all presented accounts here, there are some differences about who really was a personal witness of events and where.

Muhammad Ibrahim al-'Ali notes that he was personally present in Hafiz al-Asad's office when the latter spoke with 'Abd al-Karim al-Jundi, who during that telephone conversation committed suicide. Al-Asad apparently heard the shot (Muhammad Ibrahim al-'Ali, Vol. 3, p. 335).

Muhammad Haydar notes on the other hand that 'Ali Zaza, Head of the Military Intelligence Branch, was the one with whom 'Abd al-Karim al-Jundi was speaking by telephone, when he (Haydar) heard al-Jundi shoot himself (p. 180).

Mustafa Talas, finally, notes that he heard the shot when he was in the office of Hafiz al-Asad, who spoke through an internal line with General 'Ali Zaza, who in turn spoke with al-Jundi (Vol. 3, p. 116).

Marwan Habash notes that 'Abd al-Karim al-Jundi told 'Ali Zaza: 'Report to General Hafiz that I leave the country up to him.'[26]

Muhammad Ibrahim al-'Ali does not mention anyone else but himself being present in the office with Hafiz al-Asad when the shot was fired. He notes that afterwards both Muhammad Haydar and 'Abd al-Halim Khaddam entered the office of the minister of defence and reported about their visit to 'Ali Zaza, where they had come to know that 'Abd al-Karim al-Jundi had committed suicide.

Mustafa Talas writes, however, that he was the one who was in Hafiz al-Asad's office, and that Muhammad Ibrahim al-'Ali, Muhammad Haydar and 'Abd al-Halim Khaddam were at that moment with 'Ali Zaza, and came to the office of Hafiz al-Asad later on. Mustafa Talas, however, is not mentioned in the account of Muhammad Ibrahim al-'Ali here at all.

Taking as a point of departure that all mentioned authors wrote their stories in good faith, it just shows that human memory is not always perfect, however much the authors themselves may be convinced of the authenticity of their respective versions.

As most of the main participants of the Syrian Ba'thist period 1963–70 have already reached an advanced age, or have died, this era is also coming to a close as far as the publication of their personal memoirs and observations is concerned.[27]

Appendix A

A Ba'thist analysis of sectarianism, regionalism and tribalism.[1]

The party's answer to the state of ignorance (jahiliyah) and clannishness is Arabism

The introduction of sectarianism was a criminal attempt to change the party into its antithesis

When the party introduced the principle of 'socialist nationalism' it defined the nature of the struggle in which it would have to engage in order to achieve it. It also defined the sort of struggle which the Arab people would have to undertake. It considered this struggle to consist of two related phases: on the one hand a struggle between the deprived toiling class and its exploiters and on the other a struggle between the working class and imperialism and the exploiting class which profits from divisiveness and the misfortune of the social situation.

Taking this definition as its point of departure, the party considered any struggle which did not take place on this basis to be a departure from the struggle which would realise the interests of the people; [a departure] which would increase its divisiveness, diffuse its efforts, and hinder its potential for progress. Based on this point of view, the party stated from the beginning that regionalism, sectarianism and tribalism were dangerous social diseases to be combated by any method because they seriously increased and deepened the fragmentation of society.

[The party] also considered that any social struggle that was based on regionalism, sectarianism or tribalism would be a struggle that would threaten the livelihood and existence of the people. It therefore stated that Arabism in its humanitarian sense is the fundamental bond which binds people together and that any other loyalty is a deviation because it is at the expense of that bond and is incompatible with the principles of nationalism which guarantee the progress of the Arab people.

Throughout its struggle, the party has believed in class struggle as an historical reality, which on the one hand realises national existence and on the other hand is marked by humanitarian principles.

After the outbreak of the Revolutions of Ramadan [i.e. the Ba'thist coup in Iraq of 8 February 1963] and March [i.e. the 8 March 1963 coup in Syria], imperialism and Arab reactionaries both felt threatened by this party, as well as by the principles it upholds and the actions it takes towards their realisation. They did all they could and used all available weapons to combat this party and its two Revolutions. But whereas they were able to defeat the Ramadan Revolution, they were not able to defeat the March Revolution, nor were they able to destroy the party in Iraq.

The enemies of the people realised that armed conspiracy would only make the party stronger and more determined. Even if they were victorious their victory could only be temporary. Therefore, the imperialist media and Arab reactionaries concentrated on attacking the Revolution at all levels: in the field of the principles which it upholds and of the party which constitutes the active instrument with which these principles are realised. The media persistently employed a rightist and individualist mentality [i.e. the mentality of the deposed National Command, and of Amin al-Hafiz] in order to crush them. They also exploited sectarianism, regionalism and tribalism to their furthest limits as a means to bring an end to the party, both as a [way of] thought and as an instrument.

With the help of sectarianism, regionalism and tribalism, those forces were able to realise a number of goals, the most important of which were:

1. To kindle an internal struggle in society which would divert the attention of the people and move them far away from the class struggle which the party advocates.

2. To divide society along vertical lines in reaction to the horizontal separation between the exploited and the exploiting classes, as promoted by the party.

Thus, by sustaining sectarianism, the bonds between a farmer or worker on the one hand and a feudalist or capitalist on the other, who belong to one and the same religious community, are strengthened in such a manner that the members of that religious community become one bloc which opposes another religious community. The class struggle is thereby brought to an end. It also hinders the spreading of any political movement among the popular masses, as happened, for instance, in Lebanon.

3. Membership of a religious, regional or tribal community becomes an alternative to being an Arab. In this way the potential for national struggle is paralysed, while the threat which Arab nationalism constitutes to imperialism and [the forces of] reaction is removed.

4. If concepts such as these infiltrate the minds of the party

members, the party will be torn to pieces and it will lose some of its members.

Therefore, the news and rumour-mongering imperialist media and the Arab reactionaries have applied themselves with assiduity and concentration to the task of attributing sectarian significance, and sometimes regional and tribal significance, to any steps that are taken by the Revolution, be they forward or backward. They show no eagerness to brand the party with a permanent imprint such as sectarianism or regionalism but use these labels with flexibility in order to obtain the greatest profit from them in each region according to the particular sensitivities of the local peoples. In this way, the media sometimes describe the party in terms that give the impression that the Sunni community has been victorious over the Shi'i religious communities, as in Iraq and in Syria during certain stages of the Revolution. At other times, as in Syria, they make it seem as though the Shi'i and Christian communities have been victorious over the Sunnis.

In the regions which are not easily influenced by sectarianism, the circulation of rumours is usually on a regional or tribal basis: So-and-so acts thus because he is a *Tikriti* [i.e. from Tikrit in Iraq], someone else acts thus because he is a *Rawi* [i.e. from Rawa in Iraq], a third person acts so because he is a *Dayri* [i.e. from Dayr al-Zur] or a *Hamwi* [i.e. from Hama], or a *Hawrani* [i.e. from Hawran], etc.

Our comrades remember how these rumours gave the impression that the Sunnis had won a victory when [the Alawi General Muhammad] 'Umran was expelled; and that the Shi'i communities had won a victory when [the Sunni President, General Amin] al-Hafiz was arrested, notwithstanding the fact that 'Umran was [also] arrested. Moreover, they remember how these rumours made it seem that the land seizure, distribution and nationalisation measures were a victory for some [specific] religious communities [i.e. religious minorities against the Sunnis]. These impressions and the strong emphasis placed on them aroused the attention of party members at all stages.

These rumours were not only spread by the imperialists and reactionaries, but sometimes also by groups who described themselves as progressive and did not hesitate to use this weapon when fighting the party and the Revolution.

The media have exploited the contradictions which were apparent in the Commands of the party and Revolution, and have used them to such an extent as to incite some leaders to play the card of sectarianism and regionalism, particularly those party members who lacked both party logic and party means to support their points of view and behaviour and thus took up positions from where they clashed with the party and its institutions. These members have tried to put the situation on a sectarian basis and have cooperated to deepen it with the party apparatus. Notwithstanding the fact that they found little response among the party's rank and file, there were still some elements whose belief in the party was not yet strong enough or who saw it as something of personal use. The pollution was thus able to seep through into the minds of some people and undermined the ideals of many to such an extent that they felt no shame or hesitation in dealing with the party's affairs on a sectarian or regional basis. They thus strayed into the treacherous quagmire of deviation and became, whether they knew it or not, a tool for the fifth column.

This phenomenon reached its climax within the party shortly before and after the measures taken by the National Command [on 21 December 1965]. Amin al-Hafiz and Muhammad 'Umran both played an important role in kindling it to such an extent that sectarianism was explicitly brought up during party meetings, during meetings of the former regional secretary in the military Air Force Branch, as well as in other branches.

They did not even hesitate to form blocs of party and non-party members on this basis, particularly in the Army, as the preliminary investigations have revealed.[2]

The 23 February Movement came not only as an answer to rightist and individualist mentalities, but also to the introduction of sectarianism. The party's rank and file have stood firm and have shown their disapproval of the undermining elements by proceeding with the Movement and gaining victory.

The 23 February Movement has proved practical evidence of the fact that the party's power of resistance is too strong to be crushed by vile slogans. Those who executed and supported it came from all provinces of the [Syrian] region and also included those who had previously been arrested or expelled from the country: they did not come from one specific group or religious community. No, it showed a clear distinction between people who believed in the party as a goal and an instrument and people who did not hesitate to use principles that are alien to those of the party or who illicitly contacted other political groups and incited them against it. Nevertheless, the 23 February Movement was not spared accusations of sectarianism and sometimes of regionalism. The fifth column even made desperate efforts to portray it as such, profiting thereby from party members who had been wronged by the murder of a relative but were denied blood revenge (ba'd al-hizbiyin al-mawturin) and using them to implant seditious ideas.

Those party members had been blinded by their relations, and their notions spoiled; some of them reached a point from where they would not hesitate to cooperate [even] with the devil in order to finish off the party and its Revolution.

In spite of our absolute faith in the awareness and steadfastness of the party's rank and file and in the party's ultimate victory over its enemies, our duty as Party Command obliges us to eliminate those whose ideals have been poisoned, even if they represent only one element within the party, and irrespective of their past as strugglers. Man is determined not only by his past but also by his present; we believe that a struggler is a man who not only has taken an honourable stand in the past but who also adheres to the struggle for the sake of the principles in which he believes for as long as he lives.

O Comrades,

The Extraordinary Regional Congress [held in Damascus in March 1966], taking into account the gravity of the fact that some party comrades have introduced slogans which are alien to and incompatible with the principles of the party, has agreed to the following recommendation:

'To pursue all elements which introduce sectarian, regional or tribal points of view and to take the most severe punitive measures against them, particularly in the case of party members. Persons who treat the affairs of the party and the Revolution with such wrong logic deserve the severest punishment. Negligence of such elements by the higher or indirect Commands is considered a crime against the party and its principles, as well as against the people and their interests.

'To play the card of sectarianism, tribalism and regionalism is a vile method which only serves imperialism's plans to tear up society. It is in no way permissible to accept as a [party] comrade a person who adopts such an orientation towards our affairs. Such a person should be punished as though he were an enemy of the people.'

On the basis of this recommendation we ask that all party Commands announce the holding of party meetings to discuss this phenomenon and to explain the ideas and aims on which it is based. And that they submit any information they have about those who approach party affairs from a sectarian, regional or tribal viewpoint, so that we can proceed to cut them off from the party and to purge them. Subsequently, criminal law can be brought into force against the dangerous elements amongst them.

Party Commands at all levels are responsible for combating any complicity with, or toleration of, such rotten elements. They are therefore requested to make all haste in submitting information, after having first ascertained its correctness, together with suggestions which are in keeping with this recommendation.

O comrades,

The era of weakness and irresolution is over. To build up the party in a firm, positive and homogeneous fashion is a matter for which all Commands are responsible. Any Command which shows laxity and is tolerant of those rotten elements whose conceptions are alien to the principles of the party shall be accountable to the Regional Command for its inefficiency and shall even be considered as acting in collusion against the party and its safety.

Therefore, let us [strive for] a maximum of supervision and guidance; for a maximum of control and resolution in [calling people] to account; and for maximum effort in the interest of our Arab nation. May our mission be eternal.

The Organisational Party Bureau

Appendix B

Confessions about sectarianism in the army units of Hama[1]

Sectarianism

The psychological method was one of those used in order to prepare an atmosphere conducive to a military operation. It was oriented towards the Army, and particularly towards enemies of the party. These people were urged to adopt deviant attitudes [e.g. sectarianism], despite the fact that this was in contradiction with the simplest of party principles, its constitution and its internal regulations. The party has to combat both such deviant attitudes and any [other] discrimination that is intended to fragment the Arab people and its toiling masses.

Apart from being used among the party's rank and file, interrogations held among officers and soldiers stationed in Hama have shown that this [psychological] method was also applied to them. The following are examples of their confessions.

1. First Lieutenant Ahmad Kallas of Battalion 237 m/t said: 'About twenty days ago an evening gathering was held at the house of Captain 'Abd al-Jawad. There was a varied conversation, which included the following:

> The wife of Lieutenant Ghassan Hamwi spoke about the bloc formation of the Alawis. She told what she knew of Alawi women forming blocs in the House for Female Teachers during their studies. At that moment the conversation was about sectarian factionalism in the Army. Either 'Abd al-Jawad or Ghassan Hamwi said that the Alawis were trying to dominate the Army and that this made it necessary for us to form an opposing bloc.

2. First Sergeant Mustafa 'Ajnabji of the same battalion told the following:

> The first man who contacted me on this subject was Master Sergeant al-'Itr. That was on 9 February 1966. He told me that he was responsible for informing Captain 'Abd al-Jawad about all meetings that took place.

Then he said: 'Master Sergeant Hamshu contacted me and said, "You must observe what the Alawis are doing so that we can inform Captain 'Abd al-Jawad." Adjutant 'Abd al-Rahman Yasin has contacted me also, and has said to me: "The issue, O 'Ajnabji, is not that of a party but of religion. You must defend your religion and your womenfolk." The following day First Sergeant Muhammad Hassun repeated the words of Adjutant Yasin and Master Sergeant Hamshu. He also said: 'The [party] organisation will be abolished and replaced by a new organisation.'

3. Recruit 'Abd al-Jalil al-Abrash of the same battalion said:

Before the Feast of Breaking the Ramadan Fast ['Id al-Fitr], First Lieutenant Ghassan Hamwi and Sergeant Muhammad Hassun came to my tent, while recruit Salim Aba Zayd and Ibrahim al-Rushaydat were sitting with me and we were playing cards. The Lieutenant said to us: 'Be watchful and pay attention.' Then he started to warn us. That was during the first meeting. As to the second meeting, he came to me in the presence of the [other] men and said: 'The Alawis are dominating the regime, and there will come a day when they will betray the Sunnis and annihilate them.' Then on a certain day, Sergeant Muhammad Hassun came to my tent on the orders of Lieutenant Ghassan Hamwi and said to me: 'Take these keys which belong to the arms depot. Then go and bring a rifle with two full magazines.' I indeed went, brought it and hung it up in the tent. Lieutenant Ghassan ordered me to hide it, however, which I did. Then he said to me, 'God willing [In Sha' Allah] we shall leave it [i.e. the rifle] with you, because we are meeting at your tent without weapons and we fear that the Alawis might stage an operation to arrest and kill us.' Therefore we hid this rifle in order to use it against the Alawis in case of surprise.

4. Sergeant Dib Babat of the same battalion said:

I heard Master Sergeant Muhammad 'Abbas and private Muhammad Dib Sa'd say: 'We are going to slaughter the Alawis in the third company so that they will not be able to lift their heads.' [He also said]: '[The issue of] sectarianism was not raised before the coming of Captain 'Abd al-Jawad Najjar.'

5. First Soldier Dib Khalil Sa'd of the same battalion said:

For three years I have been a [Ba'th] party member and I paid no heed to sectarianism, except that about two months ago, after the dissolution of the [Syrian] Regional Command [on 21 December 1965] and during one of the call-ups, First Sergeant Muhammad Hassun came to me and said that there were problems in the Army that were becoming critical, notably those between the Sunni community and the other religious communities and that we had to cooperate to protect our religion. I felt that he was convinced of what he was saying and that he conveyed these words from Captain 'Abd al-Jawad, so I demonstrated my readiness to help.

6. Private 'Id Birjis of the same battalion said:

On 1 January 1966, Sergeants Muhammad Hassun, Riyad Salim and Muhammad 'Abbas said to me: 'Are you a Muslim?'[2] I said: 'Yes'. Then they said: 'If you are truthful, then you defend your religion. By your family honour [wa 'ardak] you see that the Alawis and Druzes want to take power and that they try to remove [the Sunni President, Lieutenant-General Amin] al-Hafiz, in order to take over.' Then I answered them: 'If your action is for the sake of religion then I am with you, but if it is for political matters then I will have nothing to do with it.' Then they were joined by Lieutenant Ghassan Hamwi and others.

7. First Sergeant 'Ali Fadil of the battalion said:

Directly after the dissolution of the [Syrian] Regional Command and after the National Command took its place, I started to hear rumours among the people of the city about a dispute between the two Commands. Thereupon Adjutant 'Abd al-Rahman Yasin started to confirm these reports to me, that there was sectarian[ism] between the bloc of Lieutenant-General al-Hafiz, i.e. the Sunni bloc and the Alawi bloc; that the Alawis were forming a bloc against Islam and that if they should take over power they would humiliate and subdue us; that we had to be watchful and observe them so that their domination could not be completed; and that Captain Mustafa 'Abdu represented the Lieutenant-General [Amin al-Hafiz] in Hama and that we had to follow and support him in order to defend Islam and support religion. He told me that these words came from the Commander of the Battalion. From the civilians I heard that, if necessary, Captain Mustafa 'Abdu would arm the people to defend the bloc of Lieutenant-General al-Hafiz.

8. First Sergeant Muhammad Hassun, a non-party member of Bat talion 237 m/t, said:

When the [Syrian] Regional Command was formed [in August 1965], it was composed of different groups. But as time went by and the country came to be ruled by the non-Sunni [religious] communities, some men in the National Command became aware of the seriousness of the situation. They dissolved the [Regional] Command and seized power in the country. It is noteworthy that Lieutenant-Colonel Mustafa Talas used to cooperate with the Alawis in spite of his being a Sunni Muslim. But he is not to be blamed, because his mother was of Alawi origin. Then he [i.e. Captain 'Abd al-Jawad Najjar] started to accuse the battalion for not being alert and watchful and said that we knew this and that most of the

other units knew it and were wakeful, whereas we were asleep. We had
to cleanse ourselves of these dishonours and should always be wakeful;
we should examine our history and remember the Islamic victories and
conquests and the like, and how many Muslims had died as martyrs for
the sake of their religion and the law of Islam [*Shari'ah*]. We were like
them, and we were to allow nobody to trample on our religion. The
Captain also said to me: 'I see that you are weak. Therefore, when we
give you orders, we will ask you to answer with two words in order to
define your stand: either you are with us or against us. In the latter case
your fate will be the same as theirs [i.e. of the non-Sunnis]: you will be
machine-gunned.' Then he sent us to Lieutenant Ghassan Hamwi, and
I told him: 'Captain 'Abd al-Jawad has sent us to you because on this
very night the Alawi group will try to slaughter Islam.' Then he said to
me, 'You non-party members must not think that the Command is not
interested in you. You can be sure that there will come a day on which
the National Command will issue a secret resolution to dissolve the party
definitively and to rebuild it. When that happens we shall know who we
will organise in the party.'

9. Captain 'Abd al-Jawad Najjar, chief of staff of Battalion 237 m/t,
   said:

During the period in which the Regional Command was dissolved I
contacted Sergeant Muhammad Hassun, who is a non-party member. I
told him to pay attention to the meetings of the Alawis and started a
conversation with him on the subject of Alawi bloc formation. I did the
same with Lieutenant Ghassan Hamwi and others. And he told me: 'I
have started to appoint security men on the basis of their being Sunnis.
They, in turn, have started to become active in order to enlarge the
[Sunni] bloc. I have informed the Commander of the Battalion Captain
Mustafa 'Abdu of this, and he consented to the idea.'

Appendix C

An analysis of the Syrian armed forces[1]

The Army is a subject on which we must dwell closely and at length, for the simple reason that the Army – any army – is the shield which ruling organisations erect around themselves in order that they may actively develop their achievements, that they may be protected against surprises, whether internal or external, and that they may even strike, when necessary, all those who attempt to obstruct the functioning of their organisation. In this sense the army is a double-edged weapon: either it is a people's army representing the toiling classes and safeguarding their accomplishments or, if it is a professional or bourgeois army it is a sword drawn against the neck of those classes.

It is for that reason that political blocs impose as a condition the distribution among themselves of the 'regime's seats' or the 'army's brigades and battalions' as a guarantee of their continued existence and of acceptance of their point of view. (The Socialist Unionists imposed similar conditions on Salah al-Din Bitar as a condition of their entering the National Council and participating in government.)

Therefore, world imperialism and its agents make desperate efforts to maintain the bourgeois composition of the armies in the developing countries. They do so by excluding people who belong to the poor and deprived classes from leading and influential positions (as officers and non-commissioned officers) which are monopolised by feudalists, capitalists and the haute bourgeoisie, i.e. by introducing a spirit of professionalism and blind obedience into military concepts and by excluding the army from politics (*returning the army to its barracks*), in order that such armies may form a safety valve which imperialism uses whenever its interests are threatened, as in Ghana and Indonesia and other countries of the Third World.

The replacement of the concept of the classical bourgeois 'professional army' by that of the '*ideological army*' was the greatest blow aimed in modern times at world imperialist interests in the developing countries.

'*Force*' is a method to which man has recourse in defending the '*point of view*' which he believes to be the truth. In that sense his capacity to implement that force is totally related to his belief that his point of view is the right one and to the strength of the obstacles which he has to overcome in order to realise it. In other words, it is dependent on the forearm which carries the weapon and not on the weapon itself. The technical competence of a military man therefore becomes a secondary precondition to his ideological competence.

And if someone forms the idea that the truth is a relative and unsolved question, the answer is that such a thought would be correct if we were merely scholars evaluating and classifying things from the outside. However, if we are consciously and voluntarily members of a revolutionary organisation, then the matter of the truth becomes clear to us. There is no room for doubt or ambiguity, for it is a question of the deprived toiling Arab generations who represent the majority of the people. It is a matter of defending the targets of these masses and of using various revolutionary means in their realisation. It is a matter of abolishing the injustice, oppression, tyranny and disgrace which for hundreds of years have been held over the head of Arab man, degrading his humanity, curbing his capabilities and stifling his aspirations.

The ideological soldier whom we have in mind must be educated on the basis of these principles in order to be entrusted with the weapon he carries and to be an unsurmountable barrier against all enemies: the enemies of the Arab nation, the enemies of the deprived toiling classes, the enemies of Unity, Freedom and Socialism, whether they come from within or without.

O comrades, in the ideological army the classical professional ways based on mercenariness and blind force disappear and are replaced with new relationships based on attachment, mutual understanding and a shared belief in a common destiny.

Among the most outstanding accomplishments of the People's Revolution of 8 March was the ideological transformation and even ideological revolution which it brought about in the ranks of the Syrian Arab Army among officers, non-commissioned officers and men. It made this army a guiding example for all countries of the Third World, next to the peoples' armies of Russia and China. The objective situation in the Arab world, bearing the impediments of backwardness, divisiveness and imperialism, made the *Revolution* the only way by which that ill reality could be changed. Revolution is the method by which present reality is being improved *essentially* rather than *quantitatively*. It means overcoming reformist ways towards [creating] a *revolutionary movement* which brings together those sons of the people who first perceived the diseases of their society and conceived its ideal future; [a revolutionary movement] which concentrates most of the deprived toiling masses around itself and prepares to attack the positions of the economic and political right, with the key intention of subsequently *assuming power*.

The revolutionary movement's takeover of power is a fundamental and necessary precondition to realising and consolidating the *Revolution*. Hence, its need for a *People's Army* of its own kind and nature, initially to help it attack the rightist and imperialist reactionaries and later to defend the processes of socialist nationalist social transformation, as justification for the staging of a revolution and a guarantee of its survival and continuance. Hence, in their plans to regain their positions, all hostile forces first aimed to overthrow the Revolution by 'pounding' its 'fortified exterior' and actively corrupting its 'popular social composition' and socialist infrastructure. They applied various, extremely shrewd means: they threw their gates wide open to receive members of the revolutionary movement and to drown them in a 'surge of cheap banalities'; they furthermore attempted to 'bribe' them and buy them directly with money. In this way they [attempted to] break through the ideological shield of the *military man* and demoralise his socialist psychological constitution. Thus, the arms which bear weapons and the hands which work the hammer gradually slacken; the best man stumbles, and then disaster happens.

O comrades,

It is suitable for us to turn for a while to the subject of our Syrian Arab Army, the Army of the [8] March Revolution, the Revolution of the Arab Ba'th Socialist Party, in order that we may analyse its situation and grasp its sound and weak points, and may try to keep it from the frightful abysses which our enemies have designed for it.

The nature of the independence struggle, and the fact that clearcut class distinctions did not exist in our society, opened the possibility for a group of sons of farmers, labourers and people with small incomes to penetrate into the *Military Academy* in addition to members of important trading and bourgeois families, and later to become the revolutionary *core* of the Army, enabling it to realise its [historic] role of supervising the life of this country and of the Arab nation and even that of the whole Third World.

Since 1949, the political history of the Syrian Arab region appears like a '*political slaughter*' between the right, the reactionaries and the bourgeoisie on the one hand, and the working classes and the party on the other hand. The main goal for the bourgeoisie was to correct that *historical mistake* – the mistake of allowing the sons of the poor classes to reach the Armed Forces Command – whereas for the party and the working classes it was to preserve that great gain. The series of revolutions which continued to take place on the political stage were but a result of that struggle between the two parties. The *'Qatana Insurrection'²* *[of 1957] was an important turning point in the history of the Syrian Arab Army.* It had both its negative and positive sides: on the one hand it showed the strength of the group of officers who as a whole appeared to be committed to the socialist nationalist policy of the party, and substantially demonstrated their distinctive presence for the first time; on the other hand it uncovered this strength and turned it into a direct target for imperialism and the bourgeoisie. The vehemence of this struggle in the Army therefore increased after that insurrection and reached its climax when the subject of unity with Egypt was introduced. This time victory also fell to the party, preventing weakness and bargaining from penetrating the unity negotiations [which it considered to be] a sacred people's cause, [determining their] destiny.

When the unity regime [of the United Arab Republic (UAR)] expelled our comrades from the Army Command, and replaced them by people belonging to prominent families and the bourgeoisie, and by mercenaries and professionals, the disaster of [Syria's] separation [from the UAR] took place. Notwithstanding the fact that our comrades were at the time dispersed and banished, they soon changed it into an overwhelming victory on the morning of 8 March 1963. It is well known, of course, that a great many unionist elements who were not members of the party participated with us in the 8 March Movement. They clashed with the party, however, for considerations which cannot be discussed here, and [consequently] it became necessary to purge them, not so much because they were not unionist or socialist, but because there is nothing more lethal to the Revolution than mutual contradiction and irresolution.

The Revolution, which allowed itself to abolish all existing bourgeois institutions at one stroke, had to pay the price for that directly and swiftly by acts of socialist, social and nationalist transformation. Therefore, it had to act swiftly in order to achieve the goals for the sake of which it took over power. And this could be attained only if it undertook to purge its ranks and remove the contradictions which paralysed its [executive] instrument.

The Regional Command, having studied the conditions which existed in the Army during its ideological transformation in the preceding period, [now] offers its fundamental comments on the subject to the comrades. In essence, they have been taken from the report which the Provisional Regional Command submitted to the latest Extraordinary Regional Congress [held in Damascus in March 1966], and approved after some alterations had been made:

1. The circumstances under which the Revolution [of 8 March

1963] was carried out, as well as the fact that it did not emanate directly from the official party organisation, caused many of the military comrades who staged the Revolution in the name of the party to feel that they were more responsible for protecting the Revolution than were their civilian comrades. This had negative effects on the party which for some took the form of Army tutelage over the party and for others the disdain and disrespect of the civilian party organisation. As a result the military organisation was for a long period closed to [predominantly civilian] organisational commands.

2. The initial circumstances following the Revolution and its attendant difficulties urged the calling up of a large number of military reserve officers and non-commissioned officers, party members and supporters, to fill the gaps resulting from purges of opponents and to consolidate and defend the party's position.

This urgency made it impossible at the time to apply objective standards in the calling-up operation. Rather, friendship, family relationships and sometimes mere personal acquaintance were the basis [of admission], which led to the infiltration of a certain number of elements who were alien to the party's logic and points of departure; once the difficult phase had been overcome, this issue was exploited as a weapon for slandering the intentions of some comrades and for casting doubts on them.

3. After the Revolution the party organisation started to expand without possessing an internal system of regulations which explained party relations and laid down the limits between these and the military. This encouraged chaos; moreover, there was no homogeneity in party work methods among the various Army units in that the method of organisation in each unit was determined by the opinions of its leading elements and their particular understanding of party work.

4. The admission of non-party elements, and the direct granting to them of the rank of active member (*'udw 'amil*) and giving the party command thereafter primarily to those with higher rank irrespective of their party ties, period [of membership], rank or [other] characteristics, has made it easy for many unqualified – and occasionally irresponsible – persons to obtain access to party congresses and to take part in determining the party's destiny by nominating or choosing [candidates], and subsequently gaining entry to its highest commands. A number of such people have helped to facilitate the predomination of an immoral reasoning over that of the party; they have fallen into the trap of collateral contacts, factionalism and individualism because they did not achieve complete detachment from the sphere and circumstances in which they existed before they became party members.

5. Taking into consideration the leading role played by the first

Military Committee following the Revolution and the many competences and roles it filled in the party, Army and government, and the particular positions thus acquired by its members, all this created a certain sensitivity between these comrades and other comrades holding lower ranks who had carried arms on the morning of 8 March, and between them and other comrades of various ranks who for a number of reasons pre-dating the Revolution could not carry arms.

6. This sensitivity among the comrades grew daily and the Military Committee's neglect of the organisation's affairs, its preoccupation with the affairs of government, its participation in the endless struggle among the leaders of the party and the Revolution and its aloofness from the military rank and file, caused that sensitivity to deepen, and moved the rank and file towards taking an almost completely negative view of the Committee and withdrawing their confidence from it – as an institution – at the [military] congress of al-Kiswah [held in April or May 1965].[3]

7. Due to accumulated mistakes, and partly as a result of disparities in membership levels and in understanding of the party's ideology through the experience of practical struggle, the party organisation in the army began to suffer from general weakness at all levels and ranks. These mistakes were not allowed to be rectified, because of the existing contradictions, which we have already mentioned, within the party and the Revolution. These were even encouraged by some and exploited in fights against others. With many comrades [in the military party organisation] specific concepts, such as sectarianism, tribalism, regionalism, etc., which were completely alien to the party's concepts and logic, started to prevail to such an extent that many comrades who had lost the power of self-control became well disposed towards those who sought to ensnare them and were skilled in contriving rumours, in distorting the true state of affairs and in speaking in grandiloquent style. The issue of sectarianism was one of the ugliest and most painful 'traps' that were set by our enemies and by the imperialists for comrades such as these.

8. *The sectarianism issue was among the plans that were followed in order to tear the Army apart in an effort to divest it of its vanguard role.* This is not the place for a sociological study of the phenomenon. It is certain, however, that in this country our people, by virtue of the degree of political maturity that has been achieved, have relinquished worn-out imperialist heresies such as these and have adopted new social and political values based on replacing those worn-out ties, which time has obliterated, with nationalist and class ties.

This does not preclude that specific mistakes are made and that non-party points of view sometimes and in various forms – such as

regionalism, sectarianism and tribalism – replace the true revolutionary
party values, whether at the Army level or at that of the civilian party
organisation. What has made these mistakes into 'unprecedented' affairs at the Army level is that some elements leading the Army and
Revolution have pursued these pathological phenomena and have exploited them to obtain specific objects of their desire and to execute
particular plans.

O comrades,

The attempt to sow seeds of discord among us by bringing up such
worn-out slogans is the greatest humiliation our enemies can inflict on
our honour. The weapon of sectarianism could be effectively used
during the Middle Ages or in the centuries of decline. In the twentieth
century, however, and particularly in the Arab Ba'th Socialist Party, it
is the ugliest and most despicable thing that could be directed not
only against the party's struggle over a quarter of a century, but against
the struggle of the entire Arab nation since the dawn of its awakening,
against each martyr who died for the sake of the Arab cause and even
against each drop of blood shed at the altar of Unity, Freedom and
Socialism.

*We warn all comrades about the consequences of falling into anything
resembling these worn-out imperialist traps. The responsibility for overcoming this issue rests on the shoulders of each person individually*, officers,
non-commissioned officers, soldiers and recruits alike, irrespective of
the fact that, first, the Army Command and, second, the officer comrades are to take upon themselves their entire share [of responsibility]
for its settlement, both in the short and the long term.

9. The party's military rank and file did not for long remain aloof
from the struggles between the upper civilian and military commands.
Thus it was not long before some exploiters were able to drive this
immature rank and file onto the battleground of the struggle. It began
during the crisis between the National Command and the Regional
Command in the past year [1965], as those who contended with one or
the other worked energetically and actively to win the Army's rank
and file for themselves, presenting problems to them by various non-
party methods. This facilitated the introduction of factionalism into
the ranks of the comrades. From time to time it came to be used to
cover up personal opportunism or other controversies. This was
reflected in the military standard of the Army: discipline weakened
and the level of training fell as a result of preoccupation with the
controversies and blandishments which were dictated by the interests
of the existing factions.

10. Lack of supervision and the failure to call party members to

account has encouraged carelessness and has frustrated responsibility. This had led many of the best of our comrades to fall into dangerous pitfalls. In some cases the only remedy has been to cut them off [from the party organisation].

11. Lack of understanding of the party's experience within the Army had caused many to confuse party and military concepts, mixing them up in daily party or military activities. This had a negative effect on both concepts simultaneously.

12. The realisation by some military comrades that their contemporary civilian comrades had reached specific ranks and had assumed important responsibilities in the Revolution opened their minds to unlawful desires and induced them to compensate for what they had missed by means of their party positions in a Military Committee, Military Bureau or any other sphere.

13. It should be pointed out that all hostile political groups as well as the fifth column have done their utmost to create, increase and deepen all negative aspects in the Army. They have particularly concentrated on some of our prominent comrades, surrounding them with a suffocating atmosphere of rumour and innuendo intended to damage their reputations and to cause their being purged, consequently harming the reputation of the party and Revolution and weakening its resistance.

14. The group of non-party members in the Army, who for a long period after the Revolution continued to be active in the purely military sphere without daring to participate in any political or factional activity (in view of the initial circumstances of the Revolution, the solidarity of our army comrades, and the non-existence of rifts within their ranks), eventually became restless and started to take clear and tangible action. They realised that there were some among party members who flattered, extolled and courted them, demanding that justice should be done to them and that they should be granted rights which they themselves would never have asked for were it not for the fact that some party leaders incited them and opened the way for them to make such demands. These non-party members thus became aware of their significance in the struggle that raged between the party's factions; they became a group to be reckoned with and were courted by their rivals. Their objective, notwithstanding their participation in deepening the controversies and fanning their fire, has remained definitely and clearly the same: notably, to get rid of all rival party groups in order to make the Army again prey to them and to the enemies of the Revolution, as was the case before the Revolution of 8 March.

15. *Finally, O comrades, the Regional Congress, taking as its point of departure the need to overcome all negative aspects and matters which have*

accompanied the experiences of our Ideological Army during the past period, has laid down the foundations which it considers will guarantee the realisa- tion of that aim and will achieve a new situation which is to be preferred in degree and kind, both at the party and at the Army level. They are:

1. Congress denounces all previous efforts which were intended to foil the ideological experience in the Army and to cause its return to the form of a professional army such as exists in some developing countries, where foreign and capitalist monopolies rely on it as a force with which to suppress liberation movements. Likewise, it denounces all suspect efforts to change the class structure of the Army, and has decided to implement the following fundamental recommendations in this sector:

a) To apply the texts which Party Congresses have decided upon in defining the tasks of the Army and in separating military from civilian powers, with the exception that the Minister of Defence and the Chief of General Staff are not expected to relinquish their military functions.
b) To preserve the class composition of the Army and to orient its present cadres in a people's and revolutionary direction.
c) To concentrate on ideological education and to ensure success in this respect in the ranks of non-commissioned officers and soldiers.
d) To put a resolute end to symptoms of luxury and bureaucracy, to make an end to extravagant spending and to apply the principle of accurate accounting.
e) To give the Army the opportunity to participate in the process of socialist construction and transformation by putting into practice the maxim that the Army should render [society] prosperous, ac- cording to a practical and studied plan.
f) To give the Ideological Army the opportunity to participate in elaborating the party's policy through its representation at Party Congresses, according to resolutions which have been taken at pre- vious congresses.

2. To tie the Army organically to the party by pursuing the following procedures:

a) Setting up a Military Bureau whose work shall be confined to party affairs, and which shall be made up of military and civilian men according to what is necessary. The Regional Command shall determine the number and ratio of those who devote themselves exclusively to [party work] (*mutafarrighun*). One of the members of the Regional Command shall be head of the Bureau. (It is of course not an essential precondition that he should be a military [officer].)

b) The appointment to each military [party] branch of political instructors who shall devote themselves exclusively to this task. The
   Regional Command will select them from among capable people
   who are [organisationally] linked to it through the Military Bureau.
c) To make the Army participate in the party's congresses in the ratio
   determined by the Eighth National Congress.[4] Selection shall take
   place by way of representation and not by way of appointment.
d) To deepen the experience of the Ideological Army and of the socialist line of action by teaching the party ideology and principles in
   schools, institutes and the Army academies, as part of the educational programmes.
e) To have the military party members participate in the party training
   schools.
f) To re-examine the system of military party regulations at present
   in force and to submit it to the next Ordinary Regional Congress,
   or to convene an Extraordinary Regional Congress in order to reach
   agreement on the changes which are proposed in the light of past
   experience.
g) To denounce the method of collateral contacts. Congress recommends the use of the most resolute and strong punishments in
   order to make an end to this phenomenon which threatens the
   integrity of the organisation.
h) Non-commissioned officers and the soldiers constitute the fundamental basis of the Army which should be in line with the
   Revolution and the party. Congress therefore recommends that it is
   necessary to take care of this working sector, to educate it and to
   propagate the party's experience among its members.

3. To review the party organisation in the Army in the light of
experiences, in such a way as to ensure that the sabotaging elements
which have infiltrated it shall be eliminated, according to objective
standards which shall be determined by the [Party] Command.

4. To ensure that each party member's behaviour is controlled by
the party and not [independently] by himself; and to have all those
who harm the party's moral practices and its code of behaviour account
sternly [for their deeds].

O, comrades,
The fact that the Army is ideological should strengthen its military
standards and not weaken them. The struggle for Palestine is near.
Therefore it is necessary for us to make all military arrangements to
enter into it.
A military man's party membership should not give him privileges

over others. Relations between party members and non-party members should always be disciplined. Elements of respect, attachment and democracy which have entered into military relations should not be at the expense of military discipline and the party's ability to embark on the liberation struggle. The Army Command must be resolute regarding matters which violate the Army's security and militarism.

Notes

Preface

1. In this study sectarianism, regionalism and tribalism are defined as follows: *sectarianism (ta'ifiyah)*: acting or causing action on the basis of membership of a specific religious community; *regionalism (iqlimiyah)*: acting or causing action on the basis of a specific regional origin; *tribalism ('asha'iriyah)*: acting or causing action on the basis of membership of a specific tribe, tribal section or family. The latter might also be called *familism ('a'iliyah)*.

2. Cf. President Hafiz al-Asad in a speech broadcast by Radio Damascus on 12 April 1976; Morroe Berger, *The Arab World Today* (New York, 1962), p. 265; Moshe Ma'oz, "Alawi Military Officers in Syrian Politics, 1966–1974', *Military and State in Modern Asia* (Jerusalem, 1976), p. 279.

3. 'Abd al-Karim Zahr al-Din, *Mudhakkirati 'an Fatrat al-Infisal fi Suriyah ma bayn 28 Aylul 1961 wa 8 Adhar 1963* (Beirut, 1968), p. 345; Hizb al-Ba'th al-'Arabi al-Ishtiraki, al-Qutr al-Suri, al-Qiyadah al-Qutriyah, *Muqarrarat al-Mu'tamar al-Qutri al-'Adi al-Thani lil-Qutr al-Suri wa al-Mun'aqid bayn 18/3–4/4/65: al-Taqrir al-Tanzimi, al-Taqrir al-Siyasi, al-Taqrir al-Iqtisadi al-Ijtima'i* (Damascus, 1966) (hereafter quoted as *al-Taqrir al-Tanzimi 1965*), p. 18.

1. Introduction

1. The percentile representation of the major religious and linguistic groups in Syria used in this study has been taken from Gabriel Baer, *Population and Society in the Arab East* (London, 1964), p. 109. For a discussion of the reliability of available Syrian population statistics, see J. C. Dewdney, 'Syria: patterns of population distribution', in: J. I. Clarke and W. B. Fischer (eds), *Populations of the Middle East and North Africa* (New York, 1972), pp. 130–42; E. Wirth, *Syrien: Eine Geographische Landeskunde* (Darmstadt, 1971), pp. 170, 171. For other figures on Syria's major religious and linguistic groups see I. Nouss, *La Population de la République Syrienne. Etude démographique et géographique*, *Thèse d'Etat* (Paris, 1951); *US Army Area Handbook for Syria* (Washington, DC, 1965); and Statistisches Bundesamt Wiesbaden, Allgemeine Statistik des Auslandes, Länderkurzberichte, *Syrien* (Stuttgart/ Mainz, 1967, 1969), as quoted in Wirth, *Syrien*, p. 452.

2. The following discussion is based mainly on A. H. Hourani, *Minorities in the Arab World* (London, 1947), pp. 15–22.

3. Elie Kedourie, *The Chatham House Version and other Middle Eastern Studies* (London, 1970), pp. 386–7.

4. L. C. Biegel, *Minderheden in het Midden-Oosten, hun betekenis als politieke factor in de Arabische wereld* (Deventer, 1972), pp. 61, 332.

5. Hourani, *Minorities in the Arab World*, p. 22.

6. Ibid., pp. 23–9.

7. Cf. Shakeeb Salih, 'The British-Druze Connection and the Druze Rising of 1896 in the Hawran', *Middle Eastern Studies*, Vol. 13, No. 2, May 1977, pp. 251–7.

8. Hourani, *Minorities in the Arab World*, p. 24.

9. Cf. Zaki al-Arsuzi, 'al-Tajribah al-Siyasiyah fi Liwa' al-Iskandarun', *al-Mu'allafat al-Kamilah*, Vol. 3 (Damascus, 1974), pp. 341–62.

10. Cf. Munir Mushabik Mousa, *Etude sociologique des 'Alaouites ou Nusairis* (Thèse Principale pour le Doctorat d'Etat, Paris, 1958), pp. 924–6.

11. Jacques Weulersse, *Paysans de Syrie et du Proche Orient* (Paris, 1946), p. 77. Cf. Jacques Weulersse, *Le Pays des Alaouites* (Tours, 1940), pp. 49, 73, 288.

12. Michael H. Van Dusen, 'Political Integration and Regionalism in Syria', *Middle East Journal*, Vol. 26, No. 2, Spring 1972, pp. 123, 125–6.

13. Cf. Moshe Ma'oz, 'Society and State in Modern Syria', in: Menahem Milson (ed.), *Society and Political Structure in the Arab World* (New York, 1973), pp. 29–91; Moshe Ma'oz, 'Attempts at Creating a Political Community in Modern Syria', *Middle East Journal*, Vol. 26, No. 4, Autumn 1972, pp. 389–404.

14. Van Dusen, 'Political Integration and Regionalism in Syria', pp. 123–4.

15. Ibid., pp. 124, 125.

16. Ibid., pp. 124, 127.

17. Hourani, *Minorities in the Arab World*, p. 14.

18. In this study, unless otherwise indicated, '*Latakia region, district or province*' is used to indicate the coterminous administrative unit that existed until 1966, when the new Tartus Province was constituted. Earlier, the Province of Latakia had also included the district (*mantiqah*) Masyaf and the sub-district (*nahiyah*) Wadi al-Nasara. Nowadays, Masyaf is part of the Province of Hama and the Wadi al-Nasara has been added to the Province of Homs as part of the *mantiqah* of Talkalakh. Wadi al-Nasara (Valley of the Christians) lies to the south-east of the Alawi Mountains and is mainly inhabited by Greek Orthodox Christians. '*Aleppo region*' is used to indicate the coterminous Aleppo Province together with the Province of Idlib. '*Dayr al-Zur region*' is used to indicate the area of the provinces of Dayr al-Zur, al-Raqqah and al-Hasakah together.

19. Cf. *Statistical Abstract 1976*, pp. 45, 63; *Statistical Abstract 1971*, pp. 7, 32.

20. Weulersse, *Le Pays des Alaouites*, p. 66. The following discussion on the Syrian Alawis is mainly based on Weulersse, ibid.; Mousa, *Etude sociologique des 'Alaouites ou Nusairis*; and Munir al-Sharif, *al-Muslimun al-'Alawiyun. Man Hum? wa Ayn Hum?* (Damascus, 1961, third printing). For a history of the Alawis see Muhammad Amin Ghalib al-Tawil, *Tarikh al-'Alawiyin* (Beirut, 1966, second printing), with a commentary by the Syrian Alawi Shaykh 'Abd al-Rahman al-Khayyir. See also Chapter 8, note 13.

21. Mousa, *Etude sociologique des 'Alaouites ou Nusairis*, p. 237, also mentions the Alawi sect called the *Klaziyah*. Cf. Peter Gubser, 'Minorities in Power: The Alawites of Syria', in: R. D. McLaurin (ed.), *The Political Role of Minority Groups in the Middle East*, New York, 1979, pp. 17–48.

22. Cf. Issam Y. Ashour, *The Remnants of the Feudal System in Palestine, Syria, and Lebanon* (master's thesis, American University of Beirut, Beirut, 1946), Chapter 4, 'The Metayer System and the Survival of Certain Feudal Features', pp. 54–75.

23. Van Dusen, 'Political Integration and Regionalism in Syria', p. 132; Weulersse, *Le Pays des Alaouites*, p. 325. See also Haytham Manna, 'Syria: Accumulation of Errors?', *Middle Eastern Studies*, Vol. 23, No. 2, April 1987, pp. 211–14.

24. Alasdair Drysdale, 'The Regional Equalization of Health Care and Education in Syria since the Ba'thi Revolution', *International Journal of Middle East Studies*, Vol. 13 (1981), pp. 93–111. Cf. Alasdair Drysdale, 'The Syrian Political Elite, 1966–1976: A Spatial and Social Analysis', *Middle Eastern Studies*, Vol. 17, No. 1, January 1981, pp. 3–30. For a study that deals with socio-economic change in the Syrian rural areas since 1963, and which takes Latakia Province as an example, see Raymond A. Hinnebusch, 'Local Politics in Syria: Organization and Mobilization in Four Village Cases', *Middle East Journal*, Vol. 30, No. 1, Winter 1976, pp. 1–24. See also Raymond A. Hinnebusch Jr., 'Elite-Mass Linkage: The Role of the Mass Organizations in the Syrian Political System' (n.p., n.d.); and Raymond A. Hinnebusch, *Peasant and Bureaucracy in Ba'thist Syria: The Political Economy of Rural Development* (San Francisco, 1989).

25. Patrick Seale, *Asad*, p. 454. Seale quotes the French social anthropologist Françoise Métral, who discovered that in the western Ghab, inhabited by Alawis, between 34 and 41 per cent of girls attended school, while in the eastern Ghab, inhabited by Sunnis, the percentage was as low as 0 to 7 per cent.

26. As a clear example of pro-Alawi favouritism, Sadiq reports that in the late 1970s, when a group of 200 students from Tartus Province was sent to the Soviet Union for studies, 198 of them were Alawis, the other two being respectively a Sunni and a Christian. When the (Sunni) assistant secretary-general of the Syrian Regional Command of the Ba'th Party, Muhammad Jabir Bajbuj, objected to the composition of the delegation and its disproportionate number of Alawis, a severe dispute broke out between him and Rif'at al-Asad, the brother of the (Alawi) Syrian President. Rif'at strongly denied Bajbuj's accusations of selecting students on a sectarian basis instead of Ba'th Party membership. Mahmud Sadiq, *Hiwar hawl Suriyah*, pp. 86, 95.

27. Cf. M. Talal Akili, *Die Syrischen Küstengebiete. Eine Modelluntersuchung zur Regionalplanung in den Entwicklungsländern* (Berlin, 1968), pp. 68–84; and Weulersse, *Le Pays des Alaouites*, pp. 341–2.

28. According to an analysis of Alain Chouet, 'L'espace tribal alaouite à l'épreuve du pouvoir. La désintégration par le politique', *Maghreb-Machrek*, No. 147, January–March 1995, p. 105, the percentage of Alawis in Syrian coastal cities in 1990 was approximately as follows: Tartus 70 per cent, Banyas and Jablah 65 per cent, and Latakia 55 per cent.

29. Those Christians who fled from Lebanon simultaneously with the Druzes have the same customs, the same dress, and the same dialect. Those who lived in the 'Mountains of Hawran' before the arrival of the Druzes have a different dialect and customs which are similar to those of the people of the lower plain of Hawran ('Arif al-Nakadi (ed.), *al-Ta'rif bi-Muhafazat al-Suwayda'* (Damascus, 1962), p. 127). For a history of the Druzes and their religion see: Philip K. Hitti, *The Origins of the Druze People and Religion* (New York, 1928); Sami Nasib Makarem, *The Druze Faith* (New York, 1974); and Robert B. Betts, *The Druze*, New Haven, 1988. Cf. *Al-Anba'* (Beirut), 14 December 1968, in which the Druzes are declared to be Muslims according to a *fatwa* issued by al-Azhar.

30. Van Dusen, 'Political Integration and Regionalism in Syria', p. 125.

31. Salamah 'Ubayd, *al-Thawrah al-Suriyah al-Kubra (1925–1927)* (Damascus, 1971), pp. 60–63. 'Ubayd provides a map of the Jabal al-Duruz indicating which areas were influenced by specific Druze notable families.

32. Shibli al-'Aysami in: 'Arif al-Nakadi (ed.), *al-Ta'rif bi-Muhafazat al-*

Suwayda', pp. 20, 55–77, 115. Cf. Haytham al-'Awdat, *Intifadat al-'Ammiyah al-Fallahiyah fi Jabal al-'Arab* (Damascus, 1976).

33. For a vivid description of such social events see Shibli al-'Aysami, in: 'Arif al-Nakadi (ed.), *al-Ta'rif bi-Muhafazat al-Suwayda'*, pp. 94–6.

34. Weulersse, *Le Pays des Alaouites*, pp. 341, 342, 369, 370.

35. Wirth, *Syrien*, pp. 176, 177, 363, 365, 395. Cf. Mahmud Amin, *Salamiyah fi Khamsin Qarnan* (Damascus, 1983).

36. See also Chapter 10. Cf. Raymond A. Hinnebusch, *Authoritarian Power and State Formation in Ba'thist Syria: Army, Party, and Peasant* (San Francisco, 1990); Raymond A. Hinnebusch, 'Class and State in Ba'thist Syria', in: Richard T. Antoun and Donald Quataert (eds), *Syria: Society, Culture and Polity* (Albany, New York, 1991), pp. 29–48; Michael H. Van Dusen, *Intra- and Inter-Generational Conflict in the Syrian Army* (PhD dissertation, Baltimore, Maryland, 1971); Ronald R. Macintyre, *The Arab Ba'th Socialist Party: Ideology, Politics, Sociology and Organization* (PhD thesis, Australian National University, 1969); Ronald R. Macintyre, 'Syrian Political Age Differentials 1958–1966', *Middle East Journal*, Vol. 29, No. 2, Spring 1975, pp. 207–13.

37. The views of the Syrian Ba'thists, who assumed power on 23 February 1966, on the problems of sectarianism, regionalism and tribalism as a social and political disease, are given in *al-Munadil*, No. 3, April 1966, p. 13. A translation of the article concerned is given in Appendix A.

38. Cf. Kedourie, *The Chatham House Version and other Middle Eastern Studies*, pp. 386–7.

39. For a discussion of the concepts of religious community, tribe and socio-economic class, their similarities and differences, see Nasif Nassar, *Nahwa Mujtama' Jadid. Muqaddamat Asasiyah fi Naqd al-Mujtama' al-Ta'ifi* (5th ed., Beirut, 1995). See also: Burhan Ghalyun, *Nizam al-Ta'ifiyah: Min al-Dawlah ila al-Qabilah*, Beirut, 1990; James A. Bill, 'Class Analysis and the Dialectics of Modernization in the Middle East', *International Journal of Middle East Studies*, 3 (1972), pp. 417–34; Ilya F. Harik, 'The Ethnic Revolution and Political Integration in the Middle East', *International Journal of Middle East Studies*, 3 (1972), pp. 303–23; and C. A. O. van Nieuwenhuijze (ed.), *Commoners, Climbers and Notables. A Sampler of Studies on Social Ranking in the Middle East* (Leyden, 1977), pp. 1–82, 248–67.

40. Weulersse, *Paysans de Syrie et du Proche Orient*, p. 85.

2. The rise of minorities in the Syrian armed forces and in the Ba'th party

1. Bashir al-Da'uq (ed.), *Nidal al-Ba'th*, Vol. 1, second impression, Beirut, 1970, pp. 172–6.

2. Shibli al-'Aysami, *Hizb al-Ba'th al-'Arabi al-Ishtiraki, 1, Marhalat al-Arba'inat al-Ta'sisiyah 1940–1949* (Beirut, 1975), pp. 86–99; Sami al-Jundi, *al-Ba'th* (Beirut, 1969), p. 38; Jalal al-Sayyid, *Hizb al-Ba'th al-'Arabi* (Beirut, 1973), p. 30; Jalal al-Sayyid, *Haqiqat al-Ummah al-'Arabiyah wa 'Awamil Hifziha wa Tamziqiha* (Beirut, 1973), pp. 394–405; Munif al-Razzaz, *al-Tajribah al-Murrah* (Beirut, 1967), p. 158; Muta' Safadi, *Hizb al-Ba'th, Ma'sat al-Mawlid Ma'sat al-Nihayah* (Beirut, 1964), pp. 68–71; R. R. Macintyre, *The Arab Ba'th Socialist Party*, pp. 93–100; John F. Devlin, *The Ba'th Party, A History from its Origins to 1966* (Stanford, CA, 1976), p. 39. Cf. Van Dusen, 'Political Integration and Regionalism in Syria', p. 129.

3. Muta' Safadi, *Hizb al-Ba'th*, p. 68.

4. Sami al-Jundi, *al-Ba'th*, pp. 39–40.

5. Ibid., p. 38.

6. Sylvia Haim, *Arab Nationalism, an Anthology* (Berkeley and Los Angeles, 1964), p. 57; A. R. Kelidar, 'Religion and State in Syria', *Asian Affairs*, Vol. 61 (new series Vol. 5), Part I, February 1974, p. 22.

7. Hourani, *Syria and Lebanon, A Political Essay* (third impression, London, 1954), p. 128.

8. Michel 'Aflaq, *Fi Sabil al-Ba'th* (third impression, Beirut, 1963), p. 58. It should be noted that the Greek Orthodox Christian founder and first Secretary-General of the Ba'th Party, Michel 'Aflaq, because of his religious background, for a long time symbolised secularism and equalitarianism among different religious groups within the Ba'thist Arab nationalist movement. In later life 'Aflaq converted in silence to Islam: he was buried as a Muslim in Baghdad, after having died in exile in Paris on 23 June 1989 at the age of 79. The issue of 'Aflaq's conversion was hardly discussed at the time of his death, and it is not clear whether his unusual step of becoming a Muslim at an advanced age symbolised to some Ba'thists the failure of secular Arabism, or whether it was just seen as an individual step. Cf. Michel 'Aflaq, *Fi Sabil al-Ba'th*, 2nd edn, pp. 53–4. Cf. Zuhayr al-Maridini, *al Ustadh, Qissat Hayat Michel 'Aflaq* (The Teacher. The Story of Michel 'Aflaq), London, 1988, pp. 120–36, 151, 195. Al-Maridini (p. 195) notes that in 1949 'Aflaq, apparently during a moment of despair, wanted to resign as secretary-general of the Ba'th Party because he felt it inappropriate 'that a Christian should fulfil such a crucial position in an Arab nationalist party in conservative Damascus, whose overwhelming majority of inhabitants, like the rest of the Arab world, consisted of Muslims'. However, see also Dhuqan Qarqut, *Michel 'Aflaq, al-Kitabat al-Ula*, Beirut, 1993, pp. 250–1, who quotes a will apparently written by 'Aflaq in 1979, in which the latter explains how he was inspired by Islam, and actually stopped being a Christian when only 15 years old. 'Aflaq refers to the speech he gave in 1943 on the occasion of the birthday of the 'Arab Prophet' Muhammad (*Fi Dhikra al-Rasul al-'Arabi*), in which he stated that 'all Arabs should be like [the prophet] Muhammad'. After the Syrian Ba'thist military coup of 23 February 1966, Michael 'Aflaq's position as founder and ideologist of the Ba'th Party was no longer respected by the new rulers. As an alternative they promoted the retired Alawi schoolteacher Zaki al-Arsuzi (born in the Alexandretta district when it was still part of Syria) as being the spiritual father of the Ba'th Party. Sami al-Jundi, *al-Ba'th*, p. 19, has suggested that the aged al-Arsuzi was exploited by the (predominantly Alawi) military Ba'thist rulers because of his Alawi origin. See also: Zaki al-Arsuzi, *al-Mu'allafat al-Kamilah*, 4 vols, Damascus, 1972–74 (published by the Syrian Armed Forces Political Department Press); Nafidh Suwayd, *Zaki al-Arsuzi al-Ab al-Ruhi li-Hizb al-Ba'th al-'Arabi al-Ishtiraki*, Damascus, 1992; Antoine Audo, *Zaki al-Arsouzi: Un Arabe face à la modernité* (Beirut, 1988).

9. Cf. Muhammad 'Umran, *Tajribati fi al-Thawrah* (Beirut, 1970), p. 8; Biegel, *Minderheden in het Midden-Oosten*, pp. 97–104.

10. Mustafa Talas, *Mir'at Hayati, 1948–1958*, p. 324, note 1.

11. Cf. Muhammad Talab Hilal, *Dirasah 'An Muhafazat al-Jazirah min al-Nawahi al-Qawmiyah, al-Ijtima'iyah, al-Siyasiyah*, n.p., n.d.; Ismet Chérif Vanly, *La Persécution du Peuple Kurde par la Dictature du Baas en Syrie*, Amsterdam, 1968, and *Le Problème Kurde en Syrie: Plans pour le génocide d'une minorité nationale*, n.p.,

1968; Ismet Chérif Vanly, *Kurdistan und die Kurden*, Vol. 3, Göttingen, 1988; Mustafa Nazdar, 'Die Kurden in Syrien', in Gérard Chaliand (ed.), *Kurdistan und die Kurden*, Vol. 1, Göttingen, 1988, pp. 395–412, also in Gérard Chaliand (ed.), *People Without a Country: The Kurds and Kurdistan*, London, 1980, pp. 211–19, as 'The Kurds in Syria'; Sa'd Naji Jawad, *al-Aqalliyah al-Kurdiyah fi Suriya*, Baghdad, 1988. See also Haytham Manna', *Halat al-Akrad fi Suriyah* (The Situation of the Kurds in Syria), n.p. [Cairo Centre for Human Rights Studies], n.d. [1995], who notes that in 1989 the governor of al-Hasakah issued an official decree (No. 1865/S/25, dated 3 December 1989) forbidding the local use of languages other than Arabic during working hours, and prohibiting non-Arab manifestations, including the singing of non-Arab songs during parties and weddings. With the apparent aim of further Arabising the Kurds, the Syrian authorities, according to Haytham Manna', in 1992 started a practice of occasionally refusing to register Kurdish children under original Kurdish names. Cf. the memoirs of the Syrian Kurdish author Salim Barakat (i.e. Sullo Pavi Ghazzo), *Hatihi 'Aliyan, Hat al-Nafir 'ala Akharih (Sirat al-Saba)* (Beirut, 1982), pp. 8, 63, 78–81, 115–19.

12. Cf. Volker Perthes, 'Syria's Parliamentary Elections: Remodelling Asad's Political Base', *Middle East Report*, January–February 1992, pp. 15–18, 35; and Volker Perthes, *Staat und Gesellschaft in Syrien, 1970–1989*, pp. 262–3, 272–8.

13. See *Qadaya al-Khilaf fi al-Hizb al-Shuyu'i al-Suri* (Beirut, 1972), p. 415. Cf. Muhammad Talab Hilal, *Dirasah 'an Muhafazat al-Jazirah min al-Nawahi al-Qawmiyah, al-Ijtima'iyah, al-Siyasiyah* (n.p., n.d.), pp. 91–4.

14. Cf. Hourani, *Syria and Lebanon*, p. 144; Hourani, *Minorities in the Arab World*, p. 36; Biegel, *Minderheden in het Midden-Oosten*, p. 112.

15. *Al-Taqrir al-Tanzimi 1965*, p. 28.

16. See Hanna Batatu, 'Some Observations on the Social Roots of Syria's Ruling, Military Group and the Causes for its Dominance', *Middle East Journal*, Vol. 35, Summer 1981, p. 339.

17. Ibid., p. 28.

18. Cf. *Al-Taqrir al-Tanzimi 1965*, p. 29. See also A. Ben-Tsur, 'Composition of the Membership of the Ba'th Party in the Kuneitra Region', *Hamizrah Hehadash*, Vol. XVIII (1968), pp. 269–73. According to 'Abd Allah al-Ahmad, former member of the Syrian Regional Command, the establishment of the Suburbs' Branch was a logical consequence of the fact that the Governorate of Rural Damascus had only recently been constituted, and that each governorate was supposed to have its own party branch. Interview with 'Abd Allah al-Ahmad, Damascus, 5 November 1995.

19. Muta' Safadi, *Hizb al-Ba'th*, p. 341; *al-Hayat*, 24 April 1964. See also *al-Zaman*, 21 April 1964; and Fu'ad al-Atrash, *al-Duruz, Mu'amarat wa Tarikh wa Haqa'iq* (Beirut, 1975), p. 374.

20. *Al-Taqrir al-Tanzimi 1965*, p. 31. According to 'Abd Allah al-Ahmad it was impossible, according to party regulations, to set up a separate party branch for the Hama countryside because, unlike the case of the Governorate of Rural Damascus, the Hama countryside did not constitute a governorate separate from the city. Interview with 'Abd Allah al-Ahmad, Damascus, 5 November 1995.

21. Mustafa Talas, *Mir'at Hayati, al-'Aqd al-Thani 1958–1968*, pp. 527–9.

22. *Al-Munadil*, No. 2, December 1965, p. 10.

23. Cf. Sari Hanafi, *Les ingénieurs en Syrie, modernisation, technobureaucratie et identité*, Thèse pour le doctorat en sociologie, Paris (EHESS), 1994, p. 115, who has noted, for instance, that in the town of Salamiyah, which is inhabited by both

Sunnis and Isma'ilis, the 'Syrian Communist Party – Political Bureau' of Riyad al-Turk was almost exclusively composed of Sunnis, whereas the 'Party for Communist Action' recruited its members mainly from the local Isma'ili community.

24. Jalal al-Sayyid, *Hizb al-Ba'th al-'Arabi*, Beirut, 1973, pp. 252–3.

25. According to Munif al-Razzaz the number of officially registered full party members at the time was between 500 and 600. Interview with Munif al-Razzaz, Amman, 5 September 1971. According to former Ba'thist leader Jamal al-Atasi the number was not more than 400 (interview with Jamal al-Atasi, Damascus, 9 November 1995). Zuhayr al-Maridini, *al-Ustadh. Qissat Hayat Michel 'Aflaq*, London, 1988, p. 287, mentions the number of 200 civilian full members. This number was, according to al-Maridini, increased within a short period to more than 10,000, and according to some estimates even to 20,000. Ba'thists who have ruled Syria after 1966 generally dispute the above low numbers, claiming that they were in fact much higher. They have not, however, provided any alternative statistics.

26. For details see: Nikolaos van Dam, *De Rol van Sektarisme, Regionalisme en Tribalisme bij de Strijd om de Politieke Macht in Syrië (1961–1976)*, pp. 84–9. Cf. Muta' Safadi, *Hizb al-Ba'th*, pp. 291, 294, 327, 328; *al-Munadil*, appendix, No. 5, June 1966, p. 4; Nikolaos van Dam, 'The Struggle for Power in Syria and the Ba'th Party (1958–1966)', *Orient*, 1973/1, March 1973, pp. 11, 12. Mustafa Talas, *Mir'at Hayati, al-'Aqd al-Thani, 1958–1968*, Damascus, 1995, pp. 607, 873, 889, notes the special relationship which developed between General Salah Jadid and some prominent Ba'thists from Dayr al-Zur, notably Fawzi Rida, Muslih Salim, Yusuf Zu'ayyin, Muhammad 'Ashawi and Fayiz al-Jasim, whom he describes as the 'Dayr al-Zur block' or the 'Dayr al-Zur Troika' in the Syrian Regional Command (i.e. Yusuf Zu'ayyin, Muhammad 'Ashawi and Fayiz al-Jasim).

27. Bashir al-Da'uq (ed.), *Nidal Hizb al-Ba'th al-'Arabi al-Ishtiraki 'abr Mu'tamaratih al-Qawmiyah, al-Mu'tamar al-Qawmi al-Thamin (Nisan 1965)* (Beirut, 1972), pp. 221, 224, 232. Cf. *al-Taqrir al-Tanzimi 1965*, p. 45.

28. Munif al-Razzaz, *al-Tajribah al-Murrah*, p. 110.

29. Itamar Rabinovich, *Syria under the Ba'th 1963–66; The Army-Party Symbiosis* (Jerusalem, 1972), p. 230.

30. *Al-Taqrir al-Tanzimi 1965*, p. 34.

31. Ibid., p. 17.

32. Ibid., p. 11.

33. Ibid., p. 43.

34. For more details on the *Munshaqqun*, see Chapter 4.

35. Ibid., pp. 22, 41–3.

36. Ibid., pp. 42, 43, 44.

37. Ibid., p. 44. For a survey of Syrian electoral practices in the 1950s see Ralph Crow, *'A Study of Political Forces in Syria based on a Survey of the 1954 Elections'* (unpublished, Beirut, May 1955).

38. Circular of the Organisational Bureau of the Syrian Regional Command to the sub-branch commands (mimeographed, 6 March 1967), classified as 'very secret'. For more details on the situation in the Idlib Branch in 1967 see: Van Dam, *De Rol van Sektarisme, Regionalisme en Tribalisme*, pp. 95–7.

39. *Al-Taqrir al-Tanzimi 1965*, pp. 41–2.

40. Ibid., pp. 32–3.

41. For statistics on Alawi members of the Syrian Regional Commands after 8 March 1963 see Tables 3, 5, 6 and 7 and Chapters 6 and 9.

42. Sami al-Jundi, *al-Ba'th*, p. 113.

43. Cf. Muhammad 'Umran, *Tajribati fi al-Thawrah*, p. 22.

44. Cf. Morris Janowitz, *The Military and the Political Development of New Nations* (Chicago, 1964), pp. 52–3; Eliezer Be'eri, *Army Officers in Arab Politics and Society* (New York and London, 1970), p. 334.

45. Patrick Seale, *The Struggle for Syria; A Study of Post-War Arab Politics (1945–1958)* (London, 1965), p. 37.

46. N. E. Bou-Nacklie, 'Les Troupes Spéciales: Religious and Ethnic Recruitment, 1916–46', *International Journal of Middle East Studies*, Vol. 25, 1993, p. 656.

47. J. C. Hurewitz, *Middle East Politics: The Military Dimension* (New York, Washington, London, 1969), p. 153.

48. Seale, *The Struggle for Syria*, p. 37.

49. Mousa, *Etude Sociologique des 'Alaouites ou Nusairis*, pp. 924–6; Be'eri, *Army Officers in Arab Politics and Society*, pp. 336, 337.

50. Gordon H. Torrey, 'Aspects of the Political Elite in Syria', in George Lenczowski (ed.), *Political Elites in the Middle East* (Washington, 1975), p. 157; Seale, *The Struggle for Syria*, p. 37.

51. Be'eri, *Army Officers in Arab Politics and Society*, p. 336; Hurewitz, *Middle Eastern Politics: The Military Dimension*, p. 153.

52. Fadl Allah Abu Mansur, *A'asir Dimashq* (Beirut, 1959), p. 51.

53. Hanna Batatu, 'Some Observations on the Social Roots of Syria's Ruling Military Group and the Causes for its Dominance', *Middle East Journal*, Vol. 35, No. 3, Summer 1981, pp. 340–43. See also Andrew Rathmell, *Secret War in the Middle East: The covert struggle for Syria, 1949–1961*, London, 1995, p. 198, who quotes Burhan Qassab Hasan, formerly (1954) director of information and education of the Syrian army, as saying that at the time '70–80 per cent of the army's NCOs were from the minorities'.

54. Fadl Allah Abu Mansur, *A'asir Dimashq*, p. 68; cf. Nadhir Fansah, *Ayyam Husni al-Za'im*, Damascus, 1994, p. 98.

55. In the purge after the military coup which caused the fall of President al-Shishakli in February 1954, Kurdish officers were reportedly removed from the highest positions in the Syrian Army (Hurewitz, *Middle Eastern Politics: The Military Dimension*, p. 153).

56. Patrick Seale, *The Struggle for Syria*, p. 135.

57. Interview with Jasim 'Alwan, Cairo, 5 February 1995. Cf. Andrew Rathmell, *Secret War in the Middle East: The covert struggle for Syria, 1949–1961*, pp. 87–8, who notes that a 'large proportion of the officers whom Shishakli distrusted came from the minorities, especially the 'Alawi and the Druze. The 'Alawis had been angered by the murder of Muhammad Nasir, regarded as their leader, in July 1950 and the Druze added Shishakli's repression in the Jabal [al-Duruz] to their list of grievances.'

58. Cf. Ahmad 'Abd al-Karim, *Adwa' 'ala Tajribat al-Wahdah* (Damascus, 1962), p. 97; Van Dusen, *Intra- and Inter-Generational Conflict in the Syrian Army*, pp. 375–414; Van Dusen, 'Political Integration and Regionalism in Syria', p. 125; Seale, *The Struggle for Syria*, p. 320, n. 8.

59. Cf. Gordon H. Torrey, *Syrian Politics and the Military 1945–1958* (Columbus, Ohio, 1964), pp. 350, 355; Seale, *The Struggle for Syria*, pp. 238–46; Khalid al-'Azm, *Mudhakkirat Khalid al-'Azm*, Vol. 2 (Beirut, 1973), pp. 501–3.

60. Cf. Zahr al-Din, *Mudhakkirati*, p. 66; Van Dusen, *Intra- and Inter-Generational Conflict in the Syrian Army*, pp. 375–414.

61. Zahr al-Din, *Mudhakkirati*, pp. 60, 61. The Damascene general Muti' al-Samman later vehemently denied and denounced Zahr al-Din's account as 'an unacceptable way of promoting sectarianism', arguing that Zahr al-Din had been selected as Commander-in-Chief only because of his better qualities. It remains unclear, however, why Zahr al-Din should have been willing to undervalue his qualifications in his own memoirs. Therefore his account appears to be true. See the memoirs of Muti' al-Samman, *Watan wa 'Askar*, Beirut, 1995, pp. 54–63. Elsewhere in his memoirs Zahr al-Din writes that during the Syrian-Egyptian union, the Egyptian-dominated Army Command also objected to the appointment of non-Sunni Muslim Syrian officers to the position of Commander of the First (i.e. Syrian) Army of the United Arab Republic. Thus, when it was suggested that Nasserist Lieutenant-Colonel Jadu 'Izz al-Din might be suitable for this position, he was rejected mainly because of his being a Druze. (Zahr al-Din, *Mudhakkirati*, p. 43.)

62. Ibid., pp. 22–4. Cf. Ahmad 'Abd al-Karim, *Hisad Sinin Khasibah wa Thimar Murrah*, Beirut, 1994, p. 420; Bashir al-'Azmah, *Jil al-Hazimah. Bayn al-Wahdah wa al-Infisal. Mudhakkirat*, London, 1991, pp. 224–6; Ghassan Zakariya, *al-Sultan al-Ahmar*, London, 1991, pp. 181–268, 283–6.

63. Cf. Zahr al-Din, *Mudhakkirati*, pp. 66, 221.

64. Zahr al-Din, *Mudhakkirati*, pp. 215–16; cf. Muti' al-Samman, *Watan wa 'Askar*, p. 129, who does not deny Zahr al-Din's account on this issue; Rabinovich, *Syria under the Ba'th 1963–66*, pp. 32, 33; Van Dusen, *Intra- and Inter-Generational Conflict in the Syrian Army*, pp. 375–414.

65. Zahr al-Din, *Mudhakkirati*, p. 372.

66. Cf. Munif al-Razzaz, *al-Tajribah al-Murrah*, p. 159.

67. Be'eri, *Army Officers in Arab Politics and Society*, p. 337. According to Muti' al-Samman, *Watan wa 'Askar*, p. 63, the Ba'thists had only one Damascene officer in the Army at the time, Colonel Bashir Sadiq.

68. Munif al-Razzaz, *al-Tajribah al-Murrah*, pp. 158, 159.

69. The highest leadership of the Ba'thist Military Committee, founded in 1959 during the Syrian-Egyptian union by Ba'thist officers who had been transferred to Egypt, at first consisted of five officers, of whom three were Alawis, i.e. Muhammad 'Umran, Salah Jadid and Hafiz al-Asad, and two Isma'ilis, i.e. 'Abd al-Karim al-Jundi and Ahmad al-Mir. Later, when the Military Committee was expanded to 15 members, its composition was as follows: *five Alawis*, Muhammad 'Umran from al-Mukharram (Homs), Salah Jadid from Duwayr Ba'abda (Latakia), Hafiz al-Asad from al-Qardahah (Latakia), 'Uthman Kan'an from the Alexandretta region, and Sulayman Haddad from Hamman al-Qarahilah (Latakia); *two Isma'ilis*, 'Abd al-Karim al-Jundi from Salamiyah (Hama) and Ahmad al-Mir from Masyaf (Hama); *two Druzes* from the Jabal al-Duruz, Salim Hatum from Dhibin and Hamad 'Ubayd; *six Sunnis*, of whom three were from Hawran, Musa al-Zu'bi, Mustafa al-Hajj 'Ali and Ahmad Suwaydani; *two from Aleppo*, Amin al-Hafiz and Husayn Mulhim; and *one from Latakia*, Muhammad Rabah al-Tawil. Most members of the Military Committee had rural backgrounds and came from poor families. Salah Jadid and 'Abd al-Karim al-Jundi were exceptions, coming from prominent local middle-class families. Jadid's father was commissioner of the district of Banyas, while his grandfather had been one of the leaders of the Alawi tribal confederation of the Haddadun. For more details on the Ba'thist Military Committee and the backgrounds of its members see: Mustafa Talas, *Mir'at Hayati, al-'Aqd al-Thani, 1958–1968*, pp. 156–7; Muhammad Ibrahim al-'Ali, *al-Ghajariyah (al-Murabi "5")*, Damascus, 1995,

pp. 275–94; *al-Jadid*, 16 September 1966; Van Dusen, 'Political Integration and Regionalism in Syria', p. 132; Van Dusen, *Intra- and Inter-Generational Conflict in the Syrian Army*, pp. 336–40, 409; Muhammad 'Umran, *Tajribati fi al-Thawrah*, pp. 18, 19; Munif al-Razzaz, *al-Tajribah al-Murrah*, p. 87; Sami al-Jundi, *al-Ba'th*, p. 85; Van Dam, 'The Struggle for Power in Syria and the Ba'th Party (1958–1966)', p. 10; Van Dam, 'De Ba'thpartij in Syrië (1958–1966)', *Internationale Spectator*, XXV–20, 22 November 1971, p. 1892. Macintyre, *The Arab Ba'th Socialist Party*, pp. 202, 248, unjustly names the Ba'thist Military Committee as the 'Alawite Officer Committee', suggesting that its members were only Alawis or that only its Alawi members exercised real power. This was certainly not the case as far as the pre-1967 period, which Macintyre describes, is concerned.

70. Hizb al-Ba'th al-'Arabi al-Ishtiraki, al-Qutr al-Suri, al-Qiyadah al-Qutriyah, *Azmat al-Hizb wa Harakat 23 Shubat wa In'iqad al-Mu'tamar al-Qutri al-Akhir* (Damascus, 1966) (henceforth *Azmat al-Hizb wa Harakat 23 Shubat*), p. 20. For a translation see Appendix C.

71. Cf. Rabinovich, *Syria under the Ba'th 1963–66*, p. 76, n. 1.

72. Macintyre, *The Arab Ba'th Socialist Party*, pp. 247, 248.

73. Mahmud Sadiq, *Hiwar hawl Suriyah*, London, 1993, pp. 5–6.

74. Munif al-Razzaz, *al-Tajribah al-Murrah*, pp. 87, 158. Amin al-Hafiz was not made a member of the Military Committee until after the 8 March 1963 coup.

75. Cf. Muta' Safadi, *Hizb al-Ba'th*, p. 312; Biegel, *Minderheden in het Midden-Oosten*, pp. 226–7; Rabinovich, *Syria under the Ba'th 1963–66*, p. 25. See also Macintyre, *The Arab Ba'th Socialist Party*, p. 249.

76. Interview with Amin al-Hafiz, Baghdad, 12 September 1973.

77. The purged Independent Unionist officers Lu'ayy al-Atasi and Ziyad al-Hariri, and the Nasserist officers Muhammad al-Sufi, Rashid al-Qutayni and Fawwaz Muharib, who had all been members of the National Council of the Revolutionary Command set up as the supreme authority of the state after the 8 March 1963 coup, as well as Jasim 'Alwan and Muhammad al-Jarrah, two leading Nasserist officers, were indeed all Sunnis.

78. Among the Alawi officers who helped to suppress the Nasserist coup were Sulayman Haddad, Sulayman al-'Ali and 'Ali Mustafa. Cf. *al-Ba'th*, 19 July 1963.

79. Cf. the falsified declaration ascribed to the well-known Alawi Shaykh 'Abd al-Rahman al-Khayyir, published in *al-Hayat*, 19 May 1968; Sa'd Jum'ah, *Mujtama' al-Karahiyah* (Beirut, n.d.), pp. 62–75; Fu'ad al-Atrash, *al-Duruz, Mu'amarat wa Tarikh wa Haqa'iq*, pp. 344–51. See also the reaction of al-Shaykh 'Abd al-Rahman al-Khayyir to Sa'd Jum'ah, published in *Risalah tabhath fi Masa'il Muhimmah hawl al-Madhhab al-Ja'fari: "al-'Alawi" (Min Turath al-Shaykh 'Abd al-Rahman al-Khayyir)* (Damascus, 1994), pp. 97–110. Cf. Chapter 4, p. 58.

80. Muta' Safadi, *Hizb al-Ba'th: Ma'sat al-Mawlid Ma'sat al-Nihayah* (Beirut, 1964), p. 69. Safadi argues, for instance, that the Ba'th was originally a sectarian movement which had designs on supplanting the traditional order in which Sunnis were dominant. He writes that the religious minorities, with Alawis in the first place, followed by Druzes, Isma'ilis and Christians, 'were most ambitious to overthrow the order of traditional society in which urban Sunni Muslims dominated.' For a later view of Safadi on political developments in Syria see: 'Nahwa Suriyah Hadithah', *Milaff al-Nahar*, No. 61 (al-'Alam al-'Arabi al-Yawm, 7), 6 March 1971. Safadi's criticism of the Syrian Ba'th is discussed in detail in Van Dam, *De Rol van Sektarisme, Regionalisme en Tribalisme*, pp. 62–81. See also: *al-Muharrir*, 15 July

1963; Qadri Qal'aji, *Watha'iq al-Naksah taht Adwa' al-Tajribah al-Murrah* (Beirut, 1969); Muhammad Sa'id al-Najdi, *Hasilat al-Inqilabat al-Thawriyah fi ba'd al-Aqtar al-'Arabiyah* (Beirut, 1966); Khalil Mustafa, *Suqut al-Jawlan!?* ('The Fall of the Golan!?') (Amman, 1969); Khalil Mustafa, *Min Milaffat al-Jawlan?* ... ('From the Dossiers of the Golan? ... ') (Amman, 1970). Khalil Mustafa (pseudonym for Khalil Barayiz), a Syrian military officer, was abducted from Lebanon in 1971. Tried in Syria and sentenced to fifteen years in prison, he was not released when his sentence expired in 1985.

3. Sectarian polarisation in the Syrian armed forces between Sunnis and religious minorities

1. Hizb al-Ba'th al-'Arabi al-Ishtiraki, al-Qutr al-Suri, al-Maktab al-'Askari, *Mashru' Taqrir 'an Waqi' al-Hizb fi al-Tanzim al-'Askari*, 19 October 1965. For more details see Van Dam, *De Rol van Sektarisme, Regionalisme en Tribalisme*, pp. 122–4.

2. Munif al-Razzaz, *al-Tajribah al-Murrah*, p. 159.

3. Ibid.

4. Muta' Safadi, *Hizb al-Ba'th*, pp. 339–40.

5. Munif al-Razzaz, *al-Tajribah al-Murrah*, p. 159; *al-Nahar*, 9 July 1963; *al-Safa'*, 11 July 1963; *al-Muharrir*, 15 July 1963.

6. Munif al-Razzaz, *al-Tajribah al-Murrah*, p. 159; cf. Fu'ad al-Atrash, *al-Duruz, Mu'amarat wa Tarikh wa Haqa'iq*, p. 373; and Muta' Safadi, *Hizb al-Ba'th*, pp. 338–9.

7. Muta' Safadi, *Hizb al-Ba'th*, pp. 339–40.

8. Munif al-Razzaz, *al-Tajribah al-Murrah*, p. 159.

9. Hizb al-Ba'th al-'Arabi al-Ishtiraki, al-Qutr al-Suri, al-Qiyadah al-Qutriyah, *al-Taqrir al-Watha'iqi li-Azmat al-Hizb wa al-Muqaddam lil-Mu'tamar al-Qutri al-Istithna'i al-Mun'aqid bayn 10/3–27/3/1966* (Damascus, 1966) (henceforth *al-Taqrir al-Watha'iqi*), pp. 65, 85–8. See also J. C. Hurewitz, *Middle East Politics: The Military Dimension*, p. 153; and Martin Seymour, 'The Dynamics of Power in Syria since the Break with Egypt', *Middle Eastern Studies*, Vol. 6, No. 1, January 1970, p. 40.

10. Muta' Safadi, *Hizb al-Ba'th*, p. 349.

11. *Al-Taqrir al-Watha'iqi*, p. 65.

12. Circular issued by the Military Bureau to all members of military party branches and independent sub-branches, 2 October 1965 (mimeographed).

13. Radio Damascus, 8 October 1965.

14. Sami al-Jundi, *al-Ba'th*, pp. 109–10.

15. On the position of high Sunni officers such as Mustafa Talas and Naji Jamil see Chapter 5.

16. See: Rabinovich, *Syria under the Ba'th 1963–66*, pp. 165–71, 180–189; and Van Dam, 'The Struggle for Power in Syria and the Ba'th Party (1958–1966)', pp. 14–16.

17. For a detailed description of the incident see Van Dam, 'De Ba'thpartij in Syrië (1958–1966)', pp. 1919–20. For an extensive account from the viewpoint of Mustafa Talas, see his *Mir'at Hayati, 1958–1968*, pp. 626–34. Talas's memoirs, written with hindsight, do not reflect the fact that he had once been considered as a staunch supporter of Amin al-Hafiz.

18. *Al-Taqrir al-Watha'iqi*, p. 91. For a translation see Appendix B.

19. See Mustafa Talas, *Mir'at Hayati, al-'Aqd al-Awwal (1948–1958)* (Damascus,

2nd edn, 1991), pp. 282, 299; Lucien Bitterlin, *Hafez El-Assad: Le Parcours d'un Combattant* (Paris, 1986), p. 34.

20. See for instance: Mustafa Talas, *Harb al-'Isabat* (Beirut, 1969); Mustafa Talas, *al-Kifah al-Musallah wa al-Tahaddi al-Sahyuni* (Beirut, n.d.); Muhammad 'Umran, *Tajribati fi al-Thawrah*; cf. *Majallat al-Fikr al-'Askari* (Damascus). It may be noted that, especially after the takeover of power by the Ba'th in 1963, a number of Sunnis tended to 'suspect' specific Sunnis who occupied important positions in Syrian power institutions of belonging to a religious minority, whereas this was not really the case. Cf. Khalil Mustafa, *Suqut al-Jawlan!?*, p. 210, where it is suggested that 'Abd al-Halim Khaddam (a Sunni from Banyas) was an Alawi. According to Khalil Mustafa, Khaddam, being governor of al-Qunaytarah shortly before the outbreak of the June 1967 War allowed only Alawi families to evacuate from the Syrian–Israeli front to safer places, and forced members of other religious communities to stay behind. Hanna Batatu, 'Some Observations on the Social Roots of Syria's Ruling Military group and the Causes for its Dominance', *Middle East Journal*, Vol. 35, Summer 1981, p. 332, notes that 'Abd al-Halim Khaddam 'married in 1954 a woman from al-Hawwash, a family that provided the chiefs of the [Alawi] al-Matawirah in Ottoman times ... Later Khaddam apparently took for second wife a woman from the Sunni family al-Tayyarah'.

21. Munif al-Razzaz, *al-Tajribah al-Murrah*, p. 138.

22. Ibid., pp. 115–17, 137–8, 159; cf. Muta' Safadi, *Hizb al-Ba'th*, pp. 349–50.

23. Interview with Munif al-Razzaz, Amman, 5 September 1971; *Al-Taqrir al-Watha'iqi*, pp. 63, 64. Cf. Muta' Safadi, *Hizb al-Ba'th*, p. 341.

24. *Al-Taqrir al-Watha'iqi*, p. 64.

25. Ibid., pp. 63–6. According to Mustafa Talas, *Mir'at Hayati, 1958–1968*, pp. 556–9, Muhammad 'Umran was accused of preparing a military coup with the aim of monopolising power for himself.

26. *Al-Hayat*, 10 February 1965. See also 'Tariq Suriyah ba'd Dhihab 'Umran wa Madrasatih', *al-Hayat*, 26 October 1964; 'Al-Saratan al-Ta'ifi yujammid al-Dawlah wa al-Sha'b', *al-Hayat*, 5 February 1966; *al-Nahar*, 15 December 1964.

27. *Al-Thawrah*, 23 February 1965.

28. *Al-Munadil*, No. 3, April 1966, p. 13. See Appendix A.

29. Van Dusen, *Intra- and Inter-Generational Conflict in the Syrian Army*, pp. 366–8.

30. Rabinovich, *Syria under the Ba'th 1963–66*, p. 151.

31. *Azmat al-Hizb wa Harakat 23 Shubat*, p. 21. See Appendix C.

32. Interview with Munif al-Razzaz, Amman, 22 November 1974. See also Munif al-Razzaz, *al-Tajribah al-Murrah*, p. 160.

33. Ibid. Talas, *Mir'at Hayati, 1958–1968*, pp. 563–7, 626. Talas notes (p. 564) that during party meetings Amin al-Hafiz started classifying the percentages of religious communities in Syria 'just as is being done by orientalists, but not by Ba'thist combatants.'

34. *Al-Taqrir al-Watha'iqi*, pp. 88–96. A translation of fragments of these hearings is given in Appendix B.

35. *Al-Taqrir al-Watha'iqi*, pp. 34, 101, 102; cf. *al-Anwar*, 16 March 1966.

36. Interview with Munif al-Razzaz, Amman, 22 November 1974; Munif al-Razzaz, *al-Tajribah al-Murrah*, pp. 159–60.

37. For details see ibid., pp. 149–51; Rabinovich, *Syria under the Ba'th 1963–66*, pp. 161–71, 180–89; Van Dam, *De Rol van Sektarisme, Regionalisme en Tribalisme*,

pp. 117–20; Van Dam, 'The Struggle for Power in Syria and the Ba'th Party (1958–1966)', pp. 15–16.

38. Cf. Rabinovich, *Syria under the Ba'th 1963–66*, p. 182, n. 4.

39. Cf. Munif al-Razzaz, *al-Tajribah al-Murrah*, p. 160.

40. Cf. Weulersse's definition of the 'minority complex'. See Chapter 1, p. 4.

41. See Van Dam, *De Rol van Sektarisme, Regionalisme en Tribalisme*, pp. 137–8, n. 37.

42. Cf. Munif al-Razzaz, *al-Tajribah al-Murrah*, pp. 165–8, 194.

43. Hizb al-Ba'th al-'Arabi al-Ishtiraki, al-Qiyadah al-Qawmiyah, *Nashrah ila al-Rifaq al-'Askariyin*, No. 1, January 1966.

44. Dr Yusuf Zu'ayyin's Cabinet, composed mainly of supporters of Salah Jadid, had resigned on 22 December 1965, i.e. shortly after the dissolution of the Syrian Regional Command.

45. Munif al-Razzaz, *al-Tajribah al-Murrah*, pp. 181–2.

46. *Al-Taqrir al-Watha'iqi*, p. 96.

47. Interview with Munif al-Razzaz, Amman, 22 November 1974.

48. Interview with Munif al-Razzaz, Amman, 22 November 1974; interview with Shibli al-'Aysami, Baghdad, 30 August 1971; Munif al-Razzaz, *al-Tajribah al-Murrah*, p. 160; cf. Macintyre, *The Arab Ba'th Socialist Party*, pp. 370, 382; *al-Munadil*, No. 8, early September 1966, p. 13; *al-Taqrir al-Watha'iqi*, pp. 36–9, 43, 44.

49. *Al-Anwar*, 15 November 1970. Cf. Mustafa Talas, *Mir'at Hayati, 1958–1968*, p. 645, who notes that 'Amin al-Hafiz imagined that [by recalling Major-General 'Umran from Spain in order to assume the portfolio of the Ministry of Defence] he could buy off the officers from the Latakia region and be silent. It did not occur to him that there were men in the Alawi community whom he could not satisfy, except if the revolutionary, progressive and nationalist line were undoubtedly clear'.

50. Interview with Munif al-Razzaz, Amman, 22 November 1974; Mustafa Talas, *Mir'at Hayati, 1958–1968*, pp. 665–6.

51. Ibid.

52. *Al-Taqrir al-Watha'iqi*, pp. 65–6.

53. Ibid., pp. 104–8.

54. Cf. Munif al-Razzaz, *al-Tajribah al-Murrah*, p. 159; cf. *al-Taqrir al-Watha'iqi*, pp. 33–4, where it is mentioned that al-Hafiz was specifically supported by officers of the Intelligence Service, especially those who were stationed in Damascus, Homs, Aleppo, Latakia and al-Qunaytarah.

55. *Al-Munadil*, No. 11, mid-December 1966, p. 9; *al-Hayat*, 30 December 1966.

56. Cf. circulars of the Syrian Regional Command of the Ba'th Party, 14 and 17 July 1966. For a list of names of purged officers, see Van Dam, *De Rol van Sektarisme, Regionalisme en Tribalisme*, p. 143, n. 84.

4. The purge of Druze officers in the Syrian armed forces

1. Members of the Military Bureau of the deposed National Command were: Fahd al-Sha'ir (Druze), secretary; Salah Namur (Sunni), Mujalli al-Qa'id (Christian from Basir, Hawran), 'Ali Sultan, Sharif Sa'ud, and 'Ali al-Damad (Sunni from Hawran). Membership of the Military Bureau was not constant and changed several times. Thus, Lieutenant-Colonel Isma'il Hilal was also a member for a short time. Interview with Munif al-Razzaz, Amman, 22 November 1974; Hizb al-Ba'th al-

'Arabi al-Ishtiraki, al-Qiyadah al-Qawmiyah, *Muqarrarat al-Mu'tamar al-Qawmi al-Tasi' al-Mun'aqid fi al-Nisf al-Thani min Aylul 1966* (Damascus, n.d.) (henceforth *Muqarrarat al-Mu'tamar al-Qawmi al-Tasi'*), p. 70; *al-Ba'th*, 29 and 31 January 1967, 5, 15 and 28 March 1967; *al-Thawrah*, 29 January 1967.

2. *Al-Ba'th*, 6 February 1967.

3. Interview with Munif al-Razzaz, Amman, 22 November 1974.

4. *Al-Munadil*, No. 3, April 1966, p. 13. See Appendix A.

5. *Al-Hayat*, 29 March 1966.

6. Hamad 'Ubayd in an interview with Macintyre, *The Arab Ba'th Socialist Party*, pp. 293–4.

7. Interview with Munif al-Razzaz, Amman, 5 September 1971.

8. Macintyre, *The Arab Ba'th Socialist Party*, pp. 393–4; *al-Nahar*, 4 March 1966; *al-Ba'th*, 24 February 1966.

9. *Muqarrarat al-Mu'tamar al-Qawmi al-Tasi'*, p. 68.

10. *Al-Taqrir al-Watha'iqi*, pp. 104–108; *Muqarrarat al-Mu'tamar al-Qawmi al-Tasi'*, pp. 68, 69; Mustafa Talas, *Mir'at Hayati, 1958–1968*, pp. 692–9; *al-Nahar*, 27 February 1966, 4 and 8 March 1966; *al-Muharrir*, 28 March 1966. During party trials held later in 1966, Hamad 'Ubayd was found guilty of illegal enrichment and abuse of power. Cf. *al-Munadil*, appendix, No. 5, June 1966, p. 9; *al-Hayat*, 1 and 5 May 1966; *al-Jaridah*, 4 May 1966. According to *al-Hayat*, 12 June 1966, Hatum forcefully opposed the confiscation of the possessions of his co-religionist 'Ubayd.

11. Cf. *al-Nahar*, 1 March 1966 and 16 September 1966.

12. Interview with Munif al-Razzaz, Amman, 22 November 1974; *al-Thawrah*, 29 January 1967; *al-Ba'th*, 30 January 1967.

13. *Al-Taqrir al-Watha'iqi*, pp. 31–2.

14. Interview with Munif al-Razzaz, Amman, 22 November 1974; *al-Taqrir al-Tanzimi 1965*, pp. 37–9; *al-Munadil*, No. 9, mid-September 1966.

15. Sami al-Jundi, *al-Ba'th*, p. 149.

16. Interview with Amin al-Hafiz, Baghdad, 12 September 1973.

17. Interview with Munif al-Razzaz, Amman, 22 November 1974.

18. *Muqarrarat al-Mu'tamar al-Qawmi al-Tasi'*, p. 70.

19. Interview with Munif al-Razzaz, Amman, 22 November 1974.

20. Cf. *al-Munadil*, No. 9, mid-September 1966, p. 1. According to Mustafa Talas, *Mir'at Hayati, 1958–1968*, p. 745, the Military Bureau which was involved in the abortive coup of 8 September 1966 consisted of Fahd al-Sha'ir, Salim Hatum, Mustafa al-Hajj 'Ali, Talal Abu 'Asali and Sharif al-Shaqqi.

21. Interview with Munif al-Razzaz, Amman, 22 November 1974. See also Mustafa Talas, *Mir'at Hayati, 1958–1968*, pp. 741–94.

22. *Al-Munadil*, No. 9, mid-September 1966.

23. Cf. *al-Difa'* (Jerusalem), 9 September 1966; *al-Hayat*, 8 September 1966.

24. Interview with Munif al-Razzaz, Amman, 22 November 1974. See also Van Dam, *De Rol van Sektarisme, Regionalisme en Tribalisme*, p. 153.

25. Cf. *al-Munadil*, No. 9, mid-September 1966; Edouard Saab, *La Syrie ou la Révolution dans la Rancoeur* (Paris, 1968), p. 240; *al-Hayat*, 31 July 1966.

26. *Al-Munadil*, No. 9, mid-September 1966.

27. Supporters of the deposed National Command were described by the regime of the Syrian Regional Command as 'rightist elements'.

28. *Al-Ba'th*, 28 March 1967.

29. *Al-Munadil*, No. 9, mid-September 1966; *al-Ba'th*, 27 February 1967, 15

March 1967; Muhammad Ibrahim al-'Ali, *al-Ghajariyah (al-Murabi "5")*, Damascus, 1995, p. 292; *al-Jaridah*, 13 September 1966; cf. *al-Hayat*, 15 March 1966; cf. Mustafa Talas, *Mir'at Hayati, 1958–1968*, pp. 612–15.

30. *Al-Munadil*, No. 9, mid-September 1966.

31. Cf. *al-Muharrir*, 13 September 1966.

32. Talal Abu 'Asali in an interview with Muhammad Hasanayn Haykal, *al-Ahram*, 1 October 1966.

33. *Filastin* (Jerusalem), 14 September 1966; *al-Difa'*, 14 September 1966.

34. Ibid.

35. Ibid.

36. *Al-Munadil*, No. 9, mid-September 1966, p. 5.

37. *Al-Nahar*, 15 September 1966.

38. Ibid.

39. Ibid.

40. Ibid.

41. *Al-Hayat*, 29 September 1966.

42. Sa'd Jum'ah, *Mujtama' al-Karahiyah* (Beirut, 1971), pp. 62–75. Cf. Fu'ad al-Atrash, al-*Duruz, Mu'amarat wa Tarikh wa Haqa'iq*, pp. 344–51.

43. For similar propagandist accusations against Jadid as wanting to establish an Alawi state in Syria, see: *al-Hawadith*, 16 August 1968; and Sami al-Jundi, *Kisrat Khubz* (Beirut, 1969), pp. 7–18. Cf. 'Abd al-Rahman al-Khayyir, *Risalah tabhath fi Masa'il Muhimmah hawl al-Madhhab al-Ja'fari: "al-'Alawi" (Min Turath al-Shaykh 'Abd al-Rahman al-Khayyir)* (Damascus, 1994), pp. 97–110.

44. For names of purged Druze officers, see: *al-Munadil*, No. 11, mid-December 1966; Van Dam, *De Rol van Sektarisme, Regionalisme en Tribalisme*, p. 157; cf. *al-Hayat*, 11 and 13 September 1966; *al-Nahar*, 19 September 1966; *al-Safa'*, 15 September 1966.

45. Cf. *al-Hayat*, 7 and 23 October 1966; *al-Nahar*, 30 September 1966.

46. Circular of the Organisational Bureau of the Syrian Regional Command of the Ba'th Party, 6 March 1967. Cf. *al-Hayat*, 5 March 1967; *al-Safa'*, 25 February 1967.

47. *Al-Nahar*, 31 December 1966.

48. Cf. *al-Jaridah*, 13 September 1966. See also *al-Hayat*, 14 October 1966, where it is alleged that Hatum's abortive coup had also negatively affected relations between inhabitants of Hawran Province and the authorities in Damascus. Cf. Fu'ad al-Atrash, al-*Duruz, Mu'amarat wa Tarikh wa Haqa'iq*, p. 322.

49. *Al-Ba'th*, 14 March 1967.

50. *Al-Ba'th*, 28 March 1967.

51. The Druze officers against whom death sentences were demanded were reportedly: Fahd al-Sha'ir, Salim Hatum, Talal Abu 'Asali, 'Abd al-Rahim Bathish, and Fawwaz Abu al-Fadl. Cf. *al-Hayat*, 2 April 1967.

52. See Mustafa Talas, *Mir'at Hayati, 1958–1968*, pp. 865–9; *al-Ba'th*, 25 June 1967; Radio Damascus, 26 June 1967; cf. Daniel Dishon (ed.), *Middle East Record 1967* (Jerusalem, 1971), p. 496. See also Sami al-Jundi, *al-Ba'th*, p. 156. In 1968, officers and civilians who were accused of participation in Hatum's abortive coup of September 1966 and his so-called second attempt to overthrow the Syrian regime during the June 1967 War were put on trial in Damascus. *Al-Ba'th*, 8 September 1968; Dishon (ed.), *Middle East Record 1968* (Jerusalem, 1973), pp. 735, 736.

53. According to *al-Safa'*, 22 November 1966, Chief of Staff Ahmad Suwaydani

and Muhammad al-Zu'bi, both Sunnis from Hawran, were among those who were concerned about the dominant role of Alawis.

54. Circular of the Organisational Bureau of the Syrian Regional Command of the Ba'th Party, 19 March 1967. For the text see Van Dam, *De Rol van Sektarisme, Regionalisme en Tribalisme*, p. 171.

55. Hawran ministers who threatened to resign were Muhammad al-Zu'bi (Sunni), Salih Mahamid (Sunni), and Mashhur Zaytun (Christian). *Al-Hayat*, 12 March, 6 and 7 April 1967; *al-Ahrar*, 14 February 1967; *al-Jadid*, 17 March 1967.

56. *Al-Muharrir*, 26 September 1967; *The Arab World*, 11 September 1967; *al-Hayat*, 12 and 26 September 1967. See also Van Dam, *De Rol van Sektarisme, Regionalisme en Tribalisme*, pp. 170–72.

57. Mustafa Talas, *Mir'at Hayati, 1958–1968*, pp. 889–90. On the al-Asad/Jadid rivalry and the conflict between Minister of Defence Hafiz al-Asad and Chief of Staff Ahmad Suwaydani, see pp. 882–97. Cf. *al-Ba'th*, 16 February and 21 July 1968; *al-Thawrah*, 17 February 1968; *al-Rayah*, 12 July 1971.

58. Cf. *al-Hayat*, 16 February 1968; *al-Safa'*, 6 February 1968; *al-Jaridah*, 2 March 1968; cf. *al-Anwar*, 15 November 1970.

59. Cf. 'Abd al-Karim al-Jundi in an interview with *Akhbar al-Yawm*, 7 September 1968; *al-Nahar*, 20 August 1968; *al-Hayat*, 21 August 1968 and 23 July 1969; *al-Anwar*, 21 August 1968; *al-Sayyad*, 24 July 1969.

60. Cf. *al-Hayat*, 9 August 1969. Cf. al-*Ahrar*, 6 June 1970; *al-Rayah*, 12 July 1971; and Lajnat al-Difa' 'an al-Mu'taqalin al-Siyasiyin fi Suriyah, al-Maktab al-Markazi, *Min Qawafil al-Mu'taqalin al-Siyasiyin wa Akhbarihim fi al-Sujun al-Suriyah*, n.p., 1976.

61. See *al-Hayat*, 24 February 1994.

5. The struggle for power within the Alawi community

1. Cf. *al-Anwar*, 15 November 1970.

2. According to Mustafa Talas, *Mir'at Hayati, 1958–1968*, pp. 885–8, Salah Jadid tried in vain after the June 1967 War to regain his control over the army. His attempts to obtain the post of minister of defence were aborted by Hafiz al-Asad, however, whose rise to power turned out to be irreversible. Cf. *al-Rayah*, 12 July 1971, p. 17; *al-Ahrar*, 14 February 1967; *al-Anwar*, 1 and 9 February 1967; *al-Ba'th*, 12 February 1967; Radio Damascus, 13 February 1967.

3. See Dishon (ed.), *Middle East Record 1968*, pp. 711–13.

4. Ibid., pp. 711–12.

5. Minutes of the sessions of the Tenth Extraordinary National Congress of the Ba'th Party, *al-Rayah*, 5 July 1971; *al-Jaridah*, 18 October 1968; *al-Anwar*, 29 October 1968.

6. Minutes of the sessions of the Tenth Extraordinary National Congress of the Ba'th Party, *al-Rayah*, 12 July 1971.

7. *Al-Jaridah*, 8 November 1968.

8. Minutes of the sessions of the Tenth Extraordinary National Congress of the Ba'th Party, *al-Rayah*, 12 July 1971.

9. Cf. *al-Hawadith*, 1 November 1968; *al-Anwar*, 26 October 1968; *al-Hayat*, 29 October 1968; Dishon (ed.), *Middle East Record 1969–1970* (Jerusalem, 1977), pp. 1129–30. The transferred officers reportedly included several members of the Alawi Na'isah family.

10. Minutes of the sessions of the Tenth Extraordinary National Congress of the Ba'th Party, *al-Rayah*, 12 July 1971.

11. Ibid.; *al-Anwar*, 26 October 1968; *al-Hawadith*, 1 November 1968.

12. Cf. Van Dusen, 'Political Integration and Regionalism in Syria', p. 136.

13. See Chapter 2. According to Hurewitz, *Middle East Politics: The Military Dimension*, p. 154, the Alawi officers were divided into two rival groups: 'one consisting of native-born Syrians and the other of immigrants from the vilâyet of Hatay, as the district of Alexandretta became known after its assimilation by Turkey in 1939. Of these two groups, the immigrant officers, coming from families that were more urbanised and a notch or two less impoverished, filled the superior posts.' This study did not establish the existence of such a prominent Alawi officers' faction from the Alexandretta region. Rather, it demonstrated that, above all, Alawi officers from the Latakia region occupied important positions in Syrian power institutions. One of the most prominent Alawi officers from the Alexandretta region was 'Uthman Kan'an, member of the Ba'thist Military Committee that was dissolved in August 1965.

14. *Al-Rayah*, 12 June 1971.

15. Circular from the secretary-general of the Syrian Regional Command of the Ba'th Party to the Syrian party apparatus, 28 February 1969; *al-Nahar*, 5 March 1969; *al-Rayah*, 5 July 1971, p. 26; cf. *al-Ba'th*, 25 May 1969.

16. *Al-Rayah*, 19 July 1971, p. 6. Cf. Radio Damascus, 2 March 1969; *al-Thawrah*, 3 March 1969; *al-Nahar*, 5 March 1969.

17. *Al-Hayat*, 6 August 1969, interpreted the conflict between Hafiz al-Asad and Salah Jadid as 'a manoeuvre, aimed at purging the non-Alawi party leaders, and at being able to discover those elements which took a hostile attitude towards the Syrian regime'. Fabricated rumours such as these, which tried to explain almost anything by the sectarian backgrounds of the Ba'thists in power, were typical for an anti-Ba'thist conservative Lebanese daily such as *al-Hayat*.

18. Cf. *al-Sayyad*, 22 May 1969; Dishon (ed.), *Middle East Record 1969–1970*, p. 1149.

19. *Al-Rayah*, 7 June 1971.

20. *Al-Rayah*, 14 and 17 November 1970.

21. Prominent Alawi members of Hafiz al-Asad's officers' faction were: Rif'at al-Asad (his brother), 'Ali Haydar (commander of the 'special forces'), Muhammad Tawfiq al-Juhni (commander of the first division), 'Ali ('Isa) Duba (chief of military intelligence), 'Ali al-Salih (commander of air defence), and 'Ali Hammad (chief of officers' affairs). In 1975 these were members of a Military Committee which was responsible for the transfer of officers. Other prominent Alawi military supporters of Hafiz al-Asad were: 'Abd al-Ghani Ibrahim, 'Ali Aslan, Hikmat Ibrahim, and 'Ali Husayn. Several names of other military supporters of Hafiz al-Asad can be found in *al-Ba'th*, 11 March 1974, which published a list of officers who had received military distinctions as a reward for their performance during the October 1973 War. See also Van Dam, *De Rol van Sektarisme, Regionalisme en Tribalisme*, p. 184, n. 29.

22. Cf. *al-Kifah*, 23 September 1971; *Beirut*, 23, 24 and 26 September 1971; *al-Hawadith*, 7 December 1972. *Al-Dustur* (Beirut), 26 June 1972, reported the existence of Sunni officers' factions led by Minister of Defence Mustafa Talas, Air Force Commander Naji Jamil, and Prime Minister 'Abd al-Rahman Khulayfawi (a Damascene of Algerian origin), which were supposed to threaten the position of al-

Asad. Such reports appeared especially in the pro-Iraqi press after the takeover of power in Iraq on 17 July 1968 by a group of Ba'thists who were organisationally connected with those who had been deposed in Syria on 23 February 1966. See also *al-Rayah*, 1 March 1971, where it is noted that after al-Asad's coup of 13 November 1970 his supporters became divided into 'three wings'.

23. See *al-Rayah*, 14 and 28 June 1971; *al-Hayat*, 11 and 15 June 1971. On 5 January 1971, *al-Hayat* reported the retirement of twelve officers, ten of whom were Alawis, including 'Izzat Jadid.

24. *Al-Dustur* (Beirut), 26 June 1972; *al-Hawadith*, 7 December 1972; *al-Hayat*, 6 March 1972; *Beirut*, 6 March 1972; *al-Siyasah* (Kuwayt), 6 March 1972. *Al-Muharrir*, 6 March 1972, accused the Iraqi Ba'th regime of murdering 'Umran; *al-Thawrah* (Baghdad), 4 October 1976, and Radio Baghdad, 4 October 1976, likewise brought charges against the Syrian Ba'th regime. It is not clear whether the changes in the Syrian Army Command of 26 March 1972 were related to the murder of 'Umran. Cf. Mahmud Sadiq, *Hiwar hawl Suriyah* (London, 1993), pp. 26, 33.

25. *Al-Rayah*, 4 December 1972. Cf. *al-Hawadith*, 7 December 1972; *The Arab World*, 8 December 1972, pp. 11–12: 'President Assad's Worries and Problems', *L'Orient–Le Jour*, 14 December 1972. The arrested party members of the Damascus Branch were possibly also from the Latakia region.

26. *Al-Ba'th*, 11 March 1974. See Rif'at al-Asad's interview with *al-Sayyad*, 13 February 1974, about the role played by his armed units during the October War. The original name of *Saraya al-Difa'* was *Saraya al-Difa' 'an al-Matarat* ('The Airport Defence Platoons'). Cf. Mustafa Talas, *Mir'at Hayati, 1958–1968*, p. 893.

27. See for instance *al-Rayah*, 14 June 1971.

28. *Al-Nahar*, 15 April 1975.

29. *Al-Ba'th*, 16 April 1975. Cf. *al-Kifah al-'Arabi*, 8 April 1975.

30. *Al-Nahar*, 28 May 1973. According to this daily, Salma Najib, President al-Asad's brother's mother-in-law, was chosen at the same time.

31. *Al-Ba'th*, 23 January 1975.

32. *Al-Rayah*, 22 November 1971.

33. *Al-Rayah*, 10 April 1972. Cf. *al-Rayah*, 19 July 1971, 20 December 1971, 1 May 1972, and 28 August 1972.

34. On 12 April and 20 July 1976, in speeches transmitted by Radio Damascus, President Hafiz al-Asad explained the background of his decision to intervene in Lebanon. See also Sabir Falhut, *al-Mas'alah al-Filastiniyah wa al-Mawqif al-'Arabi al-Suri* (Damascus, 1977), pp. 309–14; and Ghalib Kayyali, *Hafiz al-Asad: Qa'id wa Risalah* (Beirut, 1977), pp. 179–85.

35. Cf. *al-Sumud*, as quoted in *Arab Report and Record*, 1–15 April 1976, p. 231. Cf. *Beirut*, 27 May 1976; *al-Jumhuriyah* (Cairo), 27 April 1976; *Baghdad Observer*, 11 and 19 May 1976.

36. Prominent Alawis who were assassinated included: Major 'Ali Haydar, commanding officer of the Hama garrison (killed at the end of 1976); Professor Muhammad al-Fadil, rector of Damascus University (killed on 22 February 1977); Brigadier 'Abd al-Karim Razzuq, commander of the missile corps of the Syrian army (killed on 19 June 1977); Dr 'Ali 'Abid al-'Ali, Aleppo University professor (killed on 1 November 1977); Dr Yusuf 'Id, a close relative of General Muhammad 'Id, military commander of the northern region (killed on 6 March 1978); Dr Ibrahim Nu'amah, doyen of Syrian dentists, and deputy chairman of the Soviet–Syrian Friendship Society (killed on 18 March 1978); and Lieutenant-Colonel

Ahmad Khalil, director of police at the Ministry of Interior (killed on 1 August 1978), who was very close to President Hafiz al-Asad. Both al-'Ali and Nu'amah were in-laws of the Syrian president and originated from his village neighbourhood. Cf. *Le Monde*, 1 April 1978, which also reported that General Naji Jamil, chief of national security, had apparently been deposed as vice-minister of defence and commander of the Syrian air force for not having prevented the assassinations. (Cf. *al-Ba'th*, 3 November 1977, 28 March 1978, 26 April 1978; *al-Nahar al-'Arabi wa al-Duwali*, 8 April 1978; *al-Nahar*, 28 March 1978; *Sunday Times*, 16 April 1978; Radio Baghdad, 24 April 1978; *Le Monde*, 23 August 1978.) On 6 July 1977, the government-controlled Syrian daily *Tishrin* hinted that the assassinations may have been aimed at provoking 'sectarian divisions'. (Cf. *Guardian*, 6 July 1977.)

37. Radio Damascus, 28 March 1977, 13 July 1977, 2 November 1977, and 17 September 1978. (Cf. *Baghdad Observer*, 11 July 1977, Radio Baghdad, 24 and 30 August 1978.) Towards the end of September 1978, Syrian–Iraqi propaganda warfare suddenly subsided; on 24–26 October 1978 President Hafiz al-Asad paid a reconciliatory visit to Baghdad to further the rapprochement between the two rival Ba'th regimes that had been sparked by their shared opposition to the Egyptian–Israeli agreements on 'A Framework for Peace in the Middle East' and the 'Framework for the Conclusion of a Peace Treaty between Egypt and Israel', signed at Camp David on 17 September 1978. Al-Asad's visit ended with the signing of a 'Charter for Joint National Action between Syria and Iraq'. (*Al-Ba'th*, 27 October 1978.) For a study of Syrian–Iraqi relations during that period see Eberhard Kienle, *Ba'th v Ba'th: The conflict between Syria and Iraq 1968–1989* (London, 1990).

38. Radio Cairo, 26 April 1976; *al-Jumhuriyah* (Cairo), 27 April 1976.

39. President Anwar al-Sadat in an interview with *October*, 26 March 1978; Radio Cairo, 25 March 1978. See also Chapter 4.

40. Speech by President Hafiz al-Asad, Radio Damascus, 18 August 1977.

41. Cf. *Guardian*, 22 September 1977; *Arab Report and Record*, 16–30 September 1977, p. 798; *Afrique–Asie*, 7 February 1977. According to *Arab Report and Record*, 1–15 July 1977, p. 559, Alawis were then believed to hold about 18 of the 25 army commands, i.e. 72 per cent. This percentage corresponds with our own statistical findings. See Chapter 9.

6. Sectarian and regional factionalism in the Syrian political elite: a statistical analysis

1. The political entity Syria, within its present boundaries, was formed in January 1942. The cabinet which was then in power was the thirty-first since Syria's separation from the Ottoman Empire. Therefore, in Tables 1 and 4 the number of Cabinets since 1942 starts with No. 31. In Table 2, the ministers originating from the Alexandretta district (notably the Alawis Fa'iz Isma'il, Adham Mustafa and 'Adnan Mustafa) are for the sake of convenience included in the category of ministers from the Latakia region. See also Van Dam, *De Rol van Sektarisme, Regionalisme en Tribalisme*, pp. 31–45 and 200–202, for statistical details of individual Syrian governments and Syrian Regional Commands. See also: Alasdair Drysdale, 'The Regional Equalization of Health Care and Education in Syria since the Ba'thi Revolution', *International Journal of Middle East Studies*, Vol. 13 (1981), pp. 93–111; Alasdair Drysdale, 'The Syrian Political Elite, 1966–1976: A Spatial and Social Analysis', *Middle Eastern Studies*, Vol. 17 (1981), pp. 3–30; Hinnebusch, *Authorit-*

arian Power and State Formation in Ba'thist Syria, pp. 177–89; and Macintyre, *The Arab Ba'th Socialist Party*, pp. 205–330. In the present study, sectarian representation has been regionally subdivided in the statistical tables to determine the extent to which regional and sectarian representation overlap. For other studies on the Syrian political elite see Michael H. Van Dusen, 'Syria: Downfall of a Traditional Elite', in Frank Tachau (ed.), *Political Elites and Political Development in the Middle East* (New York, 1975), pp. 114–55; Gordon H. Torrey, 'Aspects of the Political Elite in Syria', in George Lenczowski (ed.), *Political Elites in the Middle East* (Washington, DC, 1975), pp. 151–61; Bayly Winder, 'Syrian Deputies and Cabinet Ministers, 1919–1959', *Middle East Journal*, Vol. 16, No. 4, Autumn 1962, pp. 407–29, and Vol. 17, No. 1, Winter 1963, pp. 35–54; M. Mohammed Sabet Mahayni, *L'Evolution constitutionelle de la Syrie indépendante* (Thèse pour le doctorat d'état, Paris, 1972); cf. Hasan al-Hakim, *Mudhakkirati. Safahat min Tarikh Suriyah al-Hadith 1920–1958* (Beirut, 1966), Vol. 2, pp. 147–282; George Faris (ed.), *Man huwa fi Suriyah, 1949* (Damascus, 1949); Faris (ed.), *Man huwa fi Suriyah, 1951* (Damascus, 1951); Faris (ed.), *Man Hum fi al-'Alam al-'Arabi, Vol. 1, Suriyah* (Damascus, 1957); Office de Presse Arabe et de Documentation (OFA), *2e Cabinet Mahmoud Ayoubi (1er Septembre 1974), Structure, Analyse et Biographies* (Damascus, 1974); *Who's Who in the Arab World*, Second Edition, 1967–1968 (Beirut, n.d.); C. Ernest Dawn, 'The Rise of Arabism in Syria', *Middle East Journal*, Vol. 16, No. 4, Autumn 1962, pp. 145–68.

2. Sami al-Jundi, *al-Ba'th*, pp. 136–7. See also Muta' Safadi, *Hizb al-Ba'th*, p. 340, who maintains that religion was the most important standard for promotion and for obtaining key positions in government institutions under Ba'thist rule in Syria.

3. Cf. Mark W. Cowell, *A Reference Grammar of Syrian Arabic* (Washington, DC, 1964), p. 4. See also Bernard Lewin, *Notes on Cabali: The Arabic dialect spoken by the Alawis of "Jebel Ansariye"* (Göteborg, 1969), p. 8, who notes: 'The 'Alawis are qaf-speakers and my informants ridiculed the "weak" hamza-speakers of Hama'.

4. Cf. Macintyre, *The Arab Ba'th Socialist Party*, p. 254.

5. Van Dusen, 'Syria: Downfall of a Traditional Elite', p. 139.

6. Macintyre, *The Arab Ba'th Socialist Party*, p. 234, Table 25: 'Representation of Religious Communities in the Government of the United Arab Republic, 1958–61'.

7. As mentioned above, Salah Jadid was strongly supported by a great many *Qutriyun*, who were heavily represented in the regions of Latakia, Hawran and Dayr al-Zur. See Chapter 2.

8. For a further analysis of the Ba'thist military and civilian elite under Hafiz al-Asad see Chapter 9.

7. Sectarian provocation and confrontation

1. Cf. *al-Ahram*, 13 February 1976, which reported the killing of Major Muhammad Ghurrah, head of security services in Hama.

2. *Al-Nadhir*, No. 2, 21 September 1979. Cf. *al-Ba'th*, 28 June 1979; and Eric Rouleau, 'Le Mécontentement Populaire Favorise le Renouveau de l'Islam Intégriste', *Le Monde*, 20 April 1979. See also Hans Günter Lobmeyer, 'Islamic ideology and secular discourse: the Islamists of Syria', *Orient*, Vol. 32 (1991), p. 396, who concludes that 'since the mid 1970s, practically simultaneously with the start of the

armed struggle, the Islamists have increasingly used a clearly secular discourse', and that Islam was much more 'the catalyst for but not the cause of the conflict.' For a study of the *Jihad* see Rudolph Peters, *Islam and Colonialism. The Doctrine of Jihad in Modern History* (The Hague, 1979).

3. *Al-Nadhir*, No. 1, 6 September 1979, p. 3.

4. *Al-Nadhir*, No. 6, 8 November 1979, p. 1.

5. David Hirst, 'Campaign of Terror is Leading to War', *Guardian*, 8 October 1979.

6. David Hirst, 'Divisive Rulers Threaten to Send Syria along Road to Civil War', *Guardian*, 26 June 1979; *al-Ba'th*, 24 June 1979, 1 July 1979. Cf. *al-Nadhir*, No. 10, 1 February 1980, pp. 10–11, where it is alleged that at the time of the Aleppo massacre only 60 out of the 320 cadets of the Aleppo artillery school were Sunnis and the remainder Alawis. Although a high percentage of Alawi cadets would not have been surprising, it seems very improbable that there would have been only Alawis and Sunnis. Hinting at a 'high percentage' of Sunni cadets at the air force academies, *al-Nadhir* on the other hand remarked that 'correct' admission procedures had been conscientiously applied there. Cf. *Haqa'iq 'an al-Ta'ifah al-Nusayriyah fi Suriyah* (n.p., n.d.), p. 9; *al-Ikhwan al-Muslimun ... yakshifun haqiqat al-Awda' fi Suriya* (n.p., n.d.), p. 6.

7. *Financial Times*, 28 June 1979.

8. Hirst, 'Divisive Rulers', 'Campaign of Terror' and 'Heads must Roll if Asad Clean-up Succeeds', *Guardian*, 9 October 1979.

9. Radio Damascus, 7 September 1979.

10. Hirst, 'Divisive Rulers'; *al-Nahar*, 25 June 1979; 'Vague d'Agitation Confessionelle en Syrie', *Le Monde Diplomatique*, October 1979; *al-Ikhwan al-Muslimun ... yakshifun Haqiqat al-Awda' fi Suriya*, p. 6; *Haqa'iq 'an al-Ta'ifah al-Nusayriyah fi Suriyah*, p. 9; Hizb al-Ittihad al-Ishtiraki al-'Arabi fi Suriyah, *al-Qutr al-Suri yamurr bi-Azmah Wataniyah Khatirah* (internal circular exclusively for members, Damascus, 1979). See also Hans Günther Lobmeyer, *Islamismus und sozialer Konflikt in Syrien*, pp. 19, 24–5, who reports that during the 1960s many Islamic-oriented school teachers succeeded in infiltrating the educational sector, because they were enabled to fill the gaps left by many Ba'thist teachers and sympathisers who were recruited at the time for the newly built Ba'thist bureaucracy. In the 1970s, following the purge of Salah Jadid and his supporters, the Islamists were provided with a similar opportunity, and thus succeeded in increasing their influence over students for some time.

11. Radio Damascus, 22 June 1979; *al-Ba'th*, 24 June 1979.

12. Radio Damascus, 27 June 1979.

13. Cf. Johannes Reissner, 'Die Andere Ablehnungsfront: Stimmen Radikal-islamischer Kreise zur Friedensinitiative Anwar as-Sadats', *Orient*, Vol. 21, No. 2, June 1979, pp. 19–41. For a study of the Muslim Brotherhood in Syria see Johannes Reissner, *Ideologie und Politik der Muslimbrüder Syriens. Von den Wahlen 1947 bis zum Verbot unter Adib al-Shishakli 1952* (Freiburg, 1980).

14. Radio Cairo, 10 July 1979. Three of those executed were explicitly accused of carrying out earlier assassinations.

15. Cf. *Nidal al-Sha'b*, Appendix to No. 210, mid-September 1979; Mahmud Sadiq, *Hiwar hawl Suriyah*, p. 169.

16. See Chapter 5. Propaganda attacks between Egypt and Syria were only briefly interrupted in 1976 when mutual relations improved temporarily.

17. See for instance *October*, 26 March 1978; *al-Ahram*, 6 April 1979, 15 May 1979, 6 June 1979.

18. Radio Cairo, 1 May 1979.

19. *Al-Akhbar*, 24 June 1979.

20. Radio Damascus, 30 June 1979; *al-Ba'th*, 1 July 1979.

21. Speech of President al-Asad at the opening session of the Seventh Syrian Regional Congress of the Ba'th Party in Damascus, Radio Damascus, 22 December 1979. Cf. *al-Nadhir*, No. 11, 21 February 1980. For a comment by the *Mujahidin* on al-Asad's speech of 22 December 1979 see *al-Nadhir*, No. 9, pp. 26–7. On al-Asad's description of the Muslim Brothers as 'heretics' they commented: 'The word "heretics' [*Haratiqah*] is usually not used by Muslims, except when describing the Nusayris and other freethinkers and atheists [*Zanadiqah*] like them.'

22. *Al-Ba'th*, 29 October 1979.

23. *Al-Ikhwan al-Muslimun ... yakshifun Haqiqat al-Awda' fi Suriya*, p. 6. Cf. Salah al-Din al-Bitar, 'Su'al al-Sa'ah: Ma huwa al-Badil?', *al-Ihya' al-'Arabi*, No. 16, 19 May 1980.

24. Radio Damascus, 23 March 1980. Cf. interview with President al-Asad in *al-Ra'y al-'Amm*, Kuwait, broadcast by Radio Damascus, 9 March 1980.

25. Radio Damascus, 17, 23 and 29 March 1980; *al-Ba'th*, 18 March 1980.

26. Speech of President al-Asad, Radio Damascus, 8 March 1980. Cf. *al-Nadhir*, No. 2, 21 September 1979, pp. 23–5; No. 3, 7 October 1979, p. 3; R. Stephen Humphreys, 'Islam and Political Values in Saudi Arabia, Egypt and Syria', *Middle East Journal*, Vol. 33, No. 1, Winter 1979, pp. 15–18; Michael C. Hudson, *Arab Politics. The Search for Legitimacy* (New Haven and London, 1977), pp. 251–67, 395, 397.

27. Hirst, 'Campaign of Terror'.

28. Internal circular issued by the Central Committee of the Syrian Communist Party (i.e. the Riyad al-Turk faction opposing the regime) in early June 1979.

29. *Economist*, 22 March 1980. Cf. *al-Nadhir*, No. 4, 22 October 1979, p. 3.

30. Hirst, 'Divisive Rulers'. Cf. Paul Maler (i.e. Michel Seurat), 'La Société Syrienne contre son État', *Le Monde Diplomatique*, April 1980, who notes that, according to two interviewed members of the Central Committee of the Ba'th Party in Syria, 'the twelve repressive campaigns which the Movement [of 23 February 1966, i.e. the Ba'thist supporters of imprisoned Alawi General Salah Jadid] has had to confront since 1970, are the best proof that it represents the most serious danger to the regime'. As explained earlier, Jadid's former power was based mainly on Ba'thist officers from the Alawi community.

31. Cf. Munif al-Razzaz, *al-Tajribah al-Murrah* (Beirut, 1967), p. 160, quoted at the beginning of this chapter.

32. Hizb al-Ittihad al-Ishtiraki al-'Arabi fi Suriyah, *al-Qutr al-Suri yamurr bi-Azmah Wataniyah Khatirah* (internal circular exclusively for members, Damascus, 1979). 'Haddadism' in this quotation refers to the movement of Lebanese Major Sa'd Haddad, who in 1979, under Israeli protection, proclaimed the 'Free Republic of Lebanon' in an area of southern Lebanon bordering on Israel. During the civil war Haddad had deserted from the Lebanese army, and took the law into his own hands in those areas of southern Lebanon which he was able to bring under his control. Cf. Nikolaos van Dam, 'Israel and Arab National Integration: Pluralism versus Arabism', *Asian Affairs*, Vol. 10 (Old Series Vol. 66), Part 2, June 1979, pp. 144–50.

33. *Guardian*, 26 June 1979.

34. Press statement of Hammud al-Shufi, Permanent Representative of the Syrian Arab Republic to the United Nations, announcing his resignation from that post on 27 December 1979. On the issue of corruption see also: Mahmud Sadiq, *Hiwar hawl Suriyah*; Yahya M. Sadowski, 'Patronage and the Ba'th: Corruption and Control in Contemporary Syria', *Arab Studies Quarterly*, Vol. 9, No. 4, 1987, pp. 442–61; Volker Perthes, 'The Syrian Private Industrial and Commercial Sectors and the State', *International Journal of Middle East Studies*, Vol. 24 (1992), pp. 214–15; Volker Perthes, *Staat und Gesellschaft in Syrien, 1970–1989*, pp. 232–237, 303–4; and Joseph Bahout, *Les Entrepreneurs Syriens. Economie, affaires et politique*, Beirut (Les Cahiers du CERMOC No. 7), 1994, pp. 64–8.

35. *Al-Munadil*, No. 129, January 1980, p. 95.

36. Ibid., pp. 95–6.

37. Ibid., p. 21; *al-Nahar al-'Arabi wa al-Duwali*, 14–20 January 1980.

38. Other Alawi military members of the Central Committee were Ibrahim Safi, Shafiq Fayyad, 'Ali al-Salih, 'Adnan Badr al-Hasan (*Al-Munadil*, No. 129, January 1980, pp. 128–9; *al-Ba'th*, 6 January 1980). At the Seventh Regional Congress, which was attended by 518 full members, 160 represented the armed forces, i.e. more than 30 per cent of all full member delegates. They included the president's cousin 'Adnan Ibrahim al-Asad (commander of the Struggle Companies – *Saraya al-Sira'*) and other prominent Alawi officers such as 'Abd al-Ghani Ibrahim, 'Ali Husayn, and Hikmat Ibrahim. President al-Asad's brother Jamil was one of the civilian participants. According to the Organisational Report presented to the Seventh Regional Congress, civilian full members of the Syrian party apparatus at the time of the Congress numbered 45,381. At the end of 1978, party members (including categories other than full members) were estimated to total 237,501 (*Al-Munadil*, No. 129, January 1980, pp. 11, 94).

39. The new Syrian Regional Command elected on 5 January 1980 contained 14 Sunnis (including 3 military), 4 Alawis (among whom 2 military), 2 Christians and 1 Druze. Cf. Maler, 'La Société Syrienne'.

40. See Tables 5 and 6 and Chapter 6. For the first time since February 1966, two (Sunni) officers from the Aleppo region were elected to the new Regional Command, i.e. General Hikmat al-Shihabi, who had replaced General Yusuf Shakkur as chief of staff in August 1974, and General Nasir al-Din Nasir, who was appointed minister of the interior in the cabinet of Dr 'Abd al-Ra'uf al-Kasm, which was installed on 14 January 1980. Cabinets Nos. 96–103 (1976–95) of (Sunni Damascene) Premiers 'Abd al-Rahman al-Khulayfawi (1976–8), Muhammad 'Ali al-Halabi (1978–80), Dr 'Abd al-Ra'uf al-Kasm (1980–87), and of Premier Mahmud al-Zu'bi (1987–95) (Sunni from Dar'a) have not been included in Table 2. From a sectarian point of view their compositions are roughly in line with the other cabinets of the al-Asad era. From a regional point of view the number of Damascenes increased strongly (to approximately 35 per cent) in the cabinets of Mahmud al-Zu'bi. Cf. Office Arabe de Presse et de Documentation, *Le 1er Cabinet de M. Abdel Raouf Al-Kassem, Structure et Biographies* (Damascus, 1980); *Le Deuxième Cabinet de M. Mahmoud al-Zou'bi du 29 Juin 1992* (Damascus, 1992).

41. Radio Damascus, 6 January 1980. A detailed programme was given in Premier Dr 'Abd al-Ra'uf al-Kasm's government policy statement on 18 February 1980 (Radio Damascus, 18 February 1980).

42. As described in Chapter 5.

43. For a discussion of the (in various aspects similar) relationship between sectarian, regional and socio-economic categories in Iraq, see Hanna Batatu, *The Old Social Classes and the Revolutionary Movements of Iraq. A study of Iraq's Old Landed and Commercial Classes and of its Communists, Ba'thists and Free Officers* (Princeton, 1978), and Peter Sluglett and Marion Farouk-Sluglett, 'Some Reflections on the Sunni/Shi'i Question in Iraq', *British Society for Middle Eastern Studies Bulletin*, Vol. 5, No. 2, 1978, pp. 79–87.

44. Cf. Nikolaos van Dam, 'Middle Eastern Political Clichés: "Takriti" and "Sunni rule" in Iraq; "Alawi rule" in Syria. A Critical Appraisal', *Orient*, Vol. 21, No. 1, January 1980, pp. 42–57.

45. R. Stephen Humphreys, 'Islam and Political Values in Saudi Arabia, Egypt and Syria', *Middle East Journal*, Vol. 33, No. 1, Winter 1979, p. 17.

46. *Al-Nadhir*, No. 10, 1 February 1980, p. 12. Cf. *al-Nadhir*, No. 9, 8 January 1980, pp. 14–17.

47. See *al-Ihya' al-'Arabi*, No. 16, 19 May 1980.

48. Cf. Habib 'Isa, *al-Suqut al-Akhir lil-Iqlimiyin fi al-Watan al-'Arabi* (Beirut, 1979); Ra'iq al-Naqri, *al-Sawt al-Hayawi, al-Hiwar al-Awwal* (Paris, 23 January 1980).

8. Sectarian showdown: eradication of the Muslim Brotherhood

1. *Al-Taqrir al-Tanzimi 1985*, pp. 21–2.

2. Patrick Seale, *Asad: The Struggle for the Middle East*, p. 327.

3. *al-Ra'y*, Amman, 26 February 1981. Within two weeks of the assassination attempt against President Hafiz al-Asad, on 7 July 1980, the Syrian People's Assembly passed Law 49, making membership of the Muslim Brotherhood a capital offence. On the occasion of the 25th anniversary of the al-Asad regime in 1995, many Muslim Brothers were given amnesty.

4. For a detailed account of the Palmyra massacre see: *Tadmur, al-Majzarah al-Mustamirrah*, Dar al-Nadhir, 3rd edition, 1984. This publication suggests that all participants in the massacre were Alawis; in itself not surprising as the Defence Companies of Rif'at al-Asad were mostly, if not exclusively, composed of Alawis. The confessions of the two participants caught in Jordan, 'Isa Ibrahim Fayyad and Akram Bishani, were published in *al-Ra'y* (Amman), 26 February 1981. The texts published in *al-Ra'y* differ somewhat from those published in *Tadmur, al-Majzarah al-Mustamirrah*. According to a Syrian intelligence report quoted by Michel Seurat, *L'Etat de Barbarie* (Paris, 1989), p. 91, the number of prisoners killed was 1181.

5. *Jordan Times*, 26–27 February 1981, *al-Ra'y*, 26 February 1981. Salah al-Din al-Bitar, co-founder of the Ba'th Party, was assassinated in Paris on 21 July 1980, following the publication of several critical articles in his opposition journal *al-Ihya' al-'Arabi* ('The Arab Revival', being the original name of the Ba'th Party before it was officially founded in 1947). See for instance al-Bitar's articles 'Suriyah Maridah Maridah wa ta'ish Mihnah wa Ma'sah' ('Syria is very ill and is living through an ordeal and tragedy'), and 'Su'al al-Sa'ah: Ma Huwa al-Badil?' ('The Question of the Moment: What is the Alternative?'), both published in *al-Ihya' al-'Arabi* in May 1980, Nos. 15 and 16.

6. *Bayan al-Thawrah al-Islamiyah fi Suriyah wa Minhajuha*, Damascus, 9 November 1980. For a partisan description and history of the Islamic fundamentalist

opposition movement in Syria, and a translation of the above-mentioned manifesto, see Umar F. Abd-Allah, *The Islamic Struggle in Syria*, Berkeley, 1983. For further details on the Islamic opposition see Raymond A. Hinnebusch, *Authoritarian Power and State Formation in Ba'thist Syria*, Oxford, 1990, pp. 276–300; Thomas Mayer, 'The Islamic opposition in Syria, 1961–1982', *Orient*, December 1983, pp. 589–609; Hans Günther Lobmeyer, *Islamismus und sozialer Konflikt in Syrien*, Berlin, 1990. On the links of the Syrian Islamic opposition with the rival Ba'th regime in Baghdad, see Eberhard Kienle, *Ba'th v Ba'th: The Conflict between Syria and Iraq 1968–1989*, London, 1990, pp. 155–63. Hans Günther Lobmeyer notes that 'the present and past role of the secular opposition is generally neglected, even though it contributed a great deal to the near overthrow of the Asad regime at the end of the 1970s and the beginning of the 1980s ... The secular opposition became active much earlier than the Islamists and suffered from persecution at a time when the regime took hardly any notice of the Muslim Brotherhood'. See H. G. Lobmeyer, '*Al-dimuqratiyya hiyya al-hall?* The Syrian Opposition at the End of the Asad Era', in: Eberhard Kienle (ed.), *Contemporary Syria*, London, 1994, p. 84. Cf. Tamam al-Barazi, *Milaffat al-Mu'aradah al-Suriyah*, Cairo, 1994.

7. Umar F. Abd-Allah, *The Islamic Struggle in Syria*, pp. 211–12; *Bayan al-Thawrah al-Islamiyah fi Suriyah wa Minhajuha*, pp. 11–12.

8. On 16 December 1980 Muslim Brotherhood *Mujahidin* assassinated Dr Yusuf Sa'igh in his clinic in Damascus, apparently assuming that he was the personal doctor of President Hafiz al-Asad. See Talas, *Mir'at Hayati, 1948–1958*, p. 627.

9. Seale, *Asad*, p. 331; *al-Diyar*, 11 June 1995.

10. See for instance: *Haqa'iq 'an al-Ta'ifah al-Nusayriyah fi Suriyah*, n.p., n.d.; Taqi Sharaf al-Din, *al-Nusayriyah: Dirasah Tahliliyah*, Beirut, 1983; numerous issues of *al-Nadhir*; Qahtan 'Abd al-Rahman al-Duri et al., *Al-Nusayriyah Harakah Hadmiyah* ('Nusayriyah is a Destructive Movement'), Baghdad, 1986, containing papers delivered at a symposium held under that name in Baghdad in 1985 under the auspices of the Iraqi minister of higher education and scientific research, obviously with the aim of helping to undermine the rival Ba'th regime in Damascus, although Baghdad did not usually resort to sectarian propaganda as a weapon; al-Husayni 'Abd Allah, *al-Judhur al-Tarikhiyah lil-Nusayriyah al-'Alawiyah*, Cairo, 1980; Gregor Voss, *"Alawiya oder Nusairiya?' – Schiitische Machtelite und sunnitische Opposition in der Syrischen Arabischen Republik*, dissertation, Hamburg, 1987; H. Halm, 'Nusayriyya', in: *The Encyclopaedia of Islam (New Edition)*, Vol. VIII, Leyden, 1993, pp. 145–8; and Antoine Audo, *Zaki al-Arsouzi: Un Arabe face à la modernité*, Beirut, 1988, pp. 138–42.

11. These included Muhammad Amin Ghalib al-Tawil, *Tarikh al-'Alawiyin* ('History of the Alawis'), Beirut, 1966 and 1979, with a preface by the well-known Alawi Shaykh 'Abd al-Rahman al-Khayyir. See also: Munir al-Sharif, *al-Muslimun al-'Alawiyun. Man Hum wa Ayna Hum?* ('The Alawi Muslims. Who and where are they?'), Damascus, 1961, 3rd edn. Cf. Mustafa al-Shak'ah, *Islam bila Madhahib*, Cairo (8th edn), 1991, pp. 321–73. Georges Jabbur, *Safita wa Muhituha fi al-Qarn al-Tasi' 'Ashar*, Damascus, 1993, pp. 30–3, argues that Arab, including Syrian, historians could do much more to improve 'the image of Syria as a country with a unified national spirit', also with respect to the nineteenth century, and that this spirit was much stronger than foreign writers have portrayed it. Cf. Daniel Pipes, *Greater Syria: The History of an Ambition*, Oxford, 1990, pp. 158–88, for a survey and account of various opinions circulating about the Syrian Alawis and their

perceived political behaviour and motives; and Martin Kramer, 'Syria's Alawis and Shi'ism', in: Martin Kramer (ed.), *Shi'ism, Resistance, and Revolution*, Boulder, CO, 1987, pp. 237–54, on the issue of whether or not Alawis should be considered as Shi'is.

12. Voss, *"Alawiya oder Nusairiya?"*, p. 62. See also my review of Voss' study in *Die Welt des Islams*, XXIX (1989), pp. 207–9.

13. Al-Shaykh 'Abd al-Rahman al-Khayyir, *'Aqidatuna wa Waqi'una; Nahnu al-Muslimin al-Ja'fariyin 'al-'Alawiyin'*, Damascus, 3rd edition, 1992, pp. 15–18. The study of 'Uthman Hashim, *al-'Alawiyun bayn al-Usturah wa al-Haqiqah*, occupies the first place of publications mentioned in the bibliography after the earlier studies of al-Shaykh al-Khayyir himself. From this it could be concluded that the study of 'Uthman was considered as a serious work in official Alawi religious circles. See also: *Min Turath al-Shaykh 'Abd al-Rahman al-Khayyir: Risalah Tabhath fi Masa'il Muhimmah Hawla al-Madhhab al-Ja'fari: (al-'Alawi)*, Damascus, 3rd edition, 1994. Cf. al-Shaykh Ahmad Muhammad Haydar, *al-A'mal al-Kamilah*, 3 vols, Tripoli (Lebanon), 1987, 1988, 1991. Other examples of 'apologetic' writings explaining Alawi religion and history are the works of al-Shaykh 'Ali 'Aziz al-Ibrahim, *al-'Alawiyun bayn al-Ghuluw wa al-Falsafah wa al-Tasawwuf wa al-Tashayyu'*, Beirut, 1995 (prefaced by the Lebanese Shi'i Imam al-Shaykh Muhammad Mahdi Shams al-Din); and Mahmud al-Salih, *al-Naba' al-Yaqin 'an al-'Alawiyin*, 2nd edn, Damascus, 1993.

14. The manuscript was finished in 1972; its first edition was posthumously published in Damascus in 1991 by the Shaykh's son, Hani al-Khayyir. See: *Min Turath al-Shaykh 'Abd al-Rahman al-Khayyir: Naqd wa Taqriz Kitab al-'Alawiyin*, Damascus, 1992, p. 7.

15. See: Sami al-Jundi, *al-Ba'th*, pp. 144–5.

16. Al-Maktab al-I'lami lil-Ikhwan al-Muslimin, *Hamah, Ma'sat al-'Asr* ('Hama, the Tragedy of the Era'), published by the National Alliance for the Liberation of Syria, n.p., n.d. The following account is based mainly on this report, as well as *Majzarat Hamah* ('The Hama Massacre') (Cairo, n.d.), Patrick Seale, *Asad*, pp. 332–4, and official statements by the Syrian authorities. See also Thomas Friedman, *From Beirut to Jerusalem*, London, 1989, Chapter 4, 'Hama Rules', pp. 76–105; David Roberts, *The Ba'th and the Creation of Modern Syria*, London, 1987, p. 128; Raymond Hinnebusch, *Authoritarian Power and State Formation in Ba'thist Syria*, pp. 291–300; Mahmud Sadiq, *Hiwar hawl Suriyah*, pp. 37–9, 163–7; Fred H. Lawson, 'Social Bases for the Hamah Revolt', *Merip Reports*, November/December 1982, pp. 24–8; and Hanna Batatu, 'Syria's Muslim Brethren', *Merip Reports*, November/December 1982, pp. 12–23.

17. Tadmur, *al-Majzarah al-Mustamirrah*, pp. 26–7; *Hamah, Ma'sat al-'Asr*, pp. 19–21. See also: Chapter 2, 'The Great Repression, 1976 to 1982', in: Middle East Watch, *Syria Unmasked*, pp. 8–21.

18. *Majzarat Hamah*, Cairo, 1984, pp. 20–23.

19. *Hamah, Ma'sat al-'Asr*, p. 149, gives the figure of 25,000, whereas Robert Fisk, the first foreign correspondent to visit Hama during the battles, gave the estimate of 12,000 (*Times*, 19 February 1982). For a detailed account see Robert Fisk, *Pity the Nation: Lebanon at War*, London, 1990, pp. 181–7, 411–12, 415.

20. *Hamah, Ma'sat al-'Asr*, pp. 25–32, 51–7, 65, 143–60.

21. Seale, *Asad*, p. 332.

22. *Ibid.*, pp. 332–3. Cf. Elisabeth Longuenesse, 'The Syrian Working Class

Today', *MERIP Reports*, No. 134, July–August 1985, p. 23, who has noted that 'recruited workers from the surrounding rural areas [of Hama] apparently supported the regime's assault against the revolt there because of the historical antagonism between city and countryside. The contradictions and the limitations of the trade union movement can be explained primarily by this situation.'

23. *Hamah, Ma'sat al-'Asr*, pp. 56–7, 65–6, 143–60.

24. *Al-Taqrir al-Tanzimi 1985*, pp. 371–2.

25. *Hamah, Ma'sat al-'Asr*, pp. 73–4, 92, 94, 151, 279–84. Cf. *Majzarat Hamah*, pp. 20–23. According to the exiled Kurdish author Ismet Chérif Vanly, the Defence Companies of Rif'at al-Asad not only included many Kurds, but even had special 'Kurdish units'. These participated in the suppression of the revolts of Aleppo and Hama reportedly even more brutally than did the Alawi members of the Defence Companies. Afterwards, according to Vanly, Muslim Brotherhood wall-graffiti appeared occasionally in Damascus and other Syrian cities, threatening both 'Alawis and Kurds' with revenge. After the banishment of Rif'at al-Asad from Syria in 1984, the Defence Companies were disbanded, and Kurdish members were reportedly reintegrated into the regular army. People from Hama who during the Hama battle of 1982 passed themselves off as Kurds were reportedly being saved by the so-called execution squads. See Ismet Chérif Vanly, *Kurdistan und die Kurden*, Vol. 3, Göttingen, 1988, pp. 15–16.

26. *Hamah, Ma'sat al-'Asr*, pp. 150–51.

27. Batatu, 'Some Observations on the Social Roots of Syria's Ruling Military Group and the Causes for its Dominance', *Middle East Journal*, Vol. 35, No. 3, Summer 1981, p. 332. See also Chapter 9.

28. *Al-Taqrir al-Tanzimi 1985*, p. 37, Table 3.

29. The Charter of the National Alliance for the Liberation of Syria was broadcast by Radio Baghdad on 22 March 1982. Hammud al-Shufi, formerly secretary-general of the Syrian Regional Command (1963), joined the National Alliance in March 1982.

30. Radio Baghdad, 22 March 1982; Raymond Hinnebusch, *Authoritarian Power and State Formation in Ba'thist Syria*, pp. 297–9; Eberhard Kienle, *Ba'th v Ba'th*, pp. 160–61; Thomas Mayer, 'The Islamic opposition in Syria, 1961–1982', *Orient*, Vol. 24, No. 4, December 1983, pp. 604–9; Hans Günther Lobmeyer, '*Al-Dimuqratiyya hiyya al-hall?* The Syrian Opposition at the End of the Asad Era', in: Eberhard Kienle (ed.), *Contemporary Syria*, London, 1994, pp. 85–6.

31. Radio Damascus, 7 March 1982; Mustafa Talas (ed.), *Kadhalika Qal al-Asad*, 6th edition, Damascus, 1993, pp. 311–12.

32. Raymond Hinnebusch, *Authoritarian Power and State Formation in Ba'thist Syria*, p. 297.

33. Thomas Friedman, *From Beirut to Jerusalem*, pp. 100–101.

9. The power elite under Hafiz al-Asad

1. On al-Asad's obsession with loyalty, see Patrick Seale, *Asad*, pp. 149, 179–83. It could be observed that absolutist rulers in the Arab world who have insisted on full loyalty have generally stayed longer in power than those who did not. President Hafiz al-Asad was born on 6 October 1930. Details on the officers directly subordinate to the 'old guard' of highest commanding officers are scarce.

2. The following account of the al-Asad brothers is based mainly on Patrick

Seale, *Asad*, chapter 24, 'The Brothers' War', pp. 421–40. Seale's study provides the most original and detailed analysis, and is based on extensive interviews with those directly involved, including President Hafiz al-Asad himself. See also: Alasdair Drysdale, 'The Succession Question in Syria', *Middle East Journal*, vol. 39, no. 2 (1985), pp. 246–62; and Mahmud Sadiq, *Hiwar hawl Suriyah*, pp. 216–22.

3. See Patrick Seale, 'Asad: Between Institutions and Autocracy', in: Richard T. Antoun and Donald Quataert (eds), *Syria: Society, Culture and Polity*, New York, 1991, p. 98.

4. Mahmud Sadiq, *Hiwar hawl Suriyah*, pp. 98, 222.

5. Ibid., pp. 217–19.

6. President al-Asad personally went down into the streets, and drove without guards or escorts to his brother's elaborately defended positions, ordering commanding officers to return to their barracks. President al-Asad was accompanied only by his eldest son Basil, then 22 years old. (Seale, *Asad*, p. 433; Sadiq, *Hiwar hawl Suriyah*, p. 218).

7. The action programme of the League of Higher Graduates was published in its periodical *al-Fursan*, Damascus, May 1983, pp. 37–9. The official title used for Rif'at at the time was: 'Comrade Doctor Rif'at al-Asad, member of the Regional Command of the Arab Ba'th Socialist Party, Leader of the Defence Companies and President of the League of Higher Studies Graduates'.

8. Mustafa Talas, *Mir'at Hayati, 1958–1968*, pp. 583–6, 893, 894. See also *al-Thawrah* and *Tishrin*, 7 May 1994; *al-Ba'th*, 2 August 1995; and Robert Fisk, 'Assad keeps brother in the cold', *Independent*, 22 October 1992.

9. Mahmud Sadiq, *Hiwar hawl Suriyah*, pp. 220–21.

10. Ibid., pp. 79–82.

11. *Al-Taqrir al-Tanzimi 1985*, p. 357. Cf. Volker Perthes, *The Political Economy of Syria under Asad*, London, 1995, p. 157.

12. The military members of the Central Committee chosen in 1985 are separately mentioned as a group in the list published in *al-Munadil*, No. 180–81, February 1985, and included next to President Hafiz al-Asad himself: 1. Lieutenant-General Mustafa Talas (minister of defence, Sunni, reelected fifteen years later to the Central Committee in 2000 [CC 2000]; retired in 2004; replaced by General Hasan Turkmani [CC 2000] reelected twenty years later in the Central Committee of 2005 [CC 2005] under President Bashar al-Asad), 2. Lieutenant-General Hikmat al-Shihabi (chief of staff, Sunni; retired in 1998; replaced by General 'Ali Aslan [CC 2000]), 3. Major-General Ibrahim Safi [CC 2000] (commander First Division, Alawi; since early 1994 commander of the Syrian armed forces in Lebanon; was succeeded by Major-General 'Ali Hasan, Alawi, who in 1995 was succeeded by Major-General Nadim 'Abbas, Alawi), 4. Major-General Shafiq Fayyad [CC 2000] (commander Third Division, Alawi; was transferred to another key unit in 1994 and succeeded by Major-General Hikmat Idris, Alawi), 5. Major-General Subhi Haddad (commander air force, Christian; later retired), 6. Major-General 'Adnan Sulayman Hasan [CC 2000] (also named 'Adnan Badr al-Hasan) (initially commander Ninth Division [in which function he was succeeded by Major-General Jihad Sulaytin, Alawi], later chief of political security, Alawi), 7. Lieutenant-General 'Ali Aslan [CC 2000] (deputy chief of staff, chief of operations, Alawi; later promoted to chief of staff and retired in 2002), 8. Major-General 'Ali al-Salih (commander air defence forces, Alawi), 9. Lieutenant-General 'Ali ('Isa) Duba (deputy chief of staff, chief of military intelligence, Alawi; retired in February 2000; replaced by Alawi Major General Hasan

Khalil [CC 2000]), 10. Major-General 'Ali Haydar (commander of the Special Forces, Alawi; was dismissed in August 1994 and replaced by the Alawi Major-General 'Ali Habib [CC 2000, 2005], who in 2004 was appointed as chief of staff and in 2008 as minister of defence), 11. General Fu'ad 'Absi (chief of civilian intelligence, Sunni; later died; in 1995 his function was occupied by Major-General Muhammad Bashir al-Najjar, Sunni; replaced in 1998 by Alawi Major General 'Ali al-Huri [CC 2000]), 12. Major-General Mustafa Tayyarah (commander of the naval forces, Sunni), 13. Lieutenant-General Hasan Turkmani [CC 2000, 2005] (deputy chief of staff, Sunni; later promoted to chief of staff and in 2004–2008 minister of defence), 14. Major-General 'Ali Malahafji (commander air force and air defence, Sunni; retired in 1994 to become director of the Military Studies Centre), 15. Major-General Muhammad al-Khawli (deputy commander air force, chief of air force intelligence, Alawi; promoted to commander air force in 1994), and 16. Major-General Muhammad Ibrahim al-'Ali [CC 2000, 2005] (commander of the People's Army, Alawi). Rif'at al-Asad, the president's brother, was also member of the Central Committee, as were all other members of the new Regional Command, but he no longer held a military position, except for being formally the vice-president for national security affairs. Rif'at had been given that title by presidential decree on 10 November 1984, but it did not imply any real power. (*al-Munadil*, No. 180–81, January–February 1985, pp. 122–4; *al-Munadil*, No. 129, January 1980, pp. 127–33).

13. Other military key supporters belonging to the inner circle of President Hafiz al-Asad in the mid-1990s were: Major-General Muhammad Nasif Khayr Bek, leader of the important Alawi Khayr Bek clan, chief of intelligence, in charge of security; Major-General 'Adnan Makhluf, Alawi, a cousin of al-Asad's wife (Anisah Makhluf), in command of the 10,000-strong presidential guard (replaced in 1995 by Major-General 'Ali Hasan [CC 2000], Alawi; Major-General 'Adnan Ibrahim al-Asad, Alawi, the president's cousin in charge of the Struggle Companies (*Saraya al-Sira'*); Brigadier Ghazi Kan'an, head of the Syrian security apparatus in Lebanon, Alawi; Major-General Ibrahim Huwayjah [CC 2000], chief of air force security, Alawi; and Alawi Major-General Bahjat Sulayman, director of internal security in the general security apparatus who during the latter part of Hafiz al-Asad's rule spoke out in favour of the succession of Bashar al-Asad; transferred in 2005 and replaced by Major-General Khayr Bek. In 1998 Bashar al-Asad's brother-in-law, Bushra al-Asad's Alawi husband Asif Shawkat, held a position in the military intelligence apparatus, from which he rose quickly to the rank of Major-General, becoming deputy chief of military intelligence in 2001. Under President Bashar al-Asad he became one of Syria's military strongmen. Bashar's brother, Mahir al-Asad [CC 2000, 2005] also held a key military position, just like Manaf Talas [CC 2000, 2005], son of General Mustafa Talas.

For (sometimes contradictory) details on the personalities and tribal backgrounds of some of al-Asad's hard core supporters see Patrick Seale, *Asad*, pp. 428–32; Alain Chouet, 'L'espace tribal alaouite à l'épreuve du pouvoir. La désintégration par le politique', *Maghreb-Machrek*, No. 147, January–March 1995, pp. 93–119; Hanna Batatu, 'Some Observations on the Social Roots of Syria's Ruling, Military Group and the Causes for its Dominance', *Middle East Journal*, Vol. 35, Summer 1981, pp. 331–2, and 'Syria's Muslim Brethren', *Merip Reports*, November/December 1982, p. 20; 'La Nomenklatura Syrienne', *Les Cahiers de l'Orient*, Paris, 1986, pp. 233–45. Cf. Alasdair Drysdale and Raymond A. Hinnebusch, *Syria and the Middle East Peace Process*, New York, 1991, pp. 28–9. According to Batatu, Muhammad al-Khawli, 'Ali

Duba, 'Ali Aslan and 'Ali al-Salih, like Hafiz al-Asad, all belong to the al-Matawirah tribe, whereas according to Chouet and Mahmud Sadiq, *Hiwar hawl Suriyah*, p. 222, they belong to different tribes. For details on the sectarian composition of the Syrian Regional Command elected in January 1985 see David Roberts, *The Ba'th and the Creation of Modern Syria*, pp. 165–6. (Fayiz al-Nasir, a Christian from Hawran, is incorrectly described by Roberts as Sunni).

14. Hani Khalil, *Hafiz al-Asad, al-Dawlah al-Dimuqratiyah al-Sha'biyah*, Damascus, 1992, p. 440.

15. Volker Perthes, *The Political Economy of Syria under Asad*, London, 1995, p. 182.

16. Alain Chouet, 'L'espace tribal alaouite à l'épreuve du pouvoir. La désintégration par le politique', *Maghreb-Machrek*, No. 147, January–March 1995, pp. 98–111.

17. Cf. Peter Gubser, 'Minorities in Power: The Alawites of Syria', in: R. D. McLaurin (ed.), *The Political Role of Minority Groups in the Middle East*, New York, 1979, pp. 26–35; Mahmud A. Faksh, 'The Alawi Community of Syria: A New Dominant Political Force', *Middle Eastern Studies*, Vol. 20, No. 2, 1984, pp. 136–40. Safuh al-Akhras, *Tarkib al-'A'ilah al-'Arabiyah wa Waza'ifuha: Dirasah Midaniyah li-Waqi' al-'A'ilah fi Suriyah*, Damascus, 1976, p. 26, distinguishes seven levels of tribal relationships, according to closeness of blood-ties: 1. the restricted family (*al-'A'ilah al-Muhaddadah*), 2. the extended family (*al-'A'ilah al-Mumtaddah*), 3. *al-Hammulah* (a number of extended families), 4. *al-Fakhdh* (a tribal sub-section consisting of a number of *Hammulah*'s), 5. *al-Batn* (a tribal branch), 6. *al-'Ashirah* (a tribal confederation), 7. *al-Qabilah* (super-tribe).

18. Haytham Manna, 'Syria: Accumulation of Errors?', *Middle Eastern Studies*, Vol. 23, No. 2, April 1987, p. 211; Patrick Seale, *Asad*, p. 9; Hanna Batatu, 'Some Observations on the Social Roots of Syria's Ruling Military Group and the Causes for its Dominance', *The Middle East Journal*, vol. 35, no.3 (1981), p. 332; Mahmud A. Faksh, 'The Alawi Community of Syria: A New Dominant Political Force', *Middle Eastern Studies*, Vol. 20, No. 2, 1984, pp. 146, 153. Cf. Daniel Le Gac, *La Syrie du général Assad*, Brussels, 1991, p. 78–80; Alain Chouet, 'L'espace tribal alaouite à l'épreuve du pouvoir. La désintégration par le politique', *Maghreb-Machrek*, No. 147, January–March 1995, p. 96. Munir al-Sharif, *Al-Muslimun al-'Alawiyun. Man Hum? wa Ayn Hum?*, p. 122, mentions the al-Asad family as belonging to the Kalbiyah. Cf. Munir Mushabik Mousa, *Etude Sociologique des 'Alaouites ou Nusairis*, p. 567, who notes that the 'Kalbiyah clan' used to 'make use of Numaylatiyah shaykhs of the Matawirah to organise and celebrate religious ceremonies.'

19. Patrick Seale, *Asad*, p. 9.

20. Ibid. Cf. Munir Mushabik Mousa, *Etude Sociologique des 'Alaouites ou Nusairis*, pp. 16–24, 541–84.

21. See tables 8 and 9, quoted from the Organisational Report 1985. The fourth, sixth and last columns of table 9 give the percentages of the total membership and population, and have been added to the original for further clarification. Hizb al-Ba'th al-'Arabi al-Ishtiraki, al-Qutr al-'Arabi al-Suri, al-Qiyadah al-Qutriyah, *Taqarir al-Mu'tamar al-Qutri al-Thamin wa Muqarraratuh, al-Mun'aqid fi Dimashq fi al-Fatrah al-Waqi'ah bayn 5/1/1985-20/1/1985: al-Taqrir al-Tanzimi* (Damascus 1985), hereafter quoted as *al-Taqrir al-Tanzimi 1985*, pp. 56, 57; Syrian Arab Republic, Office of the Prime Minister, Central Bureau of Statistics, *Statistical Abstract 1992*, pp. 52, 61. In calculating the percentage of full party members per

regional party branch the members of the party branches of the Security Forces and the Universities of Damascus, Aleppo, and Latakia ('October University') mentioned in table 8 have been excluded, as they do not give any clear indication of the regional backgrounds of its members. Figures on sex have been dropped, as they fall outside the scope of this study. In table 9, quoted from the Organisational Report 1985, the party members of the Universities of Damascus, Aleppo and Latakia have, however, been added to the respective local party branches, thereby giving for Damascus and Aleppo in particular a substantially higher percentage of total membership than would be justified on basis of the respective number of autochthonous members. See also Raymond Hinnebusch, *Authoritarian Power and State Formation in Ba'thist Syria*, pp. 177–89, for an analysis of the social composition of the Ba'th Party membership based on the organisational report of 1985. On the sectarian composition of the population of the Golan before the Israeli occupation see: Adib Sulayman Bagh, *al-Jawlan: Dirasah fi al-Jughrafiyah al-Iqlimiyah*, Damascus, 1984, pp. 257–92, who gives the following rough estimates: Sunnis 80 per cent, Druzes 10 per cent, Alawis 4 per cent, and Christians 5 per cent.

22. *Al-Taqrir al-Tanzimi 1985*, pp. 36, 37, 57.

23. Ibid., pp. 332–3.

24. Ibid., p. 37. In the same report, pp. 371–2, it is alleged that the armed forces were hardly affected by the confrontations with the Muslim Brotherhood. See Chapter 8 above.

25. *Al-Taqrir al-Tanzimi 1985*, p. 333.

26. Cf. *al-Munadil*, No. 129, January 1980, pp. 11, 94. See Chapter 7. According to Volker Perthes, *The Political Economy of Syria under Asad*, p. 155, 'by 1992, party membership was put at around one million, a quarter of them full members.'

27. *Al-Taqrir al-Tanzimi 1985*, p. 351.

28. Raymond A. Hinnebusch, *Authoritarian Power and State Formation in Ba'thist Syria: Army, Party and Peasant*, pp. 155, 162, 301–24.

29. Shortly after Basil's death, several books were devoted to his memory. See: Riyad Sulayman 'Awwad, *al-Shahid al-Hayy Basil al-Asad* ('The Living Martyr Basil al-Asad'), Damascus, 1994; Ghazi al-Musa, *Manarat al-Ajyal: Basil Hafiz al-Asad* ('Basil Hafiz al-Asad: The Light of the Generations'), Damascus, 1994; *al-Ba'th*, special commemorative issue devoted to Basil al-Asad, March 1994; Bahjat Sulayman, *al-Manzumah al-Fikriyah lil-Batal Basil al-Asad*, Damascus, 1994; *Shahadat fi Ma'alim al-Shahid Basil al-Asad*, Damascus, 1994. Cf. *al-Diyar*, 20 April, 23 August 1994 and 17 May 1995.

30. *Al-Thawrah*, 19 February 1994; *Tishrin*, 21 February 1994.

31. Cf. Elizabeth Picard, 'Infitâh économique et transition démocratique en Syrie', in: R. Bocco and M.-R. Djalili (eds), *Moyen-Orient: migrations, démocratisation, médiations*, Paris, 1994, p. 234; Alain Chouet, 'L'espace tribal alaouite à l'épreuve du pouvoir. La désintégration par le politique', *Maghreb-Machrek*, No. 147, January–March 1995, pp. 112–16. The most high-profiled member of the *Awlad al-Sultah* (sons of those in power) who went into bussiness was Rami Makhluf (maternal cousin of Bashar al-Asad). He became one of Syria's most prominent bussinessmen. The sons of Generals Bahjat Sulayman, Hasan al-Turkmani (Bilal) and Mustafa Talas, as well as of 'Abd al-Halim Khaddam should also be mentioned as prominent *Awlad al-Sultah*, just like the immediate members of the al-Asad family (Asif Shawkat, Bushra al-Asad and Mahir al-Asad) and the members of the extended clan. See Salwa Ismail, 'Changing Social

Structure, Shifting Alliances and Authoritarianism in Syria', in Fred Lawson (ed.), *Demystifying Syria*, London, 2009, pp. 13–28.

32. Cf. *al-Hayat*, 27 September 1994; *The Middle East*, October 1994, p. 19; *Jane's Intelligence Review*, Vol. 7, No. 3, March 1995, pp. 126–7; and 'Imad Fawzi Shu'aybi, 'Kayfa Yahkum al-Ra'is al-Asad ... Biladah?', *al-Diyar*, 23 August 1994. Volker Perthes, *The Political Economy of Syria under Asad*, p. 153, notes that President Hafiz al-Asad 'has repeatedly proved that he can strip any military and security strongman of his position ... He also proved capable of dissolving power centres that tended to become independent'. The dismissal of General 'Ali Haydar could be seen as an illustration of this point.

33. Cf. *al-Hayat*, 22 February, 25 August, 6 and 27 September, 1 and 19 November 1994, 21 January 1995; *al-Ba'th*, 18 November 1994; *Le Monde*, 16 August 1994; Ben Wedeman, 'Basil's Sudden Death Threatens Syria's future', *The Middle East Times*, 31 January–6 February 1994; *al-Ahram*, 3, 4 March, 23 December 1994; *Funun*, Damascus, 2 May 1994; *The Middle East*, October 1994, p. 19; Alasdair Drysdale & Raymond A. Hinnebusch, *Syria and the Middle East Peace Process*, p. 29; cf. 'Izzat al-Sa'dani, *Basil fi 'Uyun al-Misriyin*, Cairo, 1995, pp. 178, 261–85; *al-Basil lan Yaghiba Abadan*, special issue of *Majallat Iqtisadiyat Halab*, January 1995, p. 89.

34. Ibrahim Hamidi, 'Milaffan Barizan: Lubnan wa Muharabat al-Fasad. al-Ra'id Bashar al-Asad Yaqtahim al-'Amal al-Siyasi', *al-Wasat*, No. 170, 1 May 1995. Cf. *Time*, 5 December 1994, which described Bashar al-Asad in '*The Time Global Leadership 100*' as 'inevitably ... the leading candidate to succeed the man who has ruled Syria for the past 24 years ... In Damascus, hopes are that [Bashar] ... will bring new vision to bear if he takes over the reins of a country that will play a pivotal role in any lasting Middle East peace'. See also 'Imad Fawzi Shu'aybi, 'Bashar al-Asad Najm Akhlaqi fi 'Alam al-Siyasah', *al-Shu'lah*, 16 September 1994, pp. 50–53.

35. On Bashar's meetings with, among others, the Lebanese president and the president of Lebanese Parliament, see *al-Hayat*, 22, 23, 24, 26 May, 2 June, 29 July, and 4 August 1995; *al-Hawadith*, 9 June 1995; *al-Shu'lah*, 16 September 1994. Another event symbolising strong Lebanese–Syrian governmental cooperation under full Syrian tutelage and hegemony over Lebanon was the inauguration on 1 October 1995 of a large memorial statue of Basil al-Asad in the centre of the Lebanese town of Chtaura in the Beqaa valley, on the road between Beirut and Damascus. The ceremony was held under the auspices of Lebanese President Elias al-Harawi, and was attended from the Syrian side by minister of information Dr Muhammad Salman (Alawi), representing President Hafiz al-Asad, and by Generals Ibrahim Safi and Ghazi Kan'an. In the speech given on behalf of the Lebanese president, appreciation was expressed for President Hafiz al-Asad's role in helping end the Lebanese civil war; with the death of Basil al-Asad, 'the torch was passed on to Dr Bashar'. See *al-Ba'th* and *al-Hayat*, 2 October 1995.

36. When asked in an interview in 1995 whether he considered himself to be a candidate for the Syrian presidency and was preparing himself for it, Bashar (at the time twenty-nine years old) modestly replied: 'It seems that those who mention this do not know Syria and have not read its Constitution which stipulates that those who put themselves up as a candidate for the presidency must have reached the age of forty'. Cf. *Al-Hayat*, 30 July 1995. Earlier, the Syrian author 'Imad Fawzi Shu'aybi had published a supportive editorial in the pro-Syrian Lebanese daily *al-Diyar*, claiming that Bashar had 'the mind of a grown-up man aged over forty, and was thereby

creating the impression among the Syrian people that Dr Bashar was the most ideal [successor] to President al-Asad'. See 'al-Ra'is al-Asad Madrasah fi al-Hakim al-Mas'ul wa Abna'uh Tullab Nujaba' fi Madrasatih', *al-Diyar*, 20 April 1995.

37. *Al-Hayat*, 10 February 1995. Cf. *al-Thawrah*, 19 January 1994; *Tishrin*, 21 February 1994.

38. According to Human Rights Watch/Middle East, Vol. 7, No. 4, July 1995, *Syria, the Price of Dissent*, p. 43, families of some political prisoners at the time 'resorted to visible pro-government gestures to keep security forces away ... [by] putting up pictures of Basil Asad.'

39. See: special issue of *Syria Times*, 13 November 1992.

40. *Al-Munadil*, No. 302, May–June 2000, quoted in: Radwan Ziadeh, *Rabi' Dimashq: Qadaya, Ittijahat, Nihayat*, Cairo, 2007; Radwan Ziadeh, *Power and Policy in Syria*, London, 2010, pp. 45–8. In the Central Committee chosen by the Regional Congress on 20 June 2000 the Alawi military were, as before, very strongly represented. They included the Alawi generals 'Ali Aslan, Ibrahim Safi, Shafiq Fayyad, Tawfiq Jallul, 'Ali Habib, 'Adnan Badr al-Hasan, Hasan Khalil, Ibrahim Huwayjah, Mahir al-Asad and 'Ali al-Huri.

41. Alasdair Drysdale, 'The Succession Question in Syria', *Middle East Journal*, Vol. 39, No. 2, Spring 1985, pp. 246–62; Alasdair Drysdale and Raymond A. Hinnebusch, *Syria and the Middle East Peace Process*, pp. 35–6. Cf. Volker Perthes, *The Political Economy of Syria under Asad*, pp. 250, 267–71.

42. David Roberts, *The Ba'th and the Creation of Modern Syria*, London, 1987, p. 145.

43. Cf. Daniel Pipes, 'Syrie: L'Après-Assad', *Politique Internationale*, 1993, p. 107.

44. Cf. Raymond Hinnebusch, 'State and Civil Society in Syria', *Middle East Journal*, Vol. 47, No. 2, Spring 1993, pp. 256–7; Raymond Hinnebusch, 'State, Civil Society, and Political Change in Syria', in: A. R. Norton (ed.), *Civil Society in the Middle East*, Vol. 1, Leyden, 1995, pp. 214–42.

In his study on 'Sects, Ethnicity, and Minority Groups in the Arab World' Sa'd al-Din Ibrahim concludes that 'the way out of the present dilemmas of all Arab states, but especially those with marked ethnic diversity, is a triangular formula of civil society, democracy and federalism. This strength would be further enhanced by regional peace and economic co-operation. In the mid 1990s, all the ingredients are present.' Sa'd al-Din Ibrahim, *al-Milal wa al-Nihal wa al-A'raq: Humum al-Aqalliyat fi al-Watan al-'Arabi*, Cairo, 2nd edn, 1994, pp. 16, 763. In Ibrahim's study the concept of federalism refers particularly to states with large ethnic minorities such as Iraq and Sudan. In the case of Syria, a combination of civil society and democracy would have to provide a solution.

45. Eberhard Kienle (ed.), *Contemporary Syria*, p. 10.

46. Volker Perthes, 'Stages of Economic and Political Liberalization', in: Eberhard Kienle (ed.), *Contemporary Syria*, pp. 70–71. Cf. Elizabeth Picard, 'Infitâh économique et transition démocratique en Syrie', in: R. Bocco and M.-R. Djalili (eds), *Moyen-Orient: migrations, démocratisation, médiations*, Paris, 1994, pp. 221–36; and Steven Heydemann, 'Taxation without Representation: Authoritarianism and Economic Liberalization in Syria', in: E. Goldberg, R. Kasaba and J. Migdal (eds), *Rules and Rights in the Middle East: Democracy, Law, and Society*, Seattle & London, 1993, pp. 100–101, who argues that economic reforms have bolstered the resiliency of the authoritarian regime by enhancing its patronage resources.

10. Conclusions

1. Cf. Volker Perthes, 'The Political Sociology of Syria: a Bibliographical Essay', *The Beirut Review*, 4, 1992, pp. 105-113; Joshua Landis, 'The Political Sociology of Syria Reconsidered: a Response to Volker Perthes', *The Beirut Review*, 5, 1993, pp. 143-51; Volker Perthes, 'Einige kritische Bemerkungen zum Minderheitenparadigma in der Syrienforschung', *Orient* 31/4 (1990), pp. 571-82; Elizabeth Picard, 'Y a-t-il un problème communautaire en Syrie?', *Maghreb-Machrek* 87 (janvier-mars 1980), pp. 7-21, and 'Critique de l'usage du concept d'*ethnicité* dans l'analyse des processus politiques dans le monde arabe', in: *Etudes politiques du monde arabe*, Cairo (CEDEJ), 1991, pp. 71-84; Raymond Hinnebusch, 'Class and State in Ba'thist Syria', in: Richard T. Antoun and Donald Quataert (eds.), *Syria: Society, Culture and Polity*, New York, 1991, pp. 29-47.

2. Elizabeth Picard notes that 'reflecting upon the longevity of some Arab military regimes, one should consider the huge technological progress of their armies and wonder whether the "stability" which has been remarked on since 1970 does not owe much to an increasingly pervasive state machinery, and especially state police'. See Elizabeth Picard, 'Arab Military in Politics: from Revolutionary Plot to Authoritarian State', in: Albert Hourani, Philip Khoury and Mary C. Wilson (eds), *The Modern Middle East: A Reader* (London, 1993), pp. 562-3. Cf. Andrew Rathmell, *Secret War in the Middle East: The covert struggle for Syria, 1949-1961* (London, 1995), p. 160, who notes that the world portrayed in his book dealing with the period 1949-61, 'a world of amateur spies, casual plotters, hot-headed officers and part-time terrorists, is long gone. Since at least the 1970s the Middle East's underworld has become a more serious, professional and deadly milieu … The Arab intelligence and security services, like their states, have become institutionalised, bureaucratised and increasingly ruthless. As states have tightened their grip on society these agencies have grown and their role expanded.'

3. Patrick Seale, *Asad*, p. 439.

4. Patrick Seale, 'Asad: Between Institutions and Autocracy', in: Richard T. Antoun and Donald Quataert (eds), *Syria: Society, Culture, and Polity*, p. 97.

5. Hanna Batatu, 'Some Observations on the Social Roots of Syria's Ruling, Military Group and the Causes for its Dominance', p. 344.

6. Cf. Samir 'Abduh, *Taryif al-Madinah al-'Arabiyah wa Madnanat al-Rif* ('Ruralisation of the Arab City and Urbanisation of the Countryside'), Damascus, 1989.

7. Hanna Batatu, 'Some Observations on the Social Roots of Syria's Ruling Military Group and the Causes for its Dominance', p. 337.

8. Volker Perthes, *The Political Economy of Syria under Asad*, pp. 268-9, claims that Basil al-Asad, unlike the generation of officers from peasant families that took power in the 1960s, was 'very much a Damascene, brought up, educated and networked in the capital, a facet which many conservative Damascenes overtly appreciated.' While Perthes seems correct in stating that Basil 'had, in fact, gained a certain popularity that by far exceeded the Alawi community', it remains doubtful whether he was really accepted by the autochthonous Damascenes as their own. It may be significant that after his death, Basil was not buried in his native Damascus, but in his father's birthplace al-Qardahah in the Alawi mountains. Cf. Ibrahim 'Umayri, *Silsilat al-Jibal al-Sahiliyah*, Damascus, 1995, p. 5.

9. Cf. Alasdair Drysdale, 'The Regional Equalization of Health Care and Education in Syria since the Ba'thi Revolution', *International Journal of Middle East Studies*, Vol. 13 (1981), pp. 93-111. It should be noted that living conditions in various parts of the Alawi mountains have remained extremely poor.

10. Raymond A. Hinnebusch, 'Class and State in Ba'thist Syria', in: Richard T.
Antoun and Donald Quataert (eds), *Syria: Society, Culture and Polity*, pp. 46–7. For a
thorough analysis of the changes in the socio-economic basis of the Ba'th regime, see:
Volker Perthes, *Staat und Gesellschaft in Syrien, 1970–1989*, pp. 36, 81, 220–22. See
also Elisabeth Longuenesse, 'The Class Nature of the State in Syria', *MERIP Reports*
No. 77, May 1979, pp. 3–11, 'The Syrian Working Class Today', *MERIP Reports*, No.
15, July-August 1985, pp. 17–25, and 'Les médecins syriens, des médiateurs dans une
société en crise?', in: Elisabeth Longuenesse (ed.), *Santé, Médecine et Société dans le
Monde Arabe*, Paris, 1995.

11. Raymond A. Hinnebusch, 'Class and State in Ba'thist Syria', in: Richard Antoun
and Donald Quataert (eds), *Syria: Society, Culture and Polity*, p. 43.

12. Volker Perthes, 'The Bourgeoisie and the Ba'th', *Middle East Report*, May-June
1991, pp., 31–7; and Volker Perthes, *Staat und Gesellschaft in Syrien, 1970–1989*, p.
283.

13. Cf. Volker Perthes, *Staat und Gesellschaft in Syrien, 1970–1989*, pp. 264–5,
275–80, who notes that a majority of the population seemed to take an indifferent
attitude towards the Ba'th Party and government.

14. See: Fa'iz Isma'il in his preface to Fu'ad al-'Asha, *Hafiz al-Asad: Qa'id wa
Risalah*, Damascus, 1993, p. 37.

15. See the works of Hamidi al-'Abd Allah, Fu'ad al-'Asha, Riyad Sulayman
'Awwad, Lucien Bitterlin, Ahmad 'Abd al-Salam Dabbas, 'Adil Hafiz, Hani Khalil,
Ghazi al-Musa, Safwan Qudsi, Qasim al-Rabdawi, 'Adil Rida, Ayman Sha'ban,
Mustafa Talas and others, in the bibliography.

16. Cf. Raymond A. Hinnebusch, *Authoritarian Power and State Formation in
Ba'thist Syria: Army, Party and Peasant*, p. 321.

17. In his study on 'Sects, Ethnicity, and Minority Groups in the Arab World',
published in early 1994, Sa'd al-Din Ibrahim argues that 'all the world's conflicts
since 1988, with the possible exception of Iraq's invasion of Kuwayt, have been over
internal ethnic issues ... The global awareness of the explosive nature of ethnic
politics was no doubt a factor in expediting the passage of the United Nations
General Assembly *Declaration on the Rights of Persons Belonging to National or Ethnic,
Religious and Linguistic Minorities*, adopted on 18 December 1992' (Resolution
47/135). See: Sa'd al-Din Ibrahim, *al-Milal wa al-Nihal wa al-A'raq: Humum
al-Aqalliyat fi al-Watan al-'Arabi*, Cairo, 2nd edn, 1994, p. 6. How sensitive the issue
of minorities was still perceived to be in Arab nationalist and other circles in the
1980s and 1990s can, according to Sa'd al-Din Ibrahim, be concluded from the fact
that it took the Centre for Arab Unity Studies (*Markaz Dirasat al-Wahdah
al-'Arabiyah*) in Beirut more than six years to decide not to publish his book, because
after having sought all kinds of third opinions it (not surprisingly) turned out to be
impossible to issue a so-called 'objective' version, considered satisfactory by all the
parties described.

11. Syrian Ba'thist memoirs

1. Munif al-Razzaz, *al-Tajribat al-Murrah*, Beirut, Dar Ghandur, 1967. Also
published in *Al-A'mal al-Fikriyah wa al-Siyasiyah*, Mu'assasat Munif al-Razzaz
lil-Dirasat al-Qawmiyah, n.p., 1986, Vol. 2, pp. 5–308.

2. Sami al-Jundi, *al-Ba'th*, Beirut, Dar al-Nahar, 1969.

3. See also Jalal al-Sayyid, *Hizb al-Ba'th al-'Arabi*, Beirut, 1973; Fa'iz Isma'il, *Ma'a Bidayat al-Ba'th*, Damascus, 1980; Muslih Salim, *Man Yasna' al-Aqdar* (novel), Damascus, 1975; and others.

4. General (al-Liwa') Muhammad 'Umran, *Tajribati fi al-Thawrah* (*My Experience in the Revolution*), n.p., 1970 (445 pages).

5. Mansur Sultan al-Atrash, *al-Jil al-Mudan. Sirah Dhatiyah*, Beirut, 2008, pp. 348, 393.

6. General (al-'Imad) Mustafa Talas, *Mir'at Hayati* (*The Mirror of my Life*), 5 Parts, Parts 1–3, Damascus, Dar Talas, 1991–2003; Part 4, Beirut, Dar al-Dhakirah, 2004; Part 5, Damascus, Dar Talas, 2008 (4651 pages).

7. Part 4 of *Mir'at Hayati* was published, however, in Beirut by Dar al-Dhakirah instead of by Talas's own publishing house (Dar Talas) in Damascus, apparently because it contained elements which were considered too sensitive at the time. The second edition of Part 4 was published in Damascus by Dar Talas in 2007.

8. http://www.jablah.com/modules/news/article.php?storyid=2288 (accessed 20 October 2010).

9. Marwan Habash also refers to a third abortive attempt by Salim Hatum in *Muhawalat 'Usyan al-Ra'id Salim Hatum fi al-Suwayda' Yawm 8 Aylul 1966 (2/4)*, *Kulluna Shuraka' fi al-Watan*, 8 June 2008.

10. Muhammad Ibrahim al-'Ali, *Hayati wa al-I'dam* (*My Life and Execution*), 3 vols, Damascus, 2007 (1700 pages).

11. Marwan Habash provides many interesting details not published before in *Muhawalat 'Usyan al-Ra'id Salim Hatum fi al-Suwayda' Yawm 8 Aylul 1966 (1/4)*, *Kulluna Shuraka' fi al-Watan*, 7 June 2008, and *al-Ba'th wa Thawrat Adhar*, Damascus, 2011, pp. 243–65. See also Nikolaos van Dam, *al-Sira' 'ala al-Sultah fi Suriya*, Arabic electronic edition, pp. 82–8.

12. Walid Hamdun, *Dhikrayat wa Ara'*, Damascus, 2007, p. 104.

13. From the side of the *Murshidiyin* the bridging role of Muhammad Ibrahim al-'Ali has been confirmed as well. Nur al-Mudi' al-Murshid (son of Salman al-Murshid) notes that after the 8 March 1963 revolution various Ba'th Party leaders, including Muhammad Ibrahim al-'Ali, asked Saji al-Murshid, the leader of the *Murshidiyin*, to request his followers to collectively join the Ba'th Party. Saji (elder son of Salman al-Murshid) answered that it was up to the Ba'th Party itself to recruit new members amongst the *Murshidiyin*. After all, if they would be instructed by the *Murshidiyin* leadership to join the party, their membership would not be based on conviction. Saji added, 'If you believe that the *Murshidiyin* will join the Ba'th Party on my orders, don't you believe that I can also order them to leave the Party just like they entered it?' Nevertheless, the *Murshidiyin* were encouraged by their leadership to join the Ba'th Party and many did so. See Nur al-Mudi' Murshid, *Lamahat hawla al-Murshidiyah* (*Dhikrayat wa Mushahadat wa Watha'iq*), Beirut, 2008, pp. 360–65, 397.

14. General (al-'Amid) Walid Hamdun, *Dhikrayat wa Ara'* (*Memories and Views*), Damascus, 2007 (400 pages).

15. Qaws Qazah, *Mustafa Talas: Ba'd 75 'Aman: Radin 'an Kulli ma Qumtu bihi*, *Jablah*, 9 June 2007, http://www.jablah.com/modules/news/article.php?storyid=2288 (accessed 20 October 2010).

16. Muhammad Haydar, *al-Ba'th wa al-Baynunat al-Kubra* (*The Ba'th and the Great Disunity*), n.p, 1998 (238 pages).

17. General (al-Fariq) Amin al-Hafiz, *Al-Inqilabat fi Suriya kama yaraha Amin*

al-Hafiz (*The Coups in Syria as Seen by Amin al-Hafiz*), interviews by Ahmad Mansur, *Al-Jazeera*, 2001; http://www.aljazeera.net/NR/exeres/3E3413BB-03BD-48B7-B9B2-951B0E0C754C.htm (accessed 20 October 2010).

18. Akram al-Hawrani, *Mudhakkirat Akram al-Hawrani*, Cairo, Maktabat Madbuli, 2000, pp. 3240–43.

19. Marwan Habash, *Heikal wa Cohen ... wa al-Iftira' 'ala al-Haqiqah*, *Kulluna Shuraka' fi al-Watan*, 23 April 2009; http://all4syria.info/content/view/7574/104 (accessed 20 October 2010); *Qadaya wa Ara'*, Damascus, 2010, pp. 239–51.

20. See the detailed interview with Nabil Shuwayri, *Suriyah wa Hutam al-Marakib al-Muta'aththirah: Hiwar ma' Nabil Shuwayri, Rafiq 'Aflaq wa al-Hawrani*, n.p., n.d. (99 pages); http://www.jablah.com/modules/news/article.php?storyid=22 (accessed 20 October 2010); Yusuf Zu'ayyin, *Yusuf Zu'ayyin yaftah Khazanat Asrarihi ba'd 40 'Aman*, http://www.alarabiya.net/articles/2005/06/07/13742.html (accessed 10 July 2010); and the interviews about Michel 'Aflaq by Ghassan Sharbal with 'Aflaq's daughter Razzan and leading Lebanese Ba'thists 'Abd al-Majid al-Rafi'i, Elias Firzili, Jibran Majdalani, Basharah Marhij and Ma'in Bashur, in *al-Hayat*, 5–12 July 2008, *'Awdah ila Qissat al-Qa'id al-Mu'assis lil-Ba'th*.

21. Marwan Habash, *Harakat 23 Shubat ... al-Dawa'i wa al-Asbab* (*The 23 February Movement, its Motives and Reasons*); *Muhawalat 'Usyan al-Ra'id Salim Hatum fi al-Suwayda' Yawm 8 Aylul 1966* (*The Revolt Attempt of Major Salim Hatum in al-Suwayda' on 8 September 1966*); *Harb Huzayran* (*The June War; its Preludes and Facts*); *Qadaya wa Ara'* (*Issues and Views*); and various other articles in *Kulluna Shuraka' fi al-Watan* and other media (see the bibliography for part of them).

22. Marwan Habash, *al-Qiwa al-Taqaddumiyah wa al-Tadakhkhul fi al-Urdun*, *Kulluna Shuraka' fi al-Watan*, 30 March 2009, http://all4syria.info/content/view/6383/124/ (accessed 20 October 2010); *Qadaya wa Ara'*, Damascus, 2010, pp. 37–46, 50–56.

23. Marwan Habash, *Ma Yuqarib Rub' Qarn fi al-Mu'taqal*.

24. Mansur Sultan al-Atrash, *al-Jil al-Mudan. Sirah Dhatiyah. Min Awraq Mansur Sultan al-Atrash*, edited by Rim Mansur al-Atrash, Beirut, Riyad El-Rayyes Books, 2008 (499 pages).

25. Marwan Habash, *Min Tarikh al-Hizb: Harakat 23 Shubat 1966 ... al-Dawa'i wa al-Asbab* (8/9), *Kulluna Shuraka' fi al-Watan*, 22 July 2008, http://all4syria.info/content/view/3510/124 (accessed 20 October 2010).

26. Marwan Habash, *'Abd al-Karim al-Jundi: al-Thawrah wa Khaybat al-Amal*, *Kulluna Shuraka' fi al-Watan*, 16 February 2009, http://all4syria.info/content/view/4457/124/ (accessed 20 October 2010).

27. The memoirs of Alawi General ('Amid) Shafiq Fayyad, private edition (1000 pages), were announced (but not published) in 2009 under the title *Hadatha Ma'i* ('It happened to me'), *Kulluna Shuraka' fi al-Watan*, 26 November 2009, http://all4syria.info/content/view/17603/110/ (accessed 20 October 2010).

Appendix A

1. Translation of an official party document, first published in *al-Munadil* (No. 3, April 1966, p. 13), internal organ of the Ba'th in Syria, in which the Organisational Party Bureau gave its official analysis of the situation.

2. See Appenbix B.

Appendix B

1. Translation of *al-Taqir al-Watha'iqi li-Azmat al-Hizb* ('The Documentary Report on the Party's Crisis') (pp. 88–93), an internal party brochure issued by the Syrian Regional Command of the Ba'th party in 1966, and classified as 'for members only'. It should be noted that all persons mentioned by name in Appendix B are Sunni Muslims.

2. Many Sunni Muslims consider Alawis, Isma'ilis, Druzes and other heterodox Muslims to be non-Muslims. Therefore, if a Sunni asks someone if he is a 'Muslim', he means implicitly a Sunni Muslim.

Appendix C

1. Translation of *Azmat al-Hizb wa Harakat 23 Shubat* ('The Party's Crisis and the 23 February Movement'), pp. 15–28. This document was issued by the Syrian Regional Command of the Ba'th party in 1966, and classified as a 'secret internal publication exclusively for members'.

2. For the 'Qatana Insurrection see Muhammad 'Umran, *Tajribati fi al-Thawrah*, p. 13; Sami al-Jundi, *al-Ba'th*, p. 85; Mustafa Talas, *Mir'at Hayati, al-'Aqd al-Awwal (1948–1958)*, pp. 630–44; Rabinovich, *Syria under the Ba'th 1963–66*, p. 14.

3. For the military congress of al-Kiswah see Munif al-Razzaz, *a-Tajribah al-Murrah*, pp. 132–3; Rabinovich, *Syria under the Ba'th 1963–66*, p. 158; Van Dam, *De Rol van Sektarisme, Regionalisme en Tribalisme*, pp. 115–17; Van Dam, 'The Struggle for Power in Syria and the Ba'th Party (1958–1966)', p. 14.

4. The Eighth National Congress of the Ba'th Party was held in Damascus in April 1965. It decided that during the forthcoming Syrian Regional Party Congresses the military party organisation should be represented by a ratio of maximally 20 per cent of all congress delegates. See Bashir al-Da'uq (ed.), *Nidal Hizb al-Ba'th al-'Arabi al-Ishtiraki 'abr Mu'tamaratih al-Qawniyah: al-Mu'tamar al-Qawmi al-Thamin (Nisan 1965)*, pp. 235–6.

Bibliography

Arabic newspapers and periodicals quoted in the text:

Al-Ahram, Cairo; *Al-Ahrar*, Beirut; *Al-Akhbar*, Cairo; *Akhbar al-Yawm*, Cairo; *Al-Anba'*, Beirut; *Al-Ba'th*, Damascus; *Beirut*, Beirut; *Al-Difa'*, Jerusalem; *Al-Diyar*, Beirut; *Al-Dustur*, Beirut; *Al-Fikr al-'Askari*, Damascus; *Filastin*, Jerusalem; *Funun*, Damascus; *Al-Fursan*, Damascus; *Al-Hawadith*, Beirut; *Al-Hayat*, Beirut, London; *Al-Ihya' al-'Arabi*, Paris; *Iqtisadiyat Halab*, Aleppo; *Al-'Iraq*, Baghdad; *Al-Jadid*, Beirut; *Al-Jaridah*, Beirut; *Al-Jumhuriyah*, Baghdad; *Al-Jumhuriyah*, Cairo; *Al-Kifah*, Beirut; *Al-Kifah al-'Arabi*, Beirut; *Kulluna Shuraka' fi al-Watan*; *Majlis al-Sha'b*, Damascus; *Al-Muharrir*, Beirut; *Al-Munadil*, Damascus; *Al-Nadhir*, n.p.; *Al-Nahar*, Beirut; *Al-Nahar al-'Arabi wa al-Duwali*, Paris; *Nidal al-Sha'b*, Damascus; *October*, Cairo; *Al-Rayah*, Beirut; *Al-Safa'*, Beirut; *Al-Safir*, Beirut; *Al-Sawt al-Hayawi*, Paris; *Al-Sayyad*, Beirut; *Al-Shu'lah*, Beirut; *Al-Siyasah*, Kuwayt; *Al-Sumud*, Beirut; *Al-Thawrah*, Baghdad; *Al-Thawrah*, Damascus; *Tishrin*, Damascus; *Al-Wasat*, London; *Al-Zaman*, Beirut.

Works in Arabic

'Abd al-Karim, Ahmad, *Adwa' 'ala Tajribat al-Wahdah*, Damascus, 1962.
— *Hisad Sinin Khasibah wa Thimar Murrah*, Beirut, 1994.
'Abd Allah, al-Husayni, *al-Judhur al-Tarikhiyah lil-Nusayriyah al-'Alawiyah*, Cairo, 1980.
'Abduh, Samir, *Taryif al-Madinah wa Madnanat al-Rif*, Damascus, 1989.
Abu Mansur, Fadl Allah, *A'asir Dimashq*, Beirut, 1959.
'Affash, Fadl, *al-Majalis al-Sha'biyah wa al-Niyabiyah fi al-Watan al-'Arabi. Vol. 1: Majlis al-Sha'b fi Suriyah (1928–1988)*, Damascus, 1988.
'Aflaq, Michel, *Fi Sabil al-Ba'th*, 3rd edn, Beirut, 1963.
— *Ma'rakat al-Masir al-Wahid*, Beirut, 1963.
— *Ahadith al-Amin al-'Amm al-Rafiq Michel 'Aflaq khilal Ziyaratih Baghdad Ayar 1969*, Baghdad, 1969.
— *Nuqtat al-Bidayah*, Beirut, 1971.
al-Ahmad, 'Abd Allah, 'Ila al-Safir Nikolaos van Dam', *al-Safir*, 8 June 1995.
Ahmad, Khalil, *Zaki al-Arsuzi wa Dawr al-Lisan fi Bina' al-Insan*, Damascus, 1978.
al-Ahmar, 'Abd Allah, *al-Ba'th wa al-Thawrah al-Mutajaddidah*, Damascus, 1990.
— *Khawatir wa Dhikrayat - min Sirati al-Dhatiyah*, Damascus, 1998.
al-Akhras, Muhammad Safuh, *Tarkib al-'A'ilah al-'Arabiyah wa Waza'ifuha. Dirasah Midaniyah li-Waqi' al-'A'ilah fi Suriyah*, Damascus, 1976.
'Ala' al-Sayyid, A., *al-Nukhbah al-Siyasiyah fi Suriya*, paper delivered to the Third

Annual Conference at Cairo University on 'The Political Elite in the Arab World', 11–13 November 1995.

al-'Ali, Muhammad Ibrahim, *al-Ghajariyah (al-Murabi '5')*, Damascus, 1995.

— *Hayati wa al-I'dam*, 3 vols, Damascus, 2007.

'Allush, Naji, *al-Thawrah wa al-Jamahir*, Beirut, 1962.

Amin, Mahmud, *Salamiyah fi Khamsin Qarnan*, Damascus, 1983.

'Anadani, Tawfiq, *al-Ba'th fi Durub al-Nidal*, Damascus, 1965.

al-Arsuzi, Zaki, *al-Mu'allafat al-Kamilah*, 6 vols, Damascus, 1972–76.

'Arudki, Yahya, *al-Iqtisad al-Suri al-Hadith*, Vol. 1, Damascus, 1972.

al-'Asi, Hamdan, 'I'fa' Rif'at Yatrah min Jadid Mawdu' al-Khilafah fi Suriyah', *al-Mushahid al-Siyasi*, 15–21 February 1998, pp. 8–14.

al-'Askari, al-Sayyid 'Abd al-Husayn Mahdi, *al-'Alawiyun aw al-Nusayriyah*, n.p., 1980.

al-Atasi, Jamal (ed.), *Fi al-Fikr al-Siyasi*, 2 vols, Damascus, 1963.

al-Atrash, Fu'ad, *al-Duruz, Mu'amarat wa Tarikh wa Haqa'iq*, Beirut, 1975.

al-Atrash, Mansur Sultan, *al-Jil al-Mudan. Sirah Dhatiyah. Min Awraq Mansur Sultan al-Atrash*, ed. Rim Mansur al-Atrash, Beirut, 2008.

al-'Awdat, Haytham [Manna'], *Intifadat al-'Ammiyah al-Fallahiyah fi Jabal al-'Arab*, Damascus, 1976.

al-'Azmah, Bashir, *Jil al-Hazimah. Bayn al-Wahdah wa al-Infisal. Mudhakkirat*, London, 1991.

al-'Aysami, Shibli, *Fi al-Thawrah al-'Arabiyah*, 2nd edn, Beirut, 1969.

— *al-Wahdah al-'Arabiyah min Khilal al-Tajribah*, Beirut, 1971.

— *Hawl al-Wahdah al-'Arabiyah*, 2nd edn, Beirut, 1974.

— *Ba'd al-Qadaya al-Qawmiyah*, Beirut, 1975.

— *Hizb al-Ba'th al-'Arabi al-Ishtiraki, 1, Marhalat al-Araba'inat al-Ta'sisiyah 1940–1949*, 2nd edn, Beirut, 1975.

— *Hawl al-Wahdah wa al-Tadamun wa al-Taswiyah*, Baghdad, 1976.

— *Hizb al-Ba'th al-'Arabi al-Ishtiraki, 2, Marhalat al-Numuw wa al-Tawassu', 1949–1958*, Beirut, 1978.

— *Risalat al-Ummah al-'Arabiyah*, Beirut, 1978.

— *al-'Almaniyah wa al-Dawlah al-Diniyah*, Baghdad, 1986.

— *'Urubat al-Islam wa 'Alamiyatuh*, 4th edn, Baghdad, 1986.

al-'Azm, Khalid, *Mudhakkirat Khalid al-'Azm*, 3 vols, Beirut, 1973.

Badawi, 'Abd al-Rahman, *al-Nusayriyah*, n.p., n.d.

Badr al-Din, Salah, *Hawl al-'Ilaqat al-Kurdiyah al-'Arabiyah*, n.p. (min Manshurat Hizb al-Ittihad al-Sha'bi al-Kurdi fi Suriya), July 1991.

— *Difa'an 'an al-Haqiqah wa did al-Shufiniyah wa al-'Unsuriyah*, n.p. (min Manshurat Hizb al-Ittihad al-Sha'bi al-Kurdi fi Suriya), September 1991.

— *Gharb Kurdistan, Dirasah Tarikhiyah Siyasiyah Watha'iqiyah Mujazah*, Bonn, 1998.

Bagh, Adib Sulayman, *al-Jawlan: Dirasah fi al-Jughrafiyah al-Iqlimiyah*, Damascus, 1984.

Bakdash, Khalid, *Kalimat – Ahadith – Maqalat 1984–1994*, Damascus, 1994.

Barakat, Salim, *Hatihi 'Aliyan, Hat al-Nafir 'ala Akharih (Sirat al-Saba)*, Beirut, 1982.

al-Barazi, Tamam, *Milaffat al-Mu'aradah al-Suriyah*, Cairo, 1994.

al-Barnamij al-'Arabi li-Nushata' Huquq al-Insan, *Nushata' Khalf al-Qudban, Suriya 1987–1997*, Cairo, 1998.

al-Basha, Faruq, *Jawhar al-Qawmiyah al-'Arabiyah*, Damascus, 1972.

Bashir, Iskandar, *Ilgha' al-Ta'ifiyah*, Beirut, 1993.

al-Ba'th fi 'Idiha al-Dhahabi 1946–1996, Damascus 1997.

Birah, George, *al-Mujtama' al-Madani wa al-Tahawwul al-Dimuqrati fi Suriya*, Cairo, 1995.

al-Bitar, Salah al-Din, *al-Siyasah al-'Arabiyah bayn al-Mabda' wa al-Tatbiq*, Beirut, 1960.

al-Bujayrimi, Yusuf (ed.), *Hiwarat al-Islah wa al-Infitah fi Suriya*, Damascus, 2001.

Dam, Nikolaos van, 'Isra'il wa al-Indimaj al-Qawmi', *Majallat Markaz al-Dirasat al-Filastiniyah*, Baghdad, 1979, pp. 100–107.

— 'Idha Ustuthniyat Dimashq min al-Salam Istahal al-Salam', *al-Hayat*, 13 November 1993.

— 'al-'Arab Iktashafu anna al-Salam Silah Aqwa min al-Harb', *al-Qabas*, 24 March 1994.

— *al-Sira' 'ala al-Sultah fi Suriya: al-Ta'ifiyah wa al-Iqlimiyah wa al-'Asha'iriyah fi al-Siyasah, 1961–1995*, 2nd edn, Cairo, Maktabat Madbuli, 1995.

— 'Suriyah Tawadd al-Insihab min Lubnan wa al-Ta'ifiyah ghayr Mawjudah Rasmiyan', *al-Hayat*, 12 March 1995.

— 'Kayfa Tunaqishun Kitaban Mamnu'an min al-Tadawul?', *al-Safir*, 24 May 1995.

— 'Radd 'ala al-Mufakkir al-'Arabi al-Suri 'Imad Fawzi Shu'aybi hawl *al-Sira' 'ala al-Sultah fi Suriya*', *al-Diyar*, 11 July 1995.

— 'Tarikh "*al-Sira' 'ala al-Sultah fi Suriya* ..." (1) Atlub al-Qira'ah al-Muhayidah', *al-Safir*, 17 July 1995.

— 'Tarikh "*al-Sira' 'ala al-Sultah fi Suriya* ..." (2) Ashkuruhu 'ala al-Tarwij!', *al-Safir*, 18 July 1995.

— e.a., 'Khilafat Bashar Sa'bah wa Khaddam Qad Yatara"as Intiqaliyan', *al-Mushahid al-Siyasi*, 15–21 February 1998, pp. 13–14.

Dandashli, Mustafa, *Hizb al-Ba'th al-'Arabi al-Ishtiraki, 1940–1963, Vol. 1, al-Idiyulujiya wa al-Tarikh al-Siyasi*, Beirut, 1979.

al-Da'uq, Bashir (ed.), *Nidal (Hizb) al-Ba'th*, 11 vols, Beirut, 1963–74.

— *Nidal Hizb al-Ba'th al-'Arabi al-Ishtiraki 'abr Bayanat Qiyadatih al-Qawmiyah (1955–1962)*, Beirut, 1971.

— *Nidal Hizb al-Ba'th al-'Arabi al-Ishtiraki 'abr Mu'tamaratih al-Qawmiyah (1974–1964)*, Beirut, 1971.

Dirasat fi al-Nizam al-Suri (Silsilat Barada, No. 3), n.p., n.d.

Diyab, 'Izz al-Din, *al-Tahlil al-Ijtima'i li-Zahirat al-Inqisam al-Siyasi fi al-Watan al-'Arabi: 'Hizb al-Ba'th al-'Arabi al-Ishtiraki Numudhajan'*, Cairo, 1993.

al-Duri, Qahtan 'Abd al-Rahman, e.a., *al-Nusayriyah Harakah Hadmiyah*, Baghdad, 1986.

Falhut, Sabir, *al-Mas'alah al-Filastiniyah wa al-Mawqif al-'Arabi al-Suri*, Damascus, 1977.

Farah, Elias, *Fi al-Siyasah al-'Arabiyah al-Thawriyah qabl al-Naksah wa ba'daha*, Baghdad, 1970.

— *Nazarat fi al-Malamih al-Asasiyah lil-Marhalah al-Rahinah*, Beirut, 1971.

— *Tatawwur al-Fikr al-Marksi, 'Ard wa Naqd*, Beirut, 1971.

— *Tatawwur al-Idiyulujiyah al-'Arabiyah al-Thawriyah (al-Fikr al-Qawmi)*, 2nd edn, Beirut 1972.

— *al-Fikr al-'Arabi al-Thawri amam Tahaddiyat al-Marhalah*, Baghdad, 1973.

Faris, George (ed.), *Man Huwa fi Suriyah, 1949*, Damascus, 1949.

— *Man Huwa fi Suriyah 1951*, Damascus, 1951.
— *Man Hum fi al-'Alam al-'Arabi, Vol. 1, Suriyah*, Damascus, 1957.
Fansah, Nadhir, *Ayyam Husni al-Za'im, 137 Yawman Hazzat Suriyah*, 3rd edn, Damascus, 1993.
Fayyad, Shafiq, *Hadatha Ma'i* (unpublished manuscript), Damascus, 2009.
al-Fukayki, Hani, *Awkar al-Hazimah. Tajribati fi Hizb al-Ba'th al-'Iraqi*, London, 1993.
Ghalyun, Burhan, *Nizam al-Ta'ifiyah: min al-Dawlah ila al-Qabilah*, Beirut, 1990.
al-Ghanim, Wahib, *al-Judhur al-Waqi'iyah li-Mabadi' Hizb al-Ba'th*, Damascus, 1997.
Habash, Marwan, 'Muhawalat 'Usyan al-Ra'id Salim Hatum fi al-Suwayda' Yawm 8 Aylul 1966' (4 parts), *Kulluna Shuraka' fi al-Watan*, June 2008.
— 'Min Tarikh al-Hizb: Harakat 23 Shubat … al-Dawa'i wa al-Asbab', *Kulluna Shuraka' fi al-Watan* (9 parts), July 2008.
— 'Ma bayn al-Lajnat al-'Askariyah wa al-Liwa' Ziyad al-Hariri', *Kulluna Shuraka' fi al-Watan*, 31 January 2009.
— ''Abd al-Karim al-Jundi: al-Thawrah wa Khaybat al-Amal', *Kulluna Shuraka' fi al-Watan*, 16 February 2009.
— ''Min 13 Kanun al-Thani 1963 ila 8 Adhar 1963', 8 March 2009, *Kulluna Shuraka' fi al-Watan*, 16 February 2009.
— 'al-Wahdah, al-Ba'th wa al-Thawrah' (4 parts), *Kulluna Shuraka' fi al-Watan*, 28–31 March 2009.
— 'al-Qiwa al-Taqaddumiyah wa al-Tadakhkhul fi al-Urdunn', *Kulluna Shuraka' fi al-Watan*, 30 March 2009.
— 'Hizb al-Ba'th al-'Arabi al-Ishtiraki: al-Nash'ah wa al-Takwin (2 parts), *Kulluna Shuraka' fi al-Watan*, 7, 8 April 2009.
— 'Heikal wa Cohen … wa al-Iftira' 'ala al-Haqiqah', *Kulluna Shuraka' fi al-Watan*, 23 April 2009,
— *Harb Huzayran 1967. Al-Muqaddamat wa al-Waqa'i'*, n.p., n.d.
— *Ma Yuqarib Rub' Qarn fi al-Mu'taqal*, n.p., n.d.
— *Min 28 Aylul 1961 ila 18 Tammuz 1963. Qira'ah fi al-Dhakirah wa al-Wathiqah lil-'Ilaqah bayn al-Ba'thiyin wa al-Nasiriyin min Wajhat Nazar Ba'thi*, n.p., n.d.
— *Qadaya wa Ara'*, Damascus, 2010.
— *al-Ba'th wa Thawrat Adhar*, Damascus, 2011.
Haddad, Rida, *Shahadat al-Muwatin 61: Min Awraq al-Shahid Rida Haddad ba'd 15 'Aman min al-I'tiqal*, n.p. (al-Hizb al-Shuyu'i al-Suri – al-Maktab al-Siyasi, Hay'at al-Kharij), 1997.
al-Hafiz, Amin, *Al-Inqilabat fi Suriya kama yaraha Amin al-Hafiz*, Interviews by Ahmad Mansur, *Al-Jazeera*, 2001.
al-Hafiz, Yasin, 'Hawl Tajribat Hizb al-Ba'th', in: Jamal al-Atasi (ed.), *Fi al-Fikr al-Siyasi*, Vol. 1, Damascus, 1963, pp. 175–202.
— *al-La 'Aqlaniyah fi al-Siyasah*, Beirut, 1975.
Al-Hajj Salih, Yasin, ''al-Ta'ifiyah wa al-Siyasah fi Suriyah', in: *Hazim Saghiyah, Nawasib wa Rawafid*, 2nd edn, Beirut, 2010, pp. 51–81.
al-Hajjar, Rashid, *Fi Azmat al-Mu'aradah al-Suriyah*, Paris, 1989.
al-Hakim, Hasan, *Mudhakkirati, Safahat min Tarikh Suriyah al-Hadith 1920–1958*, 2 vols, Beirut, 1965, 1966.
Hamdun, Walid, *Dhikrayat wa Ara'*, Damascus, 2007.
Hanna, 'Abd Allah, *al-Harakah al-'Ummaliyah fi Suriyah wa Lubnan, 1900–1945*, Damascus, 1973.

— *al-Ittijahat al-Fikriyah fi Suriyah wa Lubnan, 1920–1945*, Damascus, 1973.
Haqa'iq 'an al-Ta'ifah al-Nusayriyah fi Suriyah, n.p., n.d.
Haydar, Muhammad, *al-Ba'th wa al-Baynunat al-Kubra*, n.p., 1998.
Haydar, al-Shaykh Ahmad Muhammad, *al-A'mal al-Kamilah*, 3 vols, Tripoli (Lebanon), 1987, 1988, 1991.
al-Hawrani, Akram, *Mudhakkirat Akram al-Hawrani*, Cairo, Maktabat Madbuli, 2000.
Hilal, Muhammad Talab, *Dirasah 'an Muhafazat al-Jazirah min al-Nawahi al-Qawmiyah, al-Ijtima'iyah, al-Siyasiyah*, n.p., n.d.
Hilan, Rizq Allah, *Suriyah bayn al-Takhalluf wa al-Tanmiyah*, Damascus, 1973.
Hindi, Ihsan, *Kifah al-Sha'b al-'Arabi al-Suri (1908–1948)*, Damascus, 1962.
al-Hindi, Hani, *Jaysh al-Inqadh*, Beirut, 1974.
Hizb al-Ba'th al-'Arabi al-Ishtiraki, *Fi al-Tanzim wa al-Tarbiyah al-Hizbiyah*, Beirut, 1971.
Hizb al-Ba'th al-'Arabi al-Ishtiraki, al-Qiyadah al-Qawmiyah, *Ba'd al-Muntalaqat al-Nazariyah allati aqarraha al-Mu'tamar al-Qawmi al-Sadis fi Tishrin al-Awwal 1963*, 2nd edn, Damascus, 1967.
— *Silsilat al-Taw'iyah al-Ishtirakiyah*, Vol. 3, *al-Tahwil al-Ishtiraki fi al-Rif*, Damascus, 1967.
— *Dirasah Tahliliyah Mujazah li-Nidal Hizb al-Ba'th al-'Arabi al-Ishtiraki 1943–1971*, Damascus, 1973.
— *Ihtifalat al-Dhikra al-Khamisah wa al-'Ishrin li Ta'sis Hizb al-Ba'th al-'Arabi al-Ishtiraki*, Damascus, 1973.
— *Muqarrarat al-Mu'tamar al-Qawmi al-Tasi' al-Mun'aqid fi al-Nisf al-Thani min Aylul 1966*, Damascus, n.d.
— *Mas'alat al-Aqalliyat al-Qawmiyah*, Baghdad, 1979.
— *Min Tarikh al-Hizb, al-Bidayat fi Dhakirat Fayiz Isma'il*, Damascus, 1980.
Hizb al-Ba'th al-'Arabi al-Ishtiraki, al-Qiyadah al-Qawmiyah, Lajnat al-Tawjih al-Hizbi, Silsilat al-Tawjih al-Hizbi (1), *al-Hizb al-Thawri*, Damascus, 1970.
— Silsilat al-Tawjih al-Hizbi (2), *al-Inhiraf wa al-Zawahir al-Inqisamiyah fi al-Hizb wa Dawr al-Yamin al-Takhribi*, Damascus, n.d.
— Silsilat al-Tawjih al-Hizbi (3), *Mafhum al-Idarah al-Dimuqratiyah li-Wasa'il al-Intaj*, Damascus, 1970.
Hizb al-Ba'th al-'Arabi al-Ishtiraki, al-Qiyadah al-Qawmiyah, Maktab al-Thaqafah wa al-I'dad al-Hizbi, *al-Qutr al-'Arabi al-Suri, Dirasah 'Ammah* (Silsilat al-Watan al-'Arabi, Vol. 2), Damascus, 1984.
Hizb al-Ba'th al-'Arabi al-Ishtiraki, al-Qutr al-Suri, al-Qiyadah al-Qutriyah, *Azmat al-Hizb wa Harakat 23 Shubat wa In'iqad al-Mu'tamar al-Qutri al-Akhir*, Damascus, 1966.
— *Muqarrarat al-Mu'tamar al-Qutri al-'Adi al-Thani lil-Qutr al-Suri wa al-Mun'aqid bayn 18/3–4/4/65. Al-Taqrir al-Tanzimi, al-Taqrir al-Siyasi, al-Taqrir al-Iqtisadi al-Ijtima'i*, Damascus, 1966.
— *Al-Taqrir al-Watha'iqi li-Azmat al-Hizb wa al-Muqaddam lil-Mu'tamar al-Qutri al-Istithna'i al-Mun'aqid bayn 10/3–27/3/1966*, Damascus, 1966.
Hizb al-Ba'th al-'Arabi al-Ishtiraki, al-Qutr al-'Arabi al-Suri, al-Qiyadah al-Qutriyah, *Taqarir al-Mu'tamar al-Qutri al-Thamin wa Muqarraratuh, al-Mun'aqid fi Dimashq fi al-Fatrah al-Waqi'ah bayn 5/1/1985–20/1/1985: al-Taqrir al-Tanzimi, al-Taqrir al-Siyasi, al-Taqrir al-Iqtisadi*, Damascus, 1985.
— *Al-Harakah al-Tashihiyah al-Majidah fi al-Dhikra al-Khamisah wa al-'Ishrin*, Damascus, 1995.

Hizb al-Ittihad al-Ishtiraki al-'Arabi fi Suriyah, *al-Qutr al-Suri yamurr bi Azmah Wataniyah Khatirah*, internal circular exclusively for members, Damascus, 1979.

Humsi, Nazihah, *Al-Jannah al-Da'i'ah. Mudhakkirat Nazihah al-Humsi*, n.p., n.d.

Husayn, Harbi Musa and Qazanji, Fu'ad Yusuf, *Masadir Turath Hizb al-Ba'th al-'Arabi al-Ishtiraki*, Baghdad, 1977.

Husayn, Khalid Muhammad, *Suriyah al-Mu'asirah 1963–1993*, Damascus, 1996.

al-Husri, Sati', *al-Iqlimiyah. Judhuruha wa Budhuruha*, 2nd edn, Beirut, 1964.

al-Ibrahim, (al-Shaykh) 'Ali 'Aziz, *al-'Alawiyun bayn al-Ghuluw wa al-Falsafah wa al-Tasawwuf wa al-Tashayyu'*, Beirut, 1995.

Ibrahim, Farhad, *al-Ta'ifiyah wa al-Siyasah fi al-'Alam al-'Arabi. Numudhaj al-Shi'ah fi al-'Iraq*, Cairo, 1996.

Ibrahim, Sa'd al-Din, *Ta'ammulat fi Mas'alat al-Aqalliyat*, Cairo, 1992.

— *al-Milal wa al-Nihal wa al-A'raq: Humum al-Aqalliyat fi al-Watan al-'Arabi*, 2nd edn, Cairo, 1994.

al-Ikhwan al-Muslimun ... yakshifun Haqiqat al-Awda' fi Suriya, n.p., n.d.

'Isa, Habib, *al-Suqut al-Akhir lil-Iqlimiyin fi al-Watan al-'Arabi*, Beirut, 1979.

Isma'il, Fa'iz, *Min Tarikh al-Hizb: al-Bidayat fi Dhakirat Fayiz Isma'il*, Damascus, 1980.

— *Ma'a Bidayat al-Ba'th*, 2nd edn, Damascus, 1989.

Isma'il, Muhammad Khayr, *Dalil al-Ansab al-Sharkasiyah*, Damascus, 1994.

Jabbur, Georges, *al-Fikr al-Siyasi al-Mu'asir fi Suriyah*, 2nd edn, Beirut, 1993.

— *Safita wa Muhituha fi al-Qarn al-Tasi' 'Ashar*, Damascus 1993.

al-Jami'ah al-Amrikiyah fi Bayrut, *al-Watha'iq al-'Arabiyah, 1963–1973*, Beirut, 1964–75.

Jawad, Sa'd Naji, *al-Aqalliyah al-Kurdiyah fi Suriya*, Baghdad, 1988.

Jum'ah, Sa'd. *Mujtama' al-Karahiyah*, Beirut, n.d.

al-Jundi, Sami, *al-Ba'th*, Beirut, 1969.

— *Kisrat Khubz*, Beirut, 1969.

— *Atahadda ... wa Attahim*, Beirut, 1970.

— *Suriyah ... Ra'idat Kifah*, Beirut, 1971.

Khaddur, Adib, *al-Sahafah al-Suriyah*, Damascus, 1973.

al-Khashsh, Sulayman and Maqdisi, Antun, *al-Marksiyah, 'Ard wa Tahlil*, Damascus, 1968.

al-Khayyir, (al-Shaykh) 'Abd al-Rahman, *Min Nida' al-Iyman*, 3rd edn, Damascus, 1985.

— *Kitab al-Salat wa al-Siyam Wafq al-Madhhab al-Ja'fari (al-'Alawi)*, 8th edn, Damascus, 1991.

— *'Aqidatuna wa Waqi'una Nahnu al-Muslimin al-Ja'fariyin 'al-'Alawiyin'*, 3rd edn, Damascus, 1992.

— *Naqd wa Taqriz Kitab Tarikh al-'Alawiyin* (Min Turath al-Shaykh 'Abd al-Rahman al-Khayyir), Damascus, 1992.

— *Risalah Tabhath fi Masa'il Muhimmah hawl al-Madhhab al-Ja'fari (al-'Alawi)* (Min Turath al-Shaykh 'Abd al-Rahman al-Khayyir), 3rd edn, Damascus, 1994.

al-Khayyir, Hani, *Adib al-Shishakli, Sahib al-Inqilab al-Thalith fi Suriya*, Damascus, 1994.

Lajnat al-Difa' 'an al-Mu'taqalin al-Siyasiyin fi Suriyah, al-Maktab al-Markazi, *Min Qawafil al-Mu'taqalin al-Siyasiyin wa Akhbarihim fi al-Sujun al-Suriyah*, n.p., 1976.

al-Madani, Sulayman, *Ha'ula' Hakamu Suriyah (1918–1970)*, Damascus, 1995.

— *Muhakamat Cohen*, Damascus, 1995.
— *Khafaya wa Asrar 8 Adhar*, Damascus, 1997.
Mahadir Jalasat Mubahathat al-Wahdah, Cairo, 1963.
Majzarat Hamah, Cairo, 1984.
al-Ma'had al-Duwali lil-Dirasat al-Suriyah, *al-Ba'th al-Shi'i*, n.p., 2008.
al-Maktab al-I'lami lil-Ikhwan al-Muslimin, *Hamah, Ma'sat al-'Asr*, n.p., n.d.
al-Maliki, Riyad, *Dhikrayat 'ala Darb al-Kifah wa al-Hazimah*, Damascus, 1972.
al-Malluhi, *Akram al-Hawrani, 'Arrab al-Inqilabat fi Suriyah. Mudhakkirat*, Damascus, 1995.
Manna' (al-'Awdat), Haytham, *al-Dahiyah wa al-Jallad*, Cairo, 1995.
— *Halat al-Akrad fi Suriyah*, n.p. [Cairo Centre for Human Rights Studies], n.d. [1995].
Marhij, Basharah, *Safa' al-Khatir, Maqalat fi al-Siyasah wa al-Fikr*, Beirut, 2009.
al-Maridini, Zuhayr, *al-Ustadh. Qissat Hayat Michel 'Aflaq*, London, 1988.
Mawsili, Mundhir, *'Arab wa Akrad, Ru'yah 'Arabiyah ... lil-Qadiyah al-Kurdiyah, al-Akrad fi Watanihim al-Qawmi wa fi al-Jiwar al-'Iraqi-al-Turki-al-Irani ... wa fi Suriyah wa Lubnan*, 3rd edn, Beirut, 1995.
Muhakamat Ba'i' al-Jawlan, n.p. [Dar Barada lil-Nashr], 1982.
Murshid, Nur al-Mudi', *Lamahat hawla al-Murshidiyah (Dhikrayat wa Mushahadat wa Watha'iq)*, Beirut, 2008.
Mustafa, Khalil, *Suqut al-Jawlan*, Amman, 1969.
— *Min Milaffat al-Jawlan?* ... Amman, 1970.
Naddaf, 'Amad, *Khalid Bakdash ... Yatahaddath ... hawl ba'd Qadaya al-Tarikh wa al-Fikr wa al-Siyasah wa al-Adab*, Damascus, 1993.
al-Naddawi, Sa'd 'Abbas, 'Ahmad Mishil 'Aflaq wa Hawiyat al-'Arab al-Qawmiyah', *al-'Iraq*, 22 June 1996.
Na'isah, Haydar Muhammad, *Suwar Rifiyah min al-Ladhiqiyah*, Damascus, 1994.
al-Najdi, Muhammad Sa'id, *Hasilat al-Inqilabat al-Thawriyah fi ba'd al-Aqtar al-'Arabiyah*, Beirut, 1966.
al-Nakadi, 'Arif (ed.), *al-Ta'rif bi-Muhafazat al-Suwayda'*, Damascus, 1962.
Nassar, Nasif, *Nahwa Mujtama' Jadid. Muqaddamat Asasiyah fi Naqd al-Mujtama' al-Ta'ifi*, 5th edn, Beirut, 1995.
Nifiyudifa, N.K., *'Ala al-Mabda'. Nidal al-Hizb al-Shuyu'i al-Suri min Ajl al-Jabhah al-Wataniyah al-Muwahhadah 1936–1966* (trans. Ziyad al-Mulla), Damascus, 1992.
Nur al-Din, 'Isam, *Zaki Najib al-Arsuzi. Hayatuhu wa Ara'uhu fi al-Siyasah wa al-Lughah*, Beirut, 1996.
Qadaya al-Khilaf fi al-Hizb al-Shuyu'i al-Suri, Beirut, 1972.
Qal'aji, Qadri, *Watha'iq al-Naksah taht Adwa' al-Tajribah al-Murrah*, Beirut, 1969.
Qarqut, Dhuqan, *Michel 'Aflaq, al-Kitabat al-Ula*, Beirut, 1993.
Qasimiyah, Khayriyah (ed.), *Mudhakkirat Fawzi al-Qawuqji 1914–1932*, Vol. 1, Beirut, 1975.
— *Filastin fi Mudhakkirat al-Qawuqji*, Vol. 2, Beirut, 1975.
Qissat al-Thawrah fi al-'Iraq wa Suriyah, Baghdad, 1963.
Qiyadat al-Thawrah al-Islamiyah fi Suriyah, *Bayan al-Thawrah al-Islamiyah fi Suriyah wa Manahijuha*, Damascus, 1980.
al-Rabdawi, Qasim, *Dimashq: al-Tahawwulat al-Dimughrafiyah wa al-Ijtima'iyah wa al-Iqtisadiyah 1950–1992*, Damascus, 1994.
al-Razzaz, Munif, *Tatawwur Ma'na al-Qawmiyah*, Beirut, 1960.

— *al-Hurriyah wa Mushkilatuha fi al-Buldan al-Mutakhallifah*, Beirut, 1965.

— *Ma'alim al-Hayat al-'Arabiyah al-Jadidah*, 5th edn, Beirut, 1966.

— *al-Tajribah al-Murrah*, Beirut, 1967.

— *Ahadith fi al-'Amal al-Fida'i*, Beirut, 1970.

— *Alif Ba' al-Ba'th*, Beirut, 1970.

— *al-Sabil ila Tahrir Filastin*, Beirut, 1971.

— *al-Wahdah al-'Arabiyah, Hal laha min Sabil?*, Beirut, 1971.

— *Hawl Siyasat al-Tahwil al-Ishtiraki li-Hizb al-Ba'th al-'Arabi al-Ishtiraki*, Beirut, 1973.

— 'al-Wahdah ba'd Harb Ramadan', *Qadaya 'Arabiyah*, No. 1, April 1974, pp. 7–16.

— *Filastin wa al-Wahdah 1969–1975*, Beirut, 1975.

— *Falsafat al-Harakah al-Qawmiyah al-'Arabiyah*, 2 vols, Beirut, 1977–78.

— *al-A'mal al-Fikriyah wa al-Siyasiyah*, 3 vols, Amman (Mu'assasat Munif al-Razzaz lil-Dirasat al-Qawmiyah), 1985–86.

Sa'adah, Jibra'il, *Muhafazat al-Ladhiqiyah*, n.p., n.d.

Sa'b, Edouard, 'al-Ba'th: Hizb am Hukm', *al-Qadaya al-Mu'asirah*, Vol. 1, July 1969, pp. 129–35.

al-Sabbagh, Layla, *al-Mujtama' al-'Arabi al-Suri fi Matla' al-'Ahd al-'Uthmani*, Damascus, 1973.

Sadiq, Mahmud, *Hiwar hawl Suriyah*, London, 1993.

Safadi, Muta', *Hizb al-Ba'th, Ma'sat al-Mawlid Ma'sat al-Nihayah*, Beirut, 1964.

— 'Nahwa Suriyah Hadithah', *Milaff al-Nahar*, No. 61, al-'Alam al-'Arabi al-Yawm (7), 6 March 1971.

Saghiyah, Hazim (ed.), *Nawasib wa Rawafid. Munaza'at al-Sunnah wa al-Shi'ah fi al-'Alam al-Islami al-Yawm*, 2nd edn, Beirut, 2010.

Salamah, Ibrahim, 'al-Ba'th min al-Madaris ila al-Thuknat', *Milaff al-Nahar*, No. 25, 18 March 1969.

al-Salih, Mahmud, *al-Naba' al-Yaqin 'an al-'Alawiyin*, 2nd edn, Damascus, 1993.

Salim, Muslih, *Man Yasna' al-Aqdar*, Damascus, 1975.

Sallam, Qasim, *al-Ba'th wa al-Watan al-'Arabi*, Paris, 1980.

al-Samman, Muti', *Watan wa 'Askar: Qabl an tudfa' al-Haqiqah fi al-Turab. Mudhakkirat 28 Aylul 1961–8 Adhar 1963*, Beirut, 1995.

al-Sayyid, Jalal, *Haqiqat al-Ummah al-'Arabiyah wa 'Awamil Hifziha wa Tamziqiha*, Beirut, 1973.

— *Hizb al-Ba'th al-'Arabi*, Beirut, 1973.

al-Shak'ah, Mustafa, *Islam bila Madhabib*, 8th edn, Cairo, 1991.

Sharaf al-Din, Taqi, *al-Nusayriyah: Dirasah Tahliliyah*, Beirut, 1983.

al-Sharif, Jalal Faruq, *Mujaz al-Tarikh al-Nidali li-Hizb al-Ba'th al-'Arabi al-Ishtiraki*, Damascus, 1983.

al-Sharif, Munir, *al-Muslimun al-'Alawiyun. Man Hum? wa Ayn Hum?*, 3rd edn, Damascus, 1961.

Shu'aybi, Fawzi, *Shahid min al-Mukhabarat al-Suriyah min 'Am 1955–1968*, n.p., n.d.

Shu'aybi, 'Imad Fawzi, 'Munaqashah li-Kitab Safir Hulanda fi Misr: *'al-Sira' 'ala al-Sultah fi Suriya'*, Mu'alajah bi-Ruh al-Tafkik … wa al-Fatnah', *al-Safir*, 28 April 1995.

— 'Radd 'ala al-Safir al-Hulandi fi Misr: *al-Sira' 'ala al-Sultah fi Suriya* Kitab La Yahtarim Qari'ah', *al-Diyar*, 11 June 1995.

— 'Hal yahkum al-Ra'is Bashar al-Asad Suriyah.!!!', *al-Sharq al-Awsat*, 4 July 2004.

Shuwayri, Nabil, *Suriyah wa Hutam al-Marakib al-Muta'aththirah: Hiwar ma' Nabil Shuwayri, Rafiq 'Aflaq wa al-Hawrani*, n.p., n.d.

al-Siba'i, Badr al-Din, *'al-Marhalah al-Intiqaliyah' fi Suriyah. 'Ahd al-Wahdah 1958–1961*, Beirut, 1975.

Subhi, Muhyi al-Din, *Malamih al-Shakhsiyah al-'Arabiyah fi al-Tayyar al-Fikri al-Mu'adi lil-Ummah al-'Arabiyah*, n.p. [al-Dar al-'Arabiyah lil-Kitab], n.d.

Sultan, Zubayr, *al-Qadiyah al-Kurdiyah min al-Dahhak ila al-Maladh*, Dayr al-Zur, 1995.

Suwayd, Nafidh, *Zaki al-Arsuzi al-Ab al-Ruhi li-Hizb al-Ba'th al-'Arabi al-Ishtiraki*, Damascus, 1992.

Tadmur al-Majzarah al-Mustamirrah, 2nd edn, n.p., 1984.

Talas, Mustafa, *Harb al-'Isabat*, Beirut, 1969.

— *al-Kifah al-Musallah wa al-Tahaddi al-Sahyuni*, Beirut, n.d.

— *al-Rasul al-'Arabi wa Fann al-Harb*, Damascus, 1972.

— *Mir'at Hayati, al-'Aqd al-Awwal, 1948–1958*, 2nd edn, Damascus, 1991.

— *al-Mu'jam al-Jughrafi lil-Qutr al-'Arabi al-Suri*, 5 vols, Damascus, 1992–93.

— *Mir'at Hayati, al-'Aqd al-Thani, 1958–1968*, Damascus, 1995.

— *Mir'at Hayati, al-'Aqd al-Thalith, 1968–1978*, 2 vols, Damascus, 2003.

— *Mir'at Hayati, al-'Aqd al-Rabi', 1988–1998*, Beirut, 2004; 2nd edn, Damascus, 2007.

— and 'Iddi, Nadim, *Mu'jam al-Asma' al-'Arabiyah*, 3rd edn, Damascus, 1995.

— *Mir'at Hayati, al-'Aqd al-Khamis, 1988–1998*, 2 vols, Damascus, 2008.

al-Tawil, Muhammad Amin Ghalib, *Tarikh al-'Alawiyin*, 2nd edn, Beirut, 1966.

'Ubayd, Salamah, *al-Thawrah al-Suriyah al-Kubra 1925–1927*, Damascus, 1971.

'Umayri, Ibrahim, *Silsilat al-Jibal al-Sahiliyah*, Damascus, 1995.

'Umran, Muhammad, *Tajribati fi al-Thawrah*, Beirut, 1970.

'Uthman, Hashim, *al-'Alawiyun bayn al-Usturah wa al-Haqiqah*, 2nd edn, Beirut, 1985.

Yusuf, Rafiq, *al-Mat'un bi-Sharafihim*, Sharjah, 2000.

Zahr al-Din, 'Abd al-Karim, *Mudhakkirati 'an Fatrat al-Infisal fi Suriyah ma bayn 28 Aylul 1961 wa 8 Adhar 1963*, Beirut, 1968.

Zakariya, Ghassan, *al-Sultan al-Ahmar*, London, 1991.

Zarqah, Muhammad 'Ali, *Qadiyat Liwa' al-Iskandarunah*, 3 vols, Beirut, 1993–95.

Zartuqah, Salah Salim, *Anmat al-Istila' 'ala al-Sultah fi al-Duwal al-'Arabiyah. Al-Namat al-Wirathi – al-Namat al-Inqilabi – Anmat Ukhra 1950–1985*, 2nd edn, Cairo, 1993.

Zayn al-'Abidin, Bashir, *al-Fasad fi Suriyah (1963–2000). Haqa'iq wa Arqam*, Markaz al-Dirasat al-Islamiyah, Birmingham, n.d.

Ziadeh, Radwan, *Rabi' Dimashq: Qadaya, Ittijahat, Nihayat*, Cairo, 2007.

— *Sanawat al-Khawf. Al-Haqiqah wa al-'Adalah fi Qadiyat al-Mukhtafin Qasriyan fi Suriyah*, n.p., n.d.

Works in Arabic on Hafiz al-Asad and family

al-'Abd Allah, Hamidi, *Istratijiyat al-Asad: Dirasah fi al-Tawazun al-Istratiji bayn Suriyah wa Isra'il*, Beirut, 1995.

al-Akhras, Muhammad Safuh, *al-Hurriyah wa al-Rumuz al-Hadariyah al-Kubra fi Falsafah wa Fikr al-Qa'id al-Ramz Hafiz al-Asad*, Damascus, 1995.

'Ali, Ahmad, *Suriyah Masirat al-Huzn al-Watani*, n.p., n.d.

'Ali, Ma'n Salah al-Din (ed.), *Ahdab Fajrik*, Damascus, 1998.

— *al-Hikmah fi Fikr al-Ra'is Hafiz al-Asad*, Damascus, 1998.

al-Amin, Fawzi, *Hafiz al-Asad wa Dawruhu al-Qawmi fi Lubnan*, Beirut, 1983.

al-Asad, Hafiz, *Majmu'at Khutab al-Fariq al-Qa'id Hafiz al-Asad, al-Kitab al-Awwal, 24/11/1970–30/8/1971*, Damascus, 1971.

al-As'ad, Ahmad, *al-Takamul bayn Marhalatayn: Qira'ah Minhajiyah fi Masirah Kifahiyah lil-Qa'idayn al-'Arabiyayn Jamal 'Abd al-Nasir wa Hafiz al-Asad*, Damascus, 1981.

— *al-Wahdah Tariq al-'Arab lil-Mustaqbal: Qira'ah Wahdawiyah fi Fikr al-Qa'idayn al-'Arabiyayn Hafiz al-Asad wa Jamal 'Abd al-Nasir*, Damascus, 1995.

al-'Asha, Fu'ad, *Hafiz al-Asad: Qa'id wa Risalah*, 2nd edn, Damascus, 1993.

'Awwad, Riyad Sulayman, *al-Fada' 'Arin al-Asad*, Damascus, 1987.

— *Nidal al-Munazzamat al-Sha'biyah min Fajr al-Tashih hatta al-Yawm*, Damascus, 1990.

— *al-Dimuqratiyah wa al-Salam fi Nahj Hafiz al-Asad*, Damascus, 1992.

— *Hafiz al-Asad wa Tajribat al-Jabhah al-Wataniyah al-Taqaddumiyah fi Suriyah*, Damascus, 1992.

— *al-Nafis fi Siyasat Hafiz al-Asad*, Damascus, 1993.

— *Dhikrayat Wafa' lil-Faris al-Ramz Basil al-Asad*, Damascus, 1994.

— *al-Shahid al-Hayy Basil al-Asad*, Damascus, 1994.

— *Hafiz al-Asad wa al-Nizam al-Dawli al-Jadid*, Damascus, 1995.

— *Hafiz al-Asad wa al-Salam fi al-Sharq al-Awsat*, Damascus, 1995.

— *Harakat al-Tarikh wa Wahdat al-Ummah fi Fikr Hafiz al-Asad*, Damascus, 1995.

— *Harakat al-Tarikh wa Wahdat al-Ummah fi Fikr Hafiz al-Asad*, 2 vols, Damascus, 1995.

— *Hafiz al-Asad, Rajul al-Sharq al-Awhad*, Damascus, 1996.

— *Hafiz al-Asad, Rajul al-Sharq al-Awsat*, Damascus, 1996.

— *Hafiz al-Asad wa Tajribat al-Idarah al-Mahalliyah fi Suriya*, Damascus, 1996.

— *al-Nahj al-Qawmi fi Fikr Hafiz al-Asad*, Homs, 1996.

Babilli, Ahmad 'Ali, *Shams Tishrin*, Damascus, 1998.

al-Barazi, Riyad Ibrahim, *al-Asad … Sayyid al-Sharq al-Awsat*, Damascus, 1997.

Basil al-Asad fi Dhakirat al-Watan, Damascus, n.d.

Basil al-Asad: Malhamat Faris, Damascus, n.d.

Basil al-Asad: Sirat Faris Miqdam wa Hayat Mubdi' Khallaq, Damascus, 1995.

al-Basil lan Yaghiba Abadan, special issue of *Iqtisadiyat Halab*, Aleppo, January 1995.

Bitterlin, Lucien, *Hafiz al-Asad: Masirat Munadil*, 2nd edn, Damascus, 1992.

—— *al-Hurub wa al-Salam fi al-Sharq al-Awsat: Hafiz al-Asad wa al-Tahaddiyat al-Thalath: Lubnan - Filastin - al-Khalij*, Damascus, 1997.

Dabbas, Ahmad 'Abd al-Salam, *Adwa' 'ala al-Mas'alah al-Idariyah. Muqtatafat Idariyah min Aqwal al-Ra'is Hafiz al-Asad*, Damascus, 1992.

al-Dayah, Ibrahim, *al-Asad fi al-Khitab al-Misri. Al-'Ilaqat al-Suriyah al-Misriyah*, Cairo, 1995.

Fadil, 'Imad, *Hafiz al-Asad wa 'Abd al-Nasir: Dirasah Muqarinah*, Damascus, 1990.

al-Faris al-Basil. Al-Dhikra al-Ula lil-Rahil, special issue of *Tishrin*, Damascus, 21 January 1995.

Hafiz, 'Adil, *Hafiz al-Asad: Qa'id wa Ummah*, Damascus, 1993.

al-Hajj 'Ali, Ahmad, 'Qiyadat Hafiz al-Asad - Muqawwimat al-Bina' wa Muqaddimat al-Tafa'ul wa al-Iqtida", *al-Nadwah al-Fikriyah al-Rabi'ah*, al-Qiyadah al-Qutriyah, Damascus, 1992.

Hammadi, Hashim and Qutrayb, Hasan (eds), *Anta lana Watan*, Damascus, 1997.

al-Hariri, Marwan, *Basil Hafiz al-Asad. Dirasah wa Tawthiq*, MA thesis, University of Damascus, 1995.

al-Harrah, Ahmad As'ad, *Jinahahu Tishrinan*, Damascus, 1998.

Hizb al-Ba'th al-'Arabi al-Ishtiraki, al-Qutr al-'Arabi al-Suri, al-Qiyadah al-Qutriyah, *Al-Basil Mawkib al-Majd wa al-Shahadah*, Damascus, n.d.

'Isa, Ayyub, *Alf Nashid wa Ughniyah li-Hafiz al-Asad*, 2 vols, Damascus, 1997, 1998.

'Izz al-Din, Fayiz Hilal, *Hafiz al-Asad wa al-Jamahir*, Damascus, 1992.

— *Hafiz al-Asad al-Dimuqratiyah wa al-Mutaghayyirat al-Duwaliyah*, Damascus, 1997.

Jabbur, Georges, *Hafiz al-Asad wa Qadiyat Filastin*, Damascus, 1988.

Kayyali, Ghalib, *Hafiz al-Asad: Qa'id wa Risalah*, Beirut, 1977.

Khalil, Hani, *Hafiz al-Asad: al-Idanah al-Tarikhiyah al-Thawriyah lil-Irhab al-Duwali*, Damascus, 1990.

— *Hafiz al-Asad: al-Dawlah al-Dimuqratiyah al-Sha'biyah*, 3rd edn, Damascus, 1992.

— *Hafiz al-Asad: al-Idiyulujiyah al-Thawriyah wa al-Fikr al-Siyasi*, 3rd edn, Damascus, 1992.

al-Khuri, Nasir, *li-Majdika Yahlu al-Wafa'*, Damascus, 1997.

Luqa, Iskandar, *Hafiz al-Asad: Qiyam Fikriyah Insaniyah*, Damascus, 1986.

— 'Afkar wa Qiyam Hafiz al-Asad', *al-Nadwah al-Fikriyah al-Rabi'ah*, al-Qiyadah al-Qutriyah, Damascus, 1992.

— *Sha'b wa Qa'id*, Damascus, 1992.

Majallat Basil al-Asad li-'Ulum al-Handasah, Wizarat al-Ta'lim al-'Ali, Damascus, 1998.

Majallat Basil al-Asad lil-'Ulum al-Handasiyah al-Zira'iyah, Wizarat al-Ta'lim al-'Ali, Damascus, 1998.

Majallat Basil al-Asad li-'Ulum al-Lughat wa Adabiha, Wizarat al-Ta'lim al-'Ali, Damascus, 1998.

Markaz al-Ma'lumat al-Qawmi, *al-Qa'id al-Qawmi Hafiz al-Asad*, Damascus, 1996.

— *Waqa'i' al-Sayyid al-Ra'is Hafiz al-Asad, Ra'is al-Jumhuriyah al-'Arabiyah al-Suriyah, al-Mujallad al-Awwal, '1966–1994'*, Damascus, 1996.

— *Waqa'i' al-Sayyid al-Ra'is Hafiz al-Asad, Ra'is al-Jumhuriyah al-'Arabiyah al-Suriyah, al-Mujallad al-Thani, '1995'*, Damascus, 1996.

— *Khutab wa Kalimat wa Tasrihat al-Sayyid al-Ra'is Hafiz al-Asad, Ra'is al-Jumhuriyah, 1966–1995*, 10 vols (including CD-ROM), Damascus, 1997.

Muhakamat Ba'i' al-Jawlan, n.p. [Dar Barada lil-Nashr], 1982.

al-Musa, Ghazi, *Manarat al-Ajyal: Basil Hafiz al-Asad*, Damascus, 1994.

al-Naqib, Mahmud, *al-Basil al-Khalid*, n.p., n.d.

al-Qudsi, Safwan, *al-Batal wa al-Tarikh: Qira'ah fi Fikr Hafiz al-Asad al-Siyasi*, Damascus, 1984.

— *al-Shaja'ah wa al-'Aqilah wa al-Hikmah al-Jasurah. Ta'ammulat fi Madrasat Hafiz al-Asad al-Fikriyah wa al-Siyasiyah*, 2nd edn, Damascus, 1993.

al-Rabdawi, Qasim, *Hafiz al-Asad wa al-Qawmiyah al-'Arabiyah*, Damascus, 1995.

Rida, 'Adil, *al-Tarikh la Tuharrikuh al-Sudfah: Qira'ah fi Fikr al-Asad*, Cairo, 1993.

al-Rifa'i, Muhammad Ihsan, al-Qa'id al-Ramz: *Dirasah fi Susiyulujiyat al-Qiyadah 'ind Hafiz al-Asad*, Damascus, 1997.

Sabbagh, Mazin Yusuf, *Liqa' al-Nusur: al-Qahirah – Dimashq ... 'Ilaqah Mutamayyizah*, n.p., 1997.

al-Sa'dani, 'Izzat, *Basil fi 'Uyun al-Misriyin*, Cairo, 1995.

Sanqar, Salihah, *al-Ma'alim al-Tarbawiyah fi Fikr al-Qa'id Hafiz al-Asad*, Damascus, 1992.

Seale, Patrick, *al-Asad: al-Sira' 'ala al-Sharq al-Awsat*, Beirut, 1992.

Sha'ban, Ayman, *al-Hilm al-Thawri*, Damascus, 1995.

Shahin, Kawthar, *Qasa'id ila Basil Hafiz al-Asad al-Faris al-Dhahabi al-Ra'id*, n.p., n.d.

al-Shammas, 'Isa, *Madrasat al-Qa'id Hafiz al-Asad: Dirasah Tahliliyah Muqarinah min Manzur Tarbawi li-Khutab al-Qa'id wa Kalimatihi wa Ahadithihi ma bayn 1970–1990*, Damascus, 1997.

al-Shaybani, Karim, *Hafiz al-Asad, Shakhsiyah Tarikhiyah fi Marhalah Sa'bah*, Beirut, 1972.

— *Hafiz al-Asad Za'im al-'Urubah al-Mu'asirah*, n.p., 1985.

— *Hafiz al-Asad, al-Ummah wa al-Rihan al-Tarikhi*, Latakia, 1991.

— *al-Asadiyah: Tariq al-Hadir … Rihan al-Mustaqbal*, Latakia, 1997.

Shu'aybi, 'Imad Fawzi, *'al-Ra'is al-Asad Madrasah fi al-Hakim al-Mas'ul wa Abna'uh Tullab Nujaba' fi Madrasatih'*, *al-Diyar*, 20 April 1994.

— *'Kayfa Yahkum al-Ra'is al-Asad … Biladah?'*, *al-Diyar*, 23 August 1994.

— *'Bashar al-Asad Najm Akhlaqi fi 'Alam al-Siyasah'*, *al-Shu'lah*, 16 September 1994.

Shudud, Majid Muhammad, *Hafiz al-Asad wa al-Sira' al-'Arabi al-Sahyuni*, Damascus, 1998.

Sulayman, Bahjat, *al-Manzumah al-Fikriyah lil-Batal Basil al-Asad*, Damascus, 1994.

— *Hafiz al-Asad al-Qa'id al-Insan, 1995, al-'Id al-Faddi lil-Harakah al-Tashihiyah*, Damascus, 1995.

Talas, Mustafa (ed.), *Kadhalika Qal al-Asad*, 6th edn, Damascus, 1993.

Turkmani, Muhammad, *Hafiz al-Asad, Rajul al-Salam wa al-Husam*, Damascus, 1995.

'Uthman, Aws, *Qadat al-'Alam wa Istithna'iyat al-Asad*, Damascus, 1995.

Wizarat al-I'lam, *Wa minka yantaliq al-Ghad*, Damascus, n.d.

Works in languages other than Arabic

Abd-Allah, Umar F., *The Islamic Struggle in Syria*, Berkeley, 1983.

Abu Jaber, Kamel S., *The Arab Ba'th Socialist Party: History, Ideology and Organization*, Syracuse, NY, 1966.

Abyad, Malakah, *Values of Syrian Youth. A Study Based on Syrian Students in Damascus University*, MA thesis, American University of Beirut, 1968.

Agha, Hussein J. and Khalidi, Ahmad S., *Syria and Iran: Rivalry and Cooperation*, London, 1995.

al-Akhrass, Safouh, *Revolutionary Change and Modernization in the Arab World: A Case from Syria*, Damascus, 1972.

Akili, M. Talal, *Die Syrischen Küstengebiete. Eine Modelluntersuchung zur Regionalplanung in den Entwicklungsländern*, Berlin, 1968.

Antoun, Richard T. and Quataert, Donald (eds), *Syria: Society, Culture and Polity*, New York, 1991.

Arab Report and Record, London, 1966–78.

The Arab World, Beirut, 1963–75.

Ashour, Issam Y., *The Remnants of the Feudal System in Palestine, Syria and the Lebanon*, MA thesis, American University of Beirut, 1946.

Audo, Antoine, *Zaki al-Arsouzi: Un Arabe Face A la Modernité*, Beirut, 1988.

Aoyoma, Hiroyuki, 'The Propaganda of the Syrian Muslim Brotherhood in the Anti-Regime Movement from 1976 to 1982', *Ann. of Japanese Association for Middle East Studies*, No. 9 (1994), pp. 117–41.

Badr al-Din, Salah, *Westkurdistan (Syrien)*, Dresden, 1994.

Baer, Gabriel, *Population and Society in the Arab East*, London, 1964.

Bahout, Joseph, 'Les Entrepreneurs Syriens. Economie, affaires et politique', *Les Cahiers du CERMOC*, No. 7, 1994.

Baram, Amatzia, *Culture, History and Ideology in the Formation of Ba'thist Iraq, 1968–89*, London, 1991.

— 'Neo-Tribalism in Iraq: Saddam Hussein's Tribal Policies 1991–96', *International Journal of Middle East Studies*, Vol. 29, No. 1 (1997), pp. 1–31.

al-Barazi, Riad Ibrahim, *Al-Assad: Grand Master of the Middle East*, Damascus, 1997.

Batatu, Hanna, *The Old Social Classes and the Revolutionary Movements of Iraq. A Study of Iraq's Old Landed and Commercial Classes and of its Communists, Ba'thists and Free Officers*, Princeton, NJ, 1978.

— 'Some Observations on the Social Roots of Syria's Ruling Military Group and the Causes for its Dominance', *The Middle East Journal*, Vol. 35, No. 3 (1981), pp. 331–44.

— 'Syria's Muslim Brethern', *MERIP Reports*, No. 110, Vol. 12, No. 9 (November–December 1982), pp. 12–20, 34.

— *Syria's Peasantry, the Descendants of Its Lesser Rural Notables, and Their Politics*, Princeton, NJ, 1999.

Beany, C. H., 'The Turkic Peoples of Syria', in Margareth Brainsbridge (ed.), *The Turkic Peoples of the World*, London, 1993, pp. 207–13.

Be'eri, Eliezer, *Army Officers in Arab Politics and Society*, New York and London, 1970.

Behnstedt, Peter, *Sprachatlas von Syrien*, 2 vols, Wiesbaden, 1997.

Ben-Tsur, Avraham, 'Composition and Membership of the Ba'th Party in the Kuneitra Region', *Hamizrah Hehadash*, XVIII (1968), pp. 269–73.

— 'The Neo-Ba'th Party of Syria', *Journal of Contemporary History*, Vol. 3, No. 3, July 1968, pp. 161–81.

Berey, George, 'Syria: Prospects of Democracy', *Civil Society*, Cairo, Vol. 4, No. 42, June 1995, pp. 9–11.

Berger, Morroe, *The Arab World Today*, New York, 1962.

Betts, Robert B., *Christians in the Arab East*, Athens, 1978.

— *The Druze*, New Haven, 1988.

Biegel, L. C., *Minderheden in het Midden-Oosten, hun betekenis als politieke factor in de Arabische wereld*, Deventer, 1972.

Bill, James A., 'Class Analysis and the Dialectics of Modernization in the Middle East', *International Journal of Middle East Studies*, 3 (1972), pp. 417–34.

Bitar, Salaheddin, 'The Rise and Decline of the Baath', *Middle East International*, June 1971, pp. 12–15; July 1971, pp. 13–16.

Bitterlin, Lucien, *Hafez el-Assad: Le Parcours d'un Combattant*, Paris, 1986.

Bleany, C. H., *Modern Syria: An Introduction to the Literature*, Centre for Middle Eastern and Islamic Studies, Durham, n.d.

Bolz, Reinhardt and Koszinowski, Thomas, 'Die syrisch-irakischen Einigungsbestrebungen. Hintergründe, Grenzen und Auswirkungen', *Orient*, Vol. 20, No. 3, September 1979, pp. 63–86.

Böttcher, Annabelle, *Syrische Religionspolitik unter Asad*, Freiburg, 1998.

Bou-Nacklie, N. E., 'Les Troupes Spéciales: Religious and Ethnic Recruitment, 1916–46', *International Journal of Middle East Studies*, Vol. 25, 1993, pp. 646–60.

Büren, Rainer, *Syrien und Hafiz al-Asad*, Ebenhausen, 1976.

Cahun, Léon, 'Les Ansariés', *Le Tour du Monde*, Vol. 38, 1878, pp. 368–400.

Caldenborgh, Paul, *Savage Human Beasts or the Purest Arabs? The incorporation of the Alawi community into the Syrian state during the French mandate period (1918–1946)*, PhD thesis, Nijmegen, 2005.

Carlton, Alfred, 'The Syrian coups d'état of 1949', *The Middle East Journal*, Vol. 4, No. 1, January 1950, pp. 1–11.

Carré, Olivier and Michaud, Gérard (i.e. Michel Seurat), *Les Frères musulmans*, Paris, 1983.

Chiffoleau, Sylvia (ed.), 'La Syrie au quotidien. Culture et pratiques du changement', *Revue des mondes musulmans et de la Méditerranée*, Nos 115–16, 2007.

Chouet, Alain, 'L'espace tribal alaouite à l'épreuve du pouvoir. La désintégration par le politique', *Maghreb-Machrek*, No. 147, January–March 1995, pp. 93–119.

— 'Syria: Impact of Wielding Power on 'Alawi Cohesiveness', *FBIS-NES, Daily Report Supplement*, 3 October 1995.

Cohen, Hayyim J., *The Jews of the Middle East 1960–1972*, Jerusalem, 1973.

Comités de Défense des Libertés Démocratiques et les Droits de l'Homme en Syrie, *Les droits de l'homme en Syrie. Conférence le 18 octobre 1993*, Amnesty International, Paris, 1993.

— 'Rapport Annuel 1994: Syrie', *Rapport CDF/Syrie*, No. 193, 2nd edn, April 1994.

— *Rapport Annuel 1995*, Malakoff, 1996.

Cooke, miriam, *Dissident Syria: making oppositional arts official*, Durham and London, 2007.

Cowell, Mark W., *A Reference Grammar of Syrian Arabic*, Washington DC, 1964.

Crow, Ralph, 'A Study of Political Forces in Syria based on a Survey of the 1954 Elections', Beirut (unpublished), May 1955.

Dam, Nikolaos van, 'De Ba'th ideologie. Deel I: De orthodoxe richting van 'Aflaq', *Internationale Spectator*, XXV-4, 22 February 1971, pp. 388–408.

— 'De Ba'thpartij in Syrië (1958–1966)', *Internationale Spectator*, XXV-20, 22 November 1971, pp. 1889–933.

— 'The Struggle for Power in Syria and the Ba'th Party (1958–1966)', *Orient*, 1973/1, March 1973, pp. 10–20.

— 'Integration Problems of the Federation of Arab Republics', *Orient*, 1973/3, September 1973, pp. 112–15.

— *De Rol van Sektarisme, Regionalisme en Tribalisme bij de Strijd om de Politieke Macht in Syrië (1961–1976)*, PhD thesis, University of Amsterdam, 1977.

— 'Israeli Sectarian Propaganda during the October, 1973, War', *The Muslim World*, Vol. LXVII, No. 4, October 1977, pp. 295–305. Also in: Ron D. McLaurin (ed.), *Military Propaganda: Psychological Warfare and Operations*, New York, 1982, pp. 356–65.

— 'Sectarian and Regional Factionalism in the Syrian Political Elite', *The Middle East Journal*, Vol. 32, No. 2, Spring 1978, pp. 201–10.

— 'Israel and Arab National Integration: Pluralism versus Arabism', *Asian Affairs*, Vol. 10 (Old Series Vol. 66), Part 2, June 1979, pp. 144–50.

— 'Union in the Fertile Crescent', *Middle East International*, No. 104, 20 July 1979.

— 'Middle Eastern Political Clichés: "Takriti" and "Sunni rule" in Iraq; "Alawi rule" in Syria. A critical appraisal', *Orient*, Vol. 21, No. 1, January 1980, pp. 42–57.

— 'Das Emporkommen der Alawiten als ein Politischer Machtfaktor im Gegenwärtigen Syrien', *Zeitschrift der Deutschen Morgenländischen Gesellschaft*, Supplement IV (1980), pp. 554–56.

— 'Minorities and Political Elites in Iraq and Syria', in Talal Asad and Roger Owen (eds), *Sociology of 'Developing Societies': The Middle East*, London, 1983, pp. 127–44.

— Review of Dr. Umar F. Abd-Allah, *The Islamic Struggle in Syria*, Berkely, 1983, in *Middle East Studies Association Bulletin*, Vol. 18, No. 1, 1984, pp. 57–59.

— Review of David Roberts, *The Ba'th and the Creation of Modern Syria*, New York, 1987, in *The Middle East Journal*, Vol. 42, No. 1, 1988, pp. 113–14.

— Review of Gregor Voss, *"Alawiya oder Nusairiya?' – Schiitische Machtelite und sunnitische Opposition in der Syrischen Arabischen Republik*, Disseration, Hamburg, 1987, in *Die Welt des Islams*, XXIX (1989), pp. 207–09.

— Review of Annabelle Böttcher, *Syrische Religionspolitik unter Asad* (Freiburger Beiträge zur Entwicklung und Politik, 25), Arnold Bergstraesser Institut, Freiburg i. Br., 1998, in *Bibliotheca Orientalis*, No. 3/4, May–August 1999, pp. 505–07.

— *Suriye'de İktidar Mücadelesi*, Istanbul, 2000.

— 'A personal journey to Aleppo, Bilad al-Sham and the Syrian Arab Republic (in English)', *ALL4SYRIA / Kulluna Shuraka' fi al-Watan*, 8 November 2007.

— Review of Carsten Wieland, *Syrien nach dem Irak-Krieg. Bastion gegen Islamisten oder Staat vor dem Kollaps?*, Berlin, 2004, in *Bibliotheca Orientalis*, No. 1/2, 2007, pp. 229–31.

— Review of Eyal Zisser, *Commanding Syria: Bashar al-Asad and the first years in power*, London, 2007, in *Bibliotheca Orientalis*, No.3/4, 2007, pp. 478–81 (also in *ALL4SYRIA / Kulluna Shuraka' fi al-Watan*, 17 November 2007).

— 'Reflections on the Occasion of the 400th Anniversary of the Dutch Consulate in Aleppo', *Syrian Studies Association Newsletter*, Vol. XIII, No. 2, Winter 2008, pp. 5, 16–18.

— 'Book Review Essay: Syrian Ba'thist Memoirs', *Syrian Studies Association Newsletter*, Vol. 14, No. 2 (2009), pp. 22–25.

— 'Syrian Ba'thist Memoirs, An Extended Book Review Essay', *Kulluna Shuraka' fi al-Watan / ALL4SYRIA*, 9–11 May 2009.

—, 'Syria: the Dangerous Trap of Sectarianism', *Syria Comment*, 14 April 2011.

David, Jean-Claude, 'Ingénieurs, urbanisme et pouvoirs locaux à Alep', in E. Longuenesse (ed.), *Bâtisseurs et Bureaucrates. Ingéniers et Société au Maghreb et au Moyent-Orient*, Lyon, 1990.

Dawisha, Adeed I., *Syria and the Lebanese Crisis*, London, 1980.

Dawn, C. Ernest, 'The Rise of Arabism in Syria', *The Middle East Journal*, Vol. 16, No. 4, Autumn 1962, pp. 145–68.

Deeb, Marius, *Syria's Terrorist War on Lebanon and the Peace Process*, New York, 2003.

Dekmejian, R. Hrair, 'The Anatomy of Islamic Revival: Legitimacy Crisis, Ethnic Conflict and the Search for Islamic Alternatives', *The Middle East Journal*, Vol. 34, No. 1, Winter 1980, pp. 1–12.

Devlin, John F., *The Ba'th Party. A History from its Origins to 1966*, Stanford, CA, 1976.

— *Syria: Modern State in Ancient Land*, London, 1983.

— 'Effects of leadership style on oil policy: Syria and Iraq', *Energy Policy*, November 1992, pp. 1048–54.

Dewdney, J. C., 'Syria: Pattern of Population Distribution', in J. I. Clarke and W. B. Fischer (eds), *Populations of the Middle East and North Africa*, New York, 1972, pp. 130–42.

Dishon, Daniel (ed.), *Middle East Record 1967*, Jerusalem, 1971.

— *Middle East Record 1968*, Jerusalem, 1973.

— *Middle East Record 1969–1970*, 2 vols, Jerusalem, 1977.

Donati, Caroline, *L'Exception Syrienne. Entre Modernisation et Résistance*, Paris, 2009.

Donohue, John J., 'La Nouvelle Constitution Syrienne et ses Détracteurs', *Travaux et Jours*, Beirut, April–June 1973, pp. 93–111.

Douwes, Dick, *Justice and Oppression: Ottoman rule in the province of Damascus and the district of Hama, 1785–1841*, doctoral dissertation, Nijmegen, 1994.

Drysdale, Alasdair, 'Ethnicity in the Syrian Officer Corps: A Conceptualisation', *Civilisations*, Vol. 29, No. 3/4 (1979), pp. 359–73.

— 'The Regional Equalization of Health Care and Education in Syria since the Ba'thi Revolution', *International Journal of Middle East Studies*, Vol. 13 (1981), pp. 93–111.

— 'The Syrian Political Elite, 1966–1976: A Spatial and Social Analysis', *Middle Eastern Studies*, Vol. 17, No.1 (1981), pp.3–30.

— 'The Asad Regime and its Troubles'. *MERIP Reports*, No. 110, Vol.12, No. 9 (November–December 1982), pp. 3–11.

— 'The Syrian Armed Forces in National Politics: The Role of the Geographic and Ethnic Periphery', in R. Kolkowicz and A. Korbonski (eds), *Soldiers, Peasants, and Bureaucrats*, London, 1982, pp. 52–76.

— 'The Succession Question in Syria', *The Middle East Journal*, Vol. 39, No. 2 (1985), pp. 246–62.

— and Hinnebusch, Raymond A., *Syria and the Middle East Peace Process*, New York, 1991.

— 'Syria since 1988: From Crisis to Opportunity', in Robert O. Friedman (ed.), *The Middle East After the Invasion of Kuwait*, Gainsville, CA, 1993, pp. 276–96.

— 'Transboundary interaction and political conflict in the central Middle East: The case of Syria', in Clive H. Schofield and Richard N. Schofield (eds), *The Middle East and North Africa*, London, 1994, pp. 21–34.

Dupret, Baudouin and Ghazzal, Zouhair (eds), *La Syrie au présent. Reflets d'une société*, Paris, 2006.

Dussaud, René, *Histoire et Religion des Nosairis*, Paris, 1900.

Esman, Milton J. and Rabinovich, Itamar (eds), *Ethnicity, Pluralism, and the State in the Middle East*, London, 1988.

Faksh, Mahmud A., 'The Alawi Community of Syria: A New Dominant Political Force', *Middle Eastern Studies*, Vol. 20, No. 2, 1984, pp. 133–53.

Fawaz, Leila Tarazi, *An Occasion for War – Civil Conflict in Lebanon and Damascus in 1860*, London, 1994.

Fisk, Robert, *Pity the Nation. Lebanon at War*, London, 1990.

Freitag, Ulrike, *Geschichtsschreibung in Syrien 1920–1990. Zwischen Wissenschaft und Ideologie*, Hamburg, 1991.

— 'Writing Arab History: The Search for the Nation', *British Journal of Middle Eastern Studies*, Vol. 21, No. 1, 1994, pp. 19–37.

Friedman, Thomas, *From Beirut to Jerusalem*, London, 1989.

George, Alan, *Syria. Neither Bread nor Freedom*, London and New York, 2003.

Ginat, Joseph, Shalit, Yoram and Winckler, Onn, *Modern Syria: a Pivotal Role in the Middle East*, Sussex, 1998.

Gubser, Peter, 'Minorities in Power: The Alawites of Syria', in R. D. McLaurin (ed.), *The Political Role of Minority Groups in the Middle East*, New York, 1979, pp. 17–48.

Haddad, George M., *Revolutions and Military Rule in the Middle East, Vol. II: The Arab States*, New York, 1971.

Hanafi, Sari, *Les ingénieurs en Syrie, modernisation, technobureaucratie et identité*, Thèse pour le doctorat en sociologie, Paris (EHESS), 1994.

— *La Syrie des ingénieurs technobureaucrates. Enquête d'identité*, Paris, 1996.

Harik, Ilya F., 'The Ethnic Revolution and Political Integration in the Middle East', *International Journal of Middle East Studies*, 3 (1972), pp. 303–23.

Heydemann, Steven, 'Taxation without Representation: Authoritarianism and Economic Liberalization in Syria', in E. Goldberg, R. Kasaba and J. Migdal (eds), *Rules and Rights in the Middle East: Democracy, Law, and Society*, Seattle and London, 1993, pp. 69–101.

— *Authoritarianism in Syria. Institutions and Social Conflict, 1946–1970*, Ithaca and London, 1999.

Hill, Fiona E., 'Reverse Orientalism?: Tribe and Nation in Syria', *Journal of Arabic, Islamic and Middle Eastern Studies*, Vol. 1 (1994), No. 2, pp. 59–75.

Hinnebusch, Raymond A., 'Elite-Mass Linkage: The Role of the Mass Organizations in the Syrian Political System', n.p., n.d.

— 'Local Politics in Syria: Organisation and Mobilisation in Four Village Cases', *The Middle East Journal*, Vol. 30, No. 1, Winter 1976, pp. 1–24.

— 'Party and Peasant in Syria', *Cairo Papers in Social Science*, November 1979.

— *Peasant and Bureaucracy in Ba'thist Syria: the Political Economy of Rural Development*, San Francisco, 1989.

— *Authoritarian Power and State Formation in Ba'thist Syria: Army, Party and Peasant*, San Francisco, 1990.

— 'Class and State in Ba'thist Syria', in Richard T. Antoun and Donald Quataert (eds), *Syria: Society, Culture and Polity*, New York, 1991, pp. 29–47.

— and Drysdale, A., *Syria and the Middle East Peace Process*, New York, 1991.

— 'State and Civil Society in Syria', *The Middle East Journal*, Vol. 47, No. 2 (1993), pp. 243–57.

— 'Liberalization in Syria: the Struggle of Economic and Political Reality', in Eberhard Kienle, *Contemporary Syria*, London, 1994, pp. 97–113.

— 'The Political Economy of Economic Liberalization in Syria', *International Journal of Middle East Studies*, Vol. 27, 1995, pp. 305–20.

— 'State, Civil Society, and Political Change in Syria', in A. R. Norton (ed.), *Civil Society in the Middle East*, Vol. 1, Leiden, 1995, pp. 214–42.

— 'Syria: The Politics of Peace and Regime Survival', *Middle East Policy*, Vol. 3, No. 4, April 1995, pp. 74–87.

— 'Does Syria want Peace? Syrian Policy in the Syrian–Israeli Peace Negotiations, *Journal of Palestine Studies*, Vol. 26, No. 1, Autumn 1996, pp. 42–57.

— and Ehteshami, Anoushiravan, *Syria and Iran: Middle powers in a penetrated regional system*, London and New York, 1997.

— 'Syria: the politics of economic liberalisation', *Third World Quarterly*, Vol. 18, No. 2, 1997, pp. 249–65.

Hitti, Philip K., *The Origins of the Druze People and Religion*, New York, 1928.

Hopfinger, Hans and Boeckler, Marc, 'Step by Step to an Open Economic System: Syria Sets Course for Liberalization', *British Journal for Middle Eastern Studies*, Vol. 23, No. 2, November 1996, pp. 183–202.

Hopwood, Derek, *Syria 1945–1986: Politics and Society*, London, 1988.

Hourani, A. H. *Minorities in the Arab World*, London, 1947.

— *Syria and Lebanon, A Political Essay*, 3rd edn, London, 1954.

Hudson, Michael H., *Arab Politics. The Search for Legitimacy*, New Haven and London, 1977.

Human Rights Watch / Middle East, Vol. 7, No. 4, July 1995, *Syria, The Price of Dissent*.

— Vol. 8, No. 2 (E), April 1996, *Syria's Tadmor Prison. Dissent Still Hostage To A Legacy of Terror.*

— Vol. 8, No. 4 (E), October 1996, *Syria: The Silenced Kurds.*

— Vol. 9, No. 3 (E), May 1997, *Syria / Lebanon. An Alliance Beyond the Law: Enforced Disappearances in Lebanon.*

Human Rights Watch World Report 1995, New York, 1994.

Humphreys, R. Stephen, 'Islam and Political Values in Saudi Arabia, Egypt and Syria', *The Middle East Journal*, Vol. 33, No. 1, Winter 1979, pp. 1–19.

Hurewitz, J. C., *Middle East Politics: The Military Demension*, New York, Washington and London, 1969.

Janowitz, Morris, *The Military and Political Development of New Nations*, Chicago, 1964.

Joris, Lieve, *De Poorten van Damascus*, Amsterdam, 1993.

— *Les Portes de Damas*, Arles, 1994.

Kaylani, Nabil M., 'The Rise of the Syrian Ba'th, 1940–1958: Political Success, Party Failure', *International Journal of Middle East Studies*, 3 (1972), pp. 3–23.

Kedourie, Elie, *The Chatham House Version and other Middle Eastern Studies*, London, 1970.

Kelidar, A. R., 'Religion and State in Syria, *Asian Affairs*, Vol. 61 (new series Vol. 5), Part I, February 1974, pp. 16–22.

Kerr, Malcolm, *The Arab Cold War 1958–1967, A Study of Ideology in Politics*, 2nd edn, London, 1967.

— 'Hafiz Asad and the Changing Patterns of Syrian Politics', *International Journal*, Vol. 28, 1972–3, pp. 689–706.

— 'Coup and clan in Syria', *Gazelle Review of Literature on the Middle East*, No. 7, 1980, pp. 45–7.

Kessler, Martha Neff, *Syria: Fragile Mosaic of Power*, Washington DC, 1987.

Khadduri, Majid, *Arab Personalities in Politics*, Washington DC, 1981.

Khalidi, Tarif, 'A Critical Study of the Political Ideas of Michel Aflak', *Middle East Forum*, Vol. XLII, No. 2, pp. 55–68.

Khoury, Philip S., *Urban notables and Arab nationalism: The politics of Damascus 1860–1920*, Cambridge, 1983.

— *Syria and the French Mandate: The Politics of Arab Nationalism, 1920–1945*, London, 1987.

Khuri, Fuad I., 'The Alawis of Syria: Religious Ideology and Organization', in Richard T. Antoun and Donald Quataert (eds), *Syria: Society, Culture, and Polity*, Albany, 1991, pp. 49–62.

Kienle, Eberhard, 'The Conflict Between the Baath Regimes of Syria and Iraq Prior to Their Consolidation: From Regime Survival to Regional Domination', *Ethnizität und Gesellschaft*, Occasional Papers, No. 5 (1985).

— 'Ethnizität und Machtkonkurrenz in inter-arabischen Beziehungen: Der syrisch-irakische Konflikt unter den Ba'th-Regimen', *Ethnizität und Gesellschaft*, Occasional Papers, No. 12 (1987).

— *Ba'th v Ba'th: The Conflict between Syria and Iraq 1968–1989*, London, 1990.

— 'Entre jama'a et classe. Le pouvoir politique en Syrie contemporaine', *Revue du Monde Musulman et la Méditerranée*, Vols 59–60, 1991, Nos 1–2, pp. 211–39.

— (ed.), *Contemporary Syria. Liberalization between Cold War and Cold Peace*, London, 1994.

— 'Arab Unity Schemes Revisited: Interest, Identity, and Policy in Syria and Egypt', *International Journal of Middle East Studies*, Vol. 27 (1995), pp. 53–71.

— 'Imagined Communities Legislated: Nationalism and the Law of Nationality in Syria and Egypt', in E. Cotran and C. Mallat (eds), *Yearbook of Islamic and Middle Eastern Law*, Vol. 1, 1994, London, 1995, pp. 47–67.

— 'Middle East Peace and Normalization: The Political Consequences of Unequal Solutions', in L. Blin and Ph. Fargues (eds), *L'ecchemie de la paix au Proche-Orient*, Paris, 1995, pp. 55–75.

Kischli, Muhammad, *Kapitalismus und Linke im Libanon*, Frankfurt, 1970.

Koszinowski, Thomas, 'Rif'at al-Asad', *Orient 4* (1984), pp. 465–70.

— 'Die Krise der Ba'th-Herrschaft und die Rolle Asads bei der Sicherung der Macht', *Orient 26* (1985), pp. 549–71.

Kramer, Martin, 'Syria's Alawis and Shi'ism', in Martin Kramer (ed.), *Shi'ism, Resistance, and Revolution*, Boulder, 1987, pp. 237–54.

Landis, Joshua, 'The Political Sociology of Syria reconsidered: a response to Volker Perthes', *The Beirut Review*, 5, 1993, pp. 143–51.

— *Nationalism and the Politics of Za'ama: The Collapse of Republican Syria, 1945–1949*, PhD thesis, Princeton University, 1997.

Lawson, Fred H., 'Social Bases for the Hamah Revolt', *MERIP Reports*, No. 110, Vol. 12, No. 9 (November–December 1982), pp. 24–28.

— 'Domestic Transformation and Foreign Steadfastness in Contemporary Syria', *The Middle East Journal*, Vol. 48, No. 1, 1994, pp. 47–64.

— *Why Syria Goes to War. Thirty Years of Confrontation*, Ithaca, 1996.

— (ed.), *Demystifying Syria*, London, 2009.

Le Gac, Daniel, *La Syrie du général Assad*, Brussels, 1991.

Lenczowski, George, *The Middle East in World Affairs*, New York, 1956.

— (ed.), *Political Elites in the Middle East*, Washington DC, 1975.

Lerner, Daniel, *The Passing of Traditional Society*, New York, 1964.

Lesch, David, *The New Lion of Damascus. Bashar al-Asad and Modern Syria*, New Haven and London, 2005.

Levereth, Flynt, *Inheriting Syria. Bashar's Trial by Fire*, Washington DC, 2005.

Lewin, Bernard, *Notes on Cabali: The Arabic dialect spoken by the Alawis of 'Jebel Ansariye'*, Göteborg, 1969.

Lewis, Norman N., *Nomads and Settlers in Syria and Jordan, 1800–1980*, Cambridge, 1987.

Lobmeyer, Hans Günther, 'Islamic ideology and secular discourse: the Islamists of Syria', *Orient*, Vol. 32, 1991, pp. 395–418.

— *Islamismus und sozialer Konflikt in Syrien*, Berlin, 1993 (*Ethnizität und Gesellschaft*, Occasional Papers No. 26).

— '*Al dimuqratiyya hiyya al-hall?* The Syrian Opposition at the End of the Asad Era', in Eberhard Kienle (ed.), *Contemporary Syria*, London, 1994, pp. 81–96.

— *Opposition und Widerstand in Syrien*, Hamburg, 1995.

Longrigg, S. H., *Syria and Lebanon under French Mandate*, London, 1958.

Longuenesse, Elisabeth, 'Bourgeoisie, Petite-Bourgeoisie et Couches Moyennes en Syrie', *Peuples Méditerranéens*, No. 4, July–September 1978, pp. 21–42.

— 'The Class Nature of the State in Syria', *MERIP Reports*, No. 77, May 1979, pp. 3–11.

— 'The Syrian Working Class Today', *MERIP Reports*, No. 134, July–August 1985, pp. 17–24.

— (ed.), *Bâtisseurs et Bureaucrates. Ingéniers et Société au Maghreb et au Moyent-Orient*, Lyon, 1990.

— 'Ingénieurs et médecins dans le changement social en Syrie. Mobilité sociale et recomposition des élites', *Maghreb-Machrek*, No. 146, October–December 1994, pp. 59–71.

— 'Labor in Syria: The Emergence of New Identities', in E. Goldberg (ed.), *The Social History of Labour in the Middle East*, New York, 1995.

— 'Les médecins syriens, des médiateurs dans une société en crise?', in Elisabeth Longuenesse (ed.), *Santé, Médecine et Société dans le Monde Arabe*, Paris, 1995.

Macintyre, Ronald R., *The Arab Ba'th Socialist Party: Ideology, Politics, Sociology and Organization*, PhD thesis, Australian National University, 1969.

— 'Syrian Political Age Differentials 1958–1966', *The Middle East Journal*, Vol. 29, No. 2, Spring 1975, pp. 207–13.

Mahayni, M. Mohammed Sabet, *L'Evolution Constitutionelle de la Syrie Indépendante*, Thèse pour le Doctorat d'Etat, Paris, 1972.

Mahr, Horst, *Die Baath-Partei; Portrait einer Panarabischen Bewegung*, München, 1971.

Makarem, Sami Nasib, *The Druze Faith*, New York, 1974.

Maler, Paul, (i.e. Michel Seurat), 'La société Syrienne contre son état', *Le Monde Diplomatique*, April 1980.

Manna, Haytham, 'Histoire des Frères Musulmans en Syrie', *Sou'al*, No. 5, April 1985, pp. 67–82.

— 'Syria: Accumulation of Errors?', *Middle Eastern Studies*, Vol. 23, No. 2, April 1987, pp. 211–14.

Ma'oz, Moshe, 'Attempts at Creating a Political Community in Modern Syria', *The Middle East Journal*, Vol. 26, No. 4, Autumn 1972, pp. 389–404.

— 'Society and State in Modern Syria', in Menahem Milson (ed.), *Society and Political Structure in the Arab World*, New York, 1973, pp. 29–91.

— 'Alawi Military Officers in Syrian Politics, 1966–1974', in *Military and State in Modern Asia*, Jerusalem, 1976.

— 'Hafiz al-Asad: A Political Profile', *The Jerusalem Quarterly*, No. 8, Summer 1978, pp. 16–31.

— and Yaniv, Avner (eds), *Syria under Assad*, London, 1986.

— *Asad the Sphinx of Damascus*, London, 1988.

— *Syria and Israel: From War to Peacemaking*, Oxford, 1995.

Mayer, Thomas, 'The Islamic opposition in Syria, 1961–1982', *Orient*, Vol. 24, No. 4, December 1983, pp. 589–609.

McLaurin, R. D. (ed.), *The Political Role of Minority Groups in the Middle East*, New York, 1979.

— (ed.), *Military Propaganda: Psychological Warfare and Operations*, New York, 1982.

Métral, Françoise, 'Ingénieurs et agronomes dans un projet de développement rural en Syrie', in E. Longuenesse (ed.), *Batisseurs et Bureaucrates. Ingénieurs et Société au Maghreb et au Moyent-Orient*, Lyon, 1990, pp. 231–54.

— 'State and Peasants in Syria: a Local View of a Government Irrigation Project', in Saad Eddin Ibrahim and Nicholas Hopkins (eds), *Arab Society, Social Science Perspectives*, 3rd edn, Cairo, 1992, pp. 336–54.

Michaud, Gérard, (i.e. Michel Seurat), 'The Importance of Bodyguards', *MERIP Reports*, No. 110, Vol. 12, No. 9 (November–December 1982), pp. 29–31.

Middle East Watch, *Syria Unmasked: The Suppression of Human Rights by the Asad Regime*, New Haven, 1991.

Mitchell, R. P., *The Society of the Muslim Brothers*, London, 1969.

Moubayed, Sami, *Steel and Silk. Men and Women Who Shaped Syria 1900–2000*, Seattle, 2006.

Mousa, Munir Mushabik, *Etude Sociologique des 'Alaouites ou Nusairis*, Thèse Principale pour le Doctorat d'Etat, 2 vols, Paris, 1958.

Mufti, Malik, *Sovereign Creations: Pan-Arabism and Political Order in Syria and Iraq*, Ithaca, NY, 1996.

Nashabi, Hisham A., *The Political Parties in Syria*, MA thesis, American University of Beirut, 1951–52.

Nasr, Nicolas, *Faillite Syrienne au Liban 1975–1981*, 2 vols, Beirut, 1982.

Nazdar, Mustafa, 'Die Kurden in Syrien', in Gérard Chaliand (ed.), *Kurdistan und die Kurden*, Vol. 1, Göttingen, 1988, pp. 395–412; also in Gerard Chaliand (ed.), *People Without A Country. The Kurds and Kurdistan*, London, 1980, pp. 211–19, as 'The Kurds in Syria'.

Nieuwenhuijze, C. A. O. van (ed.), *Commoners, Climbers and Notables. A Sampler of Studies on Social Ranking in the Middle East*, Leiden, 1977.

'La Nomenklatura Syrienne', *Les Cahiers de l'Orient*, Paris, 1986, pp. 233–45.

Nouss, I., *La population de la République Syrienne, Etude démographique*, Thèse d'Etat, Paris, 1951.

Office Arabe de Presse et de Documentation, *2e Cabinet Mahmoud Ayoubi (1er Septembre 1974), Structure, Analyse et Biographies*, Damascus, 1974.

— *Le 1er Cabinet de M. El-Halabi, Structure et Biographies*, Damascus, 1978.

— *Le 1er Cabinet de M. Abdel Raouf Al-Kassem, Structure et Biographies*, Damascus, 1980.

— *Le 2e Cabinet de M. Mahmoud Al-Zou'bi du 29 Juin 1992*, Damascus, 1992.

Olson, Robert, *The Ba'th and Syria, 1947 to 1982. The Evolution of Ideology, Party and State*, Princeton, NJ, 1982.

Oron, Y. (ed.), *Middle East Record: Volume II, 1961*, Jerusalem, 1966.

Palazzoli, Claude, *La Syrie, le rêve et la rupture*, Paris, 1977.

Palmer, Monte, 'The United Republic – an Assessment of its Failure', *The Middle East Journal*, Vol. 20, No. 1, Winter 1966, pp. 50–67.

Patterson, Charles, *Hafiz Al-Asad of Syria*, Englewood Cliffs, NJ, 1991.

Perthes, Volker, 'Einige kritische Bemerkungen zum Minderheitenparadigma in der Syrienforschung', *Orient* 31/4 (1990), pp. 571–82.

— *Staat und Gesellschaft in Syrien, 1970–1989*, Hamburg, 1990.

— 'The Bourgeois and the Ba'th', *Middle East Report*, May–June 1991, pp. 31–37.

— 'The Political Sociology of Syria: a bibliographical essay', *The Beirut Review*, 4, 1992, pp. 105–13.

— 'Syria's Parliamentary Elections: remodeling Asad's Political Base', *Middle East Report*, January–February 1992, pp. 15–18, 35.

— 'The Syrian Private Industrial and Commercial Sectors and the State', *International Journal of Middle East Studies*, Vol. 24 (1992), pp. 207–30.

— 'Syrie: les élections de 1990', *Maghreb-Machrek*, No. 137, 1992, pp. 3–14.
— 'The Private Sector, Economic Liberalization, and the Prospects of Democratization: the case of Syria and some other Arab countries', in Ghassan Salamé (ed.), *Democracy without Democrats?*, London, 1994.
— 'Kriegsdividende und Friendensrisiken: Überlegungen zu Rente und Politik in Syrien', *Orient*, Vol. 35, No. 3, September 1994, pp. 413–24.
— 'Stages of Economic and Political Liberalization', in Eberhard Kienle (ed.), *Contemporary Syria*, London, 1994, pp. 44–71.
— 'Arab Unity Schemes Revisited: Interest, Identity, and Policy in Syria and Egypt', *International Journal of Middle East Studies*, Vol. 27 (1995), pp. 53–71.
— 'From War Dividend to Peace Dividend? Syrian Options in a New Regional Environment', *Al-Nadwah*, January 1995, pp. 6–18.
— *The Political Economy of Syria under Asad*, London, 1995.
— *Syria under Bashar al-Asad: Modernisation and the Limits of Change*, Adelphi Papers 366, London, 2004.
Peters, Rudolph, *Islam and Colonialism. The Doctrine of Jihad in Modern History*, The Hague, 1979.
Petran, Tabitha, *Syria*, London, 1972.
Philipp, Thomas and Schaebler, Birgit (eds), *The Syrian Land: Processes of Integration and Fragmentation. Bilad Al-Sham from the 18th to the 20th century*, Stuttgart, 1998.
Picard, Elizabeth, 'Clans Militaires et Pouvoir Ba'thiste en Syrie', *Orient*, Vol. 20, No. 3, September 1979, pp. 49–62.
— 'Y a-t-il un problème communautaire en Syrie?', *Maghreb-Machrek*, 87 (Janvier–Mars 1980), pp. 7–21.
— 'Critique de l'usage du concept d'*ethnicité* dans l'analyse des processus politiques dans le monde arabe', in: *Etudes politiques du monde arabe*, Cairo (CEDEJ), 1991, pp. 71–84.
— 'Arab Military in Politics: from Revolutionary Plot to Authoritarian State', in Albert Hourani, Philip S. Khoury and Mary C. Wilson (eds), *The Modern Middle East: A Reader*, London, 1993, pp. 551–78.
— 'Infitâh économique et transition démocratique en Syrie', in R. Bocco and M.-R. Djalili (eds), *Moyen-Orient: migrations, démocratisation, médiations*, Paris, 1994, pp. 221–36.
Pipes, Daniel, 'The Alawi Capture of Power in Syria', *Middle Eastern Studies*, Vol. 25 (1989), pp. 429–50.
— *Greater Syria: The History of an Ambition*, Oxford, 1990.
— *Damascus Courts the West: Syrian Politics, 1989–1991*, Policy Papers, No. 26, The Washington Institute for Near East Policy, 1991.
— 'Syrie: L'Après Assad', *Politique Internationale*, 1993, pp. 97–110.
— 'Understanding Asad', *Middle East Quarterly*, December 1994.
— *Syria beyond the Peace Process*, Policy Papers, No. 40, The Washington Institute for Near East Policy, 1996.
Rabinovich, Itamar, *Syria under the Ba'th 1963–66; The Army–Party Symbiosis*, Jerusalem, 1972.
— 'Historiography and Politics in Syria', *Asian Affairs*, Vol. 9 (Old Series Vol. 65), Part 1, February 1978, pp. 57, 66.
— 'The Compact minorities and the Syrian State, 1918–1945, *Journal of Contemporary History*, Vol. 14, No. 4, October 1979, pp. 693–712.

— and Esman, Milton J. (eds), *Ethnicity, Pluralism, and the State in the Middle East*, London, 1988.

— *The Road Not Taken: Early Arab–Israeli Negotiations*, Oxford, 1991.

— 'Stability and Change in Syria', in R. B. Satloff, *The Politics of Change in the Middle East*, Boulder, 1993, pp. 11–29.

— *The Brink of Peace: The Israeli–Syrian Negotiations*, Princeton, NJ, 1998.

— *The View from Damascus. State, Political Community and Foreign Relations in Twentieth-Century Syria*, London, 2008.

Rabo, Annika, *A Shop of One's Own. Independence and Reputation among Traders in Aleppo*, London, 2005.

Rathmell, Andrew, *Secret War in the Middle East. The Covert Struggle for Syria, 1949–1961*, London, 1995.

Raymond, André (ed.), *La Syrie d'Aujourd'hui*, Paris, 1980.

Receuil des Archives Biographiques Permanentes du Monde Arabe, 2ème edn, Damascus, n.d.

Reilly, James A., 'Inter-Confessional Relations in Nineteenth-Century Syria: Damascus, Homs and Hama compared', *Islam and Christian–Muslim Relations*, Vol. 7, No. 2, 1996, pp. 213–24.

Reissner, Johannes, 'Die andere Ablehnungsfront: Stimmen radikal-islamischer Kreise zur Friedensinitiative Anwar as-Sadats', *Orient*, Vol. 21, No. 2, June 1979, pp. 19–41.

— *Ideologie und Politik der muslimbrüder Syriens. Von den Wahlen 1947 bis zum Verbot unter Adīb aš-Šīšaklī 1952*, Freiburg, 1980.

Roberts, David, *The Ba'th and the Creation of Modern Syria*, London, 1987.

Rubin, Barry, *The Truth about Syria*, New York, 2007.

Saab, Edouard, *La Syrie ou la Révolution dans la Rancoeur*, Paris, 1968.

Sadowski, Yahya M., 'Cadres, Guns and Money: The Eighth Regional Congress of the Syrian Ba'th', *MERIP Reports*, No. 134 (July–August 1985), pp.3–8.

— 'Patronage and the Ba'th: Corruption and Control in Contemporary Syria', *Arab Studies Quarterly*, Vol. 9, No. 4, Fall 1987, pp. 442–61.

Saint-Prot, Charles, *Les Mystères Syriens*, Paris, 1984.

Salih, Shakeeb, 'The British–Druze Connection and the Druze Rising of 1896 in the Hawran', *Middle Eastern Studies*, Vol. 13, No. 2, May 1977, pp. 251–57.

Schäbler, Birgit, *Aufstände im Drusenbergland: Ethnizität und Integration einer ländlichen Gesellschaft Syriens vom Osmanischen Reich bis zur staatlichen Unabhängigkeit*, Gotha, 1996.

Schweizer, Gerhard, *Syrien: Religion und Politik im Nahen Osten*, Stuttgart, 1998.

Seale, Patrick, *The Struggle for Syria; A Study of Post-War Arab Politics (1945–1958)*, London, 1965.

— *Asad: the Struggle for the Middle East*, London, 1988.

— 'Asad: Between Institutions and Autocracy', in Richard T. Antoun and Donald Quataert (eds), *Syria, Society, Culture and Polity*, New York, 1991, pp. 97–110.

— 'Asad's Regional Strategy and the Challenge from Netanyahu', *Journal of Palestine Studies*, Vol. 26, No. 1, Autumn 1996, pp. 27–41.

Seurat, Michel, *L'Etat de Barbarie*, Paris, 1989.

Seymour, Martin, 'The Dynamics of Power in Syria since the Break with Egypt', *Middle Eastern Studies*, Vol. 6, No. 1, January 1970, pp. 35–47.

Sluglett, Peter and Farouk-Sluglett, Marion, 'Some Reflections on the Sunni / Shi'i Question in Iraq', *British Society for Middle Eastern Studies Bulletin*, Vol. 5, No. 2, 1978, pp. 79–87.

— 'Sunnis and Shi'is Revisited: Sectarianism and Ethnicity in Authoritarian Iraq', in John P. Spagnolo (ed.), *Problems of the Modern Middle East in Historical Perspective. Essays in Honour of Albert Hourani*, Reading, 1992, pp. 259–73.

Statistisches Bundesamt Wiesbaden: Allgemeine Statistik des Auslandes, Länderkurzberichte, *Syrien*, Stuttgart / Mainz, 1967, 1969.

Syrian Arab Republic, Office of the Prime Minister, Central Bureau of Statistics, *Statistical Abstract 1971*, Damascus, 1971.

— *Statistical Abstract 1976*, Damascus, 1976.

— *Statistical Abstract 1992*, Damascus, 1992.

Tauber, Eliezer, *The Formation of Modern Syria and Iraq*, London, 1995.

Tlass, Mustapha (ed.), *Paroles d'Assad. Discours et propos du Président de la République Arabe Syrienne*, Paris, 1986.

Torrey, Gordon H., *Syrian Politics and the Military 1945–1958*, Colombus, OH, 1964.

— 'The Ba'th – Ideology and Practice', *The Middle East Journal*, Vol. 23, 1969, pp. 445–70.

— 'Aspects of the Political Elite in Syria', in George Lenczowski (ed.), *Political Elites in the Middle East*, Washington DC, 1975, pp. 151–61.

U.S. Army Area Handbook for Syria, Washington DC, 1965.

Van Dusen, Michael H., *Intra- and Inter-Generational Conflict in the Syrian Army*, PhD dissertation, Baltimore, MD, 1971.

— 'Political Integration and Regionalism in Syria', *The Middle East Journal*, Vol. 26, No. 2, Spring 1972, pp. 123–36.

— 'Syria: Downfall of a Traditional Elite', in Frank Tachau (ed.), *Political Elites and Political Development in the Middle East*, New York, 1975.

Vanly, Ismet Chérif, *La Persécution du Peuple Kurde par la Dictature du Baas en Syrie*, Amsterdam, 1968.

— *Le Problème Kurde en Syrie: Plans pour le génocide d'une minorité nationale*, n.p., 1968.

— *Kurdistan und die Kurden*, Vol. 3, Göttingen, 1988.

Vatikiotis, P. J., 'The Politics in the Fertile Crescent', in P. Y. Hammond and S. S. Alexander (eds), *Political Dynamics in the Middle East*, New York, 1972, pp. 225–42.

Velud, Christian, 'Syrie, Etat mandataire, mouvement national et tribus (1920–1936)', *Maghreb-Machrek*, No. 147, Janv. –Mars 1995, pp. 48–71.

Vernier, Bernard, 'Le rôle politique de l'armée en Syrie', *Politique Etrangère*, XXIX (1965), pp. 458–511.

— *Armée et Politique au Moyen Orient*, Paris, 1966.

Voss, Gregor, *''Alawiya oder Nusairiya?'* – Schiitische Machtelite und sunnitische Opposition in der Syrische Arabischen Republik*, dissertation, Hamburg, 1985.

Watenpaugh, Keith D., '"Creating Phantoms": Zaki al-Arsuzi, the Alexandretta Crisis, and the Formation of Modern Arab Nationalism in Syria', *International Journal of Middle East Studies*, Vol. 28 (1996), pp. 363–89.

Weismann, Itzchak, 'Sa'id Hawwa: The Making of a Radical Muslim Thinker in Modern Syria', *Middle Eastern Studies*, Vol. 29, No. 4, October 1993, pp. 602–23.

Weulersse, Jacques, *Le Pays des Alaouites*, Tours, 1940.

— *Paysans de Syrie et du Proche Orient*, Paris, 1946.

Who's Who in the Arab World, 2nd edn, Beirut, 1967–68.

Wieland, Carsten, *Syrien nach dem Irak-Krieg. Bastion gegen Islamisten oder Staat vor dem Kollaps?*, Berlin, 2004.

Winder, Bayly, 'Syrian Deputies and Cabinet Ministers, 1919–1959', *The Middle East Journal*, Vol. 16, No. 4, Autumn 1962, pp. 407–29; Vol. 17, No. 1, Winter 1963, pp. 35–54.

Wirth, Eugen, *Syrien, Eine Geographische Landeskunde*, Darmstadt, 1971.

Worren, Torstein Schiøtz, *Fear and Resistance. The Construction of Alawi Identity in Syria*, MA thesis, University of Oslo, 2007.

Yaffe-Schatzmann, Gitta, 'Alawi Separatists and Unionists: The Events of 25 February 1936', *Middle Eastern Studies*, Vol. 31, No. 1, January 1995, pp. 28–38.

Yaniv, Avner and Ma'oz, Moshe (eds), *Syria under Assad*, London, 1986.

Ziadeh, Radwan, *Power and Policy in Syria. Intelligence Services, Foreign Relations and Democracy in the Modern Middle East*, London, 2011.

Zisser, Eyal, 'The succession struggle in Damascus', *Middle East Quarterly*, Vol. 2, No. 3, 1995, pp. 57–64.

— 'Toward the post-Asad era in Syria', *Japanese Institute of Middle Eastern Economics Review*, No. 28, 1995, pp. 5–16.

— *Decision making in Asad's Syria*, Washington, 1998.

— *Asad's Legacy*, London, 2001.

— *Commanding Syria. Bashar al-Asad and the First Years of Power*, London, 2007.

Zuwiyya-Yamak, L., *The Syrian Social Nationalist Party: An Ideological Analysis*, Cambridge, MA, 1966.

Index